IDIOT'S GUIDES.
AS EASY AS IT GETS!

Plant-Based Nutrition

Second Edition

by Julieanna Hever, M.S., R.D., C.P.T. and Raymond J. Cronise

ALPHA

A member of Penguin Random House LLC

Publisher: Mike Sanders
Associate Publisher: Billy Fields
Development Editor: Monica Stone
Cover Designer: Lindsay Dobbs
Book Designer: William Thomas
Compositor: Ayanna Lacey
Proofreader: Lisa Starnes
Indexer: Brad Herriman

First American Edition, 2018
Published in the United States by DK Publishing
6081 E. 82nd Street, Indianapolis, Indiana 46250

Copyright © 2018 Dorling Kindersley Limited
A Penguin Random House Company
18 19 20 21   10 9 8 7 6 5
005-308593-January2018

Published in the United States by Dorling Kindersley Limited.

IDIOT'S GUIDES and Design are trademarks of Penguin Random House LLC

ISBN: 9781465470201
Library of Congress Catalog Card Number: 2017945450

Note: This publication contains the opinions and ideas of its author(s). It is intended to provide helpful and informative material on the subject matter covered. It is sold with the understanding that the author(s) and publisher are not engaged in rendering professional services in the book. If the reader requires personal assistance or advice, a competent professional should be consulted. The author(s) and publisher specifically disclaim any responsibility for any liability, loss, or risk, personal or otherwise, which is incurred as a consequence, directly or indirectly, of the use and application of any of the contents of this book.

Trademarks: All terms mentioned in this book that are known to be or are suspected of being trademarks or service marks have been appropriately capitalized. Alpha Books, DK, and Penguin Random House LLC cannot attest to the accuracy of this information. Use of a term in this book should not be regarded as affecting the validity of any trademark or service mark.

DK books are available at special discounts when purchased in bulk for sales promotions, premiums, fund-raising, or educational use. For details, contact: DK Publishing Special Markets, 345 Hudson Street, New York, New York 10014 or SpecialSales@dk.com.

Printed and bound in the United States of America

This book is dedicated to our collective precious plantlings: Maya, Ben, Alexia, Erin, and Danner.

Our research has shown that a whole foods plant-based diet, when combined with moderate exercise, stress management, and love/intimacy, can often reverse the progression of a wide variety of chronic conditions. These include coronary heart disease, type 2 diabetes, high blood pressure, obesity, early-stage prostate cancer, and even the aging process at a cellular level. Idiot's Guide: Plant-Based Nutrition, Second Edition, shows you how—highly recommended.

—Dean Ornish, M.D., Founder & President, Preventive Medicine Research Institute, Clinical Professor of Medicine, UCSF www.ornish.com

Contents

Foreword

A plant-based diet saved my life!

Is that too dramatic? Who cares? The question that matters is "Is it true?" It's shocking how little of an exaggeration that opening sentence is. It may even be an understatement.

A couple years ago I was over 335 pounds and even at six feet seven, that's fat. I was dying of fat. I couldn't go upstairs without panting. I kept ending up in the hospital. I was on more drugs than Keith Richards during the recording of *Their Satanic Majesties Request*—different drugs of course, mine weren't fun—and I still had blood pressure like UK voltage. My team of doctors couldn't get it under control. They strongly suggested a stomach sleeve. I was dying from eating like an idiot. I was dying from eating like an American.

CrayRay, as I call Ray Cronise—he's been my good friend for over 20 years so I've earned naming rights—showed up at exactly the right time and told me everything you're about to read in this book. How did CrayRay save my life? He didn't pull me out of sharknado quicksand full of burning bears with handguns. Pulling me out immediate danger would have saved me for a moment. What he did was better: CrayRay saved me for the rest of my life. I could still get hit by a meteor covered with blue-ringed octopuses, but the smart money—we Vegas locals always go with the smart money; we *own* the casinos—figures a plant-based diet added years, maybe decades, to my life. Most importantly, it's changed the quality of my life.

I used to think that I was Penn, and Penn lived in my body. I thought there was a mind that was me and a body that I lived in. That's nonsense. CrayRay got me eating right, and it became very clear that my body is me. When I was fat I didn't think I was depressed, but now that I'm skinny—yeah, I can use that word; wouldn't you like to?—I feel like a different, better person. I'm so much happier the way I am now that the way Fat Penn felt seems like a twentieth-century 12-tone German opera. I'm an old dad with two wonderful preteens, and when I was fat, I had to force myself to enjoy playing with my children. I no longer need to push. It's easy. It's natural. Now my children have better than Vegas house odds of having a living dad into their adulthood. That's way better than pushing me out of the way of a falling safe. Yeah, CrayRay did more than save my life. He made it more worth saving.

Julieanna Hever (I don't know her well enough yet to give her a nickname but give me time) has street cred you won't find in a Las Vegas magician or CrayRay. She's a dietitian—a plant-based dietitian. In fact, Julieanna is *the* plant-based dietitian and the author of the first edition of this book. She's been eating this way and helping people for the last decade, and when she asked CrayRay to join her on the second edition, he enthusiastically said *yes*.

Idiot's Guide: Plant-Based Nutrition is a good title, at least for me. I'm a complete idiot. I've known most of my adult life that my diet was killing me, but I didn't know how to fix it. I always tried to use moderation to get the most bad possible into my diet without going to the hospital by dessert. That's the idiot's way. How about just eat well as a habit? Why don't we all just eat in a way that makes us feel good and keeps us alive? The problem is that the standard American diet (SAD) is everywhere. It's how we were brought up, and it's where all the corporate money is. But even an idiot like me can eat right. If this were *The Smart Person's Guide to Nutrition*, the whole book could be three words: eat whole plants. That's all a smart person needs. But an idiot like me needs step-by-step instructions, and that's what Julieanna and CrayRay offer up to you on a plate in this book.

Search for "Penn Jillette of Penn & Teller" on Google images, and look at a picture of me before 2015 . . . see how fat I am? Now look at me after 2016 . . . see how healthy and happy I am? If I can do it so can you. Don't say, "I'll try to incorporate some of these plant-based ideas into my existing lifestyle," that cop-out thinking has never worked for you before, and it's not ever going to work for you, you idiot. Read this book and change your whole life. You know it's time. That's why you bought the book. It really is time. It's not easy to change everything, but you can do it. This idiot did.

Now let Julieanna and my buddy, Ray save your life. Please.

–Penn Jillette

Penn Jillette lives in Las Vegas where he does magic at the Penn & Teller Theater. He is the author of Presto!: How I Made Over 100 Pounds Disappear and Other Magical Tales. *He eats plant-based. He is finally happy and healthy.*

Introduction

For the first time in history, the number of people worldwide that are overnourished outnumber the people that are undernourished. Health care is a disaster in which we lose billions of dollars a year supporting disease symptom management. People are sicker and fatter than ever before, and ironically, we have the most access to healthful food and medical care. Although the reasons surrounding these issues may be complex, the solution might be simple. It comes down to the food on your plate.

Eating healthfully may very well be the most confusing and frustrating part of everyday life. Frequent fads and trends come and go, leaving you lost in their wake, uncertain about the failed promises of successfully achieving perfect health and ideal weight. Distinguishing between fact and fiction is virtually impossible with the never-ending onslaught of hype on television, on the internet, in magazines, in books, and through word-of-mouth. Everyone can consider themselves experts, but what are they really trying to sell? Food policy has become entirely politicized. Thus, our nutrition guidelines come indirectly from food manufacturers, not the most objective resource for information.

Physicians receive minimal, if any, nutrition education in medical school, yet they're the frontline people providing guidance and care. Western medicine has become a game of identifying a symptom and applying a remedy for that symptom (a.k.a. chronic disease management). Never before have drug manufacturers sold their prescription medications directly to the consumer as they do now. Television commercials alternate between ads for fast food, junk food, and a new medication to help alleviate your symptoms from consuming those products.

It's time to see the forest instead of the trees. Health is not merely the absence of disease, nor are symptoms of poor health to be medicated and ignored. Instead, it's time to redefine health and nutrition.

Fortunately, a movement is well underway, confirming that what you eat can and does prevent, and even reverse, chronic disease. Researchers, physicians, and dietitians have witnessed multitudes of people regain true health, ridding their dependence on medications and habitual foods. You can change your future and be responsible for how you look and feel simply by making the right food choices.

Whether this is your first foray into the plant-based world or you're a well-seasoned veteran, a plethora of facts and tips readily await you in the following chapters. Proceed through the pages to discover the most current advances in health and nutrition while you build your nutritional database and reap the rewards.

Everything you need to know to achieve optimal health is in your hands right now. Welcome to the gorgeously exciting and health-creating, plant-based world!

How This Book Is Organized

This book is divided into four parts, each representing distinct attributes of plant-based nutrition:

Part 1, The Benefits of a Plant-Based Diet, offers a comprehensive course in nutrition fundamentals, dissecting what your food consists of. This part explains what your body requires for optimal health and where to get those nutrients. Get ready for the hot-off-the-presses Food Triangle, which will redefine what you've previously experienced and give you a new set of food groups to feast your hungry eyes upon.

Part 2, Living a Plant-Based Life, debunks most of the nutritional misinformation we've been fed over the years. It offers an entirely new perspective on weight loss and clarifies the most commonly confused health information. Take a stroll down the aisles of the supermarket with a plant-based eye, and you'll discover a whole-istic approach to food shopping. Learn how and why you need to incorporate a fitness program into your schedule to achieve optimum health, and see how much more fabulous you'll feel after you've done so. Finally, get answers to your supplement concerns so you can put to rest the notion that good health equals taking the right pills.

Part 3, Special Considerations, is dedicated to everyone who has been a baby, had a baby, raised a child, succeeded in athletics, battled the bulge, and/or confronted illness. Throughout your lifespan, your health needs change. This part breaks down all the nutrition concerns that come up in different situations, providing guidance so you can take the reins and achieve a longer healthspan.

Armed with all the knowledge you've gained about what you need to do to thrive in your body, **Part 4, The Plant-Based Recipe Box,** shows you exactly how to do so. Master the art of dining out, stocking your kitchen, and nutrifying recipes to meet the guidelines described in this book. Then indulge your taste buds with whole-food recipes—more than 45 of them!—you can easily prepare and share as you learn tips to maximize your time in the kitchen, regardless of your expertise.

In the appendixes, you'll find a glossary of terms, a week's worth of sample meal plans, Dietary Reference Intake charts, and a list of handy resources for you to continue your plant-based journey.

Extras

Throughout the book, you'll find sidebars to guide you and offer additional information. Here's what to look for:

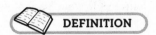 **DEFINITION**

These sidebars clarify jargon and other questionable terms.

MIXED GREENS

Miscellaneous thoughts and additives fill these sidebars.

HEALTHY HINT

These facts and tips increase your knowledge and help put the concepts into action.

PLANT PITFALL

These sidebars feature warnings and cautionary advice you should check out.

Acknowledgments

Julieanna would love to offer gratitude to several people. For giving me the opportunity to write this book (twice), I offer a huge thank you to Marilyn Allen, for believing in me right from the start. Thank you to everyone at Alpha Books for your amazing work and support. My deepest gratitude to Dr. T. Colin Campbell and John Robbins, the matches who sparked my flame, and to my mentor, Brenda Davis, whose wisdom continues to fuel my fire to do better. Thank you to Dr. Michael Greger, Dr. Neal Barnard, Dr. Joel Fuhrman, and Dina Aronson for the guidance and inspiration. Words cannot express how much appreciation I have for my electrifying co-author, Ray, and for my little plantlings, Maya and Benny.

Ray would like to thank the entire *Idiot's Guide* team. I am especially grateful to Julieanna for the invitation to collaborate on this book and all of our other amazing projects—thank you. My world forever changed directions with the help of Dr. Peter Diamandis, Michael Potter, Tim Ferriss, and Marc Hodosh, who pushed me onto the TEDMED stage. I'm grateful to my science collaborators, Dr. Andrew Bremer and Dr. David Sinclair. My health has continuously improved due to the wisdom, friendship, and support of Dr. Joel Fuhrman, Dr. Michael Klaper, Dr. Dean Ornish, and Dr. Michael Greger. I can't think of four people that have influenced my life more than Penn Jillette, Teller, Tim Jenison, and Cyan Banister. Finally, there is no one more important in my world than my mother, Lois Danner, and my children, Alexia, Erin, and Danner; your love and support mean so much to me.

Trademarks

All terms mentioned in this book that are known to be or are suspected of being trademarks or service marks have been appropriately capitalized. Alpha Books and Penguin Random House LLC cannot attest to the accuracy of this information. Use of a term in this book should not be regarded as affecting the validity of any trademark or service mark.

The Benefits of a Plant-Based Diet

More and more people are getting interested in plant-based nutrition as the numerous health benefits associated with this way of eating are coming to light. But what exactly constitutes a plant-based diet, and how do you go about exploring it for yourself? That's what Part 1 is all about. It explains how to eat a whole food, plant-based diet so you can see how easy this health-promoting way of life is.

Stay tuned for a Nutrition 101 lesson filled with everything nature has to offer. In the following chapters, we explore what your food is made of, what your body thrives on, and how to merge the two. We also help you redefine your mindset toward food and eating as you begin to switch from the confusing and irresponsible rules you've been taught your whole life to a new set of plant-based guidelines.

Find the beauty in your plate and on your palate with whole-plant foods, and see how your life grows more colorful as you incorporate the ideas into daily practice!

What is Plant-Based Nutrition?

Since the first publication of *The Complete Idiot's Guide to Plant-Based Nutrition*, the "going veg" world has exploded. While it may encompass different titles (e.g. vegetarian, vegan, plant-based, etc.) and may stem from different motivations, eating plants proffers many potential health benefits. Because of this, the food industry has responded enthusiastically to the rise of plant eaters with a variety of products targeted to meet the demand; eating plant-based is becoming increasingly more accessible. It is not uncommon to have entire menu sections filled with plant options at restaurants, ample shelf space dedicated to plant foods at supermarkets, and myriad restaurants exclusively serving up veggie food in cities around the globe. More and more healthcare professionals—and even entire healthcare organizations—are recommending plant-based diets to their patients, recognizing the surge of scientific studies supporting its health advantages.

A plant-based diet has never been easier to follow, which is electrifying for its enthusiasts. At the same time, it is important to note that the food industry is also targeting our taste buds, making it slightly trickier to identify wholesome foods. Although healthful eating is no longer synonymous with simple vegan or vegetarian labels, nothing has changed regarding the benefits of eating whole plant-based food.

In This Chapter

- A closer look at plant-based eating
- Comparing a plant-based diet and other veg diets
- Healthy versus unhealthy veg diets
- What plant-based eating can do for you

Therefore, distinguishing between fact and fiction in the marketing of these products is increasingly important. Our goal for this new edition is to provide updated tools to help you separate the health from the hype for optimal success.

Getting your nutrition from plant-based foods is one of the best things you can do for your body and your well-being. And it's easier than you might think! Get ready to be inspired by all the healthy advantages a plant-based diet offers!

What Is Plant-Based?

Before we go any further, let's look at what *plant-based* really means. Plant-based has come to represent a way of eating foods primarily or exclusively of plant origin. Simple enough, right? The addition of the words *whole food*, as in "whole food, plant-based diet," indicates the foods are as they exist in nature and have not been stripped of their original packaging.

PLANT PITFALL

Beware of junk food. Although some of it is entirely made from plants, eating a diet founded in non-nutritive foods such as white bread, potato chips, and fruit punch isn't healthy and isn't the goal here. That's where the whole-food part of the diet comes in.

A whole food, plant-based diet boasts a wide range of choices, including infinite possible combinations of vegetables, fruits, whole grains, legumes, nuts, seeds, herbs, and spices. Although these foods require very little processing and preparation, earth-harvested ingredients can tempt your taste buds in dishes ranging from fine gourmet to casual comfort food.

Additionally, while studying populations, physicians and researchers have found that a whole food, plant-based diet results in optimum health. The higher the percentage of a diet that comes from whole-plant foods, the lower the risk for cardiovascular disease, many cancers, type 2 diabetes, obesity, and autoimmune diseases. If you want to feel and look your best while savoring every bite, a whole food, plant-based diet is the win-win option.

Vegan, Vegetarian, Plant Based

Now let's look at those other "veg" diets mentioned earlier and see how they compare to a plant-based diet.

First up, *vegans.* Technically, a vegan is an exclusive plant eater, who lives solely on plant products and excludes all animal flesh, including that of poultry and fish, as well as any product made by an animal, such as milk and all other dairy products, eggs, gelatin, and honey. Typically, vegans don't wear clothing or other items made with animal products. That means no fur, leather, silk, wool, feathers, or pearls. They also avoid anything made with animal-based ingredients, such as some cosmetics, toiletries, or household goods.

A *vegetarian* doesn't eat animal flesh but may consume other animal-based foods like eggs and dairy. Vegetarianism has several subpopulations:

- Lacto-ovo vegetarians eat dairy (lacto) and eggs (ovo).

- Lacto-vegetarians eat dairy but not eggs.

- Ovo-vegetarians eat eggs but not dairy.

- Flexitarians (a contraction of the words *flexible* and *vegetarian*) eat mostly plant-based foods but occasionally eat meat, poultry, or fish, too.

- Semi-vegetarians exclude some meats (usually red meat) but still consume limited amounts of poultry, fish, or seafood.

- Pescatarians eat fish and shellfish, but no other animal flesh. They may or may not include dairy and eggs.

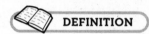 **DEFINITION**

> A **vegan** (VEE-gan) avoids consuming and using all animal products, including animal flesh, dairy, eggs, honey, leather, fur, silk, wool, and pearls. A vegetarian avoids eating meat, poultry, and fish. There are several types of vegetarianism.

When you think about it, although veganism and vegetarianism are plant-based diets for the most part, they're defined on what you *exclude* from your diet. Part of what makes a plant-based diet unique is that it defines the composition of what *is* included instead of what *isn't*.

The Health Benefits of a Plant-Based Diet

Over the last several decades, scientific studies have led to discoveries that could potentially change the landscape of healthcare. Such studies have shown that eating a whole food, plant-based diet can be the key to proactive medical care.

Disease Prevention and Reversal

After nearly a century of eating a calorie-dense, nutrient-poor standard Western diet, we have seen an unprecedented rise in chronic disease rates. Fortunately, however, there is an ever-expanding body of evidence demonstrating the benefits of adding more plant food to the diet. While no diet is a guaranteed prescription for immortality and perfect health, a plant-based diet has been shown to have the best track record.

Plant-based diets have been associated with …

- Lowering overall and ischemic heart-disease mortality.

- Supporting sustainable weight management.

- Reducing medication needs.

- Lowering the risk for most chronic diseases.

- Decreasing the incidence and severity of high-risk conditions, including obesity, hypertension, hyperlipidemia, and hyperglycemia.

- Reversing advanced coronary artery disease and type 2 diabetes.

And the list continues to grow.

We've grown accustomed to pointing at genetics as the primary insight for which diseases you're likely to contract over your lifetime. Yet it's your habits—especially what you eat—that establish whether those genes are expressed and the illness flares up or those harmful genes remain dormant. This means the food you choose to place on your plate has more control over your health than some predetermined destiny. In other words, your genes may load the gun, but your lifestyle pulls the trigger.

Cardiometabolic Disease

Cardiometabolic risk is a measure of your chances for cardiovascular disease and diabetes. Because these two conditions have individual risk factors that overlap and even impact one another, they are often grouped together in overall health assessments. A whole food, plant-based diet has powerful phytonutrients and other beneficial components that address both issues. It is not uncommon to see hypertensive or diabetic patients normalize their blood pressure or blood sugar, respectively, and completely remove the need for pharmacological intervention within months of changing their diets. And yet, many patients, dietitians, and physicians remain unaware that these dramatic results can be achieved so simply. It is a "chicken or an egg" (or, we should say, "a seed or a tree") conundrum that many healthcare professionals don't think patients are willing to make a permanent change in diet. Consequently (and tragically), patients are often not given the choice.

You must take a proactive approach with your health. While it may be true that the pharmacy is just a few steps away from the produce section in most grocery stores, a whole food, plant-based diet is a far better prescription for good health.

Weight Management

Weight management has reached a critical impasse. After decades of searching for the perfect diet, the population is growing larger and more frustrated with the contradictions between the diets. Clearly, this approach has not been successful.

 MIXED GREENS

> While nearly three out of four adults are overweight or obese in the United States, 39 percent of adults are overweight and 13 percent are obese, worldwide. Obesity is a contributing factor to many leading causes of death, including heart disease, stroke, diabetes, and some types of cancer.

Concentrating on a whole food, plant-based diet is the most advantageous solution for achieving and sustaining optimum health and weight. In fact, several studies show that this type of eating plan does, indeed, produce the most favorable outcomes. And that's *without* any other changes in exercise or portion size! In other words, you can eat vegetables, fruits, whole grains, and legumes in abundance and still achieve great weight-loss success.

A diet exclusively made of plants requires eating more food at each meal. Contrary to popular thought, eating more actually helps you maintain your ideal weight by crowding out obesogenic food sources. And that's the idea behind the whole food, plant-based diet.

Longevity and Healthspan

A plant-based diet may be the most powerful way not only to increase your lifespan, but more importantly, to expand your *healthspan*. Thus far, the only way longevity research scientists have increased the lifespan or healthspan of organisms—from yeasts to primates—is by limiting certain nutrients. Paradoxically, less is more when it comes to nutrients and a long, healthy life. Today, food is so available and ubiquitous that some have suggested it has led to a chronically fed state, which doesn't give the body time for crucial repairs and maintenance. Just like our bodies need the downtime of sleep to execute memory consolidation and other brain repairs, so, too, do our bodies need the fasted state to work efficiently. Frequent feeding, which was once the hallmark of people economically deprived of proper nutrition, has been replaced by a need to decrease meal frequency and food-calorie density. A plant-based diet is centered on increasing healthspan to *live* longer not just live *longer*.

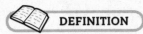 **DEFINITION**

Healthspan is the period of one's life during which one is generally healthy and free from serious disease. It addresses the number of years you live in the best health possible and is contrasted with longevity, or lifespan, which is simply the number of years you live. We want to define proper diet with the goal of *living* longer, not just living *longer*.

The Least You Need to Know

- Current research supports a whole-food, plant-based diet as the key to achieving optimum health.
- "Plant-based" describes the types of foods included in a meal plan or any type of diet that's heavy on whole-plant foods.
- A whole-food, plant-based diet is the premier option for minimizing risk of disease, achieving and maintaining optimum weight, supporting longer healthspan, and possibly even extending life span.

Breaking Down the Macro*confusion*

The colors, textures, aromas, and flavors of a delicious, freshly prepared meal all work together to stimulate your senses in anticipation of that first bite. Your mouth waters and your stomach grumbles as it eagerly looks forward to breaking down the macro- and micronutrients in every delicious morsel. Macronutrients are the calorie-providing nutrients your body requires in large amounts, including proteins, carbohydrates, and fats. Micronutrients are required in small amounts and consist of water- and fat-soluble vitamins, macrominerals, and trace elements.

In this chapter, we explain everything you need to know about the basics of macronutrition. (The micronutrients get their own chapter—Chapter 3.) So rev up your brain power and get ready for an essential lesson on nutrition!

In This Chapter

- Carbophobia
- The ABC's of Protein
- Fat Facts

Macroconfusion

The three categories of calorie-filled macronutrients—proteins, carbohydrates, and fats—are joined by a fourth zero-calorie macronutrient, water, and form the chemical basis for the structure, function, and energy of all life. Over the last century, we have embraced these labels as food groups, leading us to categorize food by the majority macronutrient, but nothing could be further from the truth. With the exception of highly processed food products, such as sugar and oil, most foods are some combination of two or more of these macronutrients. Sometimes the category given to the food doesn't even reflect the majority macronutrient (e.g. many cuts of meat are majority fat, but often listed as proteins).

The worst part of this nutritional identity crisis is that well-intentioned clinical trials shuffle around diets to determine the perfect ratio of proteins, carbohydrates, and fats. Instead of answers, we end up with contradictory diets year after year. Is it low carb or high protein? Should we skip the fat or is butter back? We are all exasperated and we'd like to untangle what we prefer to call *macroconfusion*. We propose we leave the biochemical terminology in the lab and classroom and, instead, focus our shopping lists and menus on language our great-great-grandparents would recognize as food.

Crazy Carbophobia

What do cotton, crab shells, lumber, books, baked potatoes, sugar, and grass have in common? They are all carbohydrates. No matter if it is a moth eating a sweater, a termite tearing through a tree, the voracious word appetite of a bookworm, a cow grazing in a pasture, or a bowl of Thanksgiving mashed potatoes, these items are (surprisingly) all forms of carbohydrates.

Controversy abounds over carbohydrates—or to use the shortened slang, *carbs*—and has continued to reign supreme for decades. Are they healthful, or are they fattening? Due to the evil cloud that surrounds carbs, even the name itself has been mistakenly redefined to encompass not only whole-food fruits and vegetables, but also processed foods such as donuts, cookies, cakes, crackers, chips, and candy. This misperception warrants a closer look at what makes a carbohydrate a carbohydrate and why that list of processed foods is metabolically different from whole-food carbohydrate sources.

Plants produce carbohydrates via photosynthesis during which carbon dioxide is transformed into glucose, a complex molecule composed of carbon, hydrogen, and oxygen atoms. In the process, the plant offers oxygen in return. As you might imagine, carbohydrates come in a lot of forms; therefore, let's dive into carbohydrate fundamentals to untangle some of the widely perceived carb-contradictions.

Simple Versus Complex Carbohydrates

A saccharide, commonly called *sugar*, is the most basic, repeating unit of a carbohydrate. Sugars made up of one saccharide molecule are called *monosaccharides* (*mono* meaning *one*) and those with two saccharide molecules are called *disaccharides* (*di: two*). These are often called *simple carbohydrates*, due to their simple structure.

Monosaccharides include glucose, fructose, and galactose, which are found in fruits, honey, and corn syrup. Edible disaccharides include sucrose (table sugar), lactose (milk sugar), and maltose. Disaccharides are found in cane and beet sugars, milk and milk products, and malt.

Polysaccharides (*poly: many*), or complex carbohydrates, contain three or more sugars. Complex carbohydrates include digestible starches, which are energy storage depots for plants and animals, and structural components referred to commonly as *fiber*.

Both starch and fiber are nearly identical chains of the monosaccharide glucose, a fundamental molecule that all organisms can use as fuel. These long glucose chains can be linked together in more than one way to form both cellulose (fiber) and starch. Cellulose is the primary structural component of trees, grass, and paper, while starch is the plant's energy stores and is found in potatoes, rice, or beans. These two different glucose chains, starch and fiber, hold the secret to the carbohydrate riddle discussed earlier. Various organisms seek the glucose fuel units found in fiber and starch. The need for glucose explains why a termite eats the fiber of wood, a cow eats grass, and we eat potatoes.

If we get that needed energy from a refined sugar like sucrose, the body processes it very differently than the same amount of whole-food, starchy vegetables such as potatoes, rice, squash, or beans. Much of the difference in metabolic uptake is due to the fiber, water, and other nutrients that are found in whole foods and that are removed with increased processing.

Healthful dietary starch, found in the produce or dried staples section at the supermarket, provides an excellent source of energy. Plentiful in the plant kingdom, starch shows up primarily in plant seeds and underground storage organs. Food sources of starch include potatoes, squash, beans, lentils, wheat, maize, rice, barley, cassava, tapioca, rye, oats, peas, etc.

 MIXED GREENS

Plants use underground storage organs (USOs) to retain energy produced through photosynthesis for periods when sunlight is diminished or unavailable. Tubers are starch-swollen roots such as potatoes. Corms are starch-swollen stems such as water chestnuts. Bulbs are layered storage organs such as onions and garlic. Finally, rhizomes are swollen stems that are underground such as ginger or turmeric.

Dietary fiber, or long chains of complex carbohydrates, includes the parts of the plant that are indigestible. While we can't digest fiber directly like some other animals, insects, and bacteria, it is still extremely valuable in our diet. Fibers are most simply categorized as soluble or insoluble.

Soluble fiber is the water-soluble form of dietary fiber, either dissolving or swelling to form a gel when combined with water. Pectin, gums, and mucilage are forms of soluble fiber, which can be found in oats, barley, beans, peas, apples, citrus fruits, carrots, and seaweed. Consuming soluble fiber lowers serum cholesterol levels and improves blood glucose control.

Insoluble fiber consists mainly of celluloses, hemicelluloses, and lignins, and it improves digestion and bowel health, increases satiety, and helps remove metabolic waste from the body. Foods high in insoluble fiber include vegetables, fruits, wheat bran, whole grains, legumes, nuts, and seeds.

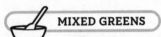 **MIXED GREENS**

Dietary fiber is found exclusively in plants and is one of the most health-promoting, disease-fighting nutrients. Yet less than 3 percent of Americans consume the minimum recommended daily intake of 25 and 38 grams for women and men, respectively.

Finally, resistant starch is a special type of starch that functions as a fiber, remaining intact throughout the cooking process and during the enzyme breakdown of digestion. Resistant starch helps control blood sugar, lowers blood cholesterol and triglyceride concentrations, improves insulin sensitivity, facilitates the growth of friendly gut bacteria, increases satiety, and reduces fat storage. Foods containing resistant starch include beans, potatoes, slightly green bananas, split peas, barley, and brown rice.

Although famous for its digestive benefits such as alleviating constipation, dietary fiber's health benefits are far more comprehensive. Eating adequate amounts of soluble and insoluble fiber helps control rates of digestion and sugar absorption; removes excess cholesterol, sex hormones, and heavy metals like mercury; enhances weight loss; and reduces risk of colorectal cancer. (See Chapter 4 for more details.) Studies have repeatedly shown that fiber supplementation doesn't match the performance of fiber-filled whole foods.

Refined Versus Whole Food

Now, here's the center of all the carb confusion. Recognizing the difference between refined or highly processed foodstuffs such as table sugar, flours, baked goods, etc... and whole-food starch sources such as grains, legumes, tubers, etc... is critical when talking about eating for health. According to the U.S. Food and Drug Administration (FDA), a *whole grain* is a cereal grain consisting of the "intact, ground, cracked, or flaked fruit whose principal components—the starchy endosperm, germ, and bran—are present in the same relative proportions as they exist in the intact grain."

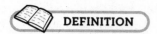 **DEFINITION**

Whole grains are derived from the seeds of grasses and include rice, oats, rye, wheat, wild rice, quinoa, barley, buckwheat, bulgur, corn, millet, amaranth, and sorghum.

Whole grains are filled with healthful starches, fiber, protein, vitamins, and minerals. They have zero cholesterol and are low in fat. They meet most of our nutritional needs and are considered essential in a health-promoting diet. They've been shown to decrease cholesterol and blood sugar levels, as well as lower risk of chronic diseases such as colon cancer, heart disease, and type 2 diabetes. Societies have survived and thrived on a whole-grain–based diet since the beginning of recorded history.

On the other hand, refined grains found in many flours and baked goods are the result of processing whole grains. The bran and germ have been removed, leaving only the endosperm. These refined products are stripped of vitamins, minerals, and fiber. A diet high in refined foods leads to increased risk of chronic disease and supports the confusing misinterpretation of the benefits of a diet rich in whole-food carbohydrate sources. In other words, a diet loaded with highly refined sugar or flour isn't comparable to a diet high in fruits, starchy vegetables, whole grains, and legumes—this is the root of the carb-versus-fat conundrum. Each side of the debate seems to pit their best plate against the other side's worst plate. Of course we see the conflicting diet advice year after year. While we often hear, "Where do you get your protein?" It turns out the more astute question is, "Where do you get your glucose?" Once you drop the "c-word" and focus your meal plan and shopping list on whole-food terminology, the confusion disappears and your plate becomes full of nutrient-packed satiety.

 MIXED GREENS

Despite the rising fear of glucose through its association with the deleterious effects of excess refined sugar in the diet, glucose remains critical for life. In a diet completely devoid of dietary carbohydrates, the body begins to break down proteins from tissue to create the needed glucose in a process called *gluconeogenesis*. Even during water-only fasting lasting over a year, blood glucose levels never go down to zero.

Power-Packed Protein

Protein is thought of as the superhero of macronutrients because of its crucial role in most—if not all—structural and functional mechanisms of the human body. There are tens of thousands of proteins in every cell in the body—muscle, organs, hair, nails, skin, teeth, ligaments, cartilage, and tendons—and they make up the enzymes, membranes, antibodies, hemoglobin, and some hormones of all organisms. Protein is the building block of life, and yet none of the 20,000 different proteins in your body came from your diet. Where did the protein come from? It was synthesized using your DNA blueprints, from a pool of protein building blocks called *amino acids*.

MIXED GREENS

In 1838, Gerrit Jan Mulder was the first to use the nutrient name, "protein," derived from the Greek word proteios, meaning "first place or primary" in a journal article, although it was Swedish chemist, Jöns Jacob Berzelius that coined the term. It's interesting that Mulder commented, "It is highly admirable that the principal substance of all animals is immediately drawn from the plants. It signifies an economy of nature in her means that is wonderful and sublime."

There's no doubt that protein is critical for life, but it's not as simple as an ingredient on food packaging. Have you noticed the protein labels everywhere? Food retailers know that protein sells. It's seen on pizza menus (pick your protein), can be overheard from every trainer at the gym, and now it's even added to water! However, just because protein is vital to our health and development, doesn't mean more is better. To properly evaluate this protein propaganda, we need to take a closer look at the protein building blocks: amino acids.

The ABCs of Amino Acids

While it seems food packages and post-workout shakes are focused on protein, what we really need from our diet are amino acids. Much like this sentence is composed of a sequence of words made from the 26 letters of the alphabet, each protein is composed of a unique sequence made from the 20 amino acids. But wait! There's a catch.

Of these 20 amino acids, your body is unable to manufacture 9, and these essential or indispensable amino acids must come from diet. Your body can produce the other 11 amino acids. Under most circumstances, we're able to synthesize the "conditionally essential" amino acids. Sometimes, though, metabolic demands are higher and the body can't make enough.

The following list breaks down all 20 amino acids into their respective categories based on whether or not they're required in your diet. The essential amino acids must be consumed to create the nonessential amino acids.

Essential:

Histidine	Phenylalanine
Isoleucine	Threonine
Leucine	Tryptophan
Lysine	Valine
Methionine	

Conditionally essential:

Arginine	Glycine
Cysteine	Proline
Glutamine	Tyrosine

Nonessential:

Alanine	Glutamic acid
Asparagine	Serine
Aspartic acid	

When you consume protein, your body breaks it down into individual amino acids and they become part of a circulating pool. When a protein needs to be built, the body restrings the amino acids together in the order required to make whatever protein is necessary at the time. It's quite a clever and efficient system!

We eat the plant or eat the animal that ate the plant to obtain essential amino acids used to build our proteins. Plants can't eat, so they must create the many organic compounds from scratch. Generally, plants need four things to grow: water, sunlight, carbon dioxide, and fertilizer. When we use compost or animal manure to fertilize a plant it must first be broken down to elemental levels so that the root system can absorb them. Nitrogen is one of the main components of fertilizer, and plants use it to create the 20 amino acids required for protein synthesis. Amino acids are simply concentrated up the food chain. All living organisms contain all 20 amino acids, though exact amounts of individual amino acid levels vary from species to species.

MIXED GREENS

Legumes (beans, lentils, peas, and peanuts) provide a critical function for all life by fixing atmospheric nitrogen into a form that a plant can easily use to synthesize amino acids. A symbiotic relationship between nitrogen-fixing bacteria and legumes kicks off the nitrogen cycle resulting in amino acid stores.

Debunking Protein Myths

Often, the first question plant eaters hear when someone discovers their diet is, "Where do you get your protein?" Most people don't really want an answer to the question, but if we take it seriously, we now have a few fun facts to begin to answer it accurately. At the highest level, the wordy answer would be: my DNA contains the blueprints for the approximately 20,000 proteins needed by my body, and they are synthesized from a pool of essential and nonessential amino acids. That is a mouthful. In fact, some proteins can last as little as a few minutes and others as long as nearly a century. All living organisms are constantly building, destroying, and rebuilding proteins. Of course, a more important question is, "Where do we get essential amino acids?"

Somehow people assume that protein comes only from animal products and that anyone avoiding them will be deficient. That's a myth! All essential amino acids originate from plants. Either you eat the plant or you eat the animal that ate the plant. Either way, the essential amino acids came from the plant. This makes sense if you take a reflective pause. No one questions if beef has protein, and yet they probably don't recall in the same thought that cows eat grass. We understand from our carbohydrate section that the real advantage an animal has over a human is the ability to extract glucose energy from the structural cellulose fiber.

There are plenty of examples of plants providing complete nutritional need for mammals—even extremely large, muscular mammals. In fact, ten of the largest, most muscular species of mammals walking this planet—3 different species of elephants, 4 rhinoceros species, the hippopotamus, the giraffe, and the gaur—all derive their complete nutritional needs, including amino acids for protein synthesis, entirely from plants.

The plant world provides complete amino acid sources, but we don't need to eat vast quantities of these nutrients to maintain superior health. Consider the fact that the very first food created specifically to nourish an infant during the stage in life when humans grow the most and at the fastest rate is low in protein. Human breast milk contains less than 1 percent protein—about 5 percent by calorie. (We will revisit dietary protein and amino acid restriction in Chapter 4.)

If you're eating enough calories from whole-plant food sources, having a diet too low in protein is nearly impossible. All whole-plant foods include protein and contain all 20 amino acids. For example, bananas contain 5 percent of their total calories from protein, white potatoes have 8 percent, and brown rice has 9 percent. These foods are categorized as "carbs," yet they can also meet dietary requirements for protein.

Furthermore, some plant foods are very high in protein, including beans, legumes, nuts, and seeds. Lentils have 36 percent, and believe it or not, leafy green vegetables have almost half their total calories from protein! The only way to become deficient in protein is either not to eat enough calories or to eat primarily processed and refined foods (i.e. sugar, flour, oil, etc.). Ultimately, if you stick to eating whole-plant foods, you don't need to worry about getting enough protein.

Protein combining is another myth. This idea to combine foods to get sufficient protein was popularized in the 1950s, but has since been repudiated. Ultimately, the human body is much more elegant than we give it credit. It's able to pool together all the amino acids it absorbs from food and re-create the proteins it requires as necessary.

It's based on the notion that certain amino acids are limited in plants and that they don't meet some ideal distribution. Animal-sourced protein is often mistakenly called a "complete protein," insinuating that it contains all amino acids and plants don't; this is simply untrue.

Both plant and animal-sourced protein contains all amino acids even though the essential amino acids occur in different concentrations. While all essential amino acids are created by plants or bacteria, animals do concentrate them in their tissue. As will be discussed later, limiting certain amino acids, particularly some essential amino acids, may be advantageous.

 MIXED GREENS

A 173 gram (medium) baked potato contains 160 calories and provides 9 percent daily value of protein. This means if one ate enough potatoes to meet their daily calorie requirement, they would get over 100 percent of required protein from this often maligned carb. In addition, the amino acid profile of a white potato scores higher than 90 percent lean beef.

How Much Do We Really Require?

The Recommended Daily Allowance (RDA) for protein set by the U.S. Department of Agriculture (USDA) is 0.8 gram per kilogram of bodyweight per day (g/kg/day) for adults 19 years old and above. The RDAs for children are higher on a gram-per-bodyweight basis than for adults:

Infants	1.5 g/kg/day
Ages 1 to 3 years	1.1 g/kg/day
Ages 4 to 13 years	0.95 g/kg/day
Ages 14 to 18 years	0.85 g/kg/day

RDAs for protein also are increased for pregnant and lactating women:

Pregnant	1.1 g/kg/day (using pre-pregnancy weight)
Lactating	1.1 g/kg/day

 **HEALTHY HINT**

To figure out how many kilograms you weigh, simply divide your weight in pounds by 2.2. For example, a 130-pound female weighs 59 kilograms (130 ÷ 2.2 = 59).

But wait! Here's some fabulous news: following a whole-food, plant-based diet automatically gives you adequate amounts of protein, carbohydrates, and fat. As long as you consume a variety of foods, you don't need to worry about calculating, weighing, measuring, or counting. This is one of the many benefits associated with eating a healthful veg diet. So put down your calculator and breathe a sigh of relief. Eat a variety of whole-plant foods, and you'll be naturally macronutrient balanced!

Super Sources of Protein

Sources of protein are abundant in the plant kingdom. Ample quantities and varieties of amino acids come packaged with phytonutrients, antioxidants, fiber, vitamins, and minerals. In animal flesh, eggs, and dairy products, protein comes along with saturated fat, dietary cholesterol, heme iron, Neu5Gc, carnitine, and none of the above-mentioned health-promoting nutrients. (More on this in Chapter 4.) The following table shares some terrific plant-based sources of protein.

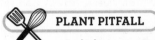 **PLANT PITFALL**

Including excessive amounts of protein not only is unnecessary, but it also can be detrimental. The kidneys, which metabolize protein, must work hard to break down the nitrogenous waste that accrues with a high protein intake. Overworking the kidneys with large quantities of protein, particularly animal-sourced protein, can lead to kidney stones and other more serious diseases.

Excellent Plant Protein Sources

Food	% Calories from Protein	Protein per Serving
Banana, 1 medium	4.6	1.2g
Brown rice, 1 cup cooked	8.5	4.9g
Barley, pearled, 1 cup cooked	9.4	16.4g
Quinoa, ½ cup cooked	14.0	11.1g
Whole-wheat bread, 1 slice	15.7	2.4g
Chickpeas, 1 cup cooked	21.6	14.5g
Lentils, 1 cup cooked	31.0	17.9g
Soy milk, 1 cup	33.4	6.6g
Broccoli, raw, ½ cup	43.3	1.3g
Tofu, raw, firm, ½ cup	43.5	19.9g
Spinach, frozen, ½ cup	44.4	3.0g

Fat: Fact and Fiction

Low fat, high fat, trans fat, saturated fat—sometimes it's difficult to keep straight all the kinds of fat, let alone know whether they're good or bad for you!

Let's make this simple so that fat makes sense. Because some fats are healthful and others are harmful, we can help you distinguish the two. It's easy to eat adequate amounts of healthy fat from whole-plant foods—and, as a bonus, it's difficult to find unhealthy fats in these foods! Here's yet another reason to celebrate the beauty of the whole-food, plant-based diet!

The Facts About Fats

Your body requires dietary fats, also known as lipids, to perform several functions. First, fat helps with the absorption of fat-soluble vitamins, minerals, and phytonutrients like carotenoids. Fat is also a major source of energy, like carbohydrates and protein. However, at 9 calories per gram (kcal/g), fat offers more than twice the amount of energy because both carbohydrates and protein supply just 4 kcal/g.

Fat also provides essential fatty acids (linoleic acid and alpha-linolenic acid) that the body can't produce on its own and, like essential amino acids, must be consumed via diet. A fatty acid is to fat what a saccharide is to a polysaccharide and amino acid to protein. Three of these single component fatty acids bond to a glycerol backbone and are transported and stored throughout the body as triglycerides. They're classified based on the length of the fatty acid chains and on their chemical composition. Additionally, some fatty acids act as precursors that help with coagulation (blood clotting), inflammation, and gene expression.

Fat in the form of triglycerides is found in both plant and animal sources. The three attached fatty acids consist of carbon atom chains that can have different types of bonds between them, which results in them being linear or kinked. When adjacent carbons have two bonds instead of one, they can't freely rotate and this may result in a kink in the chain. The fatty acids with double bonds are referred to as *unsaturated*, since hydrogens must be removed to accommodate these bonds. Long, straight chains found in saturated fats pack closely together like straight hair, while the kinked chains found in unsaturated fats are more like curly hair. The degree of saturation determines the fat's physical state: saturated fats are generally solid and unsaturated fats are generally liquid at room temperature.

Animals tend to store saturated fats since they take up less room—think lard or bacon grease. Plants, lacking a cardiovascular system to pump fats around, tend to produce unsaturated fats—like olive or peanut oils. There are exceptions to this rule. The tropical oils—coconut, palm kernel, and palm—are high in saturated fatty acids and, therefore, are solid at room temperature. Also, chemically adding hydrogens to unsaturated plant oils to make them solid at room temperatures (e.g. hydrogenated or partially hydrogenated oils, as seen in vegetable "butter" spreads) can result in trans fatty acid formation.

The USDA has not set an RDA, adequate intake (AI), or upper limit (UL) for total fat intake (except for infants). Instead, it uses the Acceptable Macronutrient Distribution Ranges (AMDR) of 20 to 35 percent for adults. Research confirms that eating a diet high in fat promotes excess weight, obesity, and chronic disease. It's associated with higher blood cholesterol levels, breast and bowel cancer, and heart disease.

However, evidence is beginning to show that the *amount* of fat consumed is not as important as the *source* of that fat. Fats derived from whole-plant foods are either neutral or health-protective; fats from animal products and processed vegetable oils are more strongly associated with chronic disease.

Types of Fats

Here are the types of fats found in food:

Monounsaturated fatty acids (MUFAs) are fatty acids that have one (mono) double bond in its structure. They are liquid at room temperature but may become cloudy and thickened in the refrigerator. Found in olives, peanuts, avocados, pecans, almonds, their oils, and canola oil, MUFAs are known for being heart healthy.

Polyunsaturated fatty acids (PUFAs) contain at least two double bonds and are usually liquid both at room temperature and in the refrigerator. PUFAs make up both the omega-3 (alpha-linolenic acid or ALA) and omega-6 (linoleic acid or LA) essential fatty acids. These are required for growth, reproduction, skin function, cholesterol metabolism, and cellular communication. Found in walnuts, flaxseeds, hempseeds, chia seeds, vegetable oils (especially canola, soybean, and flaxseed), fish, and marine oils, PUFAs protect against coronary heart disease, certain cancers, and other inflammatory diseases.

Saturated fatty acids (SFAs) have no double bonds and are primarily found in animal products. Plant sources high in SFAs are tropical oils. SFAs are known to raise blood cholesterol and promote heart disease. Consuming SFAs are unnecessary, and in fact, the Food and Nutrition Board of the Institute of Medicine recommends eating "as little as possible while consuming a nutritionally adequate diet." The American Heart Association recommends limiting SFA intake to 5 to 6 percent of total calories, which, conveniently, is what an average whole food, plant-based diet contains.

Trans fatty acids (TFAs) are a relatively new invention created from vegetable oils, but they are also found naturally in some meat and dairy products. Whether man-made or natural, it appears that trans fats are possibly the most harmful type of fat we can consume. To create them artificially, unsaturated fats found in vegetable oil are modified by a process called hydrogenation. This results in a more "straight-hair" structure that tends to solidify at lower temperatures and increase the shelf life of processed foods; even bacteria don't want to eat it!

Historically, trans fats were found in fried and fast foods; however, in 2015 the U.S. Food and Drug Administration moved to ban all trans fats by 2018. Today, if you still want to eat these banned trans fats and minimize the shelf life of your health, you'll need to consume meat and dairy to do so. If you see the words *hydrogenated* or *partially hydrogenated* on an ingredient list, put down the product and quickly walk away!

Triglycerides (TGs) are the chemical form taken by most fats both in the body and in food. When not used immediately, any excess calories consumed in a meal are transformed into TGs for transport and storage in fat cells.

The Cholesterol Conundrum

Cholesterol is a waxy substance that naturally occurs in all parts of the body and is required for normal function. It's found in cell walls or membranes throughout the entire body and is necessary to produce many hormones, vitamin D, and the bile acids that help to digest fat.

Only a small amount of cholesterol is essential for all the roles it plays in the body, and the liver produces all your body really needs. Your liver makes about 800 to 1,000 milligrams per day, so it's not necessary to consume any other cholesterol in your diet!

Excessive amounts of cholesterol in the bloodstream promotes atherosclerosis, a condition in which fat and cholesterol are deposited in the walls of the arteries throughout the body. This process eventually generates cardiovascular disease. Because cholesterol is made exclusively in the liver, it's found only in animal products.

 **HEALTHY HINT**

Phytosterols, or plant sterols found in small amounts in all whole-plant foods, are compounds similar in structure to cholesterol. But they have been shown to help block the absorption of cholesterol in the gut.

Compared to What?

Despite nearly a century of growing evidence to support the healthful and unhealthful roles of different fats, we all too often see headlines contradicting traditional advice. Are saturated fat-loaded butter and bacon back as health foods? Not so fast. Much of the confusion is often created by special interest-funded research that asks deceptive questions. All too often these studies fail to ask a simple yet key question: compared to what?

When you look at the studies making these claims, it is the use of proteins, carbohydrates, and fats as food groups that perpetuates the confusion. It's like comparing apples to orange juice.

One can invent all types of macronutrient combinations in an attempt to influence the study's outcomes. Did they add saturated, unsaturated, or trans fat in the study? Was the carbohydrate refined flours and sugars or whole-food starchy vegetables? Was the protein high or low in essential amino acids? Most of the "carbs versus fat" diet wars can be distilled down to refined sugar versus processed oils and both should be limited or eliminated from the diet. It's time to shift the discussion away from protein, carbohydrate, and fat labels and return our menus and plates back to whole food.

In general, MUFAs and PUFAs found in plant foods are the most healthful fats to consume. MUFAs have no negative effects and possible slight beneficial effects on health. Evidence suggests MUFAs might reduce blood pressure, enhance blood flow, and minimally affect blood cholesterol, making them heart healthy. PUFAs are also beneficial overall, especially when they replace TFAs and SFAs in the diet. Certain PUFAs (the essential fatty acids) are required for human survival.

SFAs and TFAs, on the other hand, are the undesirables in the fat world. These increase the risk of chronic diseases, including coronary artery disease, some types of cancers, kidney disease, type 2 diabetes, and gallstones. Two to four times more damaging than SFAs, TFAs win the gold medal for the unhealthiest fat. Harmful and disease promoting, TFAs increase heart disease risk, interfere with liver function, increase the potential of having low birth-weight babies, interrupt essential fatty acid metabolism, and worsen insulin resistance. TFAs are found primarily in processed and deep-fried fast foods.

So what does all this mean? Avoid animal products and processed or deep-fried foods. Instead, consume a variety of whole-plant foods, and you'll minimize your risk of developing chronic disease.

Essential Fatty Acid Balancing Act

The biochemistry of essential fatty acid metabolism is extremely complex. Essentially, the Standard American Diet (SAD) supplies excessive amounts of omega-6 fatty acids and inadequate amounts of omega-3 fatty acids. Omega-3 fatty acids help prevent disease, and overconsumption of omega-6 fatty acids promotes inflammation (a disease-supporting process). Thus, balancing the two is an art worth mastering! Although deficiency is rare, much research suggests the protective effects of maintaining fatty acid harmony. Following are the fundamentals you need to know to become a pro.

Foods provide two essential fatty acids: linoleic acid (LA, an omega-6 fatty acid) and alpha-linolenic acid (ALA, an omega-3 fatty acid). Your body can convert these into other compounds needed to perform various functions. LA is ubiquitous in the food world. Not consuming enough would be challenging. In fact, most people are consuming way too much. LA easily converts into highly unsaturated fatty acids (HUFAs), which are vastly active in the body and have powerful health benefits.

In contrast, ALA has a hard time converting into its final products—eicosapentaenoic acid (EPA) and docosahexaenoic acid (DHA), two extremely important long-chain fatty acids. You need an adequate supply of EPA and DHA to meet your essential fat requirements. However, plant-based eaters have no direct source for EPA and DHA in their diet. EPA and DHA come from animal products only—namely, fish, fish oils, and specialty dairy and egg products. We have to rely on the conversion from ALA to meet our goals or supplement. So what's a plant eater to do?

 **PLANT PITFALL**

Fish oil is a commonly used supplement for people trying to consume adequate omega-3 fatty acids. Although rich in EPA and DHA, it also happens to be a highly concentrated source of contaminants. Fish contain large doses of heavy metals (lead, mercury, and cadmium) and industrial pollutants (PCBs, DDT, and dioxin)—all of which may cause adverse health effects. Choose an algal-derived DHA/EPA supplement instead.

Well, several variables impact the conversion of ALA to EPA and DHA. First, you need to consume the recommended Adequate Intake levels of ALA—1.6 grams for men and 1.1 grams for women.

Another important factor is to maintain the ratio of omega-6 and omega-3 fatty acids between 2:1 and 4:1. In other words, you should consume twice to four times the amount of omega-6 fatty acids than omega-3 fatty acids. For comparison, plant eaters typically consume a ratio of 14:1 to 20:1, which is a far cry from a healthful proportion!

Whole foods high in omega-6 fatty acids include sesame seeds, tahini, sunflower seeds, pumpkin seeds, soybeans (a.k.a. edamame), wheat germ, and tofu. Good sources for omega-3 fatty acids are flaxseeds, hempseeds, chia seeds, soy foods, leafy green vegetables, walnuts, and seaweed. In fact, you can get a daily allotment of ALA from just a tablespoon of ground flaxseed! Foods with a healthful balance of omega-6 to omega-3 fatty acids include flaxseeds, leafy green vegetables, hempseeds, and walnuts.

The following table provides specific amounts of whole-plant foods you can eat to reach your daily Adequate Intake of ALA omega-3 fatty acids, whether you're a man or a woman.

Meeting Your ALA Needs

Food	ALA Content	Amount Needed to Provide 1.6g ALA	Amount Needed to Provide 1.1g ALA
Grapeseed oil, 1 TB.	0.014g	114 TB.	79 TB.
Olive oil, 1 TB.	0.103g	15.5 TB.	10.7 TB.
Avocado oil, 1 TB.	0.134g	12 TB.	8 TB.
Kale, 1 cup cooked	0.134g	11.9 cups	8.2 cups
Collards, 1 cup cooked	0.177g	9 cups	6.2 cups
Tempeh, ½ cup	0.183g	4.4 cups	3 cups
Broccoli, 1 cup cooked	0.186g	8.6 cups	5.9 cups
Tofu, firm, ½ cup	0.228g	3.5 cups	2.4 cups
Black walnuts, 2 TB.	0.312g	0.6 cup	0.4 cup
Soybeans, 1 cup	1.029g	1.6 cups	1.1 cups
Canola oil, 1 TB.	1.279g	1.25 TB.	0.9 TB.
English walnuts, 2 TB.	1.352g	2.4 TB.	1.6 TB.
Walnut oil, 1 TB.	1.414g	1.1 TB.	0.8 TB.
Hempseed oil, 1 TB.	2.240g	0.7 TB.	0.5 TB.
Flaxseeds, ground, 2 TB.	3.194g	1 TB.	0.7 TB.
Flaxseeds, whole*, 2 TB.	3.194g	1 TB.	0.5 TB.
Flaxseed oil, 1 TB.	7.249g	0.2 TB.	0.15 TB.

Flaxseeds cannot be digested whole. Grind before eating.

Furthermore, consume a nutritionally adequate diet by following the guidelines in this book. Diets including TFAs, high amounts of omega-6 fatty acids, and/or alcohol hinder conversion to EPA and DHA.

Recent evidence suggests that vegans, vegetarians, and people who have a reduced ability to convert ALA, such as the elderly, have lower levels of EPA and DHA in their bodies. Because of this, it may be beneficial to double the ALA recommendations (3.2 grams for men and 2.2 grams for women per day) and consider a supplement. Plant-based microalgae DHA and EPA supplements are now widely available to help boost intake.

Whether you're a recovering carbophobe or protein prowler, you can see how ideas have been hyped up and cause mass confusion. Essentially, all food contains some combination of protein, carbohydrates, and fat. Your red flag should go on alert when one of these essential groups of nutrients becomes the focus of attention. When you eat whole-plant foods, you automatically and effortlessly strike a healthy balance.

The Least You Need to Know

- The three macronutrients—protein, carbohydrates, and fat—make up all the calories in your diet and serve uniquely important functions in energy, metabolism, and health.
- Carbohydrates supply the body with the most efficient form of energy and the primary source of fuel for the brain when available. Whole-food sources rich in carbohydrates include the most nutrient-dense foods on the planet: vegetables, fruits, whole grains, and legumes.
- Protein is needed in a smaller amount than commonly thought, and it's impossible to be protein deficient on a whole-food, plant-based diet.
- All amino acids are present in plants and are packaged healthfully alongside fiber, vitamins, minerals, and phytonutrients.
- Fats from whole-food sources—such as nuts and seeds—provide optimal types and quantities of essential fatty acids, as long as oil and animal fats are eliminated.

Getting Your Vitamins and Minerals

Now that you're familiar with the macronutrients in Chapter 2, it's time to introduce you to the little guys. Micronutrients are a group of essential substances required in small quantities for normal metabolism. Even though you need only a trivial amount of these nutrients, they're an extremely critical component of your day-to-day functioning.

In This Chapter

- Everything you need to know about vitamins and minerals
- Fat-soluble versus water-soluble vitamins
- The big, the tiny, and the necessary minerals

Versatile Vitamins

Thirteen vitamins quietly hide in the foods you consume, awaiting absorption in the GI tract so they can kick into gear and perform their jobs. Vitamins are divided into two categories: water-soluble and fat-soluble. They are separated based on their physical properties and how they act inside the body. Of the 13, 4 are fat-soluble vitamins, while the remaining 9 are water-soluble.

> **MIXED GREENS**
>
> The Food and Nutrition Board of the National Academy of Science's Institute of Medicine sets the Recommended Dietary Allowances (RDA). These guidelines suggest the dietary intake level sufficient to meet the nutrient requirements of nearly all (97 to 98 percent) healthy individuals in a particular life stage and gender group. After an explosion of nutrition discoveries, an additional group of guidelines was established in 1998 called the Dietary Reference Intakes (DRIs). DRIs include RDAs as the target intake, adequate intake (AI), tolerable upper limit (UL) of certain nutrients, and estimated average requirement (EAR). All these recommendations are based on the objective of "minimizing risk for chronic disease."

Fat- Versus Water-Soluble Vitamins

Fat-soluble vitamins, which include A, D, E, and K, require fat for absorption, hence the name. They're stored in your body's tissues and are excreted via the feces. Excessive doses can lead to toxicity, and deficiency is possible if inadequate fat is consumed or absorbed.

Water-soluble vitamins, on the other hand, consist of the eight B-complex vitamins and vitamin C. They can be dissolved in water, are not stored in the body, and are eliminated in the urine. Therefore, you need to replenish them every day. Similarly, they're easily destroyed and washed out during storage, preparation, and cooking, so they need to be cared for delicately.

To reduce their destruction, avoid overcooking foods high in water-soluble vitamins, and steam these foods instead of boiling them. Also be sure to consume raw sources regularly. The moment a fruit or vegetable is exposed to oxygen, the vitamins begin to degrade, so use freshly picked produce as often as possible. (Purchase your produce from a farmers' market or community-supported agriculture, buy frozen, or grow a garden of your own—and consume it as quickly as possible!)

Let's take a look at each of the vitamins in a little more detail, starting with the fat-soluble vitamins.

Vitamin A

Vitamin A refers to a group of compounds essential for growth, vision, reproduction, and immune function. Preformed vitamin A is found only in animals, but provitamin carotenoids, found abundantly in fruits and vegetables, can be converted into vitamin A. Even though at least 600 of them exist in nature, only about 50 can be converted into retinol, the active form of vitamin A. Beta-carotene is the most active and most commonly known of these carotenoids. Carotenoids come in a spectrum of reds, oranges, and yellows in pigment; however, they can be found hidden by the dark-green chlorophyll color in leafy green vegetables.

Carotenoids are powerful antioxidants. Lycopene, one of the most potent antioxidants in the carotenoid family, is known to prevent and treat prostate cancer. It's also effective against other cancers, heart disease, and age-related macular degeneration. Cook your lycopene sources (found abundantly in tomatoes) to enhance its availability.

Similarly, high doses of lutein and zeaxanthin—other carotenoids—reduce the risk of age-related macular degeneration and cataracts. These carotenoids, also found in leafy green vegetables, require fat for absorption. If you're following a low-fat diet or have any issues with absorption, you may be at risk for deficiency of these important nutrients. We suggest eating your leafy greens and tomatoes with a bit of fat, like nuts, seeds, or avocados.

Beta-carotene, one of the most well-known carotenoids, is found in foods with orange and yellow hues. This carotenoid works synergistically with vitamin E to support health protection. High doses can lead to a yellowing of the skin, a harmless condition. However, when taken in high doses via supplements, beta-carotene increases the risk of cancer and heart disease in people who smoke or drink alcohol excessively.

Not surprisingly, carotenoid intake tends to be high in plant eaters. The RDA for vitamin A is 900 micrograms for men and 700 micrograms for women. Pregnant women need 770 micrograms a day and 1,300 micrograms when lactating. Excellent plant-based sources of provitamin A include tomato, pumpkin, sweet potato, butternut squash, kale, spinach, cantaloupe, mango, and apricots.

The following table gives you the vitamin A content found in certain foods.

Vitamin A

Food	Vitamin A (mcg RAE)
Tomato juice, ½ cup	28
Nectarine, 1 medium	50
Milk, whole, ½ cup	56

continues

Vitamin A (continued)

Food	Vitamin A (mcg RAE)
Broccoli, ½ cup	60
Cow's milk, 2%, ½ cup	67
Cheddar cheese, 1 oz.	75
Tomato, 1 medium	76
Mango, 1 medium	80
Apricots, raw, 3	101
Cantaloupe, ½ cup	135
Collard greens, ½ cup	148
Papaya, 1 medium	167
Bok choy, ½ cup	180
Mustard greens, ½ cup	221
Swiss chard, ½ cup	268
Beet greens, ½ cup	276
Dandelion greens, ½ cup	356
Spinach, ½ cup	472
Butternut squash, ½ cup	572
Carrots, ½ cup	665
Pumpkin, canned, ½ cup	953
Sweet potatoes, ½ cup	1,291
Kale, ½ cup	2,443

Vitamin D

Vitamin D has become the vitamin du jour as studies focus on an almost universal insufficiency. Currently, 70 to 97 percent of the U.S. population is lacking in vitamin D! This shouldn't be taken lightly. Every cell in the body contains vitamin D receptors, indicating its importance for optimal overall functioning. Two commonly known functions of vitamin D include maintaining blood levels of calcium and phosphorus and supporting the cardiovascular system. Your blood level of 25-hydroxyvitamin D (the appropriate test to request from your doctor) should be at least 20 ng/mL; optimum levels are 50 ng/mL and above.

Normally, skin produces vitamin D when exposed to sunlight. A cholesterol compound in your skin called 7-dehydrocholesterol is activated by UVB sun ray exposure. After a visit to the liver and then the kidneys, this compound is transformed into 1,25-dihydroxyvitamin D, the biologically active form of vitamin D. At this point, vitamin D is acting as a true hormone that gets busy on many fronts performing structural and functional jobs throughout the body.

People who live farther away from the equator have an increased incidence of vitamin D deficiency and are, therefore, at an amplified risk for many chronic diseases. Preformed vitamin D is found only in animal products, specifically in fatty fish and their liver oils, milk, beef liver, and egg yolks. Because vitamin D is hard to come by nutritionally, foods like dairy and plant milks, fruit juices, cereals, breads, nutrition bars, and pastas are fortified with vitamin D.

Plant eaters and meat eaters are at the same risk for vitamin D deficiency, so it's important for everyone to get their vitamin D levels checked by a blood test. The results can help you determine whether you need to consider properly increasing your sun exposure and/or adding a supplement. Populations with darker skin, breastfed infants, people with limited sun exposure, obese individuals, elderly people, and anyone with gastrointestinal absorption issues are at higher risk for vitamin D deficiency. Low vitamin D levels are consistently associated with most chronic diseases, including many cancers, heart disease, osteoporosis, type 2 diabetes, and autoimmune diseases.

How much vitamin D should you consume daily? The RDA is 600 IU (15 micrograms) per day for all populations from 1 year to 70 years of age. After 71, the RDA increases to 800 IU (20 micrograms). Many leading researchers believe higher doses are necessary to sustain optimal levels of vitamin D. (See Chapter 10 to learn more about how to ensure adequate vitamin D blood levels.)

The following table gives you the vitamin D content found in certain foods.

Vitamin D

Food	Vitamin D (mcg)
Fortified margarine, 1 tsp.	0.5
Eggs, 1 large	0.6
Fortified plant milk, 1 cup	2.5 to 3.0
Fortified cow's milk, 2%, 1 cup	2.9

MIXED GREENS

Is vitamin D a vitamin or a hormone? It's both! Because it's obtained from the diet and required for survival, vitamin D is like a vitamin. By definition, however, a vitamin can't be created by the body. A hormone, on the other hand, is a chemical substance formed in one organ and carried via the blood to another organ, where it exerts functional effects. When the sun's ultraviolet B (UVB) rays hit the skin, they kick off a chain reaction that ultimately generates the active form of vitamin D. That reaction implies that vitamin D is also a hormone. But because it's found naturally in foods, the name "vitamin D" is the accepted term for this important hormone.

Vitamin E

Vitamin E exists in eight different forms, but alpha-tocopherol is active and can meet human requirements. This form of vitamin E is a potent antioxidant. With deficiency—which is rare, thanks to its presence in many foods—red blood cells become fragile and increased free radical damage occurs, leaving the body susceptible to damage due to oxidation. Although you need oxygen to stay alive, oxygen can cause an imbalance in your cells, where reactive compounds (free radicals) outweigh the presence of antioxidants. High exposure to free radicals and oxidation initiates many disease processes, like heart disease and cancer, and speeds up aging. (See Chapter 4 for more details on this process.) Antioxidants, like vitamin E and the carotenoids, halt oxidation.

In addition to its antioxidant activities, vitamin E also participates in immune function, regulating gene expression and other metabolic processes. With ample amounts, vitamin E helps keep the inner (endothelial) lining of the blood vessels smooth. This keeps blood cell components from sticking to it, which helps prevent plaque build-up. Another heart-helpful task vitamin E performs is boosting two enzymes that increase the release of a compound called prostacyclin. Prostacyclin prevents blood clots and keeps the blood vessels open and flowing.

The RDA for vitamin E is 15 milligrams per day for both adult men and women. For children age 1 to 3 years, 3 milligrams is recommended, and from ages 4 to 8, the RDA increases to 7 milligrams. Children age 9 to 13 years require 11 milligrams. With lactation, vitamin E RDA increases to 19 milligrams per day. Plant sources of vitamin E include avocados, wheat germ, sunflower seeds, almonds and almond butter, peanuts and peanut butter, pumpkin, soybeans, olives, and leafy green vegetables.

The following table gives you the vitamin E content found in certain foods.

Vitamin E

Food	Vitamin E (mg ATE)
Pear, 1 medium	0.28
Soybeans, ½ cup	0.3
Apple, 1 medium	0.33
Kohlrabi, ½ cup cooked	0.43
Quinoa, ½ cup	0.58
Olive oil, 1 tsp.	0.65
Peanut oil, 1 tsp.	0.71
Canola oil, 1 tsp.	0.79
Mustard greens, ½ cup cooked	0.85
Kelp, ½ cup cooked	0.9
Pumpkin, canned, ½ cup cooked	1.3
Turnip greens, ½ cup cooked	1.35
Swiss chard, ½ cup cooked	1.6
Pomegranate, 1 medium	1.7
Sunflower oil, 1 tsp.	1.85
Spinach, ½ cup cooked	1.9
Avocado, raw, ½	2
Mango, 1 medium	2.3
Wheat germ, 2 TB.	2.5
Peanut butter, 2 TB.	2.9
Peanuts, ¼ cup	3
Hazelnuts, ¼ cup	4.32
Wheat germ oil, 1 tsp.	6.72
Almonds, ¼ cup	7.8
Almond butter, 2 TB.	8.3

Vitamin K

Vitamin K plays an essential role in blood clotting. In fact, its name originates from the German word *koagulation,* which is what vitamin K helps regulate in the blood. When you get a wound, vitamin K helps the blood clot and begin the healing process. On the flip side, you don't want to produce unnecessary, potentially fatal clots in your bloodstream because they lead to obstructive heart attacks, peripheral vascular disease, and strokes. Vitamin K regulates coagulation to keep you clotting only when necessary.

With the drug Warfarin (brand name Coumadin), vitamin K becomes a balancing act. If you're on this drug for anticoagulant purposes, you need to maintain a consistent intake of vitamin K to allow the drug to work properly. Ask your physician to moderate your dosage while allowing you to consume adequate green vegetables to optimize your overall health.

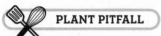 **PLANT PITFALL**

> People who are on anticoagulant drug therapy (which inhibits the clotting action of vitamin K) need to monitor their vitamin K intake carefully.

Vitamin K also assists in bone metabolism, mitigating the breakdown of bone minerals by osteoclasts and strengthening the composition of the bone. Low vitamin K levels in the blood are associated with low bone mineral density and higher rates of fractures.

Although deficiency is rare, it can affect breastfed newborn infants (which is why newborns in the United States are given a vitamin K injection right after birth), as well as adults who are suffering from malabsorption or are chronically taking antibiotics. Normally, the bacteria that live in your gut produce vitamin K. That's why the previously mentioned populations are at risk for inhibiting that process. Deficiency can lead to decreased bone mineral density and bleeding.

There are two forms of vitamin K that are significant in the human diet. Vitamin K1, known as phylloquinone, is omnipresent in the plant kingdom, especially in anything green. Vitamin K2, or menaquinone, is produced by microorganisms and converted from K1 and intestinal bacteria in small amounts. Like the other fat-soluble vitamins, foods rich in vitamin K need to be consumed with some fat. So add nuts, seeds, olives, and/or avocado to your green veggies to enhance absorption.

For adults 19 years and older, the daily adequate intake of vitamin K is 120 micrograms for men and 90 micrograms for women. Leafy green vegetables are excellent sources for vitamin K, as are broccoli, asparagus, lentils, and peas. There is increasing evidence that we may need a direct source of K2, so supplementing may be beneficial.

The following table gives you the vitamin K content found in certain foods.

Vitamin K

Food	Vitamin K (mcg)
Miso paste, 1 TB.	15
Romaine lettuce, raw, ½ cup	24
Asparagus, ½ cup cooked	45
Cabbage, ½ cup cooked	81
Brussels sprouts, ½ cup cooked	109
Broccoli, ½ cup cooked	110
Turnip greens, ½ cup cooked	265
Collard greens, ½ cup cooked	418
Spinach, ½ cup cooked	444
Kale, ½ cup cooked	531

Thiamin (Vitamin B₁)

Now let's switch to the water-soluble vitamins, starting with thiamin. Also known as vitamin B_1, thiamin acts as a *coenzyme* in the metabolism of carbohydrates and branched-chain amino acids. In other words, it helps convert carbs into energy.

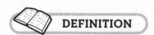 **DEFINITION**

Coenzymes are small, nonprotein molecules that enhance the action of an enzyme.

Thiamin deficiency is common in alcoholics. Many mechanisms contribute to thiamin deficiency in alcoholics, known as Wernicke-Korsakoff syndrome, including decreased intake, impaired absorption and use, and increased demand. Beriberi, a disease caused by thiamin deficiency that can lead to pain, mental confusion, and paralysis, is extremely rare because many foods are fortified with thiamin.

The RDA for thiamin is set at 1.2 and 1.1 milligrams per day in adult men and women, respectively. During pregnancy and lactation, women require 1.4 milligrams a day. Thiamin is found in whole grains such as quinoa, oats, and barley; beans, peas, and other legumes; nutritional yeast; brewer's yeast; winter squash; and tahini.

Riboflavin (Vitamin B$_2$)

Riboflavin, or vitamin B$_2$, plays a vital role as a coenzyme in energy metabolism. It's also important for growth and red blood cell formation. Although uncommon, deficiency can lead to mouth sores, a swollen tongue, inflamed and reddened skin, and a rare form of anemia.

Riboflavin is sensitive; it can be destroyed by sunlight, and substantial amounts can be lost in cooking water during boiling. So keep your produce refrigerated and use that cooking water again for soup!

The adult RDA for riboflavin is 1.3 milligrams for men and 1.1 milligrams for women. The daily requirement increases to 1.4 milligrams during pregnancy and 1.6 milligrams during lactation. Sources include nutritional yeast, fortified cereals and plant milks, barley, soybeans, mushrooms, spinach, sea vegetables, and beet greens.

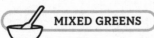

MIXED GREENS

You know when you take a multivitamin and your urine is fluorescent yellow? You can thank riboflavin for that!

Niacin (Vitamin B$_3$)

Niacin, or vitamin B$_3$, also contributes to energy by metabolizing glucose and fatty acids. (You can see why all these vitamins are in the same B family!) Used in therapeutic doses (think large), niacin helps raise HDL cholesterol levels. Niacin is also necessary in the production of DNA.

Pellagra is the disease associated with a deficiency of niacin. Symptoms of pellagra include confusion, delusion, diarrhea, inflamed mucous membranes, and scaly skin sores.

RDA for niacin in adults is 16 and 14 milligrams per day for men and women, respectively. An increase to 18 milligrams during pregnancy and then down to 17 milligrams per day for lactation is recommended. Plant-based niacin sources include fortified cereals, nutritional yeast, barley, rice, peanuts and peanut butter, brewer's yeast, tahini, tempeh, mushrooms, avocados, peas, and potatoes.

Vitamin B$_6$

Vitamin B$_6$ is comprised of three compounds (pyridoxine, pyridoxal, and pyridoxamine) that are all converted to its active forms, pyridoxal phosphate and pyridoxamine. B$_6$ functions as a coenzyme for more than 100 different enzymes that are primarily involved in amino acid metabolism. It's also essential for red blood cell metabolism and for keeping blood sugar levels stable. Vitamin B$_6$ may even have antioxidant properties. This vitamin is required for optimal function of both the nervous and immune systems. Maintaining an adequate consumption of B_6 also protects against heart disease.

Older people and individuals on a poor-quality diet may have suboptimal vitamin B_6 nutritional status. Symptoms of vitamin B_6 deficiency don't appear until later, when intake has been very low for an extended time. Signs of vitamin B_6 deficiency include dermatitis (skin inflammation), glossitis (a sore tongue), depression, confusion, and convulsions.

Adult RDA values vary according to age: from 1.3 milligrams for men and women age 19 to 50, 1.7 milligrams for men over 50, and 1.5 milligrams for women over age 50. During pregnancy, women need 1.9 milligrams daily and 2.0 milligrams daily when lactating. B_6 is found in a wide variety of foods, including fortified cereals, bananas, figs, raisins, chickpeas, lentils, sweet potatoes, tomato juice, avocados, soy products, and brewer's yeast.

The following table gives you the vitamin B_6 content found in certain foods.

Vitamin B_6

Food	Vitamin B6 (mg)
Asparagus, ½ cup cooked	0.04
Watermelon, ½ cup	0.04
Raisins, ½ cup	0.07
Peas, ½ cup cooked	0.09
Figs, 10	0.09
Nori, dried, 8g	0.1
Orange juice, ½ cup	0.1
Sunflower seeds, 2 TB.	0.1
Quinoa, ½ cup cooked	0.11
Chickpeas, ½ cup cooked	0.11
Kidney beans, ½ cup cooked	0.11
Navy beans, ½ cup cooked	0.12
Soy milk, ½ cup	0.12
Winter squash, ½ cup cooked	0.12 to 0.20
Brown rice, ½ cup cooked	0.14
Tomato juice, ½ cup	0.14

continues

Vitamin B₆   (continued)

Food	Vitamin B6 (mg)
Lima beans, ½ cup cooked	0.15
Lentils, ½ cup cooked	0.17
Plantains, ½ cup cooked	0.18
Tempeh, ½ cup cooked	0.18
Pinto beans, ½ cup cooked	0.19
Soybeans, ½ cup cooked	0.20
Spinach, ½ cup cooked	0.22
Potatoes, ½ cup cooked	0.23
Avocado, raw, ½	0.26
Wakame, dried, 8g	0.26
Sweet potatoes, ½ cup cooked	0.27
Banana, 1 medium	0.43
Kombu, dried, 8g	0.5

Folate

Folate's major role is to help produce and maintain new cells. It also helps make our genetic keys, DNA and RNA, and prevents changes in the DNA that could lead to cancer. (*Folate* is the form of the B vitamin that occurs naturally in foods. *Folic acid* is the synthetic version found in supplements and used to fortify foods.)

 **MIXED GREENS**

> Folate is named for the Latin word folium, which means "leaf"—perfect because the greatest source of folate comes from leafy green vegetables.

Pregnant women, or those who have the potential to become pregnant, are advised to maintain adequate doses of folate because deficiency, especially in the first three months of pregnancy, can lead to neural-tube defects, premature birth, and/or low birth-weight babies. Prenatal vitamins typically provide the RDA for folic acid, the synthetic form of folate.

However, recent evidence suggests that supplemental folic acid actually increases the risk for breast, colorectal, and prostate cancers, along with the risk of dying from those diseases. Studies also link folic acid supplements to an increased risk for childhood asthma and respiratory infections.

Fortunately, the natural food source (folate) does not pose any health risk and is found in abundance in the plant world. Pregnant women and everyone else can get plenty of folate without these concerns just by eating more leafy green veggies and beans. In addition, plant-based eaters tend to have superior folate intakes and status compared to omnivores!

The RDA for folate is 400 micrograms a day for both male and female adults and 600 for pregnant and 500 for lactating women. Choose spinach, asparagus, collard greens, turnip greens, beets, lentils, pinto beans, black beans, kidney beans, and black-eyed peas for deliciously rich sources of nature-made folate. There should be no reason for folate supplementation if you are regularly consuming folate rich foods, but it is important to check your multivitamin to make sure it's not an unhealthy source of folic acid. Recognizing increasing visibility of this health issue, some vitamin labels actually list folate in the dosing, but folic acid is still in the itemized ingredient list.

The following table gives you the folate content found in certain foods.

Folate

Food	Folate (mcg)
Strawberries, ½ cup	20
Tempeh, ½ cup cooked	20
Orange juice, ½ cup	24
Banana, 1 medium	24
Peanut butter, 2 TB.	24
Tomato juice, ½ cup	25
Cauliflower, ½ cup cooked	27
Tahini, 2 TB.	29
Grapefruit, 1 medium	30
Cantaloupe, 1 cup	34
Sunflower seeds, 2 TB.	40
Parsnips, ½ cup cooked	45

continues

Folate   (continued)

Food	Folate (mcg)
Brussels sprouts, ½ cup cooked	47
Orange, 1 medium	48
Mustard greens, ½ cup cooked	51
Split peas, ½ cup cooked	64
Beets, ½ cup cooked	68
Lima beans, ½ cup cooked	78
Avocado, raw, ½	81
Broccoli, ½ cup cooked	84
Turnip greens, ½ cup cooked	85
Collard greens, ½ cup cooked	88
Soybeans (edamame), ½ cup cooked	100
Black-eyed peas, ½ cup cooked	105
Kidney beans, ½ cup cooked	115
Black beans, ½ cup cooked	128
Spinach, ½ cup cooked	131
Asparagus, ½ cup cooked	134
Pinto beans, ½ cup cooked	147
Peanuts, ½ cup	176
Lentils, ½ cup cooked	179

Cobalamin (Vitamin B_{12})

Cobalamin, famously known as vitamin B_{12}, is a wildly popular topic of discussion when it comes to following a plant-based diet because it's the *only* nutrient not directly available from food or sunlight (as with vitamin D).

B_{12} is made by microorganisms, bacteria, fungi, and algae. Plants and animals cannot synthesize B_{12}. Because animals don't wash their food before eating it, they ingest these microorganisms. Ruminant animals (such as cows, goats, and sheep) have enough bacteria living in their rumen to provide adequate B_{12}. They also absorb some of the B_{12} produced by the bacteria in their intestines. Some plant foods may contain B_{12} from contamination by those B_{12}-producing bacteria in the soil, but it's unlikely in developed countries due to rigorous food washing and safety practices.

Vitamin B_{12} assists with several roles in the body, including red blood cell formation, neurological function, and DNA creation. It's unique because it requires intrinsic factor, made by the stomach, to be absorbed. With any stomach issues (as with pernicious anemia, an autoimmune disease) or intestinal issues, deficiency of vitamin B_{12} is possible. Similarly, as we age, it becomes harder to absorb the vitamin. This may lead to megaloblastic anemia and neurological disorders.

You may not realize you have a deficiency until it's too late. Symptoms include decreased sensation, dementia, difficulty walking, loss of bladder or bowel control, weakness, optic atrophy, and depression. Early detection is key to preventing irreversible neurologic damage, although this can be impossibly tricky. The liver is efficient at storing vitamin B_{12} and it may take up to five to ten years before the liver becomes depleted; however, without repletion—or for those with an inability to absorb B_{12}— deficiency will ensue. Be forewarned that during this period of time, blood test results may be skewed by other variables and irreversible damage may occur before the deficiency is caught.

While the RDA for B_{12} is 2.4 micrograms per day for adult men and women, 2.6 micrograms per day during pregnancy, and 2.8 micrograms per day with lactation, absorption varies depending on the dose and the individual. Plant-based sources include nutritional yeast and fortified plant-based milks, cereals, and meat substitutes. However, because of possible issues with absorption, it is recommended that anyone eating a plant-exclusive diet and anyone over the age of 60 use supplements to avoid deficiency. For maximum absorption, supplement with B_{12} (ideally in the cyanocobalamin form) in one of these three possible dosing schedules: 50 micrograms twice daily, 150 micrograms daily, or 2,500 micrograms once per week.

Please note that sea vegetables, algae, and spirulina act as vitamin B_{12} analogues and can actually promote deficiency. Because they look like B_{12}, they can attach to your B_{12} receptors and take up space where real B_{12} needs to be. However, these analogues have no biological activity and interfere with the absorption of the real deal.

If you don't take a B_{12} supplement or use consistent amounts of fortified products (like nutritional yeast or fortified plant milks), deficiency is also probable. See Chapter 10 for more on this. Please be steadfast and cautious about your vitamin B_{12} intake.

Biotin

Biotin serves as a coenzyme during the synthesis of glucose and fatty acids and for the metabolism of amino acids. Biotin deficiency is rare but will manifest as anorexia, glossitis, depression, nausea, and vomiting.

Limited data are available to form RDAs. Thus, the adequate intake for biotin is 30 micrograms per day for adults and 35 for lactating women. Excellent whole-food sources include oat bran, oatmeal, almonds, peanut butter, lentils, black-eyed peas, mushrooms, and spinach.

Pantothenic Acid

Pantothenic acid helps release energy from glucose, manufacture amino acids, and synthesize and degrade fatty acids. Sources are so widespread that no reliable documented deficiencies are recorded!

Adequate intakes are 5 milligrams per day for adults. The AI increases to 6 milligrams for pregnancy and 7 milligrams during lactation. Pantothenic acid can be found in high quantities in papaya, guava, mangoes, oranges, cantaloupe, broccoli, Brussels sprouts, bell peppers, and kohlrabi.

Ascorbic Acid (Vitamin C)

Vitamin C, also known as ascorbic acid, is the other water-soluble vitamin alongside the large B-family. A very busy vitamin, C functions in varied and extensive myriad roles in the body. It helps create collagen, L-carnitine, and certain neurotransmitters. Vitamin C also acts as an anti-oxidant and helps in protein metabolism, immune function, and iron absorption. Deficiency leads to scurvy, which is nearly impossible on a whole-food, plant-based diet that includes plenty of fruits and vegetables.

Plant-based eaters have no problem attaining the RDA for vitamin C, which is 90 milligrams for adult men and 75 milligrams for adult women. During pregnancy, women should consume 85 milligrams per day and then 120 milligrams when nursing. Fantastic food options include papaya, guava, pineapple, bell peppers, broccoli, Brussels sprouts, cauliflower, kiwi, oranges, strawberries, cantaloupe, kohlrabi, turnip greens, and tomatoes.

The following table gives you the vitamin C content found in certain foods.

Vitamin C

Food	Vitamin C (mg)
Asparagus, ½ cup cooked	3.5
Watermelon, ½ cup	6
Blueberries, ½ cup	7
Acorn squash, ½ cup cooked	8

Food	Vitamin C (mg)
Spinach, ½ cup cooked	9
Potatoes, ½ cup cooked	10
Banana, 1 medium	10
Okra, ½ cup cooked	13
Blackberries, ½ cup	15
Honeydew, ½ cup	15
Butternut squash, ½ cup cooked	15
Edamame, ½ cup cooked	15
Persimmon, 1 medium	16
Raspberries, ½ cup	16
Swiss chard, ½ cup cooked	16
Collard greens, ½ cup cooked	17
Beet greens, ½ cup cooked	18
Mustard greens, ½ cup cooked	18
Turnip greens, ½ cup cooked	20
Sweet potato, ½ cup cooked	21
Tomato juice, ½ cup	22
Tomato, 1 medium	23
Kale, ½ cup cooked	26
Elderberries, ½ cup	26
Tangerine, 1 medium	26
Cauliflower, ½ cup cooked	27
Cabbage, ½ cup cooked	28
Cantaloupe, ½ cup	30
Pineapple, ½ cup	40
Kohlrabi, ½ cup cooked	45
Brussels sprouts, ½ cup cooked	48
Strawberries, ½ cup	49

continues

Vitamin C   (continued)

Food	Vitamin C (mg)
Mango, 1 medium	57
Broccoli, ½ cup cooked	58
Sweet bell pepper, ½ cup cooked	60
Kiwi, 1 medium	64
Grapefruit, 1 medium	78
Orange, 1 medium	83
Guava, 1 medium	125
Papaya, 1 medium	188

Marvelous Minerals

Minerals are inorganic nutrients your body requires in continued supply for life, health, growth, and development. Thousands of different minerals exist in nature, but only about 21 have significant impact in your diet:

Arsenic	Molybdenum
Boron	Nickel
Calcium	Phosphorus
Chloride	Potassium
Chromium	Selenium
Copper	Silicon
Fluoride	Sodium
Iodine	Sulfur
Iron	Vanadium
Magnesium	Zinc
Manganese	

All minerals are derived from the soil and enter animals or humans via plants. And lucky for those on a plant-based diet, plants are loaded with minerals, including calcium, iron, zinc, and selenium. So the more plants you eat, the more minerals you acquire!

Macrominerals Versus Trace Elements

Minerals are divided into two groups based on whether you need a large amount (*macrominerals*) or small amount (*trace elements,* or *microminerals*).

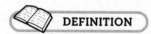

> **DEFINITION**
>
> **Macrominerals,** also considered "bulk elements," are minerals your body needs in amounts of 100 milligrams per day or greater. **Microminerals,** or **trace elements,** are present in minute amounts in the body's tissues. For optimal health, growth, and development, you need 15 milligrams per day or less.

Recommendations for intake have been established for nine essential trace elements—chromium, copper, iodine, iron, manganese, molybdenum, selenium, zinc, and fluoride. Recommendations for five potentially essential trace elements—arsenic, boron, nickel, silicon, and vanadium—haven't yet been determined.

Because you can easily attain adequate amounts of all minerals from a whole-food, plant-based diet, I focus on the three minerals that often have absorption issues: calcium, iron, and zinc. Also, because iodine tends to be low in plant eaters, we will offer some suggestions to prevent deficiency.

Calcium

Calcium is the most abundant mineral in the body—an adult human contains approximately 1,000 to 1,500 grams! Ninety-nine percent of the calcium in your body is stored in your bones and teeth, and the remaining 1 percent is throughout the rest of your body's tissues and fluids. Calcium plays an essential role in blood clotting, muscle contraction, nerve transmission, bone and tooth formation, and the secretion of hormones and enzymes.

AI recommendations for calcium in adults vary throughout the lifespan. For age 19 to 50, AI is 1,000 milligrams per day for males and females (even during pregnancy and lactation beyond the age of 19). After age 50, AI increases to 1,200 milligrams per day just for women, but the men increase at 70 years old, too. Whole-plant food sources of calcium include fortified plant milks, leafy green vegetables (especially low oxalate options such as kale, bok choy, lettuce, and cabbage), dried figs, sesame seeds and tahini, almonds and almond butter, chia seeds, beans, soybeans, soy nuts, and calcium-set tofu.

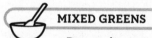

> **MIXED GREENS**
>
> Bone is dynamic and is constantly breaking down and rebuilding. Even though it's seemingly always solid and hard, bone mass is turned over as much as 15 percent every year. That shows the potential of your diet to influence the strength and density of your bones throughout your lifetime. Remember, you are what you eat!

With calcium, how much you *consume* isn't necessarily the issue. What's more important is how much you *absorb*. Calcium absorption determines risk of bone fractures and osteoporosis. Many factors influence calcium absorption, including age, how much you need, how much you take in, and other compounds that accompany the calcium when you consume it. Taking effective combinations of calcium and vitamin D improves absorption.

Only minimal research on bone status in strict plant eaters has been conducted so far. However, calcium is plentiful in plants, so you don't need to reach for harmful animal products to get your daily dose, which—because of their high protein, fat, cholesterol, and sodium content—wreak havoc on your arteries. If you eat your leafy greens and get plenty of exercise, you will have strong bones to last a lifetime.

The following table gives you the calcium content found in certain foods.

Calcium

Food	Calcium (mg)
Almonds, 2 TB.	24
Broccoli, ½ cup cooked	31
Lima beans, 1 cup cooked	32
Lentils, 1 cup cooked	38
Sweet potato, ½ cup cooked	45
Kale, ½ cup cooked	47
Orange, 1 medium	60
Bok choy, ½ cup cooked	79
Almond butter, 2 TB.	86
Turnip greens, ½ cup cooked	98
Tempeh, 3.5 oz.	111
Tahini, 2 TB.	128
Collard greens, ½ cup cooked	133
Sesame seeds, 2 TB.	140
Soybeans, 1 cup cooked	175
Dried figs, 1 cup	241
Soy milk, fortified, 1 cup	250 to 300

Food	Calcium (mg)
Fortified milk/juice, 1 cup	300
Tofu, calcium-set, 3.5 oz.	350 to 683

Iodine

Iodine deficiency is a global public health concern, affecting nearly one out of every three people worldwide. Characteristics include goiter and cretinism. Brain damage occurs when iodine deficiency happens during fetal or early childhood development, so pregnant women and preschool children in low-income settings are among the high-risk populations. Recent evidence has shown a possible increased risk of deficiency in plant eaters as well, especially raw followers.

Iodine is closely tied with thyroid function. When intake is low, production of thyroid hormones slows down. Adequate intake for infants up to 6 months is 110 micrograms per day and 130 micrograms from 6 to 12 months. The RDA for children ages 1 through 8 is 90 micrograms per day, 120 micrograms per day for children ages 9 through 13, and 150 micrograms per day for adults. Pregnant women require 220 micrograms daily and, while breastfeeding, 290 micrograms daily.

Iodine is hard to find in plant-based food. Because iodine content varies widely in soil, it's unreliable in plant foods. Sea vegetables can either have a lot of iodine or very little. Iodine deficiency was common in early twentieth-century America until salt was iodized. Salty foods like tamari, kosher salt, and processed items don't contain iodized salt. A quarter teaspoon of commercial iodized salt contains approximately 68 micrograms, or 47 percent of the adult RDA. However, since it's not advisable to use salt, you can incorporate sea vegetables (especially dulse and kelp) into your diet and monitor for iodine deficiency.

The following table gives you the iodine content found in certain foods.

Iodine

Food	Iodine (mcg)
Navy beans, ½ cup cooked	32
Potato with peel, baked, 1 medium	60
Salt, iodized, 1g	77
Cod, 3 oz.	99
Sea vegetables, dried, ¼ oz.	varies, up to 4,500

Iron

Ironically, iron is one of the most abundant metals on Earth, yet it's considered the most common nutritional deficiency worldwide! According to the World Health Organization, approximately 30 percent of the global population has iron-deficiency anemia. However, plant-based diets tend to be higher in iron than other diets. Iron is an essential component of proteins and enzymes that maintain good health, but its most important role is transporting oxygen. Almost two thirds of the iron in the body is found in hemoglobin, the protein in red blood cells that carries oxygen to the cells.

From age 19 to 50, adult men require 8 milligrams per day of iron, while adult women need 18 milligrams per day. After 51 years of age, the RDA is 8 milligrams per day for both men and women.

Diet provides two forms of iron: *heme* and *nonheme*. Heme iron is made from hemoglobin and is found in animal flesh. Nonheme iron is supplied by plants, including lentils, kidney beans, navy beans, chickpeas, pinto beans, spinach, Swiss chard, beet greens, turnip greens, pumpkin seeds, tahini, dried apricots, and blackstrap molasses.

Heme sources are absorbed better than nonheme, but this may not be advantageous. More of a good thing isn't always better, and heme iron is the perfect example of when it's not. A high blood level of stored iron has been associated with increased insulin resistance and heart disease. Furthermore, iron delivered by animal products comes with saturated fat, dietary cholesterol, steroids, hormones, and antibiotics.

Iron deficiency leads to fatigue, decreased immune function, and glossitis (inflamed tongue). Loss of iron, and its resulting anemia, usually occurs due to small intestinal bleeds or kidney disease. It can also accompany certain periods of life, including age 6 months to 4 years, adolescence, pregnancy, and menstruation. Still, dietary factors impact the absorption of iron—for better and for worse.

Dietary variables that inhibit absorption of iron include phytates in whole grains and legumes, tannic acids from tea, calcium in dairy, fiber, coffee, cocoa, and some spices (such as turmeric, coriander, chile peppers, and tamarind). To enhance iron absorption, include a source of vitamin C with your nonheme iron-rich food. For instance, enjoy salsa in your bean burrito or drizzle lemon juice over your leafy greens to maximize absorption. Other organic acids, vitamin A, and beta-carotene may also help with absorption, as does soaking and sprouting grains, beans, and seeds; leavening bread; and fermentation.

What about iron supplements, you might be wondering? They're pro-oxidative, meaning they promote oxidation. The opposite of antioxidants, they encourage free radicals to perform their mischief, thereby leading to increased risk for cancer, heart disease, aging, and other chronic diseases. Iron supplements should only be used if there's a deficiency and for as short a period as possible.

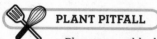 **PLANT PITFALL**

Phytates can block iron absorption up to 90 percent, making them significant inhibitors. Because they're primarily found in whole grains and legumes, phytates are prevalent in a plant-based diet. Fortunately, the higher the phytate content in a food, the higher the iron tends to be. Thus, consuming these products may not impact iron status as much as first thought. Ironically, phytates are also thought to reduce risk of various chronic diseases, including several forms of cancer!

Undoubtedly, the most telling fact about iron status in people who primarily eat a plant-based diet is that there's not much difference in incidence of iron-deficiency anemia between plant-based eaters and omnivores.

The following table gives you the iron content found in certain foods.

Iron

Food	Iron (mg)
Soy milk, ½ cup	0.55 to 0.9
Raisins, ¼ cup	0.8
Apricots, ¼ cup	0.9
Brussels sprouts, ½ cup cooked	0.9
Barley, pearled, ½ cup cooked	1.0
Cashews, 2 TB.	1.0
Collard greens, ½ cup cooked	1.1
Prunes, ¼ cup	1.2
Peas, ½ cup cooked	1.2
Sunflower seeds, 2 TB.	1.2
Tempeh, ½ cup	1.3
Beet greens, ½ cup cooked	1.4
Raisins, ½ cup	1.6
Pumpkin, ½ cup cooked	1.7
Black beans, ½ cup cooked	1.8
Black-eyed peas, ½ cup cooked	2.2
Lima beans, ½ cup cooked	2.2

continues

Iron   (continued)

Food	Iron (mg)
Navy beans, ½ cup cooked	2.3
Prunes, ½ cup	2.4
Chickpeas, ½ cup cooked	2.4
Sun-dried tomatoes, ½ cup cooked	2.4
Pumpkin seeds, 2 TB.	2.5
Tahini, 2 TB.	2.7
Spinach, ½ cup cooked	3.2
Lentils, ½ cup cooked	3.3
Blackstrap molasses, 1 TB.	3.6
Nori, dried, 8g dry weight	3.7
Dark chocolate, 1 oz.	3.9
Soybeans, ½ cup cooked	4.4
Dulse, dried, 8g dry weight	6.4
Tofu, firm, ½ cup	6.6
Kombu, dried, 8g dry weight	22.1

Selenium

Selenium is an essential trace mineral that is required for thyroid function, reproduction, and DNA synthesis, and acts as a powerful antioxidant, antimicrobial, and anti-inflammatory. While seafood and organ meats are food sources highest in selenium, plant sources vary according to soil quality. Brazil nuts are an excellent source of selenium, providing 777 percent of the RDA with just one ounce (approximately 6 to 8 nuts). When possible, eating one Brazil nut a day is an easy way to meet recommendations. Other plant sources include whole grains, legumes, vegetables, seeds, and other nuts. Adult RDAs are 55 micrograms a day, increasing to 60 micrograms when pregnant and 70 when lactating.

Zinc

Like the other minerals, zinc is needed in many metabolic processes, including the activity of about 100 enzymes, immune function, wound healing, protein and DNA creation, and cell division. You need zinc every day because your body doesn't have a special zinc-storing system. Symptoms of deficiency include growth retardation, loss of appetite, immune impairment, hair loss, delayed wound healing, and taste abnormalities.

Adult RDA for zinc is 11 milligrams per day for males and 8 milligrams for females. However, need increases for females to 11 milligrams when pregnant and 12 milligrams during lactation. Animal products contain high doses of zinc, but you can find it in plant sources, too. Cashews, chickpeas, almonds, kidney beans, and peas are all good choices. Similar to iron, zinc absorption is inhibited and enhanced by the same nutrients.

The higher incidence of zinc deficiency in plant-based eaters is due to the fact that the absorption of zinc from plants is somewhat lower than from animal products. The Food and Nutrition Board recommends that plant eaters increase their RDA by 50 percent to make up for these shortcomings.

It also recommends preparation techniques that discourage phytates from binding to zinc and increase its absorption. These techniques include soaking beans, grains, and seeds in water for several hours before cooking them and allowing them to sit after soaking until sprouts form.

You can also enhance your zinc intake by choosing leavened grain products (such as bread) instead of unleavened foods (such as crackers). Leavening partially breaks down the phytate.

The following table gives you the zinc content found in certain foods.

Zinc

Food	Zinc (mg)
Soy milk, ½ cup	0.3
Kidney beans, ½ cup cooked	0.8
Peas, boiled, ½ cup	0.8
Almonds, dry roasted, 1 oz.	1.0
Chickpeas, ½ cup cooked	1.3
Cashews, dry roasted, 1 oz.	1.6
Baked beans, canned, ½ cup	1.7

The Least You Need to Know

- Vitamin B_{12} isn't available from any plant-based food source. To get this vitamin, you need to take a supplement or eat fortified products.

- Vitamin D poses no more a risk for deficiency in strict plant eaters than in omnivores. Although sunshine is the best source, additional supplements may be required.

- Several macrominerals and trace elements have significant impact on your diet and health, and all are available from plants.

- As a plant eater, you need to remain cognizant of the minerals calcium, iron, zinc, and iodine to ensure you meet your daily needs.

You Are What You Eat (Not What You Don't)

When used together, two separate yet equally important components—consuming health-promoting nutrients and avoiding disease-advancing foods—create the ideal diet. We've said before: you are what you eat, but what you don't eat is just as important to your well-being.

In this chapter, you learn more about the supernutrients that pump up your immune system by fighting on the front lines, attacking viruses, bacteria, fungi, and cancer cells every day. You also learn why ingredients, such as refined sugars and oils, do exactly the opposite in your body and put you at risk for illness and excess weight.

In This Chapter

- Fascinating facts about fiber
- Awesome antioxidants and phytonutrients
- Compounds that are best left off the plate

What to Eat

Plants come readily equipped with bounties of fibers, antioxidants, and phytonutrients. These supernutrients, abundantly provided by Mother Nature, have been found to fight the overall process of disease. Forget potions and pills … just eat plants!

Fabulous Fiber

The word *fiber* probably stirs up thoughts of powders, capsules, and prune juice, yet fiber's fabulous benefits deserve elaboration. While it's well established that fiber keeps things moving, if you will, fiber plays other health-promoting roles, from preventing cancer to managing weight. What's more, fiber is exclusively found in plants. None (nil, nothing, zero, zilch) is found in beef, pork, chicken, fish, dairy, eggs, or other animal-derived products.

You'll remember from Chapter 2 that dietary fiber is categorized as soluble and insoluble. Soluble fiber influences positive effects on blood sugar and cholesterol levels. Soluble fibers include the following:

- Beta-glucans, found in oats, barley, and mushrooms, act as *prebiotics* and bind water.

- Gums and mucilages, including psyllium, carrageenan, and alginates from seeds and sea vegetables, are used by the food industry to stabilize, thicken, and add texture to foods.

- Pectins, found in berries and fruits, help create jellies and jams, due to their gel-forming capabilities.

- Resistant starches are found in odd places, such as unripened bananas and cooked-and-cooled cereals and potatoes, as well as in more common legumes, oats and peas.

Insoluble fibers, those well known for contributing to gastrointestinal (GI) health, help by preventing constipation, *diverticulosis,* and *hemorrhoids.* Furthermore, fiber reduces your risk of colorectal cancer and possibly even gallstones, kidney stones, varicose veins, and inflammatory bowel disease (ulcerative colitis and Crohn's disease). These insoluble fibers—celluloses, hemicelluloses, and lignins—are found in whole grains, legumes, nuts, seeds, vegetables, and fruits.

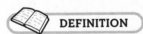 **DEFINITION**

Prebiotics are fermentable carbohydrates that encourage the growth of friendly bacteria in the microbiome of the GI tract. These bacteria and their by-products inhibit the growth of harmful bacteria and yeasts, reduce cancer-promoting compounds, improve absorption of minerals, and perhaps reduce food intolerances and allergies. **Diverticulosis** is a condition in which the colon has small outpouchings that may lead to inflammation (diverticulitis). **Hemorrhoids** are dilated veins in the anus or rectum, typically caused by constipation or strains due to diarrhea or pregnancy.

Keep in mind that proper GI health and normal bowel movements require both soluble and insoluble fiber. The insoluble fiber acts as structural material for the stool, keeping it together as it moves through the colon, and the soluble fiber holds onto some of the water so that it remains soft. Switching to an entirely plant-based diet may cause constipation due to certain fiber-rich foods—or a combination of them—causing a slowdown in the intestinal tract. Grains, cruciferous vegetables, nuts, seeds, and legumes are all fantastic for GI health, but one or more of these (or the lack thereof) may also cause an issue in some people.

Compounds named "nondigestible oligosaccharides," such as inulin and fructans (found in fruits, grains, vegetables, and legumes) are multifunctional. Some act as prebiotics, while others improve intestinal health.

Moreover, fiber removes excess sex hormones from the body, especially estrogen, and eliminates heavy metals such as mercury from the GI tract. High amounts of hormones or metals hanging out in your body increase the risk for different types of cancers.

The World Health Organization and American Heart Association recommend consuming at least 25 grams fiber a day. The Institute of Medicine recommends approximately 14 grams fiber per 1,000 calories consumed for all people over the age of 1 year. Unfortunately, the average intake of fiber is approximately 15 grams or less per day! The good news is that, by eating a heavily plant-based diet, you'll naturally and effortlessly meet—and even exceed—these recommended amounts.

Popping fiber supplements or sprinkling your processed food with fiber powder isn't the same as getting that fiber from whole-food sources. Eat a variety of beans, lentils, whole grains, vegetables, and fruits every day, and you'll reap the colossal benefits associated with high fiber intakes.

 MIXED GREENS

For every one of the approximately 10 trillion cells that comprise you, there are 10 times that number of foreign microorganisms hitchhiking through your body. These 100 trillion freeloaders living within you play a powerful role in your health. The majority of these microbes—collectively called the microbiome—live in your intestinal tract. In 2008, the Human Microbiome Project was launched to sequence the DNA of our microbiomes and to map out the complex web of their impact on our health. Surely, the implications of this project stretch far beyond the probiotics that line store shelves. The news so far is the fiber found in a plant-based diet fuels health-promoting bacteria, while a diet high in saturated fat and animal products fuels many undesirable microorganisms.

Awesome Antioxidants

You've heard the term *antioxidants* bandied about in medical news, on cereal boxes, and splashed across social media. Still, you may not really know what's so awesome about them. It all begins with the oxygen we breathe.

Ironically (and as mentioned in Chapter 3), the oxygen we require to survive also causes aging and diseases to progress. Sounds crazy, right? During respiration (breathing), *free radicals* are formed. Free radicals are highly unstable molecules that cause oxidation to occur. Think of rust forming on metal or an apple turning brown after you cut it open and it sits out for a while—these are examples of the effects of oxidation. In the body, oxidation sets off a series of reactions that create instability and keep self-perpetuating. If these reactions aren't stopped, disease ensues.

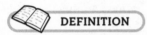

DEFINITION

Free radicals are high-energy particles with at least one unpaired electron that go wild in the body, ricocheting around trying to match up their unpaired electrons. This causes damage and leads to heart disease, cancers, autoimmune disease, macular degeneration, impaired immunity, and accelerated aging.

Free radicals also are produced during other routine body processes, like producing energy and metabolizing drugs, and by external factors such as cigarette smoke, pollution, radiation, and chemical contamination. Essentially, it's impossible to avoid exposure to oxidation. When you exercise, you take more breaths, accelerating the formation of free radicals. This increased exposure is no excuse to forego working out (or breathing, for that matter). Enjoy a diet high in antioxidants, and the benefits of exercise far outweigh any potential damage.

This is where the beauty of antioxidants comes in. These special compounds from plants sacrifice an electron, neutralizing free radicals and stopping the process of oxidation in its tracks. Potent antioxidants include carotenoids (precursors to vitamin A), vitamin E, vitamin C, and selenium. Simply eating plenty of foods with these compounds allows you to defend yourself against the consequences of free radicals.

Carotenoids represent a family of hundreds of phytonutrients that can be converted into vitamin A—although only a few are really active. They provide a continuum of color from reds, oranges, and yellows, found in watermelon, peppers, pumpkin, papaya, tomatoes, carrots, and apricots. But they're also overshadowed by the powerful dark green color present in leafy green vegetables such as kale, spinach, and broccoli. As mentioned in Chapter 3, certain carotenoids, like lycopene in tomatoes, may be absorbed better when cooked. This is why tomato sauce more effectively reduces the risk of prostate cancer than raw tomatoes themselves.

Vitamin E includes a family of eight antioxidants, but alpha-tocopherol, especially in food form, is the most influential on your health. A powerful force protecting cell membranes, this antioxidant is found in nuts, seeds, leafy green vegetables, and whole grains.

Vitamin C acts as an antioxidant by protecting cells from free radical damage and by helping other antioxidants, especially vitamin E, regenerate and maintain the ability to continue their work. Because vitamin C is water-soluble and is not stored in the body, it needs to be constantly replenished. On a daily basis, consume fruits and vegetables like citrus, guava, strawberries, peppers, broccoli, and Brussels sprouts to boost your vitamin C. But note: vitamin C is rapidly lost with exposure to oxygen.

Selenium is a trace element that plays a key role in opposing free radicals. It acts as a cofactor for the enzyme called glutathione peroxidase, where it works closely with vitamin E. Brazil nuts are excellent sources of selenium and, depending on the soil, sunflower seeds, whole grains, legumes, and some mushrooms may be good sources, too. The RDA is 55 micrograms per day for adults.

What about supplements? Unfortunately, consuming large quantities of these antioxidants as concentrated, isolated supplements turns out *not* to be beneficial—and are likely harmful, really. Beta-carotene supplements, for example, increase lung cancer risk, and alpha-tocopherol (vitamin E) supplements increased the risk of hemorrhagic stroke, prostate cancer, and death in clinical studies.

Phantastic Phytonutrients

Phytonutrients, or phytochemicals, are naturally occurring, biologically active substances found in plants. (The literal translation of the Greek prefix *phyto* is "plant.") Although they're not essential for your survival, like vitamins and minerals, phytonutrients contain potentially miraculous elements that, although meant to protect and nurture the plant they were produced for, offer those same benefits to humans. While providing color, aroma, and texture for the plants, phytonutrients also protect against predators, pests, and outside elements. In your body, their actions range from anti-inflammatory to anticancer agents, protecting you against the outside environment. (And that's just the thousands of compounds that have been discovered. Who knows how many others haven't yet come to light?)

Colorful fruits and vegetables are the record holders for all the categories of phytonutrients. The gold-medal winners in the phytonutrient competition are dark leafy greens, cruciferous vegetables (broccoli, cauliflower, cabbage, and Brussels sprouts), blue/purple fruits (blueberries, blackberries, plums, and cherries), tomatoes, garlic, onions, citrus, flaxseeds, and soybeans. These foods are bursting with compounds like flavonoids, phenolic acids, hydroxycinnamic acids, stilbenes, lignans, carotenoids, phytosterols, and glucosinolates. Now that's a mouthful (pun intended)!

MIXED GREENS

Speaking of colors, the pigments in fruits and veggies act as phytonutrients. Chlorophyll, the most abundant pigment in plants, imparts a dark green color and is known for its powerful health-promoting effects. Therapeutically used to detoxify, heal wounds, deodorize internally, and act as an antioxidant, chlorophyll is found in particularly high amounts in spinach, parsley, sea vegetables, and green olives.

Runners-up include tea, herbs, spices, legumes, nuts, seeds, and whole grains. Whole foods provide enhanced benefits when compared to supplements, since a powerful synergistic effect occurs in the combinations of nutrients.

So what do these special compounds actually do? Phytonutrients keep busy protecting your body. They help prevent cancer by blocking tumor formation, preventing cells from growing out of control, and repairing damage done to DNA. Furthermore, phytonutrients have antioxidant and anti-inflammatory actions. They boost immunity by fighting bacteria, viruses, and fungi. They even affect cardiovascular health by decreasing damage done to blood vessel walls, increasing blood flow, reducing blood clot formation and platelet stickiness, and decreasing blood cholesterol levels. Phytonutrients may reduce your risk of osteoporosis, macular degeneration, and cataracts.

To reap all the best health-promoting benefits, include a consistent supply of plant foods in your diet. Support your immune system with the limitless amount of powerful fibers, antioxidants, and phytochemicals naturally found in nature.

What to Avoid

Diet is now the number one cause of death and disability in the United States, surpassing smoking, which is now in second place. According to the World Health Organization (WHO), cardiovascular disease (CVD) remains the world's number one killer, accounting for about 31 percent of global deaths (more than 17 million deaths) per year, despite medical and procedural advances. Cancer, the second leading cause of death, accounts for almost 9 million (or one in six) deaths a year around the world. The global prevalence of type 2 diabetes, a major cause of death and disability, has risen from 4.7 percent in 1980 to 8.5 percent in 2014. What do all of these statistics have in common? Most of these deaths are preventable.

Besides piling your plate with beautiful whole-plant foods, the most proactive choice you can make for your health is to push the animal products and processed foods off your plate. Studies continue to show that animal products and processed foods are directly associated with these disease processes. This is due to compounds specifically found in these foods that are antithetical to health.

Saturated Fats, Trans Fats, and Cholesterol

As expounded upon in Chapter 2, it is well-established in the scientific literature that saturated fat, trans (or hydrogenated) fats, and dietary cholesterol promote chronic disease. Beyond these elements, other sources of overnutrition lurk primarily in animal products, tropical oils, and processed foods. Let's explore those further here.

Animal Protein versus Plant Protein

In the nineteenth century, the race was on to identify the fuels used in human metabolism. By the end of the century, Wilbur Olin Atwater, the father of American nutrition science, led the nation's push to analyze the carbohydrate, protein, and fat energy content of over 4,000 different foods. This was prior to the discovery of vitamins and minerals; therefore, the health importance of protein was emphasized. By the mid 1930s, amino acids were identified and proteins were analyzed for their amino acid composition. Essential amino acid content is generally lower in plant proteins than in animal proteins. This difference between plant and animal amino acid content is the source of the misconception that plant-food protein sources are less valuable than animal sources.

Around the same time, unrelated parallel investigations began using calorie restriction to better understand nutritional deficiency. Paradoxically, by examining the effect of rats eating a restricted diet, researchers stumbled upon a surprising result. Rats eating a restricted diet actually lived longer than rats allowed to eat freely. Nearly a century later, dietary restriction remains the only nongenetic method that extends lifespan in nearly every species studied, including yeast, flies, worms, and rodents. It has also been effective in healthspan extension of primates by reducing cardiovascular disease, tumor growth, and glucoregulatory impairment. Generally speaking, a restriction of 30 to 40 percent from a normal healthy diet resulted in an up to 50 percent longer lifespan. Data from recent first human trials suggest dietary restriction will also be beneficial for humans.

Over the last 20 years, research supporting dietary restriction has repeatedly pointed toward protein restriction. In fact, researchers have narrowed down at least some of the positive benefits to the restriction of certain essential amino acids. Despite society's mission to consume as much protein as possible, it may turn out that many of the health benefits of a plant-based diet are due to the unintentional essential amino acid restriction naturally found in plants. Some of the key amino acids to restrict are highest in chicken, eggs, and fish, the so-called healthy animal-protein choices whose consumption has risen over the last century. There are many questions left to answer, but protein and amino acid restriction seem to place you on the right track to a long, healthy life and a whole food, plant-based diet restricts these automatically. (See Chapter 16 for more information.)

Insulin-Like Growth Factor-1 (IGF-1)

Like us, animals naturally produce hormones to grow, to function, and to reproduce. While the extent to which these hormones influence human health when those animals and their byproducts are consumed has not yet been fully elucidated, we do have data supporting risk. One documented mechanism is the increased production of insulin-like growth factor-1 (IGF-1). Once we reach adulthood, growth is not an all-positive feature and can mean abnormal growth—for example in the rapid proliferation of cancerous cells. High IGF-1 levels in the blood have been associated with several types of cancer, acne, and possibly other chronic diseases. On the other side of that equation, consuming lower levels of protein (particularly animal protein) reduces growth hormone and IGF-1 and is associated with optimized healthspan and longevity.

Heme Iron

Animal products contain the heme form of iron, as opposed to the nonheme iron found in plant foods. As mentioned in Chapter 3, while heme iron may be better absorbed than nonheme, this turns out to be a disadvantage. This potent form of iron acts as a pro-oxidant and increases risk of colorectal cancer, promotes atherosclerosis, and reduces insulin sensitivity.

Chemical Contaminants

When animal flesh is cooked, harmful compounds are produced in the process. Polycyclic aromatic hydrocarbons (PAHs) are formed with high-heat methods of cooking, such as smoking, grilling, and broiling, and have been linked to increased cancer risk. Heterocyclic amines (HCAs), also considered carcinogenic, are formed when flesh is exposed to high heat (e.g. barbecuing, pan frying, and grilling), long cook times, and external charring. Finally, dietary advanced glycation end products (AGEs) contribute to oxidative stress and inflammation, kicking off and progressing the cascades of degenerative diseases. AGEs are found primarily in animal flesh, full-fat dairy products, and highly processed foods. Lower temperatures and shorter cooking times may reduce the formation of these compounds but, better yet (and to also avoid foodborne illness caused by undercooking animal products), stick to whole plants instead.

Other (Not-So) Goodies in Animal Products

A small molecule with a long name, N-glycolylneuraminic Acid (Neu5Gc), is produced by many mammals other than humans and is incorporated into humans via the consumption of meat, organ meats, and dairy products. Unfortunately, Neu5Gc promotes chronic inflammation and increases the risk of tumor formation.

Another inflammation-inducing substance commonly found in animal products is trimethyl-amine (TMA). The smell of seafood decomposing is primarily due to TMA, but that's not what really stinks about these inflammatory molecules. In our bodies, TMA becomes the compound trimethylamine N-oxide (TMAO). TMAO induces inflammation, atherosclerosis, heart attack, stroke, and death.

Carnitine, found mostly in red meat and some energy drinks, and choline, found in poultry, fish, shellfish, red meat, liver, dairy, and eggs, are metabolized by our intestinal bacteria and converted into TMAO. It should be noted that while choline is a required dietary nutrient, we do manufacture some in our bodies and too much may be just as harmful as not enough. Eggs have choline, but like many animal products they contain excessive quantities along with cholesterol, saturated fat, and methionine. Plant sources like pinto beans, broccoli, quinoa, and soy products are far better choices for dietary choline.

In dietary studies, subjects eating foods high in carnitine and choline were treated with a strong dose of antibiotics to decrease intestinal bacteria and showed no spike in TMAO. When the antibiotics were removed and the intestinal bacteria returns, so too does the TMAO. However, when long term vegans were tested with a steak (the things we do for science) they didn't produce TMAO. Proof that, ultimately, diet does drive the distribution of healthy and unhealthy intestinal bacteria.

Oil

We're going to chew the fat a little on oil. Oil is not a health food and we are not recommending you cook with it. With that said, fat plays a key role in the diet by providing essential fatty acids and enhancing fat-soluble nutrients, such as carotenoids and vitamins A, D, E, and K. Furthermore, fat adds to the culinary enjoyment of food—what chefs describe as *mouthfeel*—by mobilizing fat-soluble flavors to the taste buds. The problem with oil and cooking: we use too much. If you reach for the olive oil before the pan has even begun to heat, you'll likely overdo it. Broadly speaking, squeezing oil from olives, sugar from beets, salt from oceans, and flours from intact grains can all lead to the same issue: overuse of refined foods. Found in animals and plants alike, fat is mostly an energy storage organ, but it is also used in structural membranes and other biologically important molecules.

Most studies linking high-fat diets to chronic disease are based on the intake of fat from animal products and certain processed vegetable oils. Oil is 100 percent fat and contains 120 calories per tablespoon (nearly 2000 calories per cup). Oil is calorie rich and nutrient poor and offers no specific nutritional benefits outside of limited cases where a more harmful fat is displaced (e.g. olive oil instead of butter).

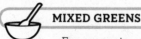 **MIXED GREENS**

For comparison, 100 grams of olives contain approximately 115 calories, 3 grams of fiber, and 11 grams of fat, and 100 grams of olive oil contain 884 calories, 0 grams of fiber, and 100 grams of fat.

Some oils contain modest amounts of vitamin E and omega-3 fatty acids, which are easily attainable from other whole-food sources such as nuts, seeds, avocados, and olives. As a bonus, when you consume whole-food sources, you also get fiber and a multitude of other nutritious deliciousness with fewer calories. (Although counting calories is unnecessary, eating a concentrated source of nutrient-poor calories is a surefire way of gaining weight.)

Remember that no type of oil is essential in the diet, and some are worse than others. Coconut oil, for example, is touted for its health properties yet contains about 83 percent of its total calories from saturated fat! Recent evidence shows that, although coconut oil has a different saturated fatty acid profile, it is still not much better than butter in terms of healthfulness. Even the universally praised olive oil isn't the superfood it is made out to be. Remember that in many of these studies, the question we need to ask is "compared to what?"

Olive oil has been hyped as a magic bullet to heart health for years, due to its role in the Mediterranean diet. But pouring oil on food is not the salient feature of this diet. Fifty years before olive oil and the Mediterranean diet became a marketing gimmick, nutrition researcher, Ancel Keys, began studying diet trends. Japanese people who immigrated to Hawaii began to experience heart disease at the same rates as seen in lifelong Americans. Their traditional, low-fat, plant-based Japanese diet was replaced by a high-fat Western diet with increased inclusion of animal products. Similarly, he noticed that Finnish farmers had increased rates of heart disease on a diet high in butter and cheese, whereas similar laborers on the Greek island of Crete, eating a mostly plant-based diet high in olive oil, had one of the lowest incidences of heart disease.

The most popular theory Keys extrapolated from this study is that monounsaturated fat-rich olive oil decreases the risk of heart disease. In each case, diets lower in animal products seemed to be protective against heart disease, while diets high in animal products resulted in significant increases in heart disease. Some scientists argued against Keys's conclusions and suggested that animal protein was a better predictor of heart disease than saturated fat. While it was later demonstrated in metabolic ward studies that saturated fat may be causal with increasing serum cholesterol, choosing plant-based sources of food still addresses both issues. Nonetheless, olive oil has received unfair credit, most likely, since the traditional Cretan Mediterranean diet consisted of fruits, vegetables, herbs, spices, beans, whole-grain breads, and fish, in addition to olive oil. The use of olive oil alone didn't cause better health outcomes. Today, olive oil is still flowing in Greece, but now the Greeks surpass the United States in heart disease.

Historically, processing olives into olive oil is a great way to concentrate energy (calories), and it is also a method to preserve the calorie for use throughout the year. This is a great strategy in times of food scarcity and certainly a good alternative to butter and lard (compared to what?). However, translating this to modern first-world societies, where there are officially more over-nourished than undernourished people around the globe and hypercaloric food is ubiquitous, an additional source of concentrated calories will not help us get healthier.

Here are some critical points to extrapolate from the decades of data on the Mediterranean diet:

- Replacing saturated with monounsaturated fats is better because you're getting less saturated fat. Health benefits aren't necessarily due to the intake of the monounsaturated fats themselves.

- You don't require monounsaturated fats to stay alive. You only need the essential fats, omega-6 and omega-3 fatty acids.

- Of olive oil's total calories, 14 percent come from saturated fat.

- Olive oil didn't give Cretans healthier hearts. Olive oil was merely one of many factors involved.

- Pouring olive oil (or any oil) on top of an unhealthy diet will *not* make you healthier.

You can get plenty of healthy fats by eating avocados, nuts, seeds, and olives instead of oils. Even leafy green vegetables contain essential fatty acids. When intact, these sources of fat maintain their other health-promoting values (phytonutrients, antioxidants, and fiber) and should be incorporated moderately into a varied, whole-food, plant-based diet.

Sodium

Sodium is an important electrolyte that regulates metabolic processes in the body. But you need only small quantities. The key word here is *small*—just 1,500 milligrams or less per day. The average 3,466 milligrams that 90 percent of Americans consume daily, according to a CDC report, is excessive. Think you don't use that much? Consider this: 1 teaspoon of salt contains 2,300 milligrams sodium!

If you eat enough food to stay alive, you'll automatically consume adequate sodium for health. If you use added salt, or if you consume high-sodium foods, know this: high intakes can lead to or exacerbate hypertension, or high blood pressure. If you have high blood pressure or take medication for your blood pressure, you must maintain a sodium-sensible diet. Processed foods and restaurant dishes tend to be high in sodium. Limit these and cook with as little salt as possible.

 **HEALTHY HINT**

Salt is well hidden in foods, especially when it is in cooked foods. For example, bread and salted potato chips have almost the same amount of sodium packed into them (490 milligrams and 527 milligrams, respectively). While potato chips taste infamously salty, the flavor is almost unnoticeable in bread. If you want something salty, but with minimal sodium, sprinkle a few granules of salt over your food right before you enjoy it, instead of adding it into the whole dish.

Limiting sodium in the diet doesn't mean eliminating the salty palate. Salt is an amazing enhancement to nature's flavors, but like oil and sugar, we often go astray with salt while cooking. Consequently, when one cooks with salt it ends up taking much more to achieve the same level of flavor as when it's added at the table, as demonstrated in the sidebar. If you choose to add sodium to your meals, do it at the table instead of the stove.

One other common mistake is caused by misleading nutrition labels; pay close attention to the serving size. For example, let's look at soy sauce (some sold as "liquid aminos"). While most soy sauces list the serving size as 1 tablespoon, with approximately 575 mg sodium in "lite" soy sauce and 920 mg sodium in regular soy sauce, another soy sauce may list the serving size as one-half teaspoon. Be careful! That 160 mg of sodium per serving is actually 960 mg per tablespoon— 40 mg more than regular soy sauce.

The most important point to emphasize is that your palate adjusts to how much sodium is consumed. The more salt you eat, the more you crave it. The good news is the less salt you eat, the saltier things taste. Keep in mind that dairy and processed meats are some of the highest-sodium foods. Following a plant-based diet can keep your sodium intake in check.

Sugar

Sugar is in nearly everything processed, from ketchup and salad dressings to protein bars and breakfast cereals. It comes hidden in many different fancy pseudonyms:

Agave	High-fructose corn syrup (or corn sugar)
Barley malt	Invert sugar
Beet sugar	Lactose
Brown sugar	Maltose
Cane syrup	Organic cane sugar
Corn syrup	Powdered or confectioners' sugar
Date Sugar	Raw sugar
Dextrose	Rice syrup
Fructose	Sucrose
Fruit juice concentrate	Turbinado sugar
Galactose	

And that's just a sampling!

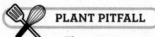 **PLANT PITFALL**

Three times as sweet as table sugar, agave nectar has become a hugely popular sweetener touted as health food. Whereas table sugar is purely sucrose, which is broken down to yield half fructose and half glucose, agave can contain up to 90 percent fructose. High-fructose corn syrup (HFCS-55) is only 55 percent fructose and is a known as a health hazard. Although agave nectar brings a lower spike in blood sugar, the fructose is metabolized in the liver and may lead to elevated triglycerides, heart disease, insulin resistance, diabetes, and weight gain.

Refined sugar and its derivatives wreak havoc on your health similar to saturated fat, with links to elevated triglycerides, blood glucose, and adrenaline. Refined sugar also promotes cancer growth, poor cholesterol profiles, diabetes, metabolic syndrome, obesity or excess weight, gastrointestinal diseases, premature aging, cardiovascular disease, gout, and acne. And if that weren't enough, it is associated with depression, anxiety, tooth and gum decay and is powerfully habit forming and physiologically addicting! Like salt, the more you sweeten things, the more sugar you desire.

One of the best things you can do for your health (after giving up animal products) is to limit or eliminate refined sugar. You'll find plenty of ways to indulge on a plant-based diet that will make you realize you're not missing anything, and whole-food fruits will become increasingly sweeter with time. Plus, it's health-promoting to cook and bake with fruits, such as dates, when more sweetness is desired—but more on that later. Refined sugar, refined oil, refined salt, and refined flours aren't poisonous, but they have become so overused in commercial and home cooking that our entire society has a shifted palate. All are better avoided and replaced with whole-food alternatives.

Artificial Sweeteners

You're born to seek out sweetness. The taste buds sensitive to sweet flavor are located at the tip of your tongue, ready to acknowledge that sweet sensation at first lick. It's a survival mechanism. Sweet represents carbohydrates, and the most efficient form of fuel comes from those carbs. You crave sweet, so you'll seek out prime energy-producing foods first.

Evolutionarily, food has never been as accessible as it is today. In the past four or five decades, food has gone from a rare and appreciated commodity to a ubiquitous inundation of daily living. Most people in developed countries no longer eat to live but, rather, live to eat. With fast-food restaurants and convenience stores on every corner, doughnuts in every break room, and vending machines on every floor, hunting and gathering are unnecessary. Instead, messages about eating bombard your life from numerous angles.

So what's the best response to these messages? More eating, of course! Instead of worrying about where the next meal will come from, the focus has shifted to how to keep eating fast and processed foods without the health consequences. And that's how artificial sweeteners were born.

They may trick your brain into thinking it's about to receive fuel, yet no fuel is taken in (unless you're drinking diet soda with french fries and a large veggie cheeseburger). People are still eating more of other calories.

Additionally, artificial sweeteners' excessive sweetness—160 to 8,000 times the sweetness of table sugar—perpetuates the cravings for sweet things and in turn diminishes the sweetness of fruits and other foods that are naturally sweet. For this reason, people who use artificial sweeteners may have no better success at controlling their weight and health than those who eat sugar and other natural sweeteners.

Reducing, if not outright avoiding, animal products, tropical oils, and processed foods minimizes their associated health risks. None of these items are necessary in the diet and you are better off without them. Don't be dismayed if at first your new diet seems a little bland. Remember, your palate is adaptable and in time, you will find whole foods tasting salty, sweet, fatty, and far more satisfying.

Cultivating the ideal nutrition plan is indeed a process. You need to nurture the two complementary components—increasing the wildly nutritious elements and decreasing the harmful have-nots. Each choice on either side is progressive and optimistic and will further your fortitude in the right direction.

The Least You Need to Know

- Plants provide plenty of fiber to prevent and reverse disease by mopping up toxins and encouraging them to move along.
- While preventing the constant barrage of illness-enhancing free radicals is impossible, your best protection is frequently consuming antioxidants and phytonutrients from fresh fruits, vegetables, and other plant sources.
- Refined oil, refined sugar, refined salt, refined flour, and other processed foods cause disease-promoting reactions in the body and hinder nutritional gains from eating whole foods.
- Acquired appetite takes precedence over natural eating. Your palate is plastic and it will change with consistency and practice.

What's on the Menu?

Dietary goals and guidelines for Americans date all the way back to 1894, when the U.S. Department of Agriculture (USDA) developed the first generation of a food composition table and guideline, *Foods: Nutritive Value and Cost.* Much of it was centered on overcoming the economic barriers that existed for food choices. In 1916, the *USDA Farmers' Bulletin 712: School Lunches* provided foods grouped for the first time to facilitate public education through discussions about appropriate preparation of balanced school lunches. At that time, the five food groups were protein-rich foods, cereals or starchy foods, fatty foods, vegetables and fruits, and simple sweets. Since starvation and undernutrition were so prevalent in children, much of this messaging centered around ensuring adequate intake. A year later, in *Food for Young Children* and a series of three bulletins entitled *How to Select Foods,* milk gained increasing emphasis across all diet recommendations, particularly for children. Food recommendations were based mostly on the USDA's charter to promote the sale of agriculture, and in all these early bulletins, it was clear that food promotion and the economy of food was as much a priority as the fledgling health recommendations.

In This Chapter

- The origin of dietary guidelines
- Introducing the Food Triangle
- Plant-based food groups to please your palate
- Eating at the top of the triangle: leafy greens and cruciferous vegetables

Over the next century, the USDA periodically updated and re-released food guides. These guides have progressed through 12 major food groups in 1933 to the *Basic Seven Food Guide* in 1942. In 1956, the seven were condensed to the "Basic Four" food groups—meat, milk, vegetables and fruits, breads and cereals—in the publication called *Essentials of an Adequate Diet*. In 1979, the *Hassle-Free Guide to a Better Diet* emphasized calories and fiber, allowing sweets, fats, and alcohol to supplement the basic four food groups in moderation. Beginning in 1980, the first *Dietary Guidelines for Americans* emerged, and this report is currently updated every 5 years.

The Food Guide Pyramid that emphasized a hierarchy of food intake recommendations was introduced in 1992. With grains as its foundation, followed by fruits and vegetables; then dairy products and meats, eggs, beans, and nuts were stacked on top. Sweets and fats appeared at the tip of the pyramid to represent their minimal recommended limited intake. This widely recognized pyramid was tipped over on its side in 2005, and in 2011, they retired the pyramid and *MyPlate* was born.

Today, you can log on to the *MyPlate* interactive website and learn about how many servings are recommended for you (based on your age and estimated calorie needs) and use their tools, such as daily checklists, quizzes, BMI calculators, and more. Yet again, the new *MyPlate* divides foods into new agriculturally centered groups of dairy, grains, vegetables, fruits, and proteins. Hey, we now know where to get our protein; it's on the plate!

Through this evolution, it has become quite clear that a conflict continues between economics and nutrition. Protein was likely used to blur the difference between beans and beef, but as we learned in Chapter 2, it's not a particularly helpful way to think about food. Recall that research demonstrates increased healthspan by limiting those essential amino acids, which result from excessive animal protein in the diet. We believe using protein as a group adds to macroconfusion and talking about food using actual food names (e.g. carrots, kale, and lentils) may be a better choice, instead.

Unfortunately, politics are involved in the making of these government guidelines and heavily influenced by lobbying and funding. Because of this, health concerns often take a secondary position when determining these recommendations. However, independent entities and practicing dietitians have developed food group guidelines based strictly on health outcomes found from sound scientific research.

One of the issues everyone faces is overcoming dietary bias. Food is an integral part of culture, family, celebration, and even self. Attempting a diet that is radically different from how you have been eating can be alarming. Even physicians and dietitians are often in a situation of unfamiliar dietary waters. We have some sources in Appendix D and even journal articles we wrote specifically to help your physician better understand the nutritional benefits of a whole food, plant-based diet. Actually, it's more difficult to overcome the bias in the discussion than to execute it in real life.

Ditch the Pyramid for a Triangle

While some might find food groups helpful, we'd like to arrange them in a slightly different way. Because the nutritional density for plant-sourced food is so much higher than most animal products, it's a lot easier to get what you need without a lot of planning. In fact, from a purely nutritional perspective, it's far easier to live exclusively on plant-sourced food than exclusively on animal-sourced food. Many of you are transitioning from a mixed, omnivorous diet and we want to take the guesswork out of your journey. Until the new diet is equally familiar, convenient, and enjoyable to your old diet, you won't have the willpower to overcome the urges; one or more of these three motivations will eventually take you back to old habits.

We'll stick with the general groups of vegetables, fruits, whole grains, legumes, nuts and seeds, and herbs and spices. To date, each of the former groupings of food have attempted to simultaneously address both agricultural economy and nutrition. Much of this advice is carried over from a time when starvation and malnourishment resulted in undernutrition. We want to arrange food purely for healthspan and that translates to sufficient nutrition with the minimum calories to meet your activity needs.

 **MIXED GREENS**

According to the World Health Organization, in 2011, we crossed a major historical milestone: the number of people worldwide who were overnourished outnumbered the people who were undernourished. In June 2017, it was reported in the New England Journal of Medicine that nearly one third of the worldwide population is overweight or obese.

We would like to introduce the Food Triangle as a new paradigm to arrange food. It was developed by one of our coauthors along with researchers at Harvard and National Institutes of Health to represent a wide range of research data supporting healthspan and longevity. In chapter 1, we discussed the role of diet in extending the lives of a wide range of organisms. The Food Triangle takes the guess work out of food choices. It's a simple tool for not only recognizing food choices that will lead to weight gain, but also a helpful reminder of how to eat to get the most nutritional bang for the buck.

The Food Triangle provides an easy way to visualize food organized by both increasing energy density and distribution of vitamins, minerals, and phytonutrients. It places emphasis on whole-food in place of macronutrient percentages.

(Used with permission from Mary Ann Liebert Publishers, Inc.)

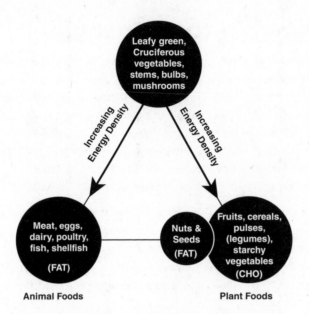

Here's how to use the Food Triangle. At the top (apex) of the triangle, you'll see the emphasis on the green side of our food palette, with leafy greens, cruciferous vegetables, bulbs, mushrooms, and stems. These should be the foundational foods for every meal and, in terms of volume, the biggest part of your plate. These foods can be eaten in nearly unlimited quantities and they are loaded with vitamins, minerals, phytonutrients, antimicrobials, antioxidants, anti-inflammatories, and fiber. All this plant goodness and you know what's missing? Calories. Hence, unlimited eating!

Now, down each side of the triangle, there is an increase in the energy-providing foods that will fuel your activity. They are divided on the left side as animal-sourced food and on the right side as plant-sourced food. This is because plants and animals concentrate nutrition differently. For example, we discussed in Chapter 4 that phytonutrients and fiber are found only in plant-based food. What plant- and animal-sourced food have in common is the calories that fuel activity. Animals tend to store energy as various fats (mostly saturated), while plants tend to store energy as starches and sugars. Foods chosen from the left side of the Food Triangle represent an Atkins-, vegetarian-, or paleo-style diet. They tend to eliminate whole-food starches and fruits (note, we didn't say carbs) from the diet. A plant-based, or vegan, diet is composed of foods down the right side of the Food Triangle. Now that we have the top and the sides of the Food Triangle defined, let's explore some of the fun of using this tool to predict our food future.

Bottom Feeders

Recall that the early guidelines for eating and balanced meals were mostly directed at overcoming malnourishment due to the economic scarcity of food that existed at the time. When we look at meals from many cultures, we see an interesting pattern: steak and potatoes, burger and fries, fish and chips, pasta and meat sauce, curried meat and rice, cheese and tortillas (quesadillas), pork and beans, eggs and pancakes. Do you see it? Yes, each of these traditional meals are composed of foods from across the bottom of the Food Triangle–bottom feeding! If calories and food are scarce, as they were a century ago, this makes perfect sense. But today, in our world of sun-up to sundown eating, this is a perfect way to pack on the pounds.

We have a simple message for you to follow: keep eating to the right! It's a straightforward formula for increasing health span and, if you ditch the salts, oils, sugars, and flours, you'll find that choosing what to eat is greatly simplified and proper weight and good health are magically achieved. We'll return to more details on weight management in Chapter 15. Let's take a closer look at our food palette and see how eating to the right is a one-stop shop for plant-powered health.

The New Palette to Please your Palate

On the right side of the Food Triangle, we find vegetables, fruits, whole grains, legumes, nuts and seeds, and herbs and spices. Although some might see a plant-based diet as restrictive, for most people, eating to the right is going to increase the variety of food, resulting in more choice. The best part of our new food palette is that macroconfusion vanishes. No more carbs to count and no need to worry about protein. By eating a wide range of intact plant-based food—apples not apple juice, beets not beet sugar, potatoes not french fries—your diet is filled with vitamins, minerals, phytonutrients, antimicrobials, antioxidants, and fiber. Let's take a closer look at all the amazing goodness each group has to offer.

Vegetables

Interestingly, the term *vegetable* isn't scientifically defined. Rather, it's a culinary term. The closest thing to a definition for *vegetable* is an edible plant or part of a plant other than a seed or sweet fruit. With that definition, categorizing certain foods such as mushrooms can be tricky.

 **MIXED GREENS**

Is corn a vegetable, fruit, or grain? Actually, it is all of these. Botanically speaking, corn is a fruit. When harvested and eaten, corn is a vegetable. If harvested when the seeds are dry, it's classified as a grain.

The vegetable category includes the following:

Underground Storage Organs (USOs) are the underground parts of plants which are rich in starch or sugar and used for plant energy storage. USOs include roots, or taproots (carrots, beets, turnips, rutabagas, parsnips, and radishes); tubers, or underground swollen stems (potatoes, sweet potatoes, yams, jicama, cassavas—manioc or yuca, Jerusalem artichokes, and celeriac); bulbs, or leaf bases (onions, leeks, garlic, and shallots); corms, or underground stems (water chestnuts, malanga, tannia, eddo, yautia, and taro); and rhizomes, or underground stems (horseradish, ginger, turmeric, and burdock).

Stems and stem shoots of the plants eaten as vegetables include celery, asparagus, kohlrabi, rhubarb, cardoon, ginger, and bamboo shoots.

Buds and flower buds are protuberances on the stems or branches of the plants. Examples are broccoli, cauliflower, Brussels sprouts, capers, globe artichokes, and cabbage.

Leaves of plants consumed as vegetables include spinach, kale, collard greens, beet greens, turnip greens, endive, lettuce, Swiss chard, watercress, arugula, purslane, rapini, radicchio, and mustard greens.

Nonsweet fruits are buds or flowers of plants that are fleshy and contain seeds. Great variation occurs with respect to appearance and composition. Vegetables in this category may include cucumbers, tomatoes, avocados, pumpkins, olives, sweet peppers, chili peppers, eggplants, breadfruits, and bitter melons.

Whole-plant sprouts are edible, germinated plant seeds usually produced by soaking seeds in a specific manner. These nutritionally dense vegetables contain high levels of vitamins, minerals, and phytochemicals. Seeds commonly sprouted and consumed are alfalfa, broccoli, chickpeas, mung beans, peas, sunflower, quinoa, clover, buckwheat, and fenugreek.

Fungi are small, plantlike organisms that lack chlorophyll and cellulose and absorb food through their cell walls. When referring to vegetables, fungi are more commonly known as mushrooms. Lauded for their numerous health benefits, gourmet mushroom varieties include portobello, shiitake, maitake, chanterelle, oyster, king oyster, crimini, porcini, enoki, button, truffle, morel, and straw. Medicinal mushrooms, typically taken in teas or powder form, include turkey tail, reishi, zhu ling, chaga, and cordyceps.

Sea vegetables, as the name implies, come from the sea and are filled with minerals, vitamins, amino acids, and fatty acids. Included in this category are nori, dulse, kombu, and wakame.

The vegetable group consists of the most nutrient-dense food available, overflowing with vitamins, minerals, starch, fiber, phytochemicals, antioxidants, amino acids, and essential fatty acids. Veggies are also very low in calories. They provide the maximum nutritional bang for your caloric buck!

HEALTHY HINT

Sprouts are superfoods. They're rich in easier-to-digest energy; bioavailable vitamins, especially B-complex, alpha-tocoherol (vitamin E), and beta-carotene (provitamin A); minerals; amino acids; proteins; enzymes; and phytochemicals because these nutrients are all necessary for a germinating plant to grow. Sprouts are easy to DIY. All you need is a clean jar, water, and some seeds, and in a few short days, you'll have sprouts.

Fruits

Colorful, sweet, and often edible, fruit is the reproductive, seed-bearing portion of a plant. Plants use fruits as a method to disperse their seeds and, using animals as the middlemen, increase proliferation.

For purposes of nutritional consideration, fruits can be divided into the following groups:

Citrus fruits are characterized by a thick rind, most of which is a bitter white pith known as *albedo*, covered by a thin, colored skin known as the *zest*. The flesh of the citrus is segmented, juicy, and acidic. Flavors range from bitter to tart to sweet. Grapefruits, lemons, limes, kumquats, oranges, and tangerines are in the citrus family.

Berries are small, juicy, antioxidant-rich fruits grown on bushes and vines. Thin-skinned berries contain many tiny seeds—so small, some are not even noticeable. Berries must be fully ripened before harvest because they won't ripen further after they're picked. Included in this category are blueberries, blackberries, raspberries, strawberries, cranberries, and currants.

Melons are members of the gourd family. The dozens of melon varieties can be divided into two general categories: sweet (or dessert) melons and watermelons. Sweet melons have a dense, fragrant flesh and a netted rind. Watermelons have a watery, crisp flesh with a thick rind. All melons are approximately 90 percent water. Included in the melon family are cantaloupe, honeydew, casaba melon, crenshaw melon, Santa Claus melon, watermelon, red seedless watermelon, and gold watermelon.

Pomes, or tree fruits, contain a central core with many small seeds and thin skin with firm flesh. Apples, pears, and quince are pomes.

Stone fruits, also known as drupes, are characterized by thin skin, soft flesh, and a single woody stone or pit. These fruits tend to be fragile, with a short shelf life. Included are apricots, peaches, nectarines, plums, and cherries.

Tropical fruits are native to regions around the world with hot, tropical, and subtropical terrain. Because of ample transportation, these fruits are available for consumption everywhere. The most commonly eaten tropicals are bananas, dates, kiwi, passion fruit, mango, papaya, and pineapple. But you can find the more exotic tropicals such as jackfruit, rambutan, lychee, cherimoya, mangosteen, durian, custard apple, dragon fruit, longan, guava, and star fruit at farmers' markets, local Asian markets, or even online. Many of these have flavors that aren't easily described; the best way is to experiment for yourself and enjoy nature's dessert.

Grapes are technically berries that grow in large clusters on vines. Thanks to the wine industry, they're the largest crop in the world. With at least a dozen varieties, grapes are classified according to the color of the skin, either white or red. Not only are grapes used to make wine, but they're commonly eaten fresh or dried (raisins). Included in the most popular varieties are Thompson seedless green grapes, Concord grapes, and red flame grapes.

Fruits are healthiest consumed fresh and as close to harvest as possible, when the nutrients are at their peak concentration. The moment a fruit is plucked, certain micronutrients begin to degrade. After fruit is cut, blended, juiced, or manipulated in any other way, oxygen exposure is maximized due to increased surface area and oxidation begins.

 **PLANT PITFALL**

> Canned fruits typically contain added syrups (sugar products), juice, and preservatives. Canned fruits are also subjected to high heat during the canning process. Make canned fruits your last choice for fruit options, and if you must use them, be sure to rinse them before consuming.

Frozen fruits may be more ideal than fresh sometimes in terms of nutrient content. Fruits are usually flash-frozen, which means they're thrown in the freezer immediately after they're picked. This process slows nutrient degradation.

Dried fruits, as the name implies, are dehydrated and are a more concentrated source of sugar without any of the satiating water content. Although they are healthy treats for most, dried fruits should be limited if you're trying to watch your weight or blood sugar. Select fresh fruits instead on most occasions.

Whole Grains

Grains are a low-cost simple staple most cultures around the world have consumed as the basis of their diets throughout history. Botanically classified as grasses that bear edible seeds, grains are also referred to as cereals. Kernels of grain are usually protected by an outer hull or husk and are composed of the germ, the endosperm, and the bran.

The germ, the smallest constituent of the grain, is the only part that contains fatty acids. The endosperm, the largest component, is high in both starch and amino acids, which is why it's the part utilized in making milled products such as flour. The bran that covers the endosperm is full of fiber and B vitamins. It (sometimes along with the germ) is removed to make refined products. To consider a grain whole, it must retain all three parts when consumed.

You can include a vast variety of whole grains in your diet. Some popular whole grains include brown rice, wild rice, barley, and oats. *Supergrains* like amaranth, quinoa, and buckwheat are excellent choices and versatile in recipes.

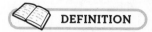 **DEFINITION**

> A **supergrain** is a grain extremely high in essential amino acids, including lysine and methionine, not common in other grains. Supergrains are also exceptionally high in fiber, vitamins, and minerals.

Legumes

Legumes are plants from the pea or pod family and include all beans, peas, lentils, and soyfoods. They are excellent sources of amino acids, fiber, vitamins, minerals, and phytonutrients. Of the hundreds of types of beans, some are used for their edible pods, while others are used to shell for fresh or dried seeds. Included in the legume category are green beans, snow peas, shelling peas, black-eyed peas, okra, all varieties of lentils, and all dried beans. Although peanuts are technically legumes, they are nutritionally and culinarily more like nuts.

It may surprise you to find items like snow peas and okra in this category. However, the definition of a legume is a fruit or seed of any bean or pea plant consisting of a casing that splits along both sides with the seeds attached to one of those sides.

Nuts and Seeds

Although nuts and seeds may get a bad rap for being high in fat (yet another victim of macro-confusion), they are extraordinarily nutritious and health promoting. A better way to think about nuts and seeds (and avocados, too) is that they are jam-packed with powerful nutrients and fat simply comes along for the ride. Paradoxically, despite the high fat and calorie content, people who consume nuts regularly tend to have lower body mass indexes and less body fat. Clinical studies have repeatedly demonstrated zero weight gain, and in some cases a weight loss, when adding nuts to the diet. Some might call them magical calories as they seem to disappear, but there is ample evidence to support that adding nuts and seeds to your diet is a net positive.

Using the Food Triangle, you will load up on the foods at the top, add enough nuts and seeds to get basic phyto-goodness and round out your diet with whole-food starches. Don't be fat-phobic, but at the same time take note that you can overeat nuts and seeds more easily than starchy vegetables or fruits. With that out of the way, let's dive in on the nutrition.

MIXED GREENS

In one clinical study, a single serving of Brazil nuts (20 grams or approximately 4 nuts), significantly lowered LDL-c ("bad" cholesterol) and raised HDL-c ("good" cholesterol) within 9 hours of consumption, and these new levels remained for 30 days!

While individual nuts and seeds boast their own nutritional profiles, generally speaking, they are loaded with essential fats, phytosterols, lignans, ellagic acid, trace minerals, vitamins, and ample antioxidants. Consuming 1 to 2 ounces (or 30 to 60 grams) per day has been shown to promote cardiovascular health and protect against type 2 diabetes, metabolic syndrome, obesity, macular degeneration, and cholelithiasis. It has even been shown to enhance life span. Seeds, too, are special in that their essential fat ratios are well balanced, and they contain multiple trace minerals and phytonutrients. We've included a table of essential nutrients found in nuts, seeds, and other high-fat plant foods. These foods make excellent bases for sauces and dressings and enhance absorption of fat-soluble nutrients. Go nuts!

Notable Nutrients from Nuts, Seeds, and Other High-Fat Plant Foods

Nutrient	Sources
Protein	Leafy greens, legumes (beans, lentils, peanuts, peas, soyfoods), nuts, seeds
Omega-3 Fats	Leafy greens, microalgae, seeds (chia, flax, hemp), soybeans and soyfoods, walnuts, wheat germ
Fiber	Avocados, dried and fresh fruits (berries, pears, papaya), legumes (beans, lentils, peanuts, peas), nuts, seeds, vegetables, whole grains
Calcium	Almonds and almond butter, blackstrap molasses, calcium-set tofu, figs, fortified plant milks, low-oxalate leafy greens (bok choy, broccoli, cabbage, dandelion, kale, watercress), sesame seeds, tahini
Iodine	Sea vegetables (arame, dulse, nori, wakame), iodized salt, supplements
Iron	Dark chocolate, dried fruits, leafy greens, legumes (beans, lentils, peanuts, peas, soyfoods), potatoes, quinoa, sea vegetables (dulse, nori), seeds (pumpkin, sesame, sunflower), tahini
Zinc	Legumes (beans, lentils, peas, peanuts, soyfoods), nuts, oats, seeds
Choline	Bananas, broccoli, legumes (beans, lentils, peanuts, peas, soyfoods), oats, oranges, quinoa
Folate	Almonds, asparagus, avocados, beets, enriched grains (bread, pasta, rice), leafy greens, nutritional yeast, oranges, quinoa

Nutrient	Sources
Vitamin B_{12}	Fortified foods (nutritional yeast, plant milks), supplements (2,500 mcg/week)
Vitamin C	Fruits (berries, cantaloupe, citrus, kiwi, mango, papaya, pineapple), leafy greens, peas, peppers (bell, chile), potatoes, tomatoes
Vitamin D	Fortified plant milks, sun, supplements (if deficient)
Vitamin K	Asparagus, avocados, broccoli, Brussels sprouts, cauliflower, leafy greens, legumes (lentils, peas), natto

Herbs and Spices

Offering minimal calories or macronutrients, herbs and spices encompass a whole category of ingredients that often goes underappreciated. These powerful gems offer not only flavor and variety, but also ample phytonutrition and disease-fighting capability. Aim to integrate more herbs and spices—such as turmeric, garlic, and ginger—into your food as a base infusion in a recipe, a seasoning sprinkled into a dish, or a topping before the first bite.

Putting Greens at The Top of Your World

The top of the Food Triangle emphasizes these truly magical foods because they're genuinely like nature's medicine. No other food group is as nutrient-dense as leafy green vegetables. Here are some of the reasons leafy greens are the superheroes of the plant-based world:

Because leafy greens are so low in calories and high in fiber, they're ideal for weight management.

They're cancer-fighting powerhouses.

Atherosclerosis, the process of clogging arteries, is hindered by leafy greens.

Leafy green intake is associated with a lower risk of type 2 diabetes.

The carotenoids hidden by the dominating chlorophyll pigment boost immunity.

Many disease processes can be ameliorated by a consistent supply of leafy green vegetables. (We'll discuss this more in Chapter 16.) Because of their strong ability to heal and reduce risk of disease, treating your body to a constant stream of greens like spinach, kale, and collard greens, will do it good. You can do this easily by making green smoothies and adding leafy greens to soups, pasta dishes, stews, salads, and virtually any recipe you make. Ask for side dishes of steamed greens when eating out, and order a salad as an appetizer or as the main dish.

Greens range from neutral to bitter in taste, so you can match them with what you're eating. Interestingly, there are two potential genetic taste oddities: Some of you may find brussels sprouts bitter, while others might think cilantro tastes like soap. There are many complex flavors in greens that will take time to appreciate if your basic palate is dominated by sugar, oil, and salt. An interesting experiment to try is steaming kale and tasting it every 30 seconds over 6 to 8 minutes. You might find that it tastes slightly bitter when raw, but at about 4 minutes, it becomes bright green and the bitter flavor is replaced by a nutty, mild flavor. For many that haven't really cared for kale, this may be a wonderful discovery.

 **PLANT PITFALL**

Oxalates are naturally occurring salts found in many plant foods such as berries, almonds, cashews, peanuts, soybeans, okra, quinoa, cocoa, tea, and chocolate, but oxalates are especially found in some leafy green vegetables, such as spinach, Swiss chard, collard greens, parsley, leeks, and beet greens. Because they may decrease absorption of calcium and other minerals, emphasize variety in foods eaten on a regular basis.

With so many different varieties and tastes, you can experiment to see which ones you prefer to eat and in what ways. Just be sure to eat them as often as possible to boost and protect your health!

The Least You Need to Know

- We have a long history of puzzling pyramids, plates, and macroconfusion.
- The Food Triangle offers a unique, super simplified tool to help guide your daily food choices.
- The focus of your plant-based diet should be on vegetables, fruits, whole grains, legumes, nuts and seeds, and herbs and spices.
- A huge variety of whole-plant foods can tempt your creativity and easily keep your nutrition sound.
- Incorporate leafy green vegetables into your day as often as possible to benefit your health in every way possible.

Living a Plant-Based Life

Confusion and controversy abound when it comes to nutrition. Unfortunately, when guidelines get complicated, the result is often a level of detachment. And really, why bother trying so hard when even the experts disagree? Instead of trying to deconstruct the details, let's keep it simple and stick to the basics.

In Part 2, you learn how to listen to your body's cues and focus on the quality of the food you eat instead of getting caught up in the numbers. We also demystify the most controversial claims in the plant-based world and show you how to make shopping for food fun and uncomplicated.

A health-promoting lifestyle would be incomplete without including exercise. That's why we added a chapter full of all the information you need to find and commit to the perfect workout program for your lifestyle.

Finally, do you really need to be popping supplements to achieve and maintain optimum health? Find out all the facts about supplementing in Chapter 10.

Stop Counting, and Start Eating

We've lost sight of the meaning of health. Health isn't merely the absence of disease; it's so much more. Our bodies are ingeniously adapted to have boundless energy, resist illness, live well into our 90s without pain or disease, and die quietly in our sleep at a ripe old age. Yet more people than ever are sick, overweight, and in pain. Health care has become little more than treating symptoms with chemistry experiments (polypharmacy) and procedures. It's time to see the forest instead of the trees, to shift the focus to prevention instead of treatment.

Do you eat at least three times a day, every day, whether you need to or not? Most of us stay in the postprandial (fed) state from waking until going to bed. Food is the direct link from the outer environment into your body. That means you literally are what you eat. The trillions of hitchhikers in your intestinal microbiota are what you eat, too, because their waste products are dumped into your absorption organ—your gastrointestinal, or GI, tract). So more specifically, you are what you absorb, and that includes both what you eat and what the symbiotic bacteria produce as metabolic waste products. Your GI tract, therefore, plays a significant role in your immune system.

In This Chapter

- You are what you absorb
- Defining metabolic and oxidative priority
- Metabolism myths
- Getting to know yourself from the inside out

Sometimes listening to your acquired or habituated appetite isn't the best approach to health. A sudden dietary change can often make you feel worse in the short term even though in the long term it might result in better health. We discussed this with salt and sugar and you may have witnessed this in someone who stops drinking alcohol or quits smoking. What's equally important to note is how we feel with the sudden addition of a food or drink back into your diet. If you haven't had broccoli or green tea for months and suddenly go on a binge, you likely won't feel hungover the next day. Anyone who has given up meat or alcohol and then suddenly adds it back into his or her diet knows that it's not a pleasant experience—even at levels once regularly consumed.

Our Obsession with Numbers

We've become obsessed with numbers. How much do you weigh? How much *should* you weigh? How many calories should you eat? What percentage of carbs is ideal? How many ounces should you eat? How many milligrams of calcium should you take to prevent osteoporosis? And on and on.

Ironically, it seems the more we count, the worse our health is becoming. Something's wrong with this picture.

The thousands of diet books on bookstore shelves today promise to make you healthier, leaner, and fitter as long as you follow the directions precisely. Unfortunately, the onslaught of new formulas and prescriptions has resulted in mass confusion and nutrition information chaos—part of this is macroconfusion. But there is more to this story. As nutritionists, our job description has been redefined as "nutrition-myth debunkers." Instead of teaching from scratch, our job has transitioned toward explaining why what's out there is false or misleading. One day, one type of fat is good for you and another is bad. The following day, avoiding fat entirely is headline news. With all these conflicting ideas, it's no wonder people are having such a hard time figuring it all out.

In addition to the lack of clarity regarding how best to eat, you'll experience the other side of health care. Physicians mostly treat symptoms by prescribing medications that manage them. Managing a disease is a win-win as it allows the patient to continue what they were doing to cause the problem and it is profitable for the health-care business. This isn't intended to cast aspersion on our health-care system, but considering the underlying economics, "sick care" is far more profitable. In medical school, students receive minimal education about nutrition; what they do learn is usually based on correcting nutrient deficiencies. If, for example, a patient comes in with a goiter, she or he has an iodine deficiency and needs a prescription for iodine. Or if a child presents signs of rickets, he or she is deficient in vitamin D and needs vitamin D supplements. Recall in our brief history review of the USDA eating guidelines that malnutrition or economically driven undernutrition was the problem that plagued society for millennia.

This is isolated, microscopic, and reductionist health care. To treat a patient, a physician needs to examine the whole person. Geoffrey Rose, an esteemed epidemiologist and promoter of preventative health care, proposed that at every office visit, there is an obligation to ask, "Why did this patient get this disease at this time?" He added, "It is an integral part of good doctoring to ask not only, what is the diagnosis, and what is the treatment, but also, why did this happen, and could it have been prevented?" Why is the patient diabetic? What is causing the hypertension? Why does the patient have high cholesterol? The source of the problem should be established and must become the focus of the treatment protocol.

When was the last time your doctor asked about your diet or exercise habits? This is rare, yet this is how health needs to be addressed to solve the health-care crisis.

The Best Nutrient Bang for Your Caloric Buck

Most of us like the process of eating. Yet the fun part is over after we swallow. Digestion is just getting started, but that is a little more like waiting around to watch the clean-up crew after the festival is over. Let's face it, everything social seems to involve food. We like to swallow together. Then we wiggle more by exercising to make up for the excessive intake. Look around and you'll see ample evidence that the swallow-and-wiggle approach isn't working very well.

We discussed the three macronutrients—protein, carbohydrate, and fat—which are included in various percentages in whole foods. While alcohol isn't one of the three macronutrients, it can be a significant source of calories. We also presented the Food Triangle that segregates animal- and plant-sourced energy at the bottom from plant food that is high in phytonutrients and fiber and low in calorie density on the top. Our daily goal is to get sufficient nutrition (vitamins, minerals, fiber, and phytonutrients) with just enough energy to supply our daily activity. If you are trying to lose weight, you need to maintain a daily energy deficit as compared to activity. If you want to maintain your current weight, you need sufficient energy as compared to daily activity. If you want to gain weight, you need enough energy to support the activity and recovery involved with increasing muscle mass (hypertrophy).

We tend to flip this entire notion upside down in our world of cheap, tasty, and excessive nutrition. We start by piling on enough food to avoid deficiency, which usually leads to excessive calorie consumption. Then, activity is increased in a vain attempt to mitigate those extra calories. We wiggle more to counter the excess swallowing. It is a futile cycle. Unless given unnatural access to food, animals only eat enough to support their activity; we're active to support more eating. We address weight loss in Chapter 15 and exercise in Chapter 9, so let's focus on a new framework for maintenance.

MIXED GREENS

The USDA *MyPlate* allows up to 10 percent of calories from added sugars. Practically speaking, this would allow a maximum of 45 grams per day (a little less than 10 teaspoons) on an 1,800-calorie diet and up to 60 grams (a little more than 14 teaspoons) of added sugars per day on a moderate 2,400-calorie diet. The World Health Organization recommends even less—no more than 5 percent of total calories from "free" sugars. The average consumer eats closer to 90 grams (or more than 22 teaspoons) per day. Considering 1 teaspoon sugar equals 4 grams and 16 calories, that's nearly 370 extra health-degrading, nutrient-devoid calories each day! Ditch the empty calories for whole-food sweetness.

Our daily goal is to get sufficient nutrition with sufficient energy. Perhaps surprisingly, achieving this goal doesn't require that we get every nutrient every day. Our diet needs a little variation to get a wider cross section of nutrition over days, weeks, and months. We also want to be certain not to eat foods that concentrate environmental toxins, like mercury in fish or arsenic in certain rices. Finally, we don't want to eat things that cause unnecessary hormonal activation like drinking hormonally active milk long after we would be normally weaned from our mothers.

The Fed, the Fasted, and the Starved

This idea that eating is over when we swallow couldn't be more incorrect. Think about grabbing that next slice of pizza, another handful of popcorn, or a chip loaded with salsa. Flavor and enjoyment peaks, and then begins to fade. You may grab a soda, beer, wine, coffee, or tea to wash it down and start all over. Some food is "paired" with a specific kind of drink. All of this swallowing is for entertainment, and adequate nutrition is an afterthought, at best.

After you eat, your body needs to get to work processing. Once you swallow food, it must go somewhere. It can be stored, metabolized (burned), or excreted (waste), but it must meet one of those three fates. You are now in the postprandial (fed) state and the body must figure out what to do with what was swallowed. During the fed state, the body is essentially running on what was just ingested. In 4 to 6 hours that process has completed and you return to the fasted state where your body once again begins using nutritional reserves that are stored in various tissue and organs. Finally, if you don't eat for a long time, your nutrition stores can be depleted and you're on the road to starvation. Starvation is death resulting from prolonged undernutrition resulting in malnutrition.

To live we need air within minutes, water within days, and food within 30 to 40 days. Most people, even the healthiest and leanest amongst us, can survive 14 to 30 days on fat reserves. When one runs out of fat stores, muscle and organ tissue is used and that results in starvation. Similarly, after weeks, one may fall short of one or more specific essential nutrients (e.g. vitamin B_{12}, essential fatty acids, essential amino acids, etc.), and this could eventually cause death by starvation. When you're rounding up coworkers at lunch, you're never "starving" despite claims to the contrary. Nutrition isn't an emergency defined in hours or even days and we get various nutrition with the wide variety of meals we eat week to week. It's interesting to note that the longest medically supervised water fast was 382 days! The patient took a multivitamin and had 276 pounds of fat to lose, but regardless, he was healthy and happy for 382 days.

Eating and Metabolic Priority

Perhaps it is easiest to illustrate metabolic priority with alcohol. After a drink, the blood alcohol begins to rise and 4 to 6 hours later, it returns to normal again. Where does the alcohol go? It's not stored as fat. It's not eliminated. The body shifts over its focus to alcohol and it is immediately metabolized. During the time it takes to eliminate the alcohol from the system, fat and glucose metabolism are diminished. In fact, one clinical trial demonstrated that alcohol alone suppressed fat utilization by 87 percent. When glucose was added (on top of the alcohol), fat utilization dropped to nearly zero for 90 mins and averaged 79 percent suppression over 4 hours. Scientists call this phenomenon oxidative priority. Here, oxidation refers to burning or metabolizing the substance to extract energy.

Similarly, there's only very limited blood plasma and cellular storage for free amino acids released by protein metabolism. Want to know why you get the metabolism spike after the high-protein meal all the fad diets recommend? You guessed it—to burn the amino acids you can't store. Yet, that protein-induced metabolic boost does little to liberate stored fat.

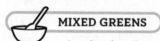 **MIXED GREENS**

It only takes the energy equivalent of an extra 168 calories of fat per week to gain 50 pounds over a 20-year period. That's equivalent to a little less than 1.5 tablespoons of olive oil per week. It is impossible to manage calories down to this level.

Let's move onto dietary sources of glucose: starches and sugars. We can store a combined about 1500 to 2000 calories as glycogen in liver and muscle tissues. Contrary to popular opinion, high glucose meals aren't stored as fat to any significant degree in humans. Once your glycogen stores are topped off, the rest is liberated through a similar shift to glucose and a rise in metabolism as we saw with the alcohol example. Dietary carbohydrate comes in as number three on our oxidative priority behind alcohol and amino acids. In each case, we see a rise in metabolism to burn what we can't store in the 4 to 6 hours following ingestion.

What about fat? It comes in last place, because you can basically store an unlimited amount of fat relative to any one meal. We can literally carry around hundreds of thousands of extra calories stored in the adipose tissue. Fat—unlike alcohol, protein (amino acids), and carbohydrate (glucose)—does not cause a great rise in metabolism after the meal nor does it shift priority significantly toward burning more fat. That happens only in the complete absence of dietary starches, sugars, proteins, and alcohol. In each case metabolic priority is given to the fuel that is the most difficult to store. Fat, of course, is our primary energy storage organ and so it's always lowest priority during the clearing of each meal.

Let's bring this back to plant-based, practical eating. You're at a party consuming a glass of fine red wine and a plate of hot, fresh gluten-free bread with black-truffle olive oil. Almost immediately upon ingestion, the wine (alcohol) becomes the top priority and combined with the glucose rise from the flour in the bread, your fat metabolism plummets. The fat in the olive oil rushes through your blood plasma to be stored away for later. Not only did you just add to your fat storage, you also suppressed the fat you would have been burning had you not eaten at all. It's a double whammy.

Rethinking Refined Food

Now you might start to better understand the reasons whole-plant foods are your best friends when it comes to nutrition. It stands to reason that *refined foods*, the polar opposite of whole-plant foods, need to be left by the wayside. Besides being nutritionally devoid of calories that lack fiber or micronutrients, refined alcohol, sugar, flour, and fat can result in overall metabolic dysfunction and suppress stored fat utilization.

The composition of refined foods can provide a possible explanation for overeating. These products have high concentrations of sugar and other refined sweeteners, refined carbohydrates, fat, salt, and caffeine—all substances that become habituated and shift the palate away from the flavor profiles of whole food. Many people can't regulate their consumption of such foods or the resulting appetite for more. This loss of control could account for the global epidemic of obesity and other metabolic disorders. Habituation to refined foods conforms to the diagnostic criteria for substance-use disorders. By redirecting your plate from refined foods to whole foods on the right side of the Food Triangle and shifting away from "bottom feeding," you can acquire a new, healthy appetite in a very short time. Sweet, oily, and salty will be redefined and you'll lose the need to adulterate every meal with highly processed additives.

Foods that can be considered refined include the majority (or totality) of what can be bought at a fast-food restaurant; foods that come packaged with ingredients you don't recognize or with more than three unrecognizable ingredients; fried foods; frozen meals; foods that appear oily, salty, or sugary; most foods from a vending machine; packaged cookies, cakes, crackers, and candies; and foods such as flour, sugar, oil, margarine, and soda.

In addition to the saturated and hydrogenated fat, sodium, and sugar or artificial sweeteners, you may find plenty of other not-so-goodies in your refined or *processed foods*. These include but are not limited to preservatives, artificial flavors, thickeners, shelf stabilizers, high-fructose corn syrup, sugar alcohols, nitrites and nitrates, and butylated hydroxyanisole.

 **DEFINITION**

Refined foods are stripped of their intact parts, as when whole grains have their bran and germ removed, leaving only the endosperm. (Think white flour and white rice.) Refined products can also be called *polished* or *processed*. **Processed foods** can technically be anything that originally comes from nature but is then manipulated via cooking, cutting, juicing, blending, or any other physical maneuver that changes its form or exposes it to oxygen or other elements. The term is typically used interchangeably with refined foods; however, healthy foods can be processed—green smoothies, for instance. So processed doesn't *always* mean harmful.

You can avoid the harmful effects of these unnatural and health-demising chemicals by sticking to a whole food, plant-based diet. A good rule of thumb is that if you can't pronounce it, don't eat it! And if you can't find it living freely in nature, avoid it! Natural isn't always good (e.g. poison ivy and hemlock tea), but for the most part, we do much better with whole-plant–sourced food than any other. So long as the processing of that food doesn't remove a large part of what it is found with at the starting point, it remains a healthy choice.

Metabolism 101: You're Not Broken

Through our never-ending drive to "increase our metabolism," it is interesting how few people can actually describe what metabolism is, and even fewer have ever measured one. Nearly every cell in your body has tiny cellular power plants called mitochondria. These generate the energy cells need for all functions. Your metabolism is the sum of this cellular activity. Scientists use an *indirect calorimeter* to measure metabolism. Interestingly, metabolism scales with weight. The more you weigh, the greater your metabolism. Thinking critically, this shouldn't be a big surprise. If you are suddenly handed 25, 50, or 100 pounds of steel to lug around all day long, wouldn't you expect your metabolism to rise to accomplish this task? It doesn't matter if that weight is made of fat or steel.

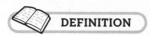 **DEFINITION**

An **indirect calorimeter** is used by scientists to monitor metabolism. When fat is metabolized it's transformed to energy, water, and carbon dioxide (CO_2), a colorless gas that's exhaled. Using sensors on a face mask or within a sealed room, the oxygen consumed on each breath and the carbon dioxide created are carefully recorded. Scientists can not only calculate your metabolism on a breath-by-breath basis, but they can also determine the fat or carbohydrate fuel mixture. Since every pound of fat you lose exits via breathing, that technically means that your lungs are the primary weight-loss organ. Get breathing!

What's equally puzzling is how often we are diagnosed with a "slow metabolism" in gyms and office visits alike, yet in none of these cases did anyone measure our metabolism. Imagine similar diagnoses for hypertension based on the idea that you just look like someone with high blood pressure without any measurement at all. Measuring a metabolism takes about 15 minutes and normally is done first thing in the morning in the fasted and rested state.

Another idea that seems to permeate the gym is that "muscle burns more energy than fat," and this is translated to mean that you can't lose fat without gaining muscle or that it's somehow easier to lose fat if one first gains muscle. It turns out adding a pound of lean muscle gives a metabolic advantage of less than 10 calories a day—a little more than a stalk of celery. Of course, we know this isn't the main driver of weight loss or gain. Otherwise, how do former bodybuilders or football players ever become overweight? Certainly they begin with more muscle mass than most people. Here's how: they eat too often, too much, and too calorically dense.

Skinny isn't the opposite of fat, as the former is insufficient muscle mass and the latter is excess adipose tissue. The physiology of the two isn't even related; one is solved by anabolism (growth) in response to tissue stress (exercise), and the other by catabolism (breakdown) of energy stores in times of deficit. We don't turn muscle into fat or vice versa. It's also important to note that most explosive moves—from weight-lifting to busting out an aerobic dance—are mostly fueled with glucose. The best exercise is to clench one's mouth tightly in the presence of fattening foods.

Living Longer with Less Food

A common practice fitness and health professionals teach is to eat frequently throughout the day to boost metabolism. This method is based on the idea that keeping your body digesting is a way to prevent overeating and maintain energy, making you lean and healthy. But what if we told you this thinking may put you at a disadvantage?

Since the 1930s, scientific experiments have confirmed that organisms live longer when put on a calorie-restricted diet. The research has also consistently shown that slimmer people tend to be healthier overall. What can we extrapolate from these data? While it was once hypothesized that lower calories resulted in lower metabolism and a longer life, we now know that this "rate of living" theory works in some organisms such as fruit flies, but not in all organisms. One explanation for why calorie restriction works seems to be related to the restriction of certain nutrients in the diet. This dietary restriction is the antithesis of the world trend towards chronic over nutrition with diets of excess. For example, plant-sourced proteins are often labeled as inferior, because they don't have the same distribution and concentration of amino acids that we find in animal proteins. It turns out reduced levels of certain essential amino acids like methionine, lysine, and leucine may be responsible for dietary restriction advantage. A whole food, plant-based diet naturally restricts the nutrients that should be restricted and at the same time boosts the fiber, phytonutrients, vitamins, and minerals.

Additionally, you must eat only as much as necessary. That means eating only when hungry and stopping before feeling overfull. You might benefit from eating at an early hour each night. Then you complete digestion before sleep, which gives your body the whole night to heal, recover, and fight disease processes.

Also, instead of eating just because it's time—breakfast, lunch, or dinner … or because others are eating—wait until your body truly feels hunger. Then provide nutritious, whole-plant foods to your prepared digestive system.

How to Hear Hunger

Inner mechanisms for regulating eating are long lost in most people and need to be relearned. Abandon any pre-existing rules you've set in your mind.

Are any of these commonly touted ideas part of your mind-set?

- Eat breakfast as soon as possible, even if you're not hungry.

- Eat every 3 or 4 hours to prevent hunger from kicking in.

- Eat three square meals and two snacks each day.

- Finish your meal before you have dessert.

- Eat 4 ounces protein, 1 cup starch, and 1 cup vegetables at every meal.

- For every pound of your ideal body weight, eat 10 calories per day.

What all these rules have in common is their disconnect from your body's needs. Your nutrient requirements are impacted by your daily life. When you're sick or fighting illness, your body needs to focus on immune function. Anyone with pets or observing animals in nature quickly realizes animals stop eating when they are sick. We force-feed the sick. Digestion and absorption will divert energy away from your immune system, so eating less may be beneficial. Plus, you're probably naturally less hungry when you're under the weather, so listen to your body.

Conversely, a great workout causes your body to send larger, louder hunger signals. Your body needs to replenish energy stores and to rebuild and repair the microdamage to the muscles and bones during your workout. Your body wants permission to ignore the rules.

You can gauge your hunger on a scale from 0 to 10: 0 means you're starving and 10 means Thanksgiving-full. Optimally, you should eat starting at 1 or 2 and stop at about 6 or 7. Eat only when you feel true hunger—but *not* at the point that you feel weak, shaky, headache-y, or ill—and stop when you feel comfortably satiated.

 **HEALTHY HINT**

If you're not hungry enough to eat an apple, you're probably not really hungry.

Like anything, practice makes perfect. If you tune in, your body's natural signals will get louder and brighter and, ultimately, impossible to miss. Start every day with an open mind, and allow your body to become hungry before that first meal. Then indulge your hunger with a colorful, phytochemical festivity to make your cells sing blissfully. Eat until you feel good and then move along with the next part of your day. You may not feel hungry again for several hours, depending on how much exercise and daily activity you engage in, how much your individual body needs to stay at its current weight, and how much you slept the night before.

Because we are creatures of habit and so many variables come into play, you can see why it's senseless to follow arbitrary rules designed around historic agricultural, work, and school schedules. Bask in your uniqueness. Honor it, and respect your individuality. Your body will thank you by maintaining superlative weight and health.

Quality Over Quantity

Quality of food needs to dominate over quantity. Clearly, counting and quantifying is ineffective. Choosing from whole-plant foods every time your body tells you it's hungry nourishes your cells, provides satiety, and sustains your disease-fighting mechanisms. You literally empower your immune system to fight off foreign invaders, slow the aging process, and maintain a lean physique by choosing nutrient-dense sources of fuel. It really is that simple.

The Least You Need to Know

- Nutrition is not an emergency. Staying in the chronically fed (postprandial) state likely leads to poor health and excess weight.
- The body prioritizes which fuels are burned by the storage availability. Oxidative priority dictates that order from first to last as alcohol, protein, carbohydrate and fat.
- Maximize your health by selecting whole, nutrient-dense plant foods that remain as close to nature as possible.
- Your body knows what it needs if you've been eating healthfully. Otherwise it may be simply reminding you of acquired bad habits.

Controversies Clarified

Nutrition is one of the most controversial and dynamic sciences. Information changes daily, and experts disagree on how to interpret that information. In this chapter, we break down the most common controversial nutrition issues and provide you with the most up-to-date wisdom on each topic.

In This Chapter

- Why dairy doesn't do a body good
- Building strong bones to last a lifetime
- Dispelling soy safety rumors
- Benefits and concerns of a raw diet
- What we should eat

The Dairy Dilemma

One of the most brilliant marketing campaigns ever to saturate popular culture came from the dairy industry. From posters and handouts given to school children to star-studded television and magazine ads, we're officially convinced a healthy diet must include dairy products. Government guidelines recommend two or three servings of dairy products per day. Is it because calcium is best delivered by dairy? Or is it because the lobbying and funding of the dairy industry have tremendous influence?

Dairy is double-edge sword when it comes to nutrition. On one hand, no one can argue that milk, regardless of species of origin, is undoubtedly food. In fact, it's the only substance we can say with certainty has no other purpose other than to be consumed. When the rise in dairy industry occurred in the early twentieth century, combating childhood malnutrition and undernourishment were prime concerns, and milk was a prominent part of the solution. Not only was it a boon for agriculture, but it fit the nutritional bill for growing young children. So why would there be any question at all about dairy?

Breast milk—be it cow, goat, rat, dog, or human—is more than just a source of calories. Have you considered, for example, why human breast-milk cheese or coffee creamer isn't common? Do you pause at that idea or does it sound disgusting? Why would we pause at consuming our own species' milk and yet cow's milk seems perfectly reasonable? It's not just marketing and semantics either. Nearly 75 percent of the world population exhibits *lactose intolerance* and in some parts of the world, it's as high as 95 percent. This is not an abnormality; lactose intolerance is nature's assistance in weaning offspring. In fact, the ability to digest lactose into adulthood—lactase persistence—is most common in those of European descent and the abnormal feature of nature.

 **DEFINITION**

> **Lactose intolerance** is the inability to digest lactose, the sugar component of milk, due to the body's failure to produce the enzyme lactase. Gastrointestinal symptoms vary from mild to extreme and can include gas, bloating, cramps, diarrhea, and pain.

We are the only species that consumes another species' milk and that continues to consume milk of any kind into adulthood. Is this an evolutionary adaptive advantage? Dairy may in fact have overcome malnutrition at a time when food was economically scarce or in certain environments. Lactase persistence is most common in northwest Europe. Here's one more thing to consider: milk is naturally hormonally active. One of milk's purposes is to stimulate growth. We know, for example, that the two active proteins in cow's milk, whey and casein, stimulate a rise in fasting insulin and serum IGF-1; these have emerged as key regulators of cancer-growth pathways.

Currently, some dietitians and physicians encourage lactase enzymes or other medications so patients can push past intolerance symptoms and still consume dairy, often under the umbrella of providing dietary calcium. Plants provide plentiful sources of calcium and don't cause discomfort when consumed. In population studies, cultures that consume the highest amounts of calcium and dairy products also have the highest incidence of osteoporosis and bone fractures. Conversely, societies that exclude dairy products from their diets experience much lower rates of bone fracture. If what we're told about drinking milk is true, how could this be possible?

Optimizing Bone Density

Bone health is a complex and multifactorial process. Bone mass accumulates most during the first couple decades of life. The more bone gained during this period, the less risk of osteoporosis you face later in life. Unfortunately, this critical window closes before most young people even hear the word *osteoporosis*. If you did know to focus on bone-building during your teenage years, what would you actually do? The same things you should do at any age to optimize bone density.

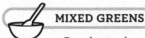 **MIXED GREENS**

Developing bones require sufficient amounts of many nutrients. Calcium has received the most attention because of its great mass present in the adult skeleton: more than 1,400 grams in males and 1,200 grams in females.

Interestingly, the number-one factor for improving and maintaining bone health isn't at all food related. The best way to build bone is to perform weight-bearing exercise regularly. Resistance exercise improves bone density more than any dietary factor. Lift weights, walk, jog, jump, or do callisthenic exercises at least three or four times a week to keep your bones, muscles, tendons, and ligaments strong and pliable.

Nutritional recommendations include eating adequate amounts of fruits and vegetables, cutting out dairy, maintaining optimal vitamin D levels, and consuming plant-based sources of calcium as well as vitamins K and B_{12}, fluoride, magnesium, phosphorus, and potassium, every day. See Chapter 3 for food sources.

Vitamin D plays an important role in bone mineralization, working with calcium to break down old bone cells and build up new ones. Milk is fortified with vitamin D; it's not a natural source of vitamin D. Other nondairy products are commonly fortified with vitamin D. You can be sure you're getting enough vitamin D with a simple blood test. See Chapter 10 for more vitamin D details.

If you're not there (like the majority of the population), try spending 15 to 20 minutes in the sun three times a week. Apply sunscreen only to your face, exposing your arms, legs, and whatever else you can reveal without offending the neighbors. The sun is the best source for vitamin D.

Sun-derived vitamin D stays in the body the longest, and you can't get vitamin D toxicity from the sun. The sun offers other health benefits—it releases feel-good endorphins and regulates your circadian rhythm.

If after a few weeks you're still testing low, consider supplementing with vitamin D_2. You can safely start out with 2,000 IU per day. If you're deficient, taking 5,000 IU per day until levels normalize is safe. Please check your blood levels before supplementing, and ask your physician to monitor to help you reach your goals.

Other Problems with Dairy

Dairy increases growth hormones in your blood. Insulin-like growth factor-1 (IGF-1) helps a baby calf double its birth weight in less than 2 months—more than three times faster than a human infant does. In human adults, IGF-1 causes undesirable growth, and a high level of IGF-1 is a known risk factor for cancer.

Early dairy consumption has been linked to type 1 diabetes, the autoimmune type typically diagnosed in childhood. Type 1 diabetes occurs when the immune system attacks pancreas cells, permanently destroying the pancreas's ability to produce insulin. Once this diagnosis is made, the person must take insulin for the rest of his or her life. Type 1 diabetics also are at increased risk for other chronic conditions later, like cardiovascular disease.

Moreover, dairy is abundant in dietary cholesterol and saturated fat. Even skim milk contains cholesterol: 1 cup contains 5 milligrams versus 25 milligrams in whole milk, which also has 5 grams saturated fat. A cup of cheddar cheese (easily found on a large piece of pizza) provides a whopping 139 milligrams cholesterol, 28 grams saturated fat, and 532 calories.

Milk products are inundated with steroids and hormones (both naturally occurring and production induced) that are linked to cancer and other potential health problems. Genetically engineered growth hormones, IGF-1, estradiol, progesterone, and testosterone fill dairy products to the brim. Even organic "no added hormone" dairy products are still potentially hormonally active, perhaps just not at the same levels.

Also in your chemical cocktail may lie antibiotic residues, pesticides, herbicides, fungicides, veterinary drugs, fertilizers, synthetic preservatives, and additives. Surprisingly, many studies find little difference between levels of the aforementioned compounds in organic dairy when compared to conventional. So just because you pay more for the organic product doesn't mean you're getting a safe, toxin-free product. Microbiological contaminants (think bacteria, viruses, parasites, and mycotoxins) can also find their way into your dairy products and other animal products.

Dairy consumption may cause iron deficiency because it inhibits absorption. (This may explain the recommendation that infants under 1 year of age not drink cow's milk.)

MIXED GREENS

White blood cells, or pus, are found in dairy products due to the infections the cows regularly acquire during the unnaturally high processing demands.

Ultimately, dairy does more damage than good. If you feel you can't give up dairy (especially cheese), blame the casein; this protein causes the same feel-good effects as opiate drugs. When consumed, casein converts into casomorphins—nature's way to ensure an infant will return to the breast for milk. In cheese, the protein (mostly casein) along with the fat and sodium content, is much more concentrated than in milk. Together, you have a powerfully addictive mixture. In fact, there have been studies using naloxone—an opiate-blocking medication used to counteract heroin and morphine overdoses—to cut cravings for cheese and other habituating foods (meat, sugar, and chocolate). Cut out dairy, and your cravings may subside within about 3 weeks.

Soy Confusing

Soy has been a favorite staple of plant-based eaters for decades. Nutritionally, soy packs a powerful punch: more protein than most other legumes, ample fiber, omega-3 fatty acids, calcium, and iron. Soy also supplies health-promoting phytonutrients like isoflavones that reduce cholesterol levels and cancer risk.

As a bean, soy can be eaten from the pod when cooked, fermented into miso paste or tempeh, curdled into tofu, or processed into milk or various other products. As an ingredient, processed soy is found in hundreds of products on the market today, including faux meats and baby formulas. It's available as textured vegetable protein, hydrolyzed vegetable protein, soy lecithin, soy flour, isolated soy protein, defatted soy flour, and soy protein concentrate.

Controversy rages when it comes to soy. Due to the wealth of nutrients and potential health claims soy has to offer, there has been an intensified explosion of studies. Intensive hype in the media makes it hard to read between the lines and know what to believe. Let's break down some of the recent concerns.

Soy contains a class of phytonutrients called *isoflavones*. Isoflavones have a similar chemical structure as estrogen, which is why they are referred to as *phytoestrogens*. However, they act differently in the body than human estrogen and appear to exert healthful effects. Consuming isoflavones during early childhood and adolescence has been shown to reduce lifetime risk of breast cancer. Furthermore, soy consumption may reduce the risk of breast cancer recurrence and improve survival from breast cancer. The American Institute of Cancer Research and American Cancer Society have concluded that consuming soy foods is safe for breast cancer patients and the general population. Beyond breast cancer, soy has been associated with a reduced risk for prostate cancer and hot flashes, as well as improved cardiovascular and skin health. There are also possible positive associations between soy consumption and bone and kidney health.

Another soy concern is its possible interference with thyroid function. Soy has been reported to cause *goiters*, hypothyroidism, and thyroid cancer. But adequate intake of *iodine* reverses any goiter-causing effect of soy in a healthy person. Plant sources include iodized salt, sea vegetables, and plants grown in iodine-rich soil. Additionally, population studies have shown a protective effect of soy on thyroid cancer. Although soy foods may interfere with the absorption of hypothyroid medication, soy can still be consumed with medication adjustments. Essentially, soy foods are not only safe for everyone (except, of course, anyone with an allergy), but they are nutrient-dense foods that may provide additional health benefits.

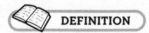 **DEFINITION**

> **Phytoestrogens** are plant compounds similar to the hormone estrogen and that look and act like estrogen in the body. A **goiter** is an abnormally enlarged thyroid gland most commonly due to iodine deficiency in the diet, but it can also occur with other thyroid diseases. **Iodine** is a trace mineral required in the diet to help with metabolism.

The media have propagated concerns about soy's effect on hormones. You may have heard how soy consumption decreases fertility or gives a male "man-boobs." But no solid evidence supports these assertions.

Similarly, fears circulated that soy-based infant formulas led to problems with sexual development, brain function, immunity, and future reproduction. No conclusive evidence supports these claims, either. Most experts are confident in recommending soy-based formulas.

To enjoy soy foods as a part of a balanced plant-based diet, do the following:

- Consume soy from whole-food or minimally processed sources such as soybeans, tofu, tempeh, miso, soybean sprouts, and soy milk.

- Use soy in moderation—less than 3 servings per day, where a serving is about 7 grams protein and 25 milligrams isoflavones, which ends up being approximately 1 cup soy milk or ½ cup soybeans, tofu, or tempeh.

- Minimize use of or avoid processed soy products, like soy protein isolates (found in protein drinks and bars, meat analogues, cereals, meal replacement products, and other processed items).

Raw Resolution

Although a raw diet is nothing new, it's all the rage nowadays with raw books, products, websites, and even restaurants popping up everywhere. Defining a raw diet depends on who you ask, but a consensus is "an eating style consisting primarily of uncooked, unprocessed foods." Some raw foodists strive to eat 100 percent of their foods raw, but technically, anything greater than 75 percent is considered a raw diet. Similarly, people who eat 50 to 74 percent of their calories from raw food sources are categorized as "high-raw foodists."

Indeed, while adding meat to the diet is often given credit for the increased calorie content that fueled the evolution of our big brains, it's far more likely that cooking should get most of the credit. When glucose is available, it's the primary fuel for the brain and will be prioritized over fat; it's not what one would expect if fat alone fueled the growth. From an evolutionary perspective, we have double the glucose transporters in the brain as compared to a chimpanzee and we have much bigger brains. On the other hand, chimpanzees have double the glucose transporters in muscle tissue compared to humans. One might respond that chimpanzees eat fruit; doesn't fruit have plenty of glucose? Yes, but fruit is seasonal, and as you may recall from Chapter 2, underground storage units are fantastic sources of dietary starch, but they must be cooked to deliver the energy density required for humans. It's likely that cooking drove year-round calorie availability, preserved our brain's thirst for glucose, and fueled our big-brain explosion.

On a raw plan, foods include fresh, dried, and frozen fruits; fresh and frozen vegetables; raw nuts and seeds; and sprouted vegetables, grains, and legumes. Common preparation techniques in the raw world are soaking, sprouting, juicing, and blending. Subpopulations under the raw umbrella emphasize fruits, sprouts, and fermented and cultured foods.

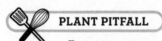 **PLANT PITFALL**

Fruitarians are a raw subgroup who eat 75 percent or more of their calories from fruit. High-fruit groups consume 50 to 74 percent of their diet from fruit. There are some nutrient adequacy concerns with a fruit diet that overlap with a cooked, vegan diet (e.g. B_{12}, D, K2, EPA/DHA, etc.) so supplement accordingly. Also be aware that because high fruit consumption can lead to tooth decay from excess sugars, it is important to practice good dental hygiene and floss, brush, and rinse after meals.

Known benefits of following a raw or high-raw diet include improved nutrient intake and minimized consumption of health-damaging foods. Raw, whole foods include all the magical nutrients this book is based on—fiber, phytonutrients, antioxidants, vitamins, and minerals. Additionally, following a raw plan automatically eliminates all the harmful compounds found in animal products and processed foods—dietary cholesterol, animal protein, refined sugars, trans fatty acids, and artificial sweeteners.

Ultimately, a raw-based diet is amazing for your health. In fact, it sounds like the perfect plan. However, some concerns should be considered before you throw away your cookware.

Raw Diets Aren't Perfect

Some people complain of lack of satiety on various diets, including raw, but those complaints tend to follow all special diets. Recognize that a raw diet does take more prep work. Of course one of the benefits of a whole food, plant-based diet (even one including cooked foods) is that a large volume of food can be eaten without weight gain. This can be a source of failure when someone moves from a more omnivorous diet to fully plant-based since serving sizes are unfamiliar and often must increase. When one moves to raw, this volume requirement goes up even more.

Fruits and vegetables are very low in calories, and you need much more food, which requires more preparation and planning. Sprouted grains and legumes are denser in calories, but it's not as easy to eat a bowl of these raw as it is when they're cooked. Some strict raw foodists compensate for the lack of calories by consuming high amounts of fat from sources such as avocados, nuts, seeds, coconut and its oil, as well as other oils. High-sugar items like dried fruits and raw agave are also sometimes consumed excessively.

Raw diets lack the science to back up any of the health claims that serve as their basis, but clearly raw diets overlap with the benefits of a whole food, plant-based diet. Concepts such as raw foods being live and having abundant enzymes are partially flawed arguments.

Yes, raw foods are high in plant enzymes. They are released when the plant's cell walls are broken down in chewing or blending. Enzyme activity is ripe and most lively the moment the cell walls are broken, immediately after cutting the plants with a blade or your teeth. This activity begins to slow down soon after being exposed to oxygen.

But it does not appear those enzymes can survive our digestive tract long enough to have a healthy impact inside the body. The stomach, where food remains for an average of 40 minutes, is very acidic and denatures, or inactivates, enzymes before the food moves down the intestinal tract for absorption. Furthermore, whether most plant enzymes are helpful to humans is unknown, even if they did survive.

Because certain nutrients are absorbed better when cooked, exclusively raw diets cannot take advantage of these. Carotenoids such as lycopene and lutein are enhanced when heated. Cooking also breaks down some nutrients, like oxalates, that prevent absorption, and it adds variety. Besides, eating soups, stews, and cooked grains is comforting, especially when it's cold outside.

Using Raw Sensibly

The small amount of research out on raw food diets shows mostly healthy improvements on the subjects. However, the raw food diet is a contrast against a standard disease-promoting diet. More convincing evidence would come from comparing raw diet practitioners to whole-food, plant-based eaters who include some cooked foods.

Eating a majority of your calories from raw foods is ideal. The health benefits of raw foods are indeed limitless. The idea that your diet must be *completely* raw to derive those health benefits may be an unnecessary step.

No Perfect Diet

When seeking answers on diet, many times it's the question that fails us. Some might ask "what did we eat?" and look to the past for guidance on a healthful human diet. But human survival has always been predicated on the question of "what can we eat?" In times of survival, our ability to process a wide range of natural materials as food has fueled human migration to every continent and to a wide range of environments, even inhospitable ones. We are the most adaptive species on the planet.

Our quest for optimal health through nutrition has focused on yet another question: "what should we eat?" This question has many answers, and sometimes they may appear as conflicting answers. Some look to the past; however, evolution is simply change over time and does not dictate diet. Our diet may be optimized for a wide range of issues: survival, health, reproduction, longevity, ideology, or even athletic competition. There is no perfect diet. We aren't "designed" to eat anything in particular. Humans can eat many things, and that is why we have inhabited such a diversity of environments. Finding a few paintings on a cave wall or a primitive tool-scraped bone isn't the final word on optimal nutrition.

"What should we eat?" opens up the conversation and allows us to consider and build upon centuries of research and to approach it from a modern perspective—a perspective that incorporates all of our accumulated knowledge and technology. At the same time, it's possible that our current dietary standards, a result of surveying humans during the last century—a time of unparalleled shift to an unhealthy diet of affluence—might have overemphasized some areas of nutrition and ignored others.

On one hand, we are focused on limiting food: not eating too much dessert, not drinking too much alcohol, or eliminating red meat. This is all done in the framework of ubiquitous social norms that involve food at nearly every celebration or interaction. The argument from the omnivorous side always seems to be centered on deficiency in this vitamin or that mineral, but in fact, chronic overnutrition may be a far bigger concern to the population.

The wide range of delicacy and palatability across many nations and cultures is evidence of the wide range of what we might call "a normal human diet." In fact, we may want to focus some effort on making a whole food, plant-based diet equally familiar, convenient, and enjoyable.

Nutrition is regularly steeped in controversy, making food choices confusing. Misinformation is commonly—and loudly—reported by organizations that reap the benefits of their own half-truths. Be wary of dollar signs and too-good-to-be-true promises. Despite that, if you stay tuned in to reliable science and listen to your own common sense, wise eating habits are attainable.

The Least You Need to Know

- Dairy may do more harm than good when it comes to your health, possibly contributing to cancer, heart disease, and other chronic diseases.
- Calcium is abundant in plants and is bone protective when consumed regularly along with a nutrient-dense diet.
- Soy foods are nutritionally dense foods that may offer health advantages.
- Following an exclusively raw diet causes some concerns, but the benefits of consuming most of your calories from raw foods are inarguable.
- There is no such thing as a "perfect diet."

Shopping Savvy

Now that you know why and how to eat whole, plant-based foods, it's time to go shopping. Filling your cart with nutritious choices is the fun part. Plus, shopping brings the theory of healthful eating to life. While at first you may feel intimidated as you carefully consider every purchase, plant-based shopping is like learning a new language. In due time, selecting the most healthful foods becomes second nature, and you'll toss items into your cart without a second thought.

In this chapter, you learn what you need to be plant perfect (or just about). Soon you won't be able to stop talking about how great your new lifestyle is!

In This Chapter

- Everything you need to know about nutrition labels
- Organic versus conventionally grown foods
- Finding sabotaging ingredients
- Plant-based shopping

Reading Nutrition Labels

What we are about to write might shock you. It goes against everything you may have heard previously. It certainly contradicts what we learned in our nutrition classes (from kindergarten through graduate school). But it will simplify your life more than any other nutrition advice ever has:

> *Never read the nutrition label on a package!*

That's right! Ignore it entirely! Everything listed there is confusing, misleading, and manipulating.

Focus on the Ingredients

The only section of a food label you should read is the list of ingredients. That's where the objective truth resides. Ingredients are listed in descending order by weight (from most to least). So those ingredients with the largest weight within the product come first, and those with the least are listed last.

Here are some tips for analyzing food products based on their ingredient lists:

- Be sure you recognize everything on the list.

- Keep it whole. Choose items with the fewest ingredients possible. The label typically shouldn't list more than a few items. Less means more.

- Watch out for the sneaky ingredients. These include all the antinutrients, artificial anything, and items you can't pronounce.

- Look for added salt and oils on bulk frozen vegetable packages. Many times, these ingredients are used as part of the blanching process to preserve color and taste.

Ultimately, most of your foods should come without ingredient lists. Vegetables and fruits are sitting out naked on the shelves in the produce section of the market; on the tables at your local farmers' market; or on the trees, bushes, and vines in your backyard. Whole grains, legumes, nuts, seeds, herbs, and spices are sold package-free in the bulk sections or in packages with one ingredient listed. And as amazing as it might sound, fresh produce doesn't have an expiration date; it's obvious when produce is expired! Real food is really easy to manage.

These whole foods are the staples of your diet. Plus, shopping is faster and easier when you don't have to analyze labels!

Making Sense of Food Labels

The nutrition facts section on a food label intends to help you make comparisons between the nutrient contents of food products and decisions about your overall diet. The nutrition facts provide information on protein, cholesterol, saturated fat, dietary fiber, and other nutrients that concern your health.

The components of the nutrition panel include both mandatory and voluntary information. Disclosing numbers for calories, total fat, total carbohydrate, and sodium is mandatory, for example. Voluntary dietary disclosures include sugar alcohol, soluble and insoluble fiber, and other essential nutrients. The absolute amount of that nutrient found per serving in the product is listed in grams or milligrams.

Nutrition Facts

8 servings per container
Serving size   2/3 cup (55g)

Amount per serving
Calories   230

	% Daily Value*
Total Fat 8g	**10%**
Saturated Fat 1g	**5%**
Trans Fat 0g	
Cholesterol 0mg	**0%**
Sodium 160mg	**7%**
Total Carbohydrate 37g	**13%**
Dietary Fiber 4g	**14%**
Total Sugars 12g	
Includes 10g Added Sugars	**20%**
Protein 3g	
Vitamin D 2mcg	10%
Calcium 260mg	20%
Iron 8mg	45%
Potassium 235mg	6%

* The % Daily Value (DV) tells you how much a nutrient in a serving of food contributes to a daily diet. 2,000 calories a day is used for general nutrition advice.

The nutrition food label represents nutrition facts mandated by the FDA's 1990 Nutrition Labeling and Education Act.

Labeling terms like *low fat, good source of calcium, reduced sodium, lean,* and *heart-healthy* are claims defined by the FDA, and carefully determined regulations specify when foods can use these statements. The problem is that you have to look up what the terms mean in order for them to make sense. *Fat-free, zero fat, no fat, and negligible source of fat* doesn't mean the food is 100 percent free of fat. Instead, the FDA allows the use of *fat-free* when a single serving has 0.5 grams of fat or less per serving. How much fat you consume depends on how much of the food you eat. Flip over that that spray can of pure olive oil labeled "fat-free cooking," and you'll see nothing but zeros in all the fat calorie categories, and yet there is 100 percent fat in the can. How do they pull off that caloric magic? Look at the serving size: spray of a ⅓ second. (For reference, it takes a 1/4 second to blink an eye.) They hit their 0.5 gram rounding number, and who among us sprays for less than a ⅓ second? These little fat bombs are hidden all over labels.

The same holds true for trans fats, a compound you should avoid altogether. That means a product can still legally include trans fatty acids without its label reflecting it! Most times, people eat more than one serving per meal, and therefore consume significant amounts of harmful trans fatty acids. This explains why you can see an ingredient like partially hydrogenated oil listed (which is, by definition, trans fat), yet the nutrition facts indicate zero trans fats. This is confusing for anyone, registered dietitians included.

The % Daily Value (%DV) column refers to how much of the specified nutrient you'll consume per serving relative to a 2,000-calorie diet. So if you're counting calories and want to be sure you're getting adequate amounts of each nutrient, you can use this column as a guideline.

One drawback of using %DV as a guideline is that not everyone eats 2,000 calories per day. Furthermore, the %DV helps only if you calculate every calorie you consume. Not only is this cumbersome and unnecessary, but how do you calculate the calories and other nutrients from, say, the salad you had at lunch? A salad usually doesn't come with a nutrition label. Technically, you'd need sophisticated nutrient software to calculate your intake accurately. And of course, you'd have to measure or weigh every portion you eat to input the correct data. No wonder diets don't work!

Nutrition facts labels are superfluous when you eat a whole food, plant-based diet. Your focus is quality not quantity. You eat nutrient-dense foods when you're hungry and stop when you're satiated. Simple. No decoding, weighing, measuring, calculating, or counting necessary. Think of all that extra time you can spend being productive—finding new recipes, cooking, exercising, etc.!

Whether and When to Buy Organic

Organic, local, and fresh are all the rage these days at discount and high-end grocery stores alike. Before we dive into organic, there's one thing you may want to keep in mind: almost all of the amazing, healthful benefits outlined in thousands of journal articles were achieved with normal, everyday vegetables and fruits. They likely weren't locally fresh, organic, or heirloom. It seems that while we can't be gamed with nutrition labels on fresh fruits and vegetables, retailers are still within reach of other labeling games. This is not to say that these labels have no meaning, but retailers know that if they toss "organic" or "protein" on the label, more product will leave the shelf.

The terms *organic* and *conventional* mostly refer to the way farmers grow and process their products. Loosely, these terms follow what might be called a natural versus an unnatural, or manmade versus artificial, approach to farming. Organic farming generally emphasizes the use of renewable and sustainable resources with the goal of protecting the soil and water for future generations. Organic production abstains from using synthetic fertilizers, bioengineering, or chemical pesticides by relying on crop rotation, biodiversity, and biological controls to manage pests. To be deemed "certified organic," a government-approved agent must inspect and approve the farm and the protocol used in production there.

In contrast, traditional farming relies on chemical pesticides, biologically superior strains of plants, synthetic fertilizers, and even genetically modified seed crops (GMOs). It all sounds pretty scary and there are economic and health issues associated with these practices. With that said, there are also the tremendous benefits that come with outstanding crop yields and new technologies, such as hydroponically grown vegetables. In the latter case, vegetables are grown with nothing more than water and a mixture of minerals, nitrogen, phosphorus and potassium— it doesn't get much more artificial or manmade than that; however, these vegetables tend to have incredible flavor and nutrient profiles.

Nonetheless, organic has its drawbacks, too. A natural, organic fertilizer is animal feces. For example, fertilizer from poultry farms contributed to the widespread arsenic contamination of rice crops. Animal feces fertilizer and fecal contamination of irrigation water is also implicated in *Salmonella* contamination through direct contact of produce or seeds with contaminated manure or animal wastes. Some might equate and promote these practices as part of a natural permaculture approach. The point here is not to cast aspersions on the ideas and notions behind organic; of course, we don't want pesticide-laden vegetables and fruits or to undermine farmers because their seed crop was contaminated by neighboring patented-GMO pollen. There is a great debate and it can't be distilled by organic versus traditional produce arguments.

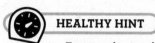 **HEALTHY HINT**

Fruits and vegetables are so powerful with disease-fighting capabilities that a recent toxicology study found an estimated 20,000 cases of cancer per year may be avoided by increasing fruit and vegetable consumption by only one serving of each per day. On the flip side, those pesticide residues people are so concerned about may result in up to 10 additional cancer cases per year.

It's definitely healthier to consume conventionally grown fruits and vegetables than not to consume them at all. Certain foods are higher in pesticides than others, so you need to prioritize which foods you buy as organic when trying to budget your purchases. If you want to buy all organic—all the better. Wash *all* produce carefully with a fruit and vegetable wash. Don't forget that *Salmonella* is 100 percent natural, organic, and locally fresh, but it will make you sick and may even kill you.

Finding Hidden Ingredients

Ingredients you want to avoid can cleverly be hidden within food products on store shelves. They have fancy names you may not be able to pronounce, or they fall under broad categories on the label that you probably would never think of. It takes a bit of homework and a lot of practice, but soon enough, you'll be able to smell a sneaky substance from an aisle away.

Products derived from animal fats and proteins are used ubiquitously, in food products, beverages, supplements, perfumes, cosmetics, skin-care products, and medications. They're even used during the production of certain products, like sugar. Because these components aren't found in the product itself, they don't have to appear in the ingredient lists. This is another reason to avoid processed foods.

In addition to animal products, harsh chemicals are sometimes used in the production of food. For example, hydrolyzed vegetable protein is made using hydrochloric acid.

Milk products are hidden in places where they really shouldn't be. Soy, almond, and rice cheeses commonly contain casein (a milk protein). This is strange, considering most people buy a cheese made from plant ingredients when they're avoiding dairy. Also, many brands of bread contain whey. Milk-containing products live under the following guises: whey, whey protein hydrolysate, casein, caseinate, butter, butter fat, cream, curds, custard, ghee, ammonium/calcium/magnesium/potassium/sodium caseinate, lactalbumin (phosphate), lactulose, lactose, milk protein hydrolysates, protein hydrolysates, nougat, and rennet.

 **MIXED GREENS**

Because of the surge in people experiencing allergies, certain foods with high allergy-causing potential have been mandated to be included at the end of the ingredient lists. This helps you easily identify certain ingredients. Milk, nuts, wheat, egg, fish, shellfish, soybeans, and peanuts are all required listings.

Gelatin, or gel, is a protein made by boiling skin, tendons, ligaments, and/or bones with water. Used as a thickener, gelatin can be found in fruit gelatin, pudding, candies, marshmallows, ice cream, cakes, and yogurts; it can also be found in the capsule holding together medication.

In addition, gelatin can be used in the processing of wine. If the product says "vegan," you can be sure there's no gelatin in the product.

Glycerin, a byproduct of soap manufacture, is normally made using animal fat. It can be found in foods and other products labeled as glycerin, glycerol, glycerides, glyceryls, glycreth-26, and polyglycol.

The terms *natural flavors* and *natural flavoring* can contain hundreds of different not-so-natural ingredients. They are defined by Title 21, Section 101, Part 22 of the Code of Federal Regulations as …

> the essential oil, oleoresin, essence or extractive, protein hydrolysate, distillate, or any product of roasting, heating or enzymolysis, which contains the flavoring constituents derived from a spice, fruit or fruit juice, vegetable or vegetable juice, edible yeast, herb, bark, bud, root, leaf or similar plant material, meat, seafood, poultry, eggs, dairy products, or fermentation products thereof, whose significant function in food is flavoring rather than nutritional.

With such a broad umbrella of "natural," you can't tell from which of the sources a natural flavor is derived. And because the word has no government-related regulation for use, food companies can use the term however they like. It's best to avoid products with "natural" ingredients.

Ultimately, the more processed the food, the more potential for hidden ingredients. Try to avoid processed foods as often as possible, relying more on whole, simple ingredients.

Plant-Based Supermarket Shopping

The secret to successful supermarket shopping is to focus on the perimeter of the store. If you picture the store where you usually shop, you'll notice produce is on the outside and processed foods are toward the center. Of course, this is an oversimplification because other foods you need are found in those center aisles, too. But the take-home message is to emphasize the fresh foods. Let's tour the market together, one aisle at a time.

To be efficient and cost effective, write a list before you hit the store so that you know exactly what items you need. Remembering everything if you just wing it is impossible (unless you have a super memory). Before you leave, decide which recipes you're going to make in the next two or three days. Then write down all the ingredients you need to purchase to prepare those recipes specifically. On the list, include staples you may be running out of. Check your pantry and refrigerator to take inventory. Got your list? Now you're ready to hit the store!

Picking Your Produce

First stop, the produce section. Stock up on any and all fresh vegetables and fruits that look appealing and fresh or that you need for a planned recipe.

The produce department is where you should indulge and experiment. If you see a food that sparks your curiosity, take it home and try it! Most everyone settles into a food comfort zone, maintaining a stable of favorites. A plant-based diet is an opportunity to explore new, previously untried foods. Challenge yourself to step outside your comfort zone. Try a new vegetable every week. Pick out a different recipe. Soak and cook dried beans just to see how easy it can be. The more open your mind, the more you'll discover and broaden your knowledge base.

Plan to spend some time in the greens section, and your cart should end up bursting with green leaves. These superfoods have a shorter lifespan than some other vegetables, so be sure to pick them up at least once a week. Then you'll have them on hand for whenever you get the craving.

After the greens, find your other veggies. Good ones to keep stocked up on are baby carrots, mushrooms, onions, bell peppers, broccoli, cauliflower, squash, celery, garlic, ginger, and potatoes of all varieties.

Find your fruits based on what you enjoy and what's available. Melons, berries, pears, pineapples, and oranges add color to your cart. Stock up on the seasonal options you look forward to all year, like figs, persimmons, and pumpkins in the fall and peaches, nectarines, and plums in the summer. The flavors of these special treats become a large part of the experience of the seasons.

Also visit the year-round regulars with permanent locations in the produce section, like bananas, apples, lettuce, cucumbers, and grapes. Don't forget your lemons and limes, which are hugely useful in so many recipes.

HEALTHY HINT

Farmers' markets are excellent places to frequent once a week. You can buy large amounts of the freshest produce for really good bargains. The produce is usually picked within the past 24 hours, so it's higher in nutrient content than supermarket produce, which is driven to the store and spends time in the back of the store before hitting the shelves. By buying at farmers' markets, you can eat produce with peak nutrition while supporting local businesses.

And don't forget the fresh herbs. Are you making Italian? Grab some basil, rosemary, and oregano. Mexican? Cilantro makes all the difference. It's good to have these and any other herbs you like on hand in the fridge because they can spice up any recipe.

Gettin' Spicy

In the spice aisle, pick up what you're out of. An exotic collection of spices can help you experiment in the kitchen. Plain salt and pepper is so passé! It's true, hot sauce—chipotle, Tabasco, Sriracha—should be its own food group. Smoked paprika, chipotle, cayenne, and various heat chili powders are amazing additions to sauces, dressings, or steamed vegetables.

From basics to blends, a shake of this or that can take your meal from blasé to fancy. A standard spice rack should contain any flavors you enjoy. Check out Chapter 18 for some spices regularly called for in plant-based recipes.

Bring on the Beans and Grains

While in the aisle with grains and legumes, have some fun. Notice how many different types of lentils you see. Pick a new one each time. Also grab some brown rice, brown jasmine rice, or wild rice. Have you discovered teff yet? Yum! Amaranth, barley, polenta, quinoa, and millet are other exotic grains.

You can find tons of recipes for these foods if you want or need them, or you can get creative and play with these foods on your own. As you experiment with new foods, the plant-based world will explode in front of you. Nothing about plants is boring. You'll enjoy more variety here than in the old-fashioned, dreary carnivorous realm.

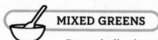

MIXED GREENS

Buy in bulk whenever possible to increase your options and save money. Specialty markets sell unusual foods (usually culture specific) at bargain prices and tend to have more bulk-buying options.

How many beans do you use on a regular basis? Have you noticed the vast selection in the bean section? Canned beans are fine to use if you don't have time to cook them from scratch. Try to find the salt-free options or, if you can't, drain and rinse them well before using.

Fun with Frozen Foods

The frozen-food section is filled with healthy, longer-lasting options ideal for a busy household. Frozen fruits and vegetables are usually flash-frozen, meaning they're frozen as soon as they're picked.

Frozen foods retain their nutrients and might even be a better choice than fresh sometimes in terms of convenience. Frozen veggies are already washed and chopped, making for easy additions to dishes. If you are new to plant-based cuisine and aren't yet familiar with recipes or various fresh green fare, then frozen vegetables are the training wheels of your new veggie bike. They are easy to steam or to toss into a large wok and can go from the freezer to the table in under 10 minutes. Frozen vegetables have come a long way since the bland TV dinners of the 70s.

Frozen fruits are perfect for smoothies and save the washing and chopping phase normally required. Plus, they give a frosty, ice-cream effect when used in a green smoothie.

Miscellaneous Finds

Other items you can pick up in your supermarket include raw nuts, raw seeds (especially hemp-seeds, flaxseeds, and sesame seeds), dates, 100 percent pure maple syrup, corn or sprouted-grain tortillas, *plant-based milks,* sun-dried tomatoes, olives, tofu, tempeh, nutritional yeast, tamari, miso, vinegars (rice, balsamic, and apple cider), mustard, low-sodium vegetable broth, tea, coffee, cocoa powder, and raw cacao nibs.

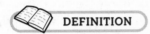 **DEFINITION**

> **Plant-based milks** are made from soy, almonds, rice, hemp, flax, vegetables, or oats and can be fortified with calcium, vitamin B_{12}, and vitamin D. Use them in the same fashion as cow's milk but without the health disadvantages.

Today, the large membership discount stores are an affordable, quick, and often overlooked option for eating green. Much of the produce is from the same sources as local grocery stores at a fraction of the price. The inventory rotates fast and large packages of leafy greens, cruciferous vegetables, mushrooms, peppers, onions, potatoes, and even exotic fruits abound! This takes most of the prep time out of large salads. (Discard the added dressing and toppings included in the package.). And don't forget those large bags of romaine lettuce hearts—they should be in every refrigerator. It may not be the latest trendy green, but it's packed with nutrition and the crunchy, sweet flavor is an outstanding start to any salad bowl. Your secret health weapon, as everyone else is buying that gallon jar of mustard they've been dreaming about, will be dashing in and out the produce section of these membership discount stores with a bountiful, fresh, colorful veggie haul.

With a bit of planning and some experience, plant-based shopping will become natural and simple. You'll find your rhythm and pick your preferences in time. Before you know it, you might even find yourself plant-perfect!

The Least You Need to Know

- Ignore the nutrition facts label, and instead focus on the ingredients. Choose products with the fewest items on the list and all ones you recognize.
- Choose organic whenever possible because organic is healthier for your body and the environment. (Plus, the difference in price grows smaller with increased demand.)
- While selecting foods with minimal ingredients is easiest, you should become acquainted with some of the names you need to avoid. Manufacturers find so many ways to sneak sketchy ingredients into food items.
- The majority of your shopping cart items should come from the perimeter of the store. Think colorful produce, whole grains, legumes, raw nuts, and raw seeds.

Plant-Perfect Fitness

When it comes to managing your health, diet prevails. However, you can't be truly healthy unless regular physical activity is a part of your life, too. Diet and exercise are the dynamic duo. Whole-plant foods flood your bloodstream with nutrients, and exercise distributes those nutrients into your cells. The innumerable benefits of staying fit make a consistent exercise program vital.

In this chapter, we explore the myriad health benefits for both mind and body resulting from an active lifestyle. While exercise can play an important role in daily activity, remember that exercise isn't a magic bullet. The opposite of sedentary isn't "working out"; the opposite is active. Exercise is a way to schedule in activity in a short period of time, but it will not mitigate a bad diet. What and how often you eat will dominate your health.

We break down the separate components that together define fitness, and show you how to incorporate each one into your routine. Remember, fitness, like a healthful diet, is a process that includes continual assessment, monitoring, and progression. Your journey to excellent health requires that you keep moving!

In This Chapter

- Why you need to be physically active
- The physical and psychological benefits of lifelong activity
- Program options for an effective workout
- Monitoring yourself for success

Why Exercise?

With approximately 640 muscles all eager to contract and expand, your body was built to move. Your heart, of course, is also a muscle, and it needs regular exercise to maintain optimal function. Your body is more likely to rust out than to wear out, so move it or lose it!

Exercise encompasses several features that together define fitness—strength, cardiovascular endurance, muscular endurance, flexibility, and balance. You need to incorporate all these factors into a program to maximize results so you thrive in every way possible. Certain types of exercise incorporate several fitness components. Walking and jogging, for example, improve balance, cardiovascular capacity, and muscular endurance all at once. You can train these attributes separately or combine them for an individualized program of your choice.

From stable energy and decreased stress to improved sleep and cognitive function, exercise has an extraordinary ability to improve your life from every angle. And consistency is key. You'll find plenty of ways to design a perfect exercise program, but the truth is, doing anything is beneficial—as long as you do it regularly. This dedication keeps all organ systems in your body conditioned.

The Physical Benefits of Exercise

Nothing feels better than post-workout euphoria. Every cell in your body rejoices for the gift you've given it. Among a multitude of physical benefits, exercise …

- Encourages nervous system communication.
- Boosts immune function.
- Increases insulin sensitivity.
- Develops positive bone turnover.
- Reduces stress.
- Protects the heart and blood vessels.
- Stimulates the endocrine system to release healthy hormones.

Metabolic Myths of Exercise

We discussed the cellular power plants, the mitochondria, that fuel all cell activity. This activity ranges from basic cellular repair functions and enzymatic activity to the coordinated functions required in the contraction of muscles during a push-up. Each cell's respiration results in the utilization of oxygen and fuel and generates carbon dioxide, water, and heat. When a lot of cellular activity is happening at once, our breath rate increases to dump all that carbon dioxide formed, and we begin to sweat to eliminate the waste heat. The unit of measure for metabolic energy and activity is the calorie (technically a kilocalorie). We see similar calorie labels on food, which indicate the amount of energy contained within a serving.

Your metabolic rate changes from minute to minute, moving up and down, to match the required energy for the current level of activity. *Basal metabolic rate* (BMR) is the lowest energy required for basic life functions and all activities will increase metabolic rate from basal. Researchers typically measure BMR first thing in the morning when the subject is rested and fasted. Even the process of digestion necessitates a "boost in *metabolism*" as so many people will ascribe to certain foods.

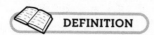 **DEFINITION**

Metabolism is the whole range of biochemical processes that occur in your body and are necessary to maintain life. **Basal metabolic rate (BMR)**, a measure of the rate of metabolism, is the minimum energy needed to sustain the metabolic activities of cells and tissues to maintain circulatory, respiratory, gastrointestinal, and renal processes. **Thermic effect of food (TEF)** is the increase in energy expenditure associated with the processes of digestion, absorption, and metabolism of food.

Seems like managing your metabolism should be pretty simple, right? Yet how many times in the past have you counted calories, busted a move in the gym, and not seen a shift on the scale? In Chapter 6 we learned about oxidative priority, how recently ingested food is metabolically disposed of based on the body's ability to store it. We also learned that during these metabolic boosts, sometimes called the *thermic effect of food (TEF)*, the metabolic energy of the rise isn't primarily coming from fat stores and consequently these boosts do little to move the scale. It turns out that the metabolic activity of exercise works much the same.

As this applies to metabolism of activity, realize that the body has reserves of glucose and fat. While both of these fuels add to the number on the scale, it's only fat loss we are after and activity largely burns glucose.

You can't out-exercise a bad diet.

Yes, eating meals boosts metabolism. Yes, exercising increases daily expenditure. Yes, the calories on food packages are generally accurate. No, you can't add all of these up into a table and easily predict weight loss or gain. It's much more complicated. An active lifestyle unquestionably promotes health span and longevity. Exercise improves overall fitness and conditions all the muscles in your body, especially your heart. These are all great reasons to be more active, but don't be fooled into believing that the metabolic magic of exercise is going to wipe out poor choices on your plate.

Immunity Influence

Immune function is greatly enhanced through active lifestyles. People who exercise regularly report fewer colds and sick days than their sedentary peers. The reason is twofold. First, running parallel to our *circulatory system* is the *lymphatic system*. Because the lymphatic system doesn't include a pump (like the heart, which acts as the pump of the circulatory system), it relies on muscle contractions to move lymph fluids throughout the body. Activity stimulates this process, which encourages the elimination of bacteria, viruses, and other immune stressors.

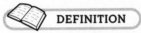 **DEFINITION**

The circulatory system consists of the heart, arteries, capillaries, and veins, and is responsible for transporting blood, oxygen, and nutrients to all cells in the body. **The lymphatic system** includes vessels and lymph nodes separate from the circulatory system that filter out microorganisms and other toxins before it returns fluid and protein to the blood. The lymphatic system carries white blood cells throughout the body to help fight infection.

Physical activity also suppresses the release of stress hormones such as cortisol, adrenaline, norepinephrine, and epinephrine, which the endocrine system secretes when tension is induced. Constant stress makes you vulnerable to illness at all levels, from colds to heart disease. Simply having an outlet for the stress through movement is also beneficial. It's impossible not to feel calmer after a workout.

Your sleep also improves with a more active life. Moreover, it enables you to reach a deeper, more restful state when you do sleep, making repair and regeneration superior. Sound sleep is essential for immune system function, among everything else. There really is no substitute for a good night's rest.

Dodging Disease

Heart-healthy cardiovascular exercise (also known as "cardio") has a major influence over risk factors for heart attack and stroke. Consistently raising and sustaining your heart rate lowers your blood pressure, "bad" (LDL) cholesterol, and total cholesterol. Interestingly, exercise is one of the few effective ways known to raise your "good" (HDL) cholesterol levels. Working out is a far superior option to taking cholesterol-lowering medications—more benefit with no harmful side effects.

Cancer risk is also reduced with exercise. Colon, breast, endometrial, prostate, and lung cancer incidence can significantly decrease with a consistent fitness plan. This may be because exercise helps maintain ideal body weight, reduces excess hormones in your blood, moderates insulin and

IGF-1 levels, boosts immunity, and suppresses inflammation. These are all cancer-promoting factors.

Once a cancer diagnosis is made, exercise may help improve outcome. Quality of life is enhanced, and fatigue is reduced. Physical activity boosts cancer survival and decreases chance of recurrence. It's never too late—and always advantageous—to kick up your activity to the next level.

Support your plant-fabulous diet with a consistent dose of exercise, and you'll maximize the benefits of both. Together they make the perfect team.

The Psychological Benefits of Exercise

An undeniable example of the interconnectedness of mind and body is the psychological response to a more active lifestyle and exercise. Moving your body positively affects the way your mind functions. All you have to do is pay attention immediately after you finish your workout. Endorphins, neurochemicals produced in the body that act as natural painkillers, flood the brain and cause a rush of calm, clear, and comfortable feelings. Mood is stabilized, stress is reduced, and cognition is enhanced.

But the bliss doesn't end right after your workout. Regular exercise has long-term benefits as well. A steady workout program can measurably minimize depression, anxiety, and stress while improving body image and self-confidence.

Being active isn't automatic. Typically, your energy levels hit peaks and valleys throughout the day, and you may struggle to keep yourself steadily vitalized. Exercise notoriously balances those waves and helps you maintain stamina all day long. Being filled with energy empowers you to be productive, sustain a level mood, handle stress, stay motivated, and sleep more efficiently. If everyone ate a whole food, plant-based diet and exercised regularly, productivity would be unparalleled!

Choose Your Physical Activity

"Active"—not "exercise"—is the opposite of "sedentary." Before we get into some of the more technical aspects of exercise, let's spend a little more time discussing an active lifestyle. You don't need to change into workout clothes or count calories, reps, or steps to be active. Instead, it is more of a mindset. From cutting the lawn to vacuuming, there are always ways to put more pep in your step and turn the mundane into activity or opportunity. Of course, there are many calisthenics that can be easily incorporated into the day. You can use apps and activity trackers to prompt you regularly with reminders to move and breathe. It's easy for repetitive exercise to become too mechanical or boring for some, so get creative. You probably know already whether or not you like the gym or the group workout environment. For those who don't gravitate to the competitive and intense, you need to make certain that regular physical activity is a priority in your life.

For physical activity, one hour of moderate exercise 5 to 7 days per week seems to be the sweet spot for health benefits. Moderate exercise should pass the "talk, not sing" test. During appropriate activity, you should be able to easily carry on a conversation but be too winded to sing. With plenty of physical activity options, you can choose activities based on what you like. You'll never have a problem finding something you love—or at least something you can tolerate:

- If you thrive in a creative environment, dancing or weight training is perfect.

- If you prefer simplicity, walking, jogging, and swimming are excellent.

- Are you competitive? Sign up for a sport or a race, or take a class at the gym.

- Need variety? Try a new activity every day, developing a varied program to keep it interesting.

- Live by the ocean? Work out on the beach or take up kayaking, windsurfing, or surfing.

- Enjoy focusing on the mind-body connection? Yoga may be right up your alley. Or try martial arts, which challenges your mind and body while getting you in fighting shape.

If you have no idea what to do and feel intimidated, personal trainers are eager to take your fitness to the next level, no matter what shape you're in. (Just be sure you choose a qualified individual—more on that later.) Ultimately, find something that makes you feel great, tickles your fancy, and keeps you going.

Let's take a look at some types of traditional exercise so you can better choose the one that's right for you.

Cardiovascular Endurance

Technically, cardiovascular endurance is defined as the ability to increase *stroke volume* and maximize *cardiac output* while reducing your resting heart rate. Simply stated, it's a well-conditioned heart.

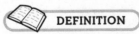 **DEFINITION**

> **Stroke volume** is the amount of blood pumped from the left ventricle of the heart with one contraction. **Cardiac output** equals the total amount of blood flow from the heart during a specified period of time, or stroke volume multiplied by heart rate. Cardiac output is regulated by the amount of nutrients and oxygen the cells require, as well as the requirement to remove wastes.

One way to measure your progress with a cardio program is by your heart rate. On average, a resting heart rate, or the number of times your heart beats when you're completely inactive, is 60 to 80 beats per minute. In physically fit individuals, this rate is lower.

Test for your resting heart rate first thing in the morning. Simply find your pulse, either by your carotid artery on the side of your throat or on your wrist. Have a stopwatch or a watch with a second hand ready. Use your pointer and middle fingers together to locate your pulse, not your thumb (it has a pulse of its own). Ideally, count the beats for an entire minute. You can also count the beats for 10 seconds and multiply the result by 6.

For maximum cardiovascular benefit, you need to keep your target heart rate between 60 and 85 percent of your maximum heart rate, or the greatest number of times your heart can beat in a minute. Your target heart rate is the recommended intensity level to ensure adequate stimulation of your cardiovascular system based on your age. Calculating target heart rate is a useful tool for setting and monitoring fitness goals. Here's the formula:

$$(220 - \text{your age}) \times .60 \text{ and } .85$$

The first number ($\times$ .60) gives you the low-end of the range, and the second result ($\times$ .85) is the high end.

An easier method of determining whether you've reached your target heart rate during exercise is to note whether you're out of breath but not gasping for air. You should find it difficult but not impossible to talk.

When your body is working hard, as during exercise, your cardiac output increases to meet your body's demands, resulting in enhanced fitness. Exercises that improve cardiovascular endurance engage the large muscle groups for a sustained period of time, allowing the heart rate to remain elevated. Endurance exercises include walking, running, swimming, cycling, jumping, hiking, and using an elliptical trainer, step mill, or stationary bicycle.

For improved endurance, exercise a 30-minute (or more) session most, and preferably all, days of the week. You can break up the time into 10-minute intervals for an accumulated total of at least 30 minutes a day. Done every day, this adds up to approximately 600 to 1,200 calories of extra energy expended per week. Of course, this depends on many variables, including your age, weight, muscle mass, and intensity of exercise.

Strength Training

Muscular strength is the ability to exert force on a physical object using muscles. Muscular endurance is the capacity of the muscles to sustain a repeated force over a period of time. These two components are individually important, and each is trained differently.

To improve strength and muscular endurance, a force needs to be applied methodically on a regular basis. A strength-increasing program positively impacts muscle endurance. However, the inverse is not true. Emphasizing endurance won't necessarily enhance strength gains. To illustrate, imagine you want to build muscle and gain strength. You develop a program in which you progressively increase the weight used for your sets. Because you lift the weight during each set for a number of repetitions, you incidentally improve endurance.

Strength training, also called resistance training, requires the use of machines, dumbbells, barbells, tubing, or your own body weight to create a force your muscles can resist. Consistency is key, as muscle is hard to build but easy to lose. Programs vary depending on goals, but ideally, you should work each major muscle group at least once a week.

 PLANT PITFALL

Strength training can lead to injury if you don't know what you're doing. If you've never worked with resistance, either hire a qualified personal trainer for a few sessions or watch an instructional video on how to do certain exercises with proper form. The last thing you want to do is sustain an injury when you're trying to boost your health.

Here are some calisthenic exercises you can do (these require no or minimal equipment):

- Pull-ups
- Push-ups (on the wall, from your knees, full push-up, with feet elevated)
- Triceps dips
- Plank holds
- Abdominal crunches
- Calf raises
- Lunges (forward, stationary, walking)
- Pliés
- Squats
- Side planks
- Bear crawls
- Wall squats
- Single-leg balances

Typically, a strength-building workout consists of 2 to 4 sets of anywhere from 4 to 10 repetitions per exercise for each muscle group. As you get stronger, you must increase the weight to continue building strength. You may need to do two to four different exercises per muscle group, depending on your objectives. When you've reached your strength goals, you can maintain them by lifting the same weight but increasing repetitions when your sets start to feel too easy.

To build endurance, use a lighter weight for longer sets, with more repetitions per set. For example, you can perform 3 sets of 15 to 25 repetitions.

Stretching

Stretching is the most neglected component of fitness. Yet the benefits are infinite, and improvements happen fast if done regularly. *Flexibility* matters because it elongates muscles, which enables movement and protects the joints.

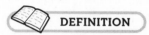 **DEFINITION**

Flexibility is a joint's ability to move freely through a full and normal range of motion. Many factors influence joint mobility, including genetics, the joint structure itself, neuromuscular coordination, and strength of the opposing muscle group.

The benefits of regular stretching include increased performance and decreased risk of injury. Training also increases blood supply and nutrients to the joints. This improves circulation and nutrient exchange and decelerates degeneration of the joint tissues.

The most effective way to stretch is to hold each stretch for at least 30 seconds, breathe deeply, and relax into it. Be sure your body is warm before you begin by warming up with a cardiovascular activity to prevent injury. Stretch each major muscle group after you use it, and be consistent. Daily practice is best, and dedicating at least 10 minutes during each session optimizes results.

Functional Fitness

Currently "functional fitness" has inundated the workout scene. And justifiably so. Taking rehabilitation and injury prevention to the next level, exercises are specifically intended to enhance activities of daily living, such as walking, sitting up, preparing meals, eating, lifting, and bending. Essentially, it's fitness aimed at surviving and thriving in the real world by preparing the body to handle physical stress.

Training functionally usually entails a lot of core work to strengthen the muscles used to protect the back and maintain posture. (Your core is the group of muscles located around the trunk of your body—the abdominal muscles: rectus abdominis, transverse abdominis, and external and internal obliques; the pelvic floor muscles; and the spinal stabilizer muscles.)

Exercises that incorporate the entire body are used as well. The focus is on improving balance, strengthening the entire body, and elongating muscles.

Sports

Engaging in sports is a great way to stay in shape without even realizing it. If you have a competitive spirit or just enjoy the challenge, you can sign up to play sports locally or round up a group of friends and start a team. Whether it's basketball, softball, or soccer, opportunities abound for everyone from the former high school jock to the seasoned athlete.

Accountability to a team will ensure you show up. Plus, you'll be motivated to maintain your fitness level, knowing your performance depends on it. Huffing, puffing, and being unable to keep up with your teammates, will inspire you to keep heading to the gym.

HEALTHY HINT

Always be sure to warm up before you play a game or practice, and stretch during and afterward. Also strengthen the muscles you use in the sport on different days with resistance training to enhance performance and prevent injury.

Just Move It!

Regardless of your workout program, always include movement throughout your day whenever possible. Get creative in finding ways to do so. Consider these examples:

- Take the stairs instead of the escalator or elevator—even if it's five floors.

- Park far from the entrance of where you're going.

- While you're talking on the phone, stretch; do squats, lunges, pliés, or calf raises; or walk up and down stairs.

- When you're in your car stopped at a stop light, squeeze your glutes and your abdominal muscles until the light turns green.

- When doing dishes or brushing your teeth, do leg swings, calf raises, or abdominal squeezes.

- Drink a lot of water all day so you get up and walk to the bathroom more often.

- When scheduling a get-together with friends or a romantic date, include an activity like a hike, a jog, or a hot new fitness class. Wall climbing or salsa dancing is sexy and fun!

- While waiting in line, squeeze, hold, and release different muscles throughout your body. Nobody notices you making isometric contractions, but you improve blood and lymph flow.

- If you watch TV, stay active while doing so. Do calisthenics on the floor. Place a minitrampoline, step, or other cardio equipment in front of the TV—and *use it!* Save movies or recorded TV shows you're excited to watch when you're exercising.

- On your way anywhere throughout the day, don't just walk. Instead, either run or do walking lunges to your destination.

- Sit on a large stability ball instead of a chair at your desk to engage your core muscles. (I, Julieanna, wrote this entire book while sitting on my big, red, stability ball.)

Go to the Gym or Work Out at Home?

You may be a gym rat or a gym-phobe—it all depends on your personality. Gym-goers may like being around other people and taking classes. Each comes with its own benefits.

Working out at the gym means you have a convenient assortment of equipment options and classes. You'll find inspiration oozing from surrounding gym members, and you'll also have the opportunity to learn new exercises by watching others or asking a trainer. Plus, there's more variety at a gym than you're likely to get at home.

If you do exercise at the gym, be sure to plan your workout before you get there. Also, schedule your workouts according to the gym's less-hectic times so you can have your choice of equipment or space in the classroom. And always bring some water and a towel.

If you prefer to work out at home, you can still achieve a progressive and balanced workout program. Literally thousands of online videos, workout DVDs, podcasts, live streams, apps, and other high-tech options are available for free or for rent or purchase in every genre of fitness. After some trial and error, you'll know which work for you and challenge you in a good way. Be sure to vary the workouts; don't get stuck on just one or two. Variety is the spice of your fitness life, so shake it up often.

You can purchase a wide assortment of workout equipment for your home, from the small and inexpensive to the large and costly. Dumbbells, kettlebells, foam rollers, exercise balls, and rubber tubing can fit easily into any home and are an affordable way to stay in shape. This equipment usually comes with instructional videos or manuals so you have an idea of how to use them. You can find additional resources online or at your local store.

On the other end of that spectrum are large pieces of equipment that may fit into your space and price range. Commercial-grade treadmills, ellipticals, and stationary bikes have come a long way in the last several years. So have other types of fitness equipment, like total body resistance machines and Pilates equipment. Ultimately, what matters most is finding something you either love or at least can commit to.

 MIXED GREENS

Many personal trainers do in-home training. In fact, that's how I worked my way through graduate school. I spent 12 years going to people's homes and getting creative using tubing, their furniture, and even their kids to make fitness fun and effective. You can hire a certified personal trainer for a short period of time to help you set up a program or, if possible, on an ongoing basis to motivate, monitor, and help you progress.

Working out at home means you can wear whatever is most comfy (even your torn-up sweats) and not have to worry about what anyone thinks. Plus, there's the convenience factor—if you're home, you're at your gym! And unless you live with others who will also work out in your gym, equipment and space in the classroom are always available. As a bonus, you can enlist the support of your family members—or even your pets!

From home, you can always go for a walk, hike, jog, bike ride, or swim if you have access to a pool. Depending on the weather, you may prefer the outdoors anyway.

Fit Tips

The take-home message here is that you need to be active. It will enhance your health in hundreds of ways and be well worth the effort. How you divide up your training (how much cardio versus strength workouts, for example) isn't as important as just doing something. Find what works for you and stick with it. The rewards will come instantly, and they'll only get better with consistency.

Keep these tips in mind while planning your workouts:

- Set goals for yourself that are realistic, measurable, and timely. Write them down, and re-evaluate them often.

- Incorporate all the components of fitness into your training regularly.

- Don't announce goals to your family, friends, or fellow gym-goers. Contrary to popular opinion the brain may view these announcements as progress, even where none is made. Let people notice your progress.

- Schedule your workout into your day and prioritize it. If possible, do it first thing in the morning, because excuses tend to build up as the day goes along.

- Keep your body guessing. The moment your workout feels easy, kick it up a notch. The only way to continue seeing results is to constantly challenge your body.

There's no need to be a fitness model or a gym rat to get the benefits of physical activity. Don't let perfection get in the way of consistent performance.

Monitoring Your Progress

Stay tuned in to your workout program. It should be a dynamic, fluid process that bears results immediately and continuously. You should always feel great afterward and see gains in endurance (you can go farther or for longer), strength (you can lift more or do more reps), flexibility (you can stretch farther), and balance (you can balance better). Keep track and be aware of your body.

Adaptation occurs quickly and often when you're doing what you're supposed to be doing in your workout program. Your exercise program should never feel easy. If it does, you won't benefit, and you'll get stuck in a plateau. Always consider adding more time, speed, weight, intensity, and/or frequency to keep your body challenged.

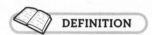 **DEFINITION**

Adaptation is your body's physiologic response to exercise. It occurs with a persistent training regimen and means your body has learned to cope with the stress you've placed on it from your current program. To avoid plateaus, change your workout frequently.

Another way to monitor your progress is to notice physical changes. You may weigh the same on the scale but fit better in your clothes. This is a great marker of muscle growth. Measuring yourself—chest, arm, waist, hips, thigh, and calf—affirms that your weight has redistributed. You may also be able to witness actual growth of muscles by looking in the mirror. Be sure to take note of how you feel, too.

And ask yourself some questions as you progress. Have you reached your current goals? What do you need to achieve the next goal? Assessment is crucial. Figure out what works and what doesn't. Do some problem-solving until you figure out what works best for you to attain your goals.

To achieve optimal health, you need a clean diet, plenty of rest, and relaxation or stress-management skills. Exercise completes the equation and adds quality to your life, pep to your step, and clarity to your mind. Embrace regular exercise—if you haven't already—and you will thrive.

The Least You Need to Know

- Incorporating physical activity into your days boosts the benefits of a plant-based diet.
- Being fit incorporates cardiovascular and muscular endurance, strength, flexibility, and balance. Include exercises to improve all these.
- It doesn't matter where or what you prefer—find any exercise program you love and will stick to, and then commit to it.
- Keep your body on its toes. As soon as something becomes easy, change it up so you continue to challenge yourself and reap the benefits.

To Supplement or Not to Supplement?

The most commonly asked question in nutrition today is whether or not supplements are necessary. In this multibillion-dollar industry, supplement manufacturers have confused the public beyond comprehension. You probably worry about whether you're getting enough nutrients from your diet alone—especially on a plant-based plan. How do you know if you're getting enough of each nutrient? Who can you trust for unbiased information? If you need a supplement, which type do you choose? Is taking more better than not taking enough? Are they safe?

In this chapter, we examine these questions in detail.

In This Chapter

- Micronutrients to consider
- Getting vitamins B_{12} and D
- Current research on supplements
- The brilliance of your body

Do You *Need* to Supplement?

Many factors determine whether your diet meets your nutrient needs. Technically, there is no such thing as a perfect diet. Furthermore, we don't typically eat the same foods nor do we necessarily meet all of our nutrient needs every single day. The standard Western diet tends to fall short on fiber, potassium, magnesium, folate, iron, and vitamins A and C. As we've discussed, a plant-based diet easily provides these nutrients; however, there are some specific nutrients that likely need to be supplemented to fill in potential gaps.

Dietary supplements need to be considered and treated as medications. If you have a nutrient deficiency, you need to determine what the origin of that deficiency is. Most of the time, a nutrient deficiency signifies either a health issue or a poor diet overall. In either of these cases, popping a supplement won't address the real problem.

Additionally, nothing comes without risk. Every drug has associated side effects, and most of the science available shows that supplements don't make you healthier. That being said, a whole food, plant-based diet that contains a wide variety of different foods every day should provide everything you need, with the exception of vitamin B_{12} and possibly vitamins D and K2, EPA, and DHA.

Boosting Your B_{12}

Vitamin B_{12} deficiency in plant-exclusive eaters is more common than it should be with a broad prevalence range of 0 to 86.5 percent of the population, depending on the subpopulation and fortified products consumed. And as discussed in Chapter 3, it can be a serious issue. Essentially, if you are excluding animal products from your diet and you don't replenish your supply of B_{12}, you will eventually become deficient. No gold standard exists to test for blood cobalamin deficiency. Currently, the most commonly used tests are serum cobalamin, MMA (methylmalonic acid), and Schilling test. Ask your physician to test you during your regularly scheduled visits, but remember blood tests may not detect a deficiency until it's too late and irreversible neurological issues can transpire during that time.

If you're plant based, the safest, cheapest, and most reliably effective way to avoid deficiency is to supplement. Consuming fortified products such as nutritional yeast or plant milks may provide some B_{12} in the diet, but it is easier to control and to ensure adequate intake with a supplement. Although the RDA for B_{12} is only 2.4 micrograms for adult men and women, supplements are not completely absorbed; this is why the recommendation for intake is higher.

Several different types of B_{12} compounds are available as supplements, and the two most commonly found are cyanocobalamin and methylcobalamin. Cyanocobalamin converts in the body to the active forms of methylcobalamin and 5-deoxyadenosylcobalamin. Evidence suggests there is no difference in bioavailability or absorption between the different forms. You can also ask your doctor for an injectable B_{12} if you have any absorption issues. Supplement with B_{12} using one of these three dosing schedules: 50 micrograms twice daily, 150 micrograms daily, or 2,500 micrograms once weekly. No tolerable upper limit has been set by the Institute of Medicine since B_{12} is water soluble and high levels are considered safe.

 MIXED GREENS

Cyanocobalamin is a precursor to the more active form of hydroxocobalamin in the body. Yet, some people are concerned about a small amount of cyanide that is released into the body from the cyanocobalamin molecule. The body has the ability to convert this into a thiocyanate, which can be easily excreted. Not only that, but hydroxocobalamin is actually used in some cases to treat cyanide poisoning.

Do's and Don'ts of Vitamin D

Vitamin D is not as cut and dried as vitamin B_{12}. A vast majority of the world's population has either insufficient or deficient levels of vitamin D. But this doesn't mean you should just pop a pill. Before you do anything, have your 25-hydroxyvitamin D blood-level tested. If you end up with a result lower than recommended, you need to determine how best to bring it up. Adequate serum 25-hydroxyvitamin D levels are 30 to 50 nmol/L (12 to 20 ng/mL).

Try using the sun as your first line of defense. Everyone responds differently to sun therapy, depending on factors such as weather, season, latitude where you live, and your skin color (the lighter your skin, the more easily you absorb vitamin D). If you live somewhere that gets a lot of sunshine throughout the year, you're at an advantage and might not have to supplement.

To maximize sun exposure safely do the following:

- Go out during the peak time of the day when the UVB rays are strongest, usually between 10 A.M. and 2 P.M.

- Protect your eyes with sunglasses.

- Apply sunscreen to your face to prevent wrinkling, but do not wear it on the other exposed parts of your body.

- Expose as much of your skin as possible without offending your neighbors.

- Never allow your skin to burn or even to turn pink. The darker your skin, the more sun exposure you require to make vitamin D, and the harder it is for you to burn.

- Do this two or three times a week at minimum.

After following these suggestions for a couple months, take a follow-up blood test. If your results go up, congratulations! Continue with the sun exposure regimen. However, if you're unable to raise your 25-hydroxyvitamin D to at least 30 nmol/L (12 ng/mL), continue with the sun exposure, but add a vitamin D supplement.

Note, this trial works best during the warmer months and in warmer climates. If you're performing the sun exposure trial during the heart of winter, you probably won't increase your levels. Your result may be situational and not a reflection of your personal ability to make vitamin D. Test this during the spring or summer seasons for optimal results. You might need to supplement only in the colder months.

Supplemental vitamin D is derived from animal sources—usually from lanolin in sheep's wool—in the form of cholecalciferol, or vitamin D_3. Now there is also a plant-derived version of D_3 commercially available sourced from lichen. An additional form called ergocalciferol, or vitamin D_2, is found in plant sources, mostly in UVB-irradiated mushrooms. Dietary supplements may contain either D_2 or D_3, both of which can be effective at raising blood levels to optimal levels in smaller doses (4,000 IU and less). Cholecalciferol (D_3) is superior when using larger doses. You can safely take 2,000 IU per day with 4,000 IU per day being the established tolerable upper limit. Physicians can prescribe high-dose supplementation in certain cases, but this needs to be monitored. Unlike vitamin B_{12}, vitamin D is fat-soluble and toxicity is possible.

PLANT PITFALL

Never double up on a multivitamin to attain optimal levels of vitamins B_{12} or D. You'll be doubling up on other compounds, too, which can be toxic.

Consider taking a moderate multivitamin that contains dietary reference intake (DRI) levels of nutrients including iodine, selenium, zinc, and K2. If the multivitamin is comprehensive, be sure folate is used instead of folic acid. There are formulas that include vitamins B_{12} and D, so you can simply take them altogether in one supplement and cover your bases. Beware of multivitamins that megadose nutrients to levels higher than DRI. Furthermore, as discussed in Chapter 3, taking a microalgal formula of EPA and DHA may be a good idea. It's optimal to have your blood tested for potential deficiencies common in the general population, including DHA, iron, zinc, and iodine. But as a universal rule, don't supplement "just in case." Instead, get your nutrients from food and monitor your blood levels regularly to confirm your nutrient intake is sufficient.

The Dangers of Supplementation

In addition to cashing in on nutrient fears, supplement manufacturers imply their products can perform miracles for your health. Herbs, botanicals, blends, powders, bars, and potions promise to stop aging, prevent cancer, replace exercise, and make you popular. If it sounds too good to be true, it probably is.

The Dietary Supplement Health and Education Act

A major force influencing the supplement industry is a piece of legislation called the Dietary Supplement Health and Education Act (DSHEA). Passed in 1994, this act took away responsibility from the government to ensure the safety of a product before it's put on the market. Instead of the FDA determining safety, as it does for foods and medications, the drug manufacturer is in charge of its own products.

If a problem comes up after a product makes it onto the shelves, only then does the FDA become responsible. But until then, buyer beware! Only the drug manufacturer that benefits from you buying and using a supplement decides whether it is safe. This possible conflict of interest has broad implications.

What's Up in Supplements?

Unless you have a deficiency, supplements don't make you healthier. In certain cases, the opposite is true. Beta-carotene, vitamin E, and folic acid have been found to be harmful in numerous trials.

After the discovery that people who ate more fruits and vegetables developed less cancer, researchers were on a mission to find out precisely what component in those foods caused the prevention. This made antioxidants all the rage in the nutrition world. In the mid-1990s, two well-designed studies compared a group at high risk for lung cancer (smokers and those exposed to asbestos) taking beta-carotene and vitamin A supplements with a control group taking no supplements. Much to the dismay of the researchers, the groups taking the supplements started developing lung cancer and dying more than the control group. They had to stop the study prematurely.

Several explanations are possible, but the results are still not completely understood. Perhaps it was due to the lack of synergistic compounds found in food sources of vitamin A. Or maybe it was because out of approximately 563 identified carotenoids, taking a large dose of only one of them (beta-carotene) prevented the others from working. The lesson to be emphasized is that isolating and concentrating a nutrient doesn't have the same effect as eating it in its original packaging.

Taking large amounts of vitamin E to ward off Alzheimer's disease and prevent oxidation is popular. But in a large meta-analysis of 19 studies performed in 2005, vitamin E was found to "increase all-cause mortality" at high doses "and should be avoided." Not only do you risk dying by taking these supplements, but many studies have shown that they don't even work to begin with.

Obstetricians advise their pregnant patients to take 600 micrograms of folic acid every day to help prevent neural-tube defects in their babies. Unfortunately, research shows that taking supplemental folic acid increases the risk of breast cancer. It may also lead to a higher risk of dying from breast cancer, as well as from all causes.

It's not the nutrient itself causing these results. Instead, it's the fact you're taking it in an unnaturally isolated, concentrated form. When consumed in its original packaging—surrounded by fiber and other nutrients—the *synergy* among all the compounds working together creates magic in your body.

 **DEFINITION**

Synergy is the effect of two or more units working together to produce a result not obtainable by each of the units independently.

Currently, taking fish oil supplements to attain high levels of the essential fatty acid DHA is the trend. Fish may be the most polluted organisms. Their muscles and livers are filled with PCBs, dioxin, mercury, organochlorines, pesticides, and DDT. All these compounds pose serious health risks to humans. If you think about it, eating one fish for dinner provides you with a dose of these toxins. In the food chain, bigger fish eat smaller fish, and those bigger fish absorb the toxins from the smaller fish. Now if you concentrate the oil from hundreds or thousands of big fish and put it into a capsule, consuming that capsule concentrates your exposure exponentially!

Lawsuits have been filed over fish oil–supplement manufacturers providing these toxins in their products. Even with the highly regarded molecular distillation process, products have still been found to contain these detrimental compounds. So far, not enough research has been done to confirm the potential health risks from taking these supplements.

Why chance it, especially when you don't need to take fish oil supplements in the first place? Be diligent about consuming ALA-rich foods (i.e. flaxseeds, hempseeds, chia seeds, walnuts, and soybeans), and also consider taking a microalgae DHA/EPA formula as a safer option than fish oil.

Knowing When to Supplement and When to Eat

The human body is the most unmistakable example of synergy. It contains 10 trillion of your cells and 100 trillion foreign cells in the microbiota, communicating with one another in a giant life symphony. The complexity of our bodies leaves even the most knowledgeable experts in awe. So many mysteries lie unsolved that we're only just beginning to scratch the surface of how exactly the body functions.

When consumed, the thousands of phytonutrients a plant contains become a part of trillions—both friendly and foreign—cells through complex, interrelated mechanisms. How, then, can you expect one isolated, concentrated compound—a vitamin, for instance—to cure disease? Yet that's precisely what the supplement industry often implies. This ignores the intricate, complicated, and synergistic workings of the human body and it's biological hitchhikers.

We are sick and overweight because of the way we eat, not because of micronutrient deficiency. Mostly we wrestle with malnourishment diseases of overnutrition, not undernutrition. You're more likely to see someone with heart disease (excess saturated fat, refined sugar, and cholesterol) than scurvy (vitamin C deficiency), with cancer (excess IGF-1, methionine, and environmental toxins) than beriberi (thiamin deficiency), and with diabetes (excess refined sugar and saturated fat) than pellagra (niacin deficiency). Popping supplements will never replace the effectiveness of correcting chronic overnutrition by eating whole-plant foods and exercising regularly for achieving and maintaining optimum health. While we can overcome certain nutritional deficiencies with supplementation, you can't expect to counteract a poor diet of excess merely by taking pills. Unfortunately, it's far more complicated.

Supplementation, when part of a proper diet, does afford us the ability to cut out certain foods that may have had some nutritional benefit packaged with nutrition of excess. Remember, just because humans ate various foods along the way to fuel our adaptive evolutionary journey, doesn't necessitate we eat those same foods now in our quest to diminish risks of certain chronic diseases. What we can eat for 45-50 years of life to reach reproductive age, reproduce, and raise our youngest offspring in a world of natural food scarcity isn't necessarily the best choice for health later in life once our genes are past. We are struggling with the chronic diseases that strike typically after our 40s.

Evolution doesn't act to perfect organisms; evolution is simply change over time. Natural selection leads to adaptation, but other somewhat random genetic forces lead only to change. We must live with those changed genes today in our world of abundance. This clash between natural scarcity and agricultural excess might be a large part of the problem. While we clearly have adapted to cope with times of scarcity, it's hard to believe that any of our genetic ancestors lived or adapted to a world of excessive food with the exception the more recent kings, queens, emperors, and pharaohs. Of course, history teaches many of these privileged few died early from disease of affluence. Today, even many poor are living the royal life when it comes to food and obesity is often a symptom of poverty.

We are fortunate to have plentiful food and the luxury of knowing those nutrients that need to be supplemented in the diet. We can supplement when desired to compliment a healthy whole food, plant-based diet and eliminate any potential shortfalls such as vitamin B_{12}. There are a limited number of known nutrients that may be deficient and these can be tested. It is likely a detriment to take large quantities of biologically active compounds at concentrations never seen in nature. At the very least, it is wasteful and excreted in the urine, but it might also accumulate in organs (e.g. kidneys, liver, and fat), where it may ultimately reach toxic levels. Perhaps instead of spending so much time and money trying to outsmart nature's harmony, the best advice is to eat whole plant foods as close as they are found in nature and avoid highly processed or refined foods even if they began as plant food.

The Least You Need to Know

- Your individual nutrient needs are based on genetics, age, makeup of your diet, and other factors.
- Vitamin B_{12} must be supplemented in a whole food, plant-based diet to avoid deficiency.
- Get your 25-hydroxyvitamin D blood level checked regularly, and treat deficiency with sun first and perhaps supplements additionally.
- The DSHEA Act of 1994 gave dietary supplement manufacturers, not the FDA, the power to determine their own products' safety.
- Ample research shows dangerous effects of taking supplemental beta-carotene, vitamin E, and folic acid.

Special Considerations

At all stages of life, from the womb to the senior years, nutritional requirements for your body adjust in subtle ways. During pregnancy, you need more of certain vitamins, minerals, and overall calories. In the later decades, you might need more vitamins and minerals but fewer calories. Then there are all the years in the middle. Between picky toddlerhood and stubborn adulthood, consider whole-plant foods your best ally. You literally are what you eat, so if you optimize every decade by eating the right foods, you'll thrive!

Beyond the timeline, Part 3 identifies the nutrient needs of other unique considerations. From athletes, who epitomize the pinnacle of what the human body can achieve, to people fighting disease, we offer suggestions on what does your body best.

We also provide a chapter about weight loss with a cutting edge approach so you can better understand the current worldwide epidemic of obesity and overweight, which impacts every population—and maybe you. No matter your age or state of health, food matters.

Plant-Based Pregnancy and Beyond

Congratulations on being pregnant! Whether or not this is your first pregnancy, get set for that journey into the unknown—the exciting roller-coaster ride that comes along with making another human being. You never know what to expect as your body undergoes major, miraculous changes. All you can do is ride the waves and provide your body and the body of your growing baby with excellent nutritional support.

In this chapter, we explain precisely what a plant-based mama needs to support a developing baby. Throughout pregnancy, your body changes, and so do your needs. Knowing which substances to avoid, which foods provide the right nutrients, and how to safely continue exercising are all laid out for you here. This chapter takes you from conception through your baby's first year, describing how you can best set up your baby's health for life.

In This Chapter

- Plant-based and pregnant!
- What to eat, how much weight to gain, and how to modify your workout
- The benefits of breast milk
- Do's and don'ts of starting on solids

Growing a Healthy Baby

Your baby's health is predetermined months—if not years—before conception. Both what you eat and what you avoid directly impact the future well-being of your baby. A whole food, plant-based diet during gestation and throughout the first 10 years is the gift that continues to give for the entirety of your child's life.

So many things have to go right to create a healthy baby. Your little human starts from the union of two cells, dividing and transforming over a series of millions of processes during the course of 9 months—or, more accurately, 40 weeks. Aside from the nausea, heartburn, constipation, discomfort, and weight gain, you're largely unaware of all the events taking place inside your womb. What can you do to help your body have everything it needs for the ultimate creation?

First, you should avoid the following, which are harmful to the developing fetus:

Caffeine: Limit your total caffeine intake from tea, coffee, soda, and chocolate to no more than 200 milligrams per day. Be careful of herbal teas because many contain medicinal effects. Mint and ginger teas, however, are safe and may help ease some of the digestive woes brought about during pregnancy.

All alcohol: No amount of alcohol consumed during pregnancy is considered safe.

Nicotine: Cigarette smoke from direct or indirect sources is dangerous.

Medications, herbs, and supplements (especially vitamin A): Be sure to tell your obstetrician (OB) about every medication, herb, and supplement you're on before pregnancy. Even over-the-counter medications, like painkillers, anti-inflammatories, and cough suppressants, may be harmful to your fetus. Discuss this in detail with your physician.

Artificial sweeteners: Use of any artificial sweeteners during pregnancy has not been proven safe.

Nitrites and nitrates: These cancer-causing compounds are found in processed (fake) meats, hot dogs, and bacon. Read the ingredient lists.

Fish, raw dairy, raw eggs, and soft cheeses: If you're on a whole food, plant-based diet, you're already avoiding these.

Nonfood items to avoid include radiation, hot tubs, saunas, cat litter, household cleaners, paint, and any other chemicals.

In addition, take these actions to support your body during pregnancy:

- Gain the right amount of weight—no more and no less.

- Be mindful and prudent regarding your nutrient intake.

- Continue your prepregnancy exercise program, but with appropriate modifications.

- Get plenty of rest.

Pregnancy is a very special time in your life when taking proper care of yourself is more crucial than ever. Prioritize your health, and both you and your baby will reap the benefits.

Gaining Weight Wisely

The extra calories needed during pregnancy go toward creating new tissue in the fetus, placenta, uterus, and breasts, as well as making amniotic fluid and blood. But contrary to popular belief, your calorie needs aren't greatly increased during pregnancy.

Gaining the right amount of weight creates an ideal condition for both you and your baby. Not gaining enough can lead to poor growth or nutrient deficiencies for your baby. On the other hand, gaining too much weight puts you at risk for *gestational diabetes* (*GDM*), more discomfort during pregnancy, and a difficult time losing the extra weight after delivery.

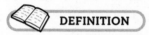 **DEFINITION**

> **Gestational diabetes (GDM)** is any degree of glucose intolerance that's first discovered during pregnancy. Although the condition usually resolves after delivery, GDM increases your risk by more than 7-fold of developing type 2 diabetes 5 to 10 years after your pregnancy. Children of moms with GDM are at increased risk of obesity, glucose intolerance, and diabetes in late adolescence and young adulthood. GDM complicates up to 9 percent of pregnancies, according to the American Diabetes Association.

Calorie needs increase throughout the trimesters. During your first trimester, you don't need to increase calories. This is the time to find ways of consuming adequate amounts of the vital nutrients despite nausea and fatigue. When your second trimester begins, increase your intake by approximately 340 calories per day. During this period, you should be adjusting to pregnancy. Typically, nausea and fatigue subside before any discomfort from weight gain begins, allowing you to eat more nutrient-dense meals. Use the slightly elevated caloric needs to take in more vegetables and fruits. When you reach your third trimester, your baby's weight gain occurs more rapidly. Add about 452 more calories a day to your diet to support his or her growth.

As you can see, the numbers aren't that large. One cup of brown rice with a cup of steamed broccoli and an apple makes up 340 calories. Of course, when you're pregnant with more than one baby, your calorie needs are slightly higher. Ideally, you'll only gain 2 to 4 pounds during the first trimester and then between 1 and 1½ pounds per week for the remaining trimesters. Ultimately, how much weight you should gain depends on your prepregnancy weight, your age, and the number of babies you're carrying.

The following guidelines support the health of both mother and baby.

Pregnancy Weight Gain Recommendations

Body Type	Weight Gain (lb.)
Normal weight	25 to 35
Underweight (< 90 percent ideal body weight)	28 to 40
Overweight (> 90 percent ideal body weight)	15 to 25
Obese (> 135 percent ideal body weight)	15
Adolescent	30 to 45
Normal weight, carrying twins	35 to 45

If you're carrying multiples (more than two) during your pregnancy, weight gain recommendations may change. Your OB will provide you with some suggestions. Regardless of how many babies you're carrying, remember that these numbers are merely guidelines. Allow your body to be your guide. When you're hungry, eat, but be careful not to overeat. Your focus should be on taking in the most nutrient-dense foods to meet your needs throughout your pregnancy.

Necessary Nutrients During Pregnancy

Unlike calories and weight gain recommendations, nutrient demands amplify greatly during pregnancy. Your body takes some nutrients directly out of its own storage; others you need to consume regularly from your diet. To prevent deficiency in both yourself and your baby, be sure to emphasize the following nutrients:

- Protein
- DHA
- Iron
- Vitamins A, C, B_6, and B_{12}
- Folate
- Niacin
- Riboflavin
- Thiamin
- Iodine
- Iron
- Zinc
- Selenium

Protein needs increase during the second and third trimesters to support tissue and fluid production. You need to consume approximately 25 grams more protein per day at this time (50 grams if you're carrying twins). Nutrient-rich sources include beans, leafy greens, nuts, and seeds.

Omega-3 fatty acids are critical for fetal brain development. The fetus takes in approximately 50 to 60 milligrams (mostly from DHA) during the last trimester. Maintain your stores of DHA by consuming walnuts, flaxseeds, hempseeds, chia seeds, and whole soy foods daily, and consider supplementing with an EPA and DHA microalgal supplement.

MIXED GREENS

In Chinese medicine, daily intake of walnuts is recommended during pregnancy because a walnut looks like the brain. Coincidentally, walnuts are filled with alpha-linolenic acid—the type that converts to the brain-building DHA.

Many women become iron-deficient for the first time during pregnancy. Iron needs at this time are nearly double what they are normally; you require 27 milligrams per day during pregnancy, as opposed to the usual 15 milligrams. All the extra blood essential for you and your baby increases your need to build hemoglobin. Emphasize iron-rich foods like your go-to leafy greens, making sure to eat them with a vitamin C–rich source, like tomatoes or citrus fruit.

However, achieving the RDA might not always be possible; supplementing might be necessary temporarily. Iron-deficiency anemia in pregnancy can lead to premature deliveries and low-birth-weight infants. Deficiency almost always resolves after delivery, especially because women typically go several months without a menstrual cycle postpregnancy. This allows the body time to restore iron levels to normal.

If you must take a supplement based on your obstetrician's recommendations, drink plenty of water and eat extra fiber to compensate for the constipating effects of concentrated iron. Also, take the iron supplements between meals and separate from tea, coffee, calcium supplements, fortified foods, and legumes.

Folic acid supplements, or prenatal vitamins containing folic acid, are given to women preventively if they're even thinking about becoming pregnant. Adequate amounts of folic acid are essential in the first few weeks of pregnancy to prevent neural tube defects, typically the time before a woman discovers she's pregnant.

In Chapter 10, we explained how folic acid supplements are harmful. However, if you're adamant about consuming your greens and beans every day, you'll never have to worry about having enough folate. A cup each of raw greens, cooked greens, and lentils eaten in a day provides more than enough folate to meet your daily requirement. You can easily reach your daily folate need of 600 micrograms when you enjoy the plant sources of folate shown in the following table.

Folate

Food	Folate (mcg)
Lentils, 1 cup cooked	358
Pinto beans, 1 cup cooked	294
Spinach, frozen, 1 cup cooked	230
Turnip greens, raw, 1 cup	107
Orange juice, 1 cup	74
Collard greens, raw, 1 cup	60
Broccoli, raw, 1 cup	50

To maintain all your nutrient levels throughout your pregnancy, stay on top of your usual whole-food, plant-based plan. Be sure you're taking vitamin B_{12} via supplement or fortified sources, and be sure your vitamin D levels are up to par. Part of routine prenatal care includes testing for micronutrient deficiency (especially iron). If you were deficient before pregnancy, odds are, you'll stay deficient, and may even become worse, during pregnancy. It takes a village of nutrients to create a little human. Be sure your village is well stocked.

Exercise During Pregnancy

Your body changes in more ways than you can predict during a pregnancy, regardless of how many times you've been through it. Structural changes occur to allow the baby to grow, expand, and, ultimately, come out to meet you. Hormones are released to enable these changes, helping relax your joints, mobilize your bones, and generally open up. The more in tune you are with your body going into pregnancy, the more control you can exert over how you handle these changes.

Being fit from the get-go is a huge advantage. You're able to continue exercising, reaping the multitude of benefits that come from maintaining your fitness level throughout pregnancy, including the following:

- Improved circulation

- Weight management before and after pregnancy

- Energy maintenance

- Better sleep quality

- Minimized joint discomfort from weight gain

- Ability to maintain endurance, strength, and flexibility

- Easier delivery

- Improved recovery postdelivery

Still, you must tailor how you work out to your pregnancy. During the first trimester, you can pretty much maintain what you were doing prepregnancy. Of course, at this time, most women are bogged down by major fatigue and nausea, thanks to the dramatic hormonal shifts. So listen to your body, and of course, speak with your OB about what you're currently doing. Move your body as much as is comfortably possible.

 **PLANT PITFALL**

Pregnancy is not the time to work on strengthening your abdominal (stomach) muscles. Not only does it put strain on your womb, but you don't want those muscles to be shortened and tight. Your abdominal cavity needs to expand at this time to allow room for the baby. Instead, focus your strengthening efforts on your back, arms, and legs. You'll have plenty of time to regain your ab muscles postdelivery, once you get the go-ahead from your OB.

During the second trimester, you should begin to ease out of the fatigue and nausea before experiencing the discomfort of carrying around extra weight—in a very awkward place on your body with respect to gravity. This is the perfect time to move more. Walking and using an elliptical, stationary bicycle, or step mill are great ways to get in your cardio. Running is not ideal because jumping may be jarring on your baby and your own body. Running also puts you at higher risk of falling because your center of gravity has shifted.

Lifting light to moderate weights is excellent to maintain muscle mass. Just be extremely careful with your form. It's easier to sustain an injury because your joints are abnormally relaxed. Don't try to lift weights heavier than you did before pregnancy; it may be best to do lighter-weight, higher-rep workouts. Hit all your major muscle groups at least a couple times a week.

Stretching should feel fabulous at this point. You may be able to stretch farther than ever before in your life—even as a child! Just be gentle, and don't force anything. But working on your flexibility (especially in your hips) may help with delivery.

It's important to remember during exercise that after 20 weeks gestation you should refrain from lying on your back because this can interfere with blood flow to your baby and the placenta. Plenty of exercises can be performed in an incline position. Use a workout bench or firm pillow to raise your head, shoulders, and back to a good angle that will protect your baby and enable you to hit muscle groups like your chest.

During your final trimester, everything changes. This is the time when your weight gain is the greatest. You may slow down and feel achy or uncomfortable. If you can, continue some form of movement. Swimming is perfect because it provides that feeling of weightlessness and gives you an opportunity for relief while getting your heart rate up.

Women may experience pregnancy in their own individual way, depending on many variables. (Julieanna recalls a woman who at 9 months pregnant was doing headstands in her yoga class.) At the other extreme, those who gain a lot of weight can barely move around through their day. Multiples pregnancies (twins or more) add extra stress to the body and should be monitored closely.

Your goal during the last few weeks is to stay comfortable, maintain movement as much as possible, and listen to your doctor's orders. Preterm labor can have potential health implications for your baby, so you want to be sure he or she is fully "cooked" before coming out. Intense exercise has the potential to increase contractions, and you don't want to push yourself into early labor just to keep up with your routine.

 **PLANT PITFALL**

If exercising brings on contractions, pain, or bleeding, stop your activity and call your OB immediately.

Walking usually feels good and improves circulation for you and your baby. Lifting light weights also enhances blood flow and helps maintain strength and functionality. Gentle stretching may help open your joints and relieve tension. During this time, be sure to get plenty of rest. Take special care of your body, and listen to its signals closely. Before you know it, you'll be holding your little one, finally having that opportunity to see who has been growing inside of you.

Postpregnancy is a great time to ease your way back into your old routine after your OB grants approval. Remember that your body has undergone major construction and deconstruction, and it may take a while to get your stamina back. Your fitness level postpregnancy depends on how fit you were beforehand. Take it one workout at a time, and your endurance, strength, and flexibility will return to normal along with your weight. Remember that it took 9 months to gain the weight, and it takes about the same amount of time, on average, to take it off. Stay consistent, and you'll see results.

Tips to Nip Nausea and Other Discomforts

The power of hormones becomes ragingly obvious the moment you become pregnant. Initially, your body surges with estrogen, progesterone, and human chorianic gonadotropin (HCG)—hormones that help maintain the pregnancy. This hormonal influx causes the feeling of nausea and sometimes vomiting. Some strategies help alleviate these symptoms.

Nausea is greater when your stomach is empty. This explains why it's typically called *morning sickness*, although the nausea can, and usually does, occur throughout the day. You wake up with no food in your stomach after an overnight fast. Eating small, regular meals throughout the day helps moderate this feeling. To help break the fast, you can keep crackers by your bedside to eat the moment you wake up.

You may notice that bland, starchy, and salty foods are the easiest to tolerate. A risky consequence of nausea is the inability to consume a wide variety of nutrient-dense foods. Do the best you can. Take advantage of less-nauseous times of the day to eat as many micronutrient-rich foods as you can find (greens, legumes, veggies, fruits, nuts, and seeds).

Also, keep the following in mind:

- Soups and cooked vegetables may be easier to tolerate than raw veggies.

- Whole-grain crackers provide more nutrients than white crackers.

- To stave off nausea, sip ginger tea or chew on ginger candy.

- Try sipping carbonated water.

- Continue drinking liquids to prevent dehydration, especially if you're vomiting.

- See your OB if you're unable to keep down any food or liquids.

 HEALTHY HINT

Ginger root is one of the very few herbs considered safe during pregnancy. It's helpful in alleviating nausea. Boil fresh ginger root in hot water for a delicious tea, buy 100 percent ginger tea bags at the store, or chew on ginger candies when you feel nauseous.

Another source of discomfort that comes with pregnancy is heartburn. Heartburn is the symptom that coincides with stomach acid being released into the esophagus. Pregnancy-induced spikes in progesterone relax the esophageal sphincter, and the uterus puts pressure on the stomach increasing the likelihood of heartburn. To help ease the discomfort, follow these tips:

- Eat your meals slowly.

- Avoid getting too full by eating small frequent meals throughout the day.

- Stay upright for at least a couple hours after you eat so the food has time to pass through your upper GI tract.

- Avoid acidic foods or those high in fats.

Constipation is another very common occurrence during pregnancy. A number of factors can contribute to the issue. It's partly those darn hormones again. Progesterone decreases muscle contractions, which slows down the movement in the intestines. A growing fetus takes up space and can interfere with normal bowel movements, too. If you're taking iron supplements, you have yet another variable keeping you stopped up.

Be sure to eat lots of fiber (impossible not to do on a whole food, plant-based diet) and drink plenty of water. Exercise also helps.

Plantlings: Raising Healthy Babies

Congratulations! After those long, intense, challenging, and sometimes uncomfortable 40 weeks, you finally get to meet and hold your baby. As you gaze into his or her eyes, you may be thinking, *so now what?*

You have the power to provide your baby with one of the greatest gifts a mother could ever give her child—superior nutrition for lifelong health! Diet in the first decade of a child's life is more significant than all the remaining years of his or her life. Massive growth occurs during these years, and cells divide at a rapid pace. This is a period of great opportunity to provide your child's cells with optimal nourishment. And a nutrient-dense diet lays the groundwork for powerful immunity and a healthy future.

Breast is Best

The very first decision you make after your baby is born (if you didn't decide before the birth) is whether you plan to breastfeed. Nothing is healthier for an infant than mother's milk. It's tailor-made for just your baby, complete with your immune system and nutrients from your plant-based diet. With a world of unique benefits, your breast milk …

- Provides antibodies that form the basis of your baby's immune system.

- Supports brain development with optimal nutrient levels (including DHA).

- Encourages good, health-promoting bacteria to form in your baby's intestinal tract.

- Offers *passive immunity* to protect your baby from infections until he or she develops his or her own immune system.

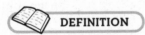 **DEFINITION**

Passive immunity is temporary protection against disease gained when one human gives already-made antibodies to another via breast milk.

- Sustains long-term health advantages, such as reducing risk of allergies, ear infections, both types of diabetes, multiple sclerosis, childhood cancers, Crohn's disease, overweight/obesity, and many other health problems.

- Gives a cost-effective alternative to formula—it's free!

- Is convenient—it's always ready to eat!

- Promotes easier postpartum weight loss for you.

- Decreases your risk of premenopausal breast cancer.

The most critical moment of breastfeeding is immediately after your milk comes in. Colostrum, the first milk to be secreted after your baby is born, is liquid gold. It's rich in antibodies that coat your baby's intestinal tract, setting up the immunity foundation.

The American Academy of Pediatrics (AAP) recommends breast milk as the sole source of food for the baby's first 6 months and then a combination of breast milk and supplemental foods for the rest of the first year. Some experts recommend breastfeeding through the age of 2, although all the health benefits have been bestowed after 1 year. Ultimately, the more breast milk you offer your baby, the better. Continue for as long as you can up until the age of 2.

Some women are unable to breastfeed due to physical or other obstacles. If this is the case, available plant-based infant formulas are fortified with all necessary nutrients. Be certain to choose one with added EPA and DHA.

Nutrify Your Breast Milk

Your breast milk is a direct reflection of what you eat. Nutrient content and toxin concentration change based on food consumption. This puts you in the driver's seat; you can maximize nutrition in your baby the entire time you breastfeed. Breast milk from strict plant-eaters is adequate in nutrients as long as you're actively taking a vitamin B_{12} supplement.

To boost the nutrition level of your breast milk, eat a wide variety of plants. Also avoid all chemicals in your food, drinks, and everyday life. Remember, if you wouldn't give it directly to your baby, don't expose yourself to it either. Stick to the goal of eating high on the nutrient-density continuum by basing your meals on greens, beans, other vegetables, fruits, whole grains, nuts, and seeds. Consume at least two sources of omega-3 fatty acids—walnuts, hempseeds, flaxseeds, chia seeds, and whole soy products—every day and consider taking a microalgae EPA/DHA supplement.

Not only are you kick-starting your baby's health, but you're also introducing tastes to your baby's pure palate. Odds are, if you love your greens and eat them daily during breastfeeding, your baby will, too. What a great way to start life!

The First Year: Nutrition No-No's

During the first year or two of life, certain foods should be avoided. No type of milk other than breast milk or baby formula is safe for your baby until after 1 year of age. This includes all types of dairy and plant-based milks.

Allergies and colic can show up in the form of gastrointestinal symptoms, rashes, or persistent crying. If you, the baby's father, or his or her siblings have a history of severe food allergies, monitor your baby carefully while breastfeeding and note any new foods you have eaten recently that may have caused a reaction in your baby.

To ease colic, consider eliminating from your diet foods that may cause discomfort to your baby, such as coffee, chocolate, onions, and cruciferous vegetables, including cabbage, broccoli, cauliflower, and Brussels sprouts.

During the first year, it's dangerous to give your baby honey or corn syrup because babies are more vulnerable to botulism. Also, never put anything in a bottle besides breast milk, formula, or water. Nourish your baby with your milk or formula for those first few months until he or she is ready to begin the culinary journey.

 PLANT PITFALL

Alcohol passes into breast milk when you drink it. Information is lacking about how much of the alcohol goes into the milk and how long it takes to be metabolized, but know that exposure to alcohol can be detrimental to your baby's development. To be safe, drink no more than one or two servings of alcohol per week while nursing.

Introducing Solids

When your baby starts to show signs that he or she is ready—usually at 4 to 6 months of age—it's time to expose your baby's palate to solid foods. (Signs of readiness to start solids include the ability to sit upright and the disappearance of the tongue extrusion reflex. Your baby may also appear curious or interested when watching you eat.)

Supplementing food displaces some of the calories that come from the milk or formula. This is one reason to wait as close to 6 months as possible. Remembering that babies have different nutrient needs, the milk or formula needs to remain the priority of the diet. Think of the solids as accessories and as eating practice.

The first taste adventure to offer is iron-enriched infant cereal. Rice cereal is the best tolerated. Mix in the milk or formula to dilute it at first until your little one develops his or her techniques. Be patient—it takes time to learn how to swallow different textures.

After your baby can take in between ⅓ and ½ cup cereal, you can begin adding other foods. Keep it to other cereals, fruits, and vegetables for the next few months. Always wait 3 or 4 days after starting one food to introduce a new one so you can monitor for allergies.

Depending on your motivation and your resources, you can make these foods at home, or you can purchase them. Brown rice, oats, and barley can be ground in a blender until very fine and then boiled in water briefly until cooked. Bananas, cooked sweet potatoes, steamed carrots, and avocados can easily be mashed. You can also use pure applesauce, steamed green beans, cooked lentils, and stewed pears.

Use this time to perk up your baby's tastes and preferences. If you start him or her eating close to nature now, you'll provide the best foreground for optimal health in the future.

The Least You Need to Know

- Your diet before conception and through breastfeeding largely impacts your baby's future health.
- During pregnancy, gain the recommended weight to prevent strain on you and your baby.
- Stay consistent with whole-plant foods throughout your pregnancy, and include food and supplemental sources of EPA and DHA, a vitamin B_{12} supplement, and vitamin D and iron if you're deficient.
- You can continue to exercise during pregnancy with a few modifications, as long as you stay tuned in to your body's signals.
- Breastfeeding provides significant health benefits to both you and your baby.
- Solid foods should be slowly and methodically introduced to your little one after the age of 4 to 6 months.

CHAPTER 12

Phyto-Rich Kids

As with adults, obesity is on the rise in children and adolescents. Approximately 9 percent of children aged 2 to 5, 17.5 percent of children aged 6 to 11, and 20.5 percent of adolescents aged 12 to 19 are obese. Puberty is starting earlier in girls than ever before—sometimes as early as age 7—due to excess body fat. Early puberty puts our daughters at an increased risk of breast cancer and other chronic diseases later in life. The prevalence of diabetes and prediabetes is rising in our youth, setting them up for a life plagued with health problems.

Why are our youth so susceptible to these health crises? Partly because they're living sedentary lifestyles. But much more significantly, it's because they're eating most of their calories from animal products and highly processed foods. The most common fruits and veggies eaten are tomatoes (via pizza), orange juice, and fried potatoes. Whole foods rarely, if ever, touch the lips of most kids on a daily basis. Childhood diet determines future health. The bottom line: we need to fix the food to save our children.

Getting kids to eat healthy can sometimes seem an impossible task. But with a little finesse and some creativity, you can succeed at getting your kids onboard with a plant-based diet.

In This Chapter

- Raising a plant-based child
- Fulfilling your little one's nutrient needs
- Feeding picky eaters
- Navigating the school system's diet woes

The Benefits of Growing Up Plant-Based

At this point in the book, you know the benefits of following a whole food, plant-based diet. And if you remember from Chapter 11, the diet consumed during the first decade of a child's life determines his or her health more than the diet consumed in the next 50 years does. Imagine, then, the opportunity you have for providing your child with all the nutrients necessary to grow and develop healthily right from the start.

Consider this fascinating example: look at families who move from a rural setting of a non-Western country to an urban, Westernized location. Take rural China, for instance. The older generations who were raised in their homeland on rice, vegetables, fruits, minimal amounts of animal products, and no highly processed foods remain slim and healthy into old age. On the contrary, their children and grandchildren, who have adapted their diets to include fast food, massive amounts of animal products, and highly processed foods, become sick and fat like their new neighbors. Their genes weren't altered on the plane ride to their new home. Their diets changed upon arrival.

Incidence of disease risk differs based on environment. You can't blame your genes. You can, however, change your destiny with the choices you make at each meal.

As a parent, you should have control over what your child eats. Until your children makes money and drive to the store on their own, you should be able to steer your children in a positive direction. Unfortunately, all too often, others—your parents, in-laws, the ex, cousins, friends, and even schools—make these decisions for you and introduce habit-forming junk food. There's nothing worse for a parent to wake up one day only to find his or her child overweight, acne-ridden, or worse, at risk for early onset nutritionally induced disease. The good news is that your children can recover and the healthy example you lead now will have more impact as they grow older.

Do as I Say *and* as I Do

The single most important factor determining how your child eats is how *you* eat. Role-modeling is an extremely effective technique for teaching. If you want your kid to love broccoli, Brussels sprouts, lentils, and lima beans, eat them and love them yourself. Do you know how many parents tell their kids to eat their veggies while they themselves fill up on junk food instead? The message it sends is contradicting and confusing. Worse, it doesn't work. You need to be passionate about your food and your health while connecting those dots for your child. When you feel the vitality within your cells, you'll want nothing less for your little one.

Inspire your family by teaching them what you know. Explain that when you eat your leafy greens, your body gets stronger and can fight off all the bad germs out there. Eating your beans makes you grow big with awesome muscles that can lift heavy things. Getting your essential fatty acids makes you so smart you'll ace all your classes in school.

Make it relevant to your child's life. Excite your child in a language he or she will understand. Of course, this changes throughout childhood, based on where your child's enthusiasm lies and his or her understanding of the world. Your child is in tune with your feelings and actions, so your best bet for compliance is your own demonstration. Represent the habits you wish to see in your children.

Practice Makes Perfect

As with anything, healthy living takes practice. Learning about nutrients and how to make nutritious delicious is a work in progress for you and your child. Why not learn and practice together? Use food shopping and cooking as learning experiences.

Spend time in the produce section with your child, talking about the plethora of health-promoting compounds surrounding you. Pick up a tomato and say, "Tomatoes have lycopene, lutein, and vitamin C." Ask your child what you should make for dinner tonight using that tomato. Include him or her in these decisions, because being actively involved infuses passion. When you get home, make the meal together. Even tiny ones can stir, hold things, hand you a spoon, or place items in a pot. The older your child gets, the more capabilities he or she will have. The longer your child is exposed to healthful eating, the deeper his or her understanding and interest will be.

 **HEALTHY HINT**

Gone are the days of the clean-plate club. Never push food on your kid. Allow his or her own hunger patterns to emerge without interference. Hunger changes based on whether it's time for a growth spurt, daily activity, and other factors. Let your child's body be the guide on when it's time to eat and how much.

Experiment with a large variety of foods and recipes, using a few family favorites. Most people rotate among one to three breakfasts, two to four lunches, and five to six dinner options every week. So find what tastes best and is easiest to prepare. Save the more labor-intensive recipes for special occasions.

Keep the options open. Availability of healthful food choices plays a significant role in a child's eating habits. Consider a few tips for increasing access to healthy options:

Keep a bowl filled with clean, fresh fruits at arm's reach at all times.

Cut veggies and fruits into bite-size pieces and keep them in the fridge next to healthy dip options (see recipes in Chapter 22).

Always have a fresh and colorful salad in the fridge with delicious dressings ready to eat.

Make extra servings when preparing meals so you have leftovers.

Create your own trail mix with your child. Choose all the nuts, seeds, and dried fruits he or she likes, and package the trail mix in baggies for easy, single-serving treats.

Stock your cabinets, fridge, and freezer with healthy alternatives so when hunger strikes, you can whip up something fast and easy.

Make recipes like Figamajigs, Fruity Nut Balls, and Unclassic Oatmeal Raisin Cookies (recipes in Chapter 23) for quick and satisfying snacks.

Eventually, as your child grows up surrounded by whole-plant foods and knows why you provide these options, a whole food, plant-based diet will be deeply rooted and more likely to stick. People often warn that when a child gets older, he or she will rebel if the diet is restricted. Rebellion happens as a result of confinement, rigidity, and hefty rules. On the contrary, enthusiasm, knowledge, and room for variety simply lead to habit. It's well established that people develop behavior based on what they learn at home. Fortunately, then, it's in your hands; create the soil you want your child's roots to grow in.

 **PLANT PITFALL**

Don't reward or bribe your kid with food or punish him or her by taking away certain foods. This adds a psychological component to food, which can affect your child later in life. Find other ways to motivate instead.

Meeting Their Macro- and Micronutrient Needs

When it comes to recommendations for what children need nutrition-wise, charts and lists from medical and government authorities abound. Their recommendations include how many servings per day from each food group, percentage of saturated fat as a maximum, and advice on taking the skin off the chicken before eating it.

Somehow, though, this information isn't translating. Parents aren't paying attention. Fast food is a daily meal for about one third of youths. That means one in three children eats fast food every single day! No matter how "happy" or "healthy" the option is at a fast-food establishment, it's impossible to achieve proper nutrient recommendations or avoid the mass quantities of saturated fat, cholesterol, and animal protein in these meals. In addition, the food is as processed as possible and as far away from nature as anything edible.

The two places where nutrition is most important—schools and hospitals—often serve the least nutritious food. Have you seen what the school cafeteria serves for lunch these days? The government-subsidized commodities are typically huge boxes of ground meats and cheeses. When the school receives its shipment, it gets to decide what to make with the items to serve the kids. Many hospitals now house fast-food chains inside their buildings. Furthermore, junk food has replaced real food in lunch boxes, in school-cafeteria lunch lines, at parties, for sports practices, and at other events.

 MIXED GREENS

Excuses for why fast food and junk food have become so prevalent include no time to cook and not enough money to afford healthy options. But these excuses fall short when you analyze the possibilities. Opening a can of beans and a jar of salsa and warming some corn tortillas in the oven takes less time than stopping at a fast-food restaurant drive-thru. Batch cooking is even more cost- and time-efficient. Buy foods in bulk (whole grains, beans, seeds, nuts, and spices) and prepare large amounts at the same time. Package, freeze, and reheat when a quick dinner is needed.

You may be wondering what children need to be healthy. Overall, they need the same thing you need to be healthy: a wide assortment of vegetables, fruits, whole grains, legumes, nuts, and seeds. Encourage and challenge your child to eat every color of the rainbow each day as a way of increasing variety. If you emphasize and provide these foods, you can easily meet all your child's nutrient needs (except for vitamin B_{12}, possibly vitamin D, and long-chain omega-3 fats).

Generally, macronutrient needs can be met with adequate calorie intake, and if you give your child the freedom to eat whenever he or she feels hungry, calorie needs will automatically be fulfilled. If you provide whole-food options at those times of hunger, macronutrient and micronutrient needs will both be met. The body is naturally self-regulating and adjusts according to activity levels and periods of growth.

Don't forget vitamins B_{12} and D. All plant eaters, regardless of age, need to supplement vitamin B_{12}. And all people—regardless of diet—need to be tested for vitamin D levels and treated if deficient. Breastfed infants should be given 400 IU vitamin D as a supplement, because their sun exposure is usually inadequate and breast milk doesn't provide enough vitamin D. The adequate intake for vitamin D is 400 IU (10 micrograms) per day for infants and 600 IU (15 micrograms) per day for anyone ages 1 through 70.

The following table lists the recommendations for vitamin B_{12} for various ages.

Vitamin B_{12} Requirements for Children

Age	Daily Requirement (mcg)
1 to 3 years	0.9
4 to 8 years	1.2
9 to 13 years	1.8
14 years and up	2.4

Pleasing Picky Palates

Children are picky eaters—and that's when they're eating everything under the sun. You might be wondering how you'll ever succeed in trying to feed them a whole food, plant-based diet.

This scenario might sound familiar: your child's hungry, so you try to feed him or her something nutritious. He or she doesn't like it and protests, asking for something not so healthful. You persist. Next comes the whining or tantrum throwing (your child, not you—although you might feel like throwing a tantrum). Finally, you give in.

This episode is common in parenting, especially with toddlers and preschoolers. The biggest problem stemming from this scenario is its self-perpetuating nature. Your child learns that whining, screaming, or begging (or all of the above) eventually works.

Remember that if you're not hungry enough to eat an apple, you're probably not really hungry. The same goes for your little one. Don't be afraid that your child won't get enough food to eat. Remember that child-size bodies are smaller than yours and don't always need as many calories. Also, when your child is hungry, he or she will eat. Children won't let themselves starve. If you try force-feeding just to calm your concern, you're only setting yourself up for frustration.

Many children get stuck on a mono diet, only wanting to choose among a few staples. Although this can be disconcerting to a concerned parent, some simple strategies may help. First and foremost, be the master of your kitchen. Stock only the foods you want your family to eat. Also, provide variations at each meal and snack. For instance, some children may be obsessed with pasta and request it for dinner daily. You can switch it up by alternating among corn, whole-wheat, rice, and quinoa noodles each night so they're exposed to different grains. You can also change up what you add to the pasta. Some nights, they find broccoli and peas in their pasta, and other nights, it's kale and lima beans.

One strategy you may try is to implement the "one-bite rule." Make it a rule that your child must taste one bite of a new food you're offering before deciding he or she doesn't like it. Stay the course, and be consistent in offering a variety of options. If your child is truly hungry, he or she will eat what you have to offer. Eventually this phase ends anyway, and your child's palate will expand.

HEALTHY HINT

> Creativity counts big time with children! Using fun names and making animals or different characters out of fruits and veggies goes a long way toward making food exciting. Think ants on a log (celery with nut butter and raisins on top), banana boats (bananas cut lengthwise and filled with nut butter, hempseeds, and dried fruit), and chocolate smoothies (with leafy greens, dates, almond milk, raw cocoa powder, and frozen fruit). Use cookie cutters to stamp out fun shapes for healthy sandwiches or whole-food cookies. Use seaweed, collard greens, or whole-grain tortillas to make fancy wraps.

Another issue is taste-bud distortion. Depending on your child's age when you introduce whole foods, those taste buds may already be biased. Regularly eating refined sugar, flour, oil, and salt causes habituation even at a young age. However, explaining the science to your little one will be senseless and not helpful. Thus, you need to be persistent, especially at the beginning of the transition. Prepare the majority of meals and snacks at home. It's already hard enough to protect your kid from junk food at school and parties, so try to have whole-food options in every other situation. Soon enough, taste buds will improve, habituation will subside, and whole foods will be appealing.

Surviving School

Schools are nutritional wastelands. With the National School Lunch Program, the School Breakfast Program, and the vast overavailability of junk food at every opportunity, you have to put on your power parenting skills to fight off the disease-inducing invaders.

Meeting government standards for the nutrient levels in the school food meals is bad enough, but when Julieanna spent some time in school food service during her dietetic internship, she was advised to increase the quantity of ketchup used in an average meal so the computer analysis would show a lower total fat percentage of calories. (Apparently, ketchup really is a fruit or vegetable serving in the school world. Or just another example of macroconfusion at work.) The requirements themselves are lenient enough; still, the actual intake numbers need to be exaggerated to appear to meet the standards.

Moreover, when produce is offered—in the form of salad bars, for instance—the presentation is unappealing and drab when sitting right next to the brightly packaged chips, sugary products, and deeply fried and reheated foods. If given those choices, which would you choose?

Furthermore, schools are still required to offer kids milk—even if the cartons are chocolate or strawberry milk at every meal. Oddly, dairy-free options are seldom, if ever, provided. No wonder the number of kids diagnosed with health complications is growing!

 MIXED GREENS

The Dietary Guidelines for Americans is the basis for menu planning in the school system. Therefore, school lunches are required to meet only the standard of no more than 30 percent total calories from fat and less than 10 percent from saturated fat. Also, schools need only offer one third of the RDAs for vitamin A, vitamin C, iron, calcium, and total calories.

What can a concerned parent do to avoid getting absorbed into this misguided, disease-promoting arrangement? Most importantly, pack your child's school lunch every day. Send healthy choices like you would provide at home, and include special treats to prevent curiosity and desire to buy food at school. Maximize your creativity here so your little one enjoys his or her lunch and doesn't feel left out.

Here are some ideas for yummy, nutrient-dense lunchbox items:

- Sprouted- or whole-grain bread or tortilla wraps with nut or seed butter and pure fruit spread or sliced bananas

- Sprouted- or whole-grain bread with hummus and sliced cucumbers and tomatoes

- Sushi rolls made with brown rice, cucumbers, avocado, and carrots

- Noritos (recipe in Chapter 20)

- Sweet Pea Guacamole (recipe in Chapter 22) with baked tortilla chips

- Homemade trail mix your child helps make with his or her favorite nuts, seeds, and dried fruits

- Roasted chickpeas

- Figamajigs (recipe in Chapter 23)

- Pineapple, peach, apple, or pear chunks

- Large, pitted olives

- Fresh fruit with a nut or seed butter or date syrup dipping sauce

- Veggie pizza on whole-grain crust with pineapple, olives, mushrooms, and/or bell peppers

- Soup in a thermos

- Oil-free, salt-free popcorn with nutritional yeast sprinkled on top

- Simply Hummus (recipe in Chapter 22) with raw, chopped or lightly blanched veggies (cherry or grape tomatoes, baby carrots, sugar snap peas, jicama sticks, button mushrooms, celery sticks, baby corn, blanched green beans, or blanched asparagus spears)

- Unclassic Oatmeal Raisin Cookies (recipe in Chapter 23)

Additionally, if your schedule allows, try to be active in the planning committees at school. Get involved in arranging class parties and events where food is involved. Argue your points with detailed facts to encourage the other parents, school faculty, and teachers to make healthier decisions. The louder your squeaky wheel, the more likely they'll listen and learn.

Finally, write letters or emails that include statistics and health information to your school; school district; and local, state, and national government officials. As a concerned and impassioned parent and citizen, you have a voice.

If we are to improve the state of our children's health, changes must be implemented. We are currently sliding downhill fast, and if we don't provide our kids with nutritious options at each meal, they'll only continue to fall. This generation is the first in recorded history predicted to live a shorter life span than the preceding generation. What does that tell you about our state of health? Take action to protect your child—loudly and backed up with facts. The only thing you have to lose is the health of your most precious commodity.

Start at home, where you have total control and branch out. Build your case by showing fellow parents the results of eating a nutrient-dense lifestyle: less sickness; improved performance in school (both academically and athletically); and happy, healthy kids. Be the role model for your child and for other parents, and change will come.

The Least You Need to Know

- Growing up on a whole food, plant-based diet sets the foundation for lifelong optimal health.
- Be the change you want to see in your child. Role-modeling is the most effective tool for inspiring and teaching healthy eating.
- Let your child gauge his or her own hunger. Children won't let themselves starve.
- Always have whole-plant options available in the house and when on the go.

- Supplement your little one's whole food, plant-based diet with a multivitamin or at least with vitamins B_{12} and D and consider a microalgal omega-3 fat formula.
- Survive school's nutritional wasteland by sending lunch to school, participating in activity planning, and being vocal about why and how to provide healthier options.

Super-Plant Seniors

The secrets to aging gracefully are surfacing, with more evidence supporting the benefits of healthy living. After recently spending time visiting a relative in a nursing home, the desperate need for reformed health management became even more blaringly obvious. What's the point of living well into old age if you're not able to enjoy it? With medical advances, people can be kept alive by invasive procedures and strong medications for decades. Unfortunately, these advancements come with a price.

The good news is it's never too late to start taking care of your body. Living a healthy lifestyle can help keep you active and youthful while avoiding cardiovascular disease, diabetes, osteoporosis, arthritis, obesity, and most cancers. A whole food, plant-based diet—together with exercise, adequate sleep, and stress management—appears to be that fountain of youth we've all been searching for.

In This Chapter

- Staying vital and active in your golden years
- Nutrient changes as you age
- Dealing with physical obstacles associated with aging
- Keeping your kitchen simple
- Managing medication complications

Living Longer Instead of Living *Longer*

Leading a vital, active life well into old age until you simply slip painlessly away is the best plan for living. Many people object to this idea, arguing that a shorter life is preferential to overhauling diet and lifestyle. Unfortunately, the choice isn't that simple. Quality of life and functional independence matter most; these objectives are precisely what you can control with your lifestyle choices.

Although how *long* you live comes with no guarantees, eating well, exercising consistently, and managing stress improves how *well* you live and how long you maintain your youth, or healthspan. The story of World Strongman Joe Rollino epitomizes this point: Joe ate a vegetarian diet while abstaining from cigarettes and alcohol. Considered one of the greatest performing strongmen ever to live, he recently was killed at the age of 104 when hit by a car during his daily 5-mile walk. Although his story is ironic, it demonstrates that lifestyle leads to vitality and health, even in your centenarian years.

 MIXED GREENS

Current life expectancy at birth is 78.8 years. The oldest documented person was a French woman who lived to the age of 122 years and 164 days. It's not clear whether "Blue Zones" longevity was because of or *in spite of* meat consumption, but what was consistent is they didn't eat much. Meat was usually served during celebrations and typically used in condiment sizes as flavoring.

Typically, after a lifetime of eating poorly and remaining sedentary, the cardiovascular system breaks down. Vascular events occur either at powerful enough levels to induce death (as in a massive heart attack or stroke) or at small degrees, which can lead to dementia, blood clots, and minimized freedom of movement. In the case of the latter, seniors can survive for many years with medications that lower blood pressure and cholesterol, stent placements in their arteries, or bypass surgeries. They may be kept alive, but how well are they living? Suffering with illness heavily influences daily life. Visiting doctors or enduring tests and procedures isn't the same as traveling, taking dancing lessons, or enjoying time with people you love.

In a nursing home environment, most residents sit around in wheelchairs or lie in their beds for most of the day. Yet our bodies have the potential for so much more than this scenario. You can find plenty of wonderful examples of fit, healthy seniors living joyously active lives. With some simple lifestyle tweaks, you can enrich your senior years and extend your capacity for deliciously living well into old age. Be defiant. Redefine the meaning of aging gracefully.

Naturally Enhanced Nutrient Needs

Your nutrient requirements change throughout your life span. Your need for many micronutrients increases after age 51 and then again after age 70. Adding to the challenge of meeting these increased needs is the fact that most people eat less as they grow older. This means you must focus on nutrient density and make every bite count.

Your metabolism slows as you age because of muscle loss, decreased physical activity, and reduced digestion efficiency. Therefore, to maintain your ideal body weight, you need to eat fewer calories. The metabolism myths presented in Chapter 6 explain why the less you eat, the slower you age. Ideally, you need to make your diet so nutrient-dense that you can get away with eating only as much as your body truly needs.

 **HEALTHY HINT**

> Muscle mass declines by approximately 1 percent per year after age 40. On average, you lose 30 percent of your strength between age 50 and 70, and another 30 percent each decade after that. Exercise combats this loss, helping you maintain muscle strength and function. Incorporating strength training into your exercise routine a few times a week is an excellent investment in your quality of life. It's never too late to start!

Your calcium and vitamin B_6 requirements increase slightly after age 51, so to enhance your intake, emphasize leafy green vegetables, broccoli, baked potatoes, bananas, oats, tofu, beans, and seeds. Circulating vitamin D levels in the blood decrease as you grow older, especially after age 70. As with every other age group, continue to stay on top of your 25-hydroxyvitamin D blood test and supplement as necessary.

Because of the higher risk of osteoporosis and fractures in later life, it's critical to maintain optimum levels of vitamin D and calcium. Supplement with vitamin D if your blood test reveals suboptimal levels, and eat plenty of calcium-rich plant foods.

Iron is harmful in excess amounts because it induces oxidation. Once women reach menopause, they stop losing iron via their monthly menstrual cycles and their iron requirements return to those of the prepuberty years. To prevent overconsumption, supplementation is necessary only as a stop-gap measure to address a deficiency for a temporary period of time. Usually, an iron deficiency indicates a medical problem instead of a nutritional imbalance.

Vitamin B_{12} deficiency is extremely common among the elderly, regardless of diet. A common condition called *atrophic gastritis* is often to blame, as are depleted vitamin B_{12} stores, insufficient intake, and inadequate absorption. Be sure to consume adequate amounts of foods fortified with B_{12} (plant milks and nutritional yeast are excellent options) and, most importantly, take a B_{12}

supplement using one of these three dosing schedules: 50 micrograms twice a day, 150 micrograms once per day, or 2,500 micrograms once per week.

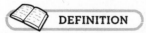 **DEFINITION**

Atrophic gastritis is chronic inflammation of the stomach lining that interferes with vitamin B$_{12}$ absorption. It affects up to half of adults over age 60.

The following tables list the recommendations for micronutrients for both men and women at various ages.

Micronutrient Needs for Older Men

Nutrient	Age 31 to 50	Age 51 to 70	Age 70 and Over
Vitamin B6	1.3mg	1.7mg	1.7mg
Vitamin D	15mcg	15mcg	20mcg
Calcium	1,000mg	1,200mg	1,200mg
Iron	8mg	8mg	8mg

Micronutrient Needs for Older Women

Nutrient	Age 31 to 50	Age 51 to 70	Age 70 and Over
Vitamin B6	1.3mg	1.5mg	1.5mg
Vitamin D	15mcg	15mcg	20mcg
Calcium	1,000mg	1,200mg	1,200mg
Iron	18mg	8mg	8mg

Dealing with Age-Related Physical Changes

Seniors have unique challenges when it comes to eating optimally. Malnutrition is common, due to multiple factors. Many medications and chronic conditions affect appetite, hydration, swallowing, digestion, and absorption. Naturally occurring physical changes of aging, like decreased appetite, chewing difficulty, decreased taste sensation, mobility limitations, and sluggish GI function, also impact food consumption. Psychological factors come into play as well. Depression, fatigue, loneliness, anxiety, and cognitive decline are common and make eating choices less of a priority.

Ideally, eating a nutrient-rich, plant-based diet prevents many of these issues. Chronic conditions that elicit the need for medications should not exist, and limitations of movement capacity should not occur. The lifelong neglect of proactive nourishment and adequate exercise is what leads to these problems. However, if you find yourself struggling with challenges, establish a solid plan to help you get the nutrients necessary to improve your health.

HEALTHY HINT

Constipation is common in older adults, thanks to sluggish digestion, medications, and inadequate food intake. Concentrate on consuming high-fiber foods like beans, whole grains, vegetables, and fruits every day, and get plenty of fluids.

Dealing with Your Diet

The more prepared you are to prepare whole, plant-based foods, the more likely you are to actually do so. If necessary, enlist the help of your friends or family, to be sure you have all the resources you need at your fingertips.

Stock your kitchen with user-friendly equipment, such as a high-powered blender, a rice cooker/steamer, a slow cooker, an automatic can opener, and assorted pots and pans. Fill your pantry, fridge, and freezer with your favorite healthful food options. If someone can help you do your shopping, you can buy more items at once. If not, simply make going to the store a part of your routine to pick up items you need for that day.

To simplify food preparation, keep frozen fruits, vegetables, and brown rice handy at all times. Frozen veggie burgers come in handy for a quick meal. Canned beans without added salt are great to include in at least one meal a day. Also stock your pantry with the following (along with a can opener to assist you):

- Canned tomatoes, tomato sauce, artichokes

- Jars of olives, marinara sauce, salsa, and crushed garlic

- Sprouted whole-grain pasta

- Whole grains (oats, brown rice, quinoa, barley)

- Dried legumes (lentils, beans, peas)

- Raw nuts and seeds and their butters

- Fortified plant-based milks

- Low-sodium vegetable broths and other soup blends

- Condiments such as vinegars, mustards, and ketchup

- Corn or rice cakes

- Whole-grain crackers

When you prepare an extra serving or two to eat the following day, you don't have to cook every day. Use recipes you're comfortable with, as long as they're nutrient-dense. If they're not, add color and substitute whole-food versions of the original ingredients. For instance, if your favorite dinner is pasta marinara, choose whole-grain pasta and marinara sauce, and stir in chopped broccoli and kale.

Many simple meals don't take too much time or effort. Keep your focus on easy. To save time, you can buy nutritious prepared foods at your local health food store or restaurant. Always seek out color, especially green, and other items that follow the recommendations in this book. And be sure to choose wisely, because you need to maximize nutrient intake for the least amount of calories to stay healthy.

Dealing with Medicine Mayhem

For many seniors, with the passage of years comes the addition of new medications to the daily regimen. As the chronic conditions pile up, so do the prescriptions. Unfortunately, the vast majority of doctors prefer to assign a condition or symptom to a pill instead of digging into the patient's lifestyle. When was the last time your doctor asked you what you eat and whether you exercise? If your doctor does that, keep him or her, and refer all your friends!

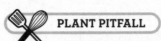

PLANT PITFALL

Polypharmacy, the use of multiple medications, is a risk to your overall health. Many medications interact with other ones by increasing or decreasing the effects or causing side effects. Be sure to tell each one of your healthcare practitioners exactly which pills you're taking, including any supplements, herbs, tonics, or elixirs. Always keep a list handy when you go to an appointment.

The main reason for this prescription-obsessed epidemic is that medical schools teach how to find the perfect pill to fix or at least quiet the symptom. Major changes to medical school curriculum, government regulations, and separation of drug companies from physician education are critical. Until these changes come to fruition, you have to look out for yourself. Doing things like reading this book and implementing our recommendations will help your lifespan *and* your healthspan.

Please know that medical care is extremely advantageous—especially in certain situations—but there's a whole world out there beyond pill popping and symptom soothing. If your body is reacting with high blood pressure, for example, something bigger is wrong, and you need to address the issue. Most of the time, a majority of indications are diet related and can be alleviated by switching to a whole-food, plant-based diet.

Certain medications interact with foods. A common example is the drug warfarin (brand name, Coumadin) and vitamin K. Warfarin is a drug commonly prescribed to thin the blood and prevent clotting. Vitamin K naturally helps the liver make blood-clotting factors. Taking warfarin prevents the liver from taking this action. You might be wondering how this interaction affects you if you're taking this medication. Consistency in your vitamin K consumption is vitally important. If you eat too many vitamin K–rich foods, you decrease the effect of the warfarin. Conversely, if you eat fewer vitamin K–rich foods, you increase the blood-thinning effect of warfarin.

Leafy green vegetables are the highest in vitamin K. Kale has the most, with 547 micrograms per cup, raw. Spinach, collard greens, broccoli, and chard are also rich sources. This doesn't mean you shouldn't eat these foods if you take warfarin; just maintain a consistent amount every day to prevent fluctuations in the effectiveness of the drug.

Here are some other points to consider with respect to medications:

- All drugs have side effects.

- Be vocal with your physician about any reactions you have to your medications, to ensure your dose and the type of drug is appropriate.

- Bring up diet with your doctor, and ask if you need to be concerned about any food-drug interactions with your current prescriptions.

As you transition to a whole food, plant-based diet, be sure you tell your doctor to supervise your medications carefully. Most people reduce or eliminate their need for their meds as their body naturally begins to heal. With drugs such as those that lower insulin or blood pressure, not monitoring carefully can be life-threatening. For example, changing your diet helps lower your blood pressure. If you remain on the dosage you started with, your blood pressure can end up too low and cause you to pass out.

The good news is that if you and your doctor are vigilant about monitoring and following the guidelines presented in this book, you have a good chance of getting off your current medications.

The Least You Need to Know

- Eating a whole food, plant-based diet and exercising regularly can help ward off chronic illnesses and physical disabilities common in the later years.

- Nutrient density is critical to your diet later in life. Metabolism slows naturally, but you still need to consume all the necessary nutrients.

- Slow the aging process by eating efficiently—high amounts of micronutrients with fewer macronutrients.

- Micronutrient needs for vitamin B_6, vitamin D, and calcium increase after age 50. Seniors also must be vigilant about getting adequate vitamin B_{12} consistently.

- Tell all your healthcare practitioners about all the medications and supplements you take, and ask about possible interactions, including potential reactions with foods.

- If you're transitioning to a whole food, plant-based diet after being on medication (especially meds that lower insulin or blood pressure), have your doctor monitor you closely for any needed adjustments.

Plant-Strong Athletes

Nutrition and athletics go hand and hand. As an athlete, the food you choose to fuel your body with may give that extra edge to separate you from the pack. And whole food, plant-based nutrition gives you what you need to push your body to its maximum intensity.

Elite athletes from many different sports have demonstrated the advantages of going plant based in their training and performance. And from what we've seen, the results of a plant-based nutrition plan are phenomenal.

Ultramarathoner Grant Campbell says, "On a plant-based diet, I can run 60 miles through mountains and enjoy running again the next day; running injuries don't haunt me anymore; and I never lose training time because I never get sick." And Carl Lewis, winner of 10 Olympic medals (9 golds) and 10 World Championship medals, is quoted as saying that his best performances came when he was 30 years old and vegan. In this chapter, you learn how you, too, can find success as a plant-based athlete.

In This Chapter

- Enhancing your performance with plant-based fuel
- The importance of timing with nutrients
- Tips for staying hydrated
- Dispelling myths about performance enhancers

Bringing Your "A" Game with Plants

Exercise has two primary impacts on the body: increased cardiovascular performance and increased tissue hypertrophy. In the latter case, physical activity breaks down tissue initiating a repair and rebuild process. It can come from intense explosive moves, as in weightlifting, or through long repetitive moves, as in lower-intensity cardiovascular exercise. Any physical stress you place on your body causes microscopic tears in your muscle tissue and that tissue is repaired and strengthened during recovery. The tougher the workout, the more damage to your muscles. The post-exercise period is a critical time when recovery, rebuilding, and enhancement occurs. At this point, providing optimal and varied nutrients that your body can easily absorb is important. This period between workouts and performances determines your improvement. If you fuel yourself properly and get adequate sleep and rest, your muscles will be stronger than before and be ready to perform more efficiently next time.

 HEALTHY HINT

The breaking down of muscle tissue is called catabolism, and the building back up is called anabolism. Both are constantly occurring throughout your body. To maximize strength, power, endurance, and agility, you want the anabolism to overpower the catabolism. Do this by emphasizing adequate and proper fuel.

Whole-plant foods provide an extra benefit because of nutrient density; plants provide a huge variety of both the macronutrients and micronutrients your body thrives on. Remember from Chapter 4 that exercise causes an increase in the presence of free radicals. This means antioxidants are required at higher levels to alleviate the stress placed on your body and support adequate recovery. The best sources for antioxidants and free radical–fighting phytochemicals are whole fruits and vegetables.

In addition, you need plenty of energy to fuel performance. Meeting appropriate energy requirements for periodized training and performance is the cornerstone of optimal sports nutrition. Processed foods and animal products provide empty calories that take up space in your digestive tract and bloodstream; a better plan is to consume actively beneficial foods. A whole food, plant-based diet is a great choice because the nutrient density of it provides a wide range of phytonutrients that scale along with energy needs—if you eat enough to support the activity, you'll likely get sufficient recovery nutrition. Body composition, size, and strength goals vary according to sport; some athletes aim to increase size or strength while others require smaller or leaner body size for biomechanical advantages or to meet weight requirements.

Keep in mind that athletes require more energy than nonathletes, but quality nutrition that minimizes highly refined fuel sources is key. Refined sources won't be eliminated completely—especially with endurance activities—but many athletes still overnourish driven by the fear of deficiency. A plant-based diet shouldn't be thought of as limiting in terms of performance. Top-level strength and endurance athletes from track and field, bodybuilding, triathlons, football, mixed martial arts, cycling, baseball, ice hockey, basketball, tennis, boxing, and more incorporate—and even break records with—a plant-based diet.

Nutrition Needs for Athletes

Sports nutrition is traditionally focused on calculating the appropriate nutrition intakes at the right times. The basis is in quantifying, counting, and measuring. We need sufficient energy to fuel physical activity and recovery, in addition to a complement of nutrients, amino acids, fatty acids, vitamins, and minerals. Too often, the focus is placed on a high level of certain macronutrient ratios, which may lead to highly refined and processed foods being substituted for quality whole-food sources.

With plant-based sports nutrition, you can broaden your body's capabilities by thinking beyond the traditional macronutrient sources. Not all foods are treated equally after they are swallowed. From digestion and absorption all the way to how your body utilizes them when they're in the bloodstream, the packaging of these nutrients matters. Why not choose energy that is wrapped together with powerful antioxidants, phytonutrients, and fiber to fight free radicals and regulate blood glucose levels? When you're applying these nutrients to a body pushing itself to extremes with training and performance, the difference in fuel choice becomes apparent: eating whole-plant foods at the right times can take your performance to new heights.

MIXED GREENS

Some of the innumerable plant-based athletes include strongman Patrik Baboumian, who broke the world record for the most weight ever carried by a human being in 2013; Alexey Voyevoda, World Armwrestling Federation champion and gold medal winner in the bobsleigh event at the 2014 Olympics; track-and-field Olympian Carl Lewis; tennis player Martina Navratilova; mixed martial artist Mac Danzig; ultramarathoners Scott Jurek and Grant Campbell; world record marathoner Fiona Oakes, the fastest female to complete a marathon on all seven continents as well as on the polar ice caps; NFL tight end Tony Gonzalez; boxers Cam F. Awesome and Keith Holmes; Ironman triathletes Brendan Brazier, Rich Roll, and Jason Lester; ice hockey player Georges Laraque; triathlete Ruth Heidrich; NFL wide receiver Desmond Howard; and bodybuilders Robert Cheeke, Torre Washington, and Robert Hazeley.

One of the most important factors in sports nutrition—besides the quality of your food choices—is adequate, but not excessive, intake. Monitor closely how much you consume, depending on your activity level, sport, and individual metabolic needs. Exercising at high intensity, frequency, and duration requires a lot of calories. Ultimately, there's no reason to change to some mythical ratio of protein, carbohydrates, or fat, but you will require adequate overall fuel for the activity. By sourcing this increased fuel requirement from whole foods whenever possible, you'll not only meet macronutrient needs, but an abundance of additional phytonutrients will aid in recovery. Instead of using a generic formula to determine how many calories you need, follow this simple protocol:

- Eat when you're hungry.

- Choose high-quality, whole-plant foods.

- Carefully plan your intake around your training (see "Nutrient Timing" later in this chapter).

- Monitor your weight. If you're at your ideal weight for your performance demands, maintain it. If you're losing weight, you're not eating enough. If you're gaining weight— and it is body fat, not muscle— either eat less or reassess the composition of your food choices.

Just as in healthy everyday life, your body knows better than any formula. Listen to your body's signals—hunger and satiation as well as performance—to determine what *you* need.

Carbohydrates: Starchy Vegetables and Fruits for Fuel and Recovery

As we explained in Chapter 5, macronutrients make poor food groups, so we aren't going to talk about "carbs" here as this word tends to group calorie foodstuff that isn't metabolically equivalent. That said, we have disputed the notion that sugar is poison or that it is the sole cause of health problems; but clearly, it's not health food for the average person and should be limited. Rather than dive into a lecture on simple versus complex carbohydrates, we are going to examine the sources of glucose within us and identify how to best replenish those internal sources with whole-food starchy vegetables and fruits when engaged in intense athletics.

As an athlete, you have two sources of glucose to consider: circulating blood glucose that results from meals or is supplied by liver glycogen and deep muscle–tissue glycogen stores. The liver can hold approximately 400 to 600 calories of glycogen stores, and muscle tissue holds approximately 1,200 to 1,500 calories of glycogen. These stores aren't shared sources of glucose. The liver uses its glycogen to maintain the approximately 4 grams of glucose that circulates in your blood daily, and muscle glycogen fuels explosive and repetitive moves. These stores need to be replenished daily.

During long-duration activity, energy is also replaced with simple, easily absorbed glucose sources such as gels, dates, or bars. Keep in mind that fueling a competitive sport requires a different strategy than the deficit goals of weight (fat) loss. Combining these two different physiologies (gaining muscle and losing fat) with competing dietary goals, may be why so many don't see the expected results (e.g. too little gain or too little loss).

MIXED GREENS

Running (or walking) requires about 100 calories per mile—or approximately 2,600 calories for a marathon (26.2 miles). If total glycogen stores are approximately 1,500 to 2,000 calories, or 60 to 75 percent of that required for the marathon, one would expect to hit the wall ("bonk") at the 15- to 20-mile mark, unless some source of glucose is provided. This is caused by the depletion of glycogen stores in the liver and muscles. Endurance training encourages the body to both source more of the energy from fat stores and store more glycogen in the tissue. Pushing activity too hard skews energy to glycogen stores and increases chances of hitting the wall.

Fueling glycogen for athletic success requires a combination of both long- and short-term strategies. Whole-food starchy vegetables and fruits are excellent sources of glucose to replenish deep tissue–glycogen stores. These sources include whole grains (brown rice, oats, barley, quinoa), potatoes, sweet potatoes, yams, corn, whole-grain pasta, sprouted bread or tortillas, beans, lentils, green bananas and plantains. For short-term fueling, the simple sugars found in Basil-Lemon Switchel, a homemade sports drink (recipe in Chapter 20) provide an instantly available glucose surge. Whole dates are also a fantastic whole-food option; they're like nature's energy gels and can rapidly replenish blood glucose. Remember that the simple sugars found in juice and even sports drinks aren't health food per se and, outside of endurance training, long-term glycogen stores are better replenished with whole-food starchy vegetables and fruits.

PLANT PITFALL

Never try anything new before a game, race, or performance. Practice what you eat and drink—and the timing in which you do so—beforehand to prevent a negative response.

Muscle: Gym-Built, Not Kitchen-Made

Stimulating muscle growth, or hypertrophy, may involve increasing volume, increasing muscle fibers, or both. This requires enough fuel for the exercise to stress the tissue and sufficient nutrition to then rebuild and repair that tissue. Of course, the first thing everyone wants to focus on is eating enough protein to build the muscle. As we learned in Chapter 2, it is the essential amino acids (the protein building blocks) that are required in our diet. The rest of the 20 amino acids can be synthesized by our body. While no animal makes every amino acid, plants must synthesize all 20 amino acids because they can't eat; therefore every whole-plant food contains all 20 amino acids. While it is true that extra amino acid sources are needed during rebuild and repair, it's not as much as everyone believes.

If you are eating whole foods and getting enough calories to support your sport, you are likely getting enough protein. Many athletes do well on a diet that is composed of 10 to 15 percent protein. To put that in perspective, beans and lentils are about 20 to 30 percent protein and soybeans (edamame) and soy products are a little over 40 percent protein. Legumes also have the advantage of being high in fiber and are packaged with starch to replenish glycogen stores. Let's not forget that amino acids and proteins are the building blocks of all things living, so every whole-food plant consumed contains protein and all amino acids.

In most sports, excessive protein consumption is considered an advantage. Yet, the research is conflicting. From what we know about the harms of high-protein intake, especially from animal sources, you may be putting your body at risk for long-term damage by following this suggestion. Interestingly, because athletes require more calories, they automatically get more protein because they eat more food. Selecting whole, unprocessed plant foods makes it's impossible not to meet adequate protein requirements. Eat enough and train hard is the best advice for packing on lean muscle mass.

Hundreds, if not thousands, of protein powders, drinks, bars, and supplements are currently on the market. These are notoriously full of hormonally active, milk-based whey and casein protein, as well as fillers, stabilizers, preservatives, sweeteners, flavors, and other compounds that wreak havoc on your body. They cost a lot of money and promise you the perfect body or ultimate performance. Yet due to the guidelines set by the Dietary Supplement Health and Education Act, manufacturers are allowed to make such health claims on the packages as "burns fat instead of storing it," "designed exactly to the needs of human metabolism," or "supplies highest quality amino acids." As tempting as these promises sound, nobody has to prove they're truthful. Nor does anyone have to prove long-term safety of their use. So if these products don't work, are expensive, and can potentially be harmful, what's the point?

Nutrient Timing

Believe it or not, *when* you eat and drink surrounding exercise may be just as important as *what* you eat. Fueling and recovering your body in a strategic manner benefits your performance.

In this section, we break down some general guidelines, but you know your body and how it functions best. Part of your training focus needs to be on which foods and drinks offer the most advantage, as well as when you should consume them. Practice makes perfect. Experiment until you know with precision what your body requires to thrive.

 **MIXED GREENS**

Professional Ironman triathlete and author Brendan Brazier says, "Quick recovery is the key to athletic success. 80 percent of the recovery process can be attributed to nutrition."

Eating and hydrating before exercise improves your performance, although you don't want to force your body to focus on digestion by filling up too much. Here are some tips for success: eat something small that's high in easily digestible starches and sugars and low in fiber, protein, and fat—such as fruit, fruit juice, white rice, or white potato—90 minutes to 2 hours before your event. Drink 1 or 2 cups fluid—preferably a beverage including carbohydrates—1 hour before an event. During an event lasting an hour, sports drinks are helpful, especially if the event occurs first thing in the morning after an overnight fast.

For events longer than 1 hour, keep the following in mind: maintain hydration by sipping water and sports drinks that contain carbohydrates consistently throughout the event. Consume carbohydrate-rich foods in the form of dried or fresh fruit, sports gels, bars, or energy drinks at 15- to 20-minute intervals.

Immediately after an event, there may be a magical time referred to as an *anabolic window of opportunity*, during which your body is ready, willing, and eager to absorb nourishment. Although the evidence is inconclusive, it is hypothesized that the 30 to 45 minutes after completion may be the most critical time to replenish stores. Plus, this is also an ideal time to reduce the free radicals that were formed during your activity by eating antioxidant-rich foods.

Excellent post-event, whole-food choices include the following:

- A green smoothie with lots of fruits, leafy greens, and coconut water
- Whole-grain pasta with oil-free marinara sauce and leafy green vegetables
- Quinoa, or other whole grain, with legumes and vegetables
- Stir-fry with brown, red, purple, or wild rice and veggies
- Veggie sushi rolls made with cucumber, avocado, seaweed, edamame, and other veggies

Whole-y Hydration

Proper hydration during exercise is critical for performance and for your safety. Dehydration, a loss of 2 percent of your body weight from fluids, can compromise your performance; impair your mental function; and even lead to serious, life-threatening consequences. Signs of dehydration include muscle cramps, spasms, decreased performance, thirst, and diminishing rate of sweat.

You lose fluids and *electrolytes* at increased levels during exercise, thanks to your increased breathing rate and sweat. Depending on the duration, the intensity, your fitness level, and the weather, the amount of fluids and electrolytes you need varies.

Preventing Dehydration and Hyponatremia

Normally, your body is extremely proficient at maintaining proper electrolyte balance. Slight fluctuations occur, but a drastic shift can have life-threatening consequences.

People with kidney disease or those who take certain medications can experience problems balancing electrolytes. However, certain behaviors can cause an imbalance as well. Consuming large amounts of water without also taking in sodium can cause a condition known as *hyponatremia,* which can cause confusion, drowsiness, muscle weakness, nausea, vomiting, brain swelling, headaches, twitches, and seizures. To prevent hyponatremia, don't overhydrate before an event or rely on water as your sole fluid source during endurance events.

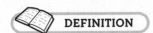 **DEFINITION**

> **Electrolytes** are minerals found in the blood that help balance fluids and maintain normal functions like your heart's rhythm and muscle contraction. The main electrolytes are sodium, potassium, chloride, magnesium, calcium, phosphate, and bicarbonate. **Hyponatremia,** also known as water intoxication, is an abnormally low concentration of sodium in the blood (less than 135 mmol per liter) that can cause cells to malfunction and can be fatal. It can result from prolonged, heavy sweating with failure to replenish sodium or from excessive water consumption, so it has become common in high-endurance athletes.

Follow these tips on maintaining proper hydration:

- At least 2 to 4 hours before you exercise, drink 2 to 4 milliliters of water per pound of body weight (5 to 10 milliliters per kilogram of body weight) to optimize hydration status.

- Because fluid needs vary greatly during exercise, you can determine your fluid requirements by routinely measuring your body weight before and after training. Weighing yourself before and after exercise can help you learn how to prevent a loss of 2 pounds over the course of the session.

- Generally, try to take in about 0.4 to 0.8 liters per hour (or approximately ½ to 1 cup) of fluids every 20 minutes during exercise.

- For athletes with high sweat rates or exercise events lasting longer than 2 hours, sodium (e.g. via a sports drink) should be ingested.

- After exercise, drink 1.25 to 1.5 liters of fluid for every kilogram of body weight lost (0.56 to 0.68 liters of fluid per pound lost).

Sports Drinks: What Type and When?

For events lasting longer than 90 minutes, sports drinks with sugars and electrolytes help spare glycogen, prevent dehydration and hyponatremia, and maintain electrolyte balance.

Several varieties are commercially available, but most of them contain large amounts of sugar, artificial colors, and artificial flavors. Instead, you can substitute coconut water or make your own sports beverage with diluted 100 percent pure fruit juice and a touch of sea salt.

Ergogenic Aids

Ergogenic aids, nutritional products that enhance performance, are widely used in the athletic community. No matter what promises the labels claim, very few of them are effective.

No pill, powder, or supplement can produce the same results as hard work and consistency in training. Worse, many of them are dangerous to your health. And some are against the rules. National and international sports organizations monitor for certain ergogenic aids with random urine testing to prevent their use in competitions.

Pushing your body to the ultimate extreme is the essence of athleticism. This population, more than any other, requires optimal nutrition to succeed in performance and recovery. Careful attention to nutrient timing and consistent hydration takes your body and your results beyond what you thought possible as an athlete. If maintaining a whole food, plant-based diet is effective when challenging your body at its maximum capacity, it represents the potential for *every* body to be plant-strong.

The Least You Need to Know

- Athletes require optimal nutrition because their bodies are constantly breaking down and rebuilding cells. Eating a whole food, plant-based diet can take your performance to the next level.

- As an athlete, you don't need excessive protein or different ratios of carbohydrates, proteins, and fats. Eating enough calories from high-quality, whole-plant foods naturally provides what your body requires.

- Whole fruits, smoothies, and starchy vegetables provide excellent fuel both before and during workouts, as well as give you post-workout replenishment.
- Proper hydration not only drastically impacts performance but is also critical for your safety. Stay well hydrated with water, and include sports drinks with sugars and electrolytes if your event lasts longer than 90 minutes.

Winning at Weight Loss

According to the *New England Journal of Medicine*, excess body weight accounted for 4 million deaths and 120 million disability-adjusted life years (the exact inverse of healthspan) around the world in 2015. Almost 70 percent of those deaths were caused by cardiovascular disease. In the United States alone, 70.7 percent of adults are overweight or obese. That means less than one third of the U.S. population is walking around at a healthy weight. Excess fat on your body puts you at risk for most chronic diseases. For the first time in history, malnutrition is due to overnourishment for a majority of the population. With unlimited access to food, we're eating too many calorie-dense foods, too much, and too often, all the while we're growing more chronically ill decade by decade.

Why are we having so much trouble winning at what seems to be a simple task: eat no more than is needed? One reason may be that humans—like every other living organism—evolved and adapted to a world of scarcity. Historically, we were naturally limited by season and availability; food, overall, had times of abundance and scarcity. Even after the rise of agriculture, food remained economically scarce for some time. But things began to change about a century ago when refrigeration and transportation entered the scene, allowing

In This Chapter

- Your body's calorie-balancing act
- Why your genes may not determine your jean size
- Choosing nutrient density over energy density
- Managing your weight by listening to your body

food to be stored and sold year-round. Consider that for the first time in history, obesity is now a symptom of poverty. The only species struggling with obesity and chronic disease are humans and the pets we keep cozy and overnourished. Unnatural access to food may be more of the problem for you and your pets than lack of willpower.

Fortunately, inherent factors of a whole food, plant-based nutrition plan naturally aid weight-loss efforts. Mind-boggling though it is—even to scientists—you can eat enough to stay satiated as you lose pounds and maintain that loss with ease.

Why Calories Count (If You Count All the Calories)

We discussed the role of metabolic macronutrient hierarchy, or oxidative priority, in Chapter 6. Recall that the energy components of the meal—alcohol, proteins (amino acids), carbohydrates (starches and sugars), and fats—are absorbed in the intestinal tract resulting in a blood plasma–concentration peak a couple of hours after eating or drinking. Those blood plasma levels return to premeal values 4 to 6 hours later. The body is constantly striving for *homeostasis* in many of its systems, and this includes the various nutrient levels in the blood. After ingesting any calorie-containing food, those calories are either stored, eliminated, or metabolized (burned) in order to maintain blood plasma–nutrient homeostasis.

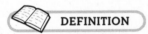 **DEFINITION**

> **Homeostasis** is the tendency to return to a stable or balanced point and is maintained by various physiological processes. For example, the rise in blood alcohol, lipids, or glucose after a meal is returned to normal pre-meal levels 4 to 6 hours after eating.

Oxidative priority explains why certain eating patterns will lead to maintenance, accumulation, or reduction of fat reserves. This understanding will take the guesswork out of gaining and losing weight. It is important to note that in the fed (postprandial) state, the body is actively trying to dispose of the energy in the food just eaten. Consequently, energy use is necessarily directed away from storage (fat) reserves accumulated during prior meals. A simplified way to conceptualize this is to imagine your body either in the fed state, lasting 4 to 6 hours after eating, or in the fasted state, and continuing that way until the next meal. Similarly, you are either disposing of a recent meal or burning off reserves. It is that latter state, burning reserves, which results in the elimination of excess fat storage.

When you eat, the body must burn, store, or eliminate the energy components of the meal. Food doesn't just hang around in the stomach or intestinal tract waiting for a push-up or a sprint to the mailbox. You might ask, "doesn't the metabolism respond to a meal?" Or wonder, "what is the importance of the metabolic boost after a high-protein meal?" Indeed, the body does respond to meals with a rise in metabolism. It is true that with a high-protein meal, your metabolism increases. It is similar for alcohol and carbohydrates. These post-meal rises are due to the energy requirement of digestion, but also to eliminate macronutrients the body can't store. These metabolic rises from meals do not lead to significant depletion of your fat reserves. Remember, the only weight loss on the scale that matters is fat loss and the only metabolic increases that help are rises fueled by fat stores (as opposed to dietary fat).

Each minute you spend in the metabolically fed state is another minute you aren't burning calorie-dense fat stores. We've all read the headlines about the latest fad calorie-burning food or how frequent meals stoke your metabolism, but the simple truth is that our fat reserves are an evolutionary resource for times of no food. With the exception of explosive exercise or when drinking alcohol, you are always burning some percentage of fat. Normally, in the fasted state, you are typically burning about half fat and half glucose. If you've been dieting for a couple of weeks without exception, fat percentage burned could rise to about 75 percent. Yes it's true, your fat percentage burned will rise during longer periods of dieting. Your fat stores are the result of an adaptive strategy for times with no food; we don't use muscle, brain, or organ tissue when faced with calorie scarcity; we use our fat from adipose tissue.

Not all calories are treated equally when it comes to digestion, absorption, and storage of food. And for those who believe a calorie isn't a calorie, the point could be somewhat correct and relevant. Scientists can, with good accuracy, account for the energy used and stored in a wide range of food products, but it requires careful analysis that is often left out of blogs, books, and news stories to the contrary. The fabulous news is that eating whole-plant foods take much of the guess work out of weight loss, make calorie counting unnecessary, and whittle away pounds with ease.

Genetics and Upbringing

Which came first—the seed or the tree? Similarly, is your weight innate or learned? The truth may lie somewhere in the middle. You may have genetic tendencies predicting how much you will weigh, and behavior patterns you learned from your family as you grew up also play a part. But which has more influence over your eating and weight? No clear-cut answer can be given yet, but no matter who you are, it's not a question of genetic doom. There is an eating volume and frequency that will comfortably maintain you at a normal, healthy weight. You're not broken.

For decades, scientists thought that genetics might be deterministic and that DNA predicted everything about your health—which diseases you're at risk for, your tendency toward obesity, how tall you'll be, and factors such as dental health and hair growth patterns. What we've come to understand is that genes can also be expressed (turned on) or silenced (turned off) through a process known as *epigenetics*. These changes can come about through diet, sleep, exercise, and even where you live. There are many factors that can cause chemical modifications of the genes, which may turn them on or off over time.

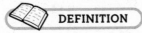

DEFINITION

Epigenetics is a trait resulting in changes in a chromosome without alterations in the DNA sequence. Epigenetic traits may be inherited, silenced, and expressed resulting in a wide range of traits and possible outcomes.

You started as a single cell in your mother's womb with genetic material from both parents. That DNA contained all the instructions for your life. As these cells grew and multiplied, all with the same DNA, some cells were turned into toes and, others, into lung tissue. In every case, individual genes were suppressed or expressed. Otherwise, you could end up with toe tissue in your lungs.

Consider the following examples. In 1981, researchers at Oxford University determined that only 2 or 3 percent of cancer risk can be attributed to genes. Children born into poverty are thought to never reach their genetic height potential due to malnutrition. Migrant studies show clearly that incidence of obesity and chronic disease change when a person moves from one society to another. Girls are starting puberty at a younger age than their mothers did. All these findings disprove the idea that your genetic tendencies are set in stone but are affected by lifestyle choices.

Your DNA is simply your book of life or your life's script. One analogy for epigenetics, is that it is like the director on a movie set with the same actor, props, and script. By directing what words and scenes to emphasize and suppress, the movie takes on a wide range of artistic and dramatic expressions. Likewise, you aren't destined by genetics for any single outcome, and the most powerful tool in your epigenetic toolbox is a healthy, whole food, plant-based diet.

Regardless of whether scientists agree, the take-home message is simple: you can, at the very least, set the stage for optimum health by managing your behaviors and lifestyle. Only positive benefits can come from making healthful choices. If you don't provide the fuel to the genetic fire (eating animal-based and processed foods, for example), lifestyle may just win over. You have absolutely nothing to lose.

Many people use their genes, age, or metabolism as an excuse to remain overweight. They give up any effort to lose weight by deciding they have no control anyway, so what's the point? The genetic component certainly complicates the question, but it's not the primary cause of failed weight loss attempts. It's well established that overweight parents can have lean, healthy kids, and vice versa. It's time we let go of this myth that's holding back a majority of the U.S. population from reaching and maintaining a healthy weight. Now is the time to take back control of your body.

Phyto Factors

As introduced in Chapter 5, the Food Triangle is a simple tool to help guide you through healthful food choices. It is also a great tool for weight loss. At the top of the Food Triangle are leafy greens, cruciferous vegetables (e.g. broccoli, kale, and bok choy), mushrooms, stems (e.g. celery and asparagus), and bulbs (e.g. garlic and onion). These can be loosely thought of as everything in the produce world except starchy vegetables and simple-sugar fruits. You can't live on the food at the top of the food triangle alone as it simply doesn't have enough energy to sustain you for long periods of time, but it does offer an abundance of vitamins, minerals, amino acids, fiber, and other phytonutrients.

Now, as we add foods from the bottom of the Food Triangle, starchy vegetables and simple sugar fruits, we are adding the energy storage components of a plant. These are the foods that will allow you to maintain your weight or even grow new tissue, depending on your goal. These bottom-right foods have many of the same phytonutrients contained in the top. Of course, this works on the left side of the Food Triangle in much the same way, except the animal-sourced food contains fat and the other storage tissues of animals without any phytonutrition or fiber. This is why people can lose weight by eliminating whole-food simple sugars (fruits) and starchy vegetables. It's also why you can lose weight by eliminating animal products.

Our simple goal for weight loss is to burn our own energy-storage adipose reserves (fat) instead of burning the storage organs of plants or animals.

Recall that "bottom feeding" (burger and fries, pasta and meat sauce, curry and rice, fish and chips, etc.) is a nearly perfect formula to gain weight; we burn the excess alcohol, amino acids, starches, and sugars, and then store the fat for later. Four to six hours later, when our body gets back to burning our internal storage reserves from previous meals, what do we do? Yes, we eat again. The cycle continues: burn a little, store a little more, and so on, until we have weeks, months, or even years of stored fuel. (Remember the man who went on a 382-day water-only fast in Chapter 6?) After 4 to 6 hours, your body naturally returns to burning its reserves. It is a myth that skipping meals causes your metabolism to crash and that you'll hold onto fat. We store fat for periods of no food and those fat reserves are a perfect complement to the low-energy plant foods from the top of the Food Triangle.

Fiber, Fasting, and Fat Loss

As you learned in Chapter 4, fiber is a dietary component that passes through your stomach and small intestine without being affected by your digestive processes, though it does feed some of the many bacteria that inhabit your digestive tract microbiome. Dietary fiber—both soluble and insoluble—keep the stool moving along. When people fast for days consuming only water, bowel movements cease. What is a little surprising to most people is that weight loss can almost reach the rate of a water-only fast when food intake is limited to the right side of the Food Triangle.

With a plant-based diet, that extra dietary fiber feels filling, keeps things moving, and causes the scale to drop.

There are many ways people describe hunger: headache, lack of focus, lethargy, irritability, or even shakiness. Here's a shocker—none are really hunger symptoms. They are very similar to the symptoms of giving up caffeine, nicotine, or even alcohol. There are many types of withdrawal, but what they have in common is a period of habituated ingestion followed by a sudden stop. That survival brain wants more and so urges surge. It turns out that after a few days or so of not getting what it wants, the brain kicks into a new expectation and the urges are silenced. For someone who has experienced a longer fast (5 to 7 days or more), they recognize that only the first couple of days are uncomfortable.

By eating on the right side of the Food Triangle, you don't need to fast a single day to lose weight. Rather, you can group your meals a little closer together, increasing the block of time between the last meal of the day and the first. Remember, it is the time after 4 to 6 hours when the body begins tapping into reserves, because the energy component of the meal is now gone. Wait, I thought everyone says to eat every 2 hours to keep my metabolism boosted?

Let's think about this critically.

We wake up at 6:00 A.M. and have breakfast (hint: we break fast) at 7:00 A.M. Now we take the next 4 to 6 hours to digest that meal. We get to work and grab a pastry and some coffee, once again 4 to 6 more hours in the fed state. Assuming there are no more coffee breaks, we eat again at noon and reset the timer for another 4 to 6 hours. At which point, it's happy hour and we grab some wine, crackers, and olives. Then, we have dinner reservations at 8:00 P.M. (another 4-6 hours from meal end) and get to bed by 11:00 P.M. Digestion is now well into your sleep period and may end about 1:00 to 2:00 A.M.! For most people, this results in a narrow window logging 5 hours of fasted time, at best. Then, it's once again time to eat all day long. Do you see why you never pay down any of that accumulated "fat debt?"

Here is an alternate day to consider: Wake and have some black coffee or tea (no sweeteners or creamers), and breakfast at noon with a large salad and a nut-based dressing. Sometime between 5:00 to 6:00 P.M., have a second meal with potatoes, steamed vegetables, and some fruit. On this day, you were in the fasted state from 10:00 P.M. until noon the next day. That's 14 hours. That's nearly 3 times the fasting period of the typical day described above spent burning fuel reserves. On which day do you think you'd burn more from the fat stores?

 **HEALTHY HINT**

If you're not positive you're hungry, you aren't hungry. Have a cup of tea instead.

We've been deluged to think that all this swallowing and wiggling is the secret to success. People want to blame the battle on food deserts, knee injuries, GMOs, broken metabolisms, and hormones. The reality is that a century ago, food was economically scarce and many handed-down, traditional recipes are built from the bottom of the Food Triangle. That's a plus when food is scarce. But, today, it is maladaptive.

Keep It Simple

Losing weight is easy if you look through our new lens. We start with the toughest part: acknowledging that if you aren't losing weight now, you are eating at a level above your minimum requirement. However, there is a wide gap between not losing and gaining weight and this may cause confusion. You can eat a lot more than you think and not gain weight, but, conversely, you may need to eat less than you think in order to lose weight. With a whole food, plant-based diet, you will be pleasantly surprised by just how much food you can eat and still lose weight every single day until you reach your goal. During this time, you may be taking in lower levels of nutrition, so limit physical activity.

Here are some simple guidelines for sustainable success:

- Eat on the right side of the Food Triangle, with an emphasis on foods from the top.

- Reduce the daily window in the fed (postprandial) state, which expands the fasted time for the body burn reserves.

- Limit nuts, seeds, and avocado to approximately ¼ cup (1 oz) and eat these whole or in sauces only with non-starchy vegetables.

- Realize it may take a couple of days to feel comfortable with your new eating patterns.

- Don't snack in between meals; even small snacks activate the digestive tract.

- Chew your food slowly, don't allow distractions while you eat (watching television, driving, etc.), and put down the fork between bites to take time to savor each bite.

- Avoid concentrated sweets like pure juices and dried fruits.

Your body is constantly in flux, striving for homeostasis, or equilibrium. We are either fed and the body is burning, eliminating, or storing the food ingested, or we are fasted and running on stored reserves. After assaults with diets and poor food choices, you may have lost touch with your intuition and actual needs. We may get away with eating more than we need without gaining weight, but the only way to extend an organism's life or increase healthspan is with dietary restriction without malnutrition. Fortunately, it's never too late to regain control. The same foods that promote optimum health naturally allow your body to reach its desirable size. Think simply, effortlessly, and healthfully, and you'll achieve your goals.

The Least You Need to Know

- All calories count, but the real test is whether or not the number on the scale is moving down every few days.
- Metabolic boosts after meals do little to dispose of energy (fat) stored away from previous meals
- Eating on the right side of the Food Triangle, with an emphasis placed on foods from the top, is the most rapid way to lose weight.
- Consuming fiber is the single factor experts agree on that helps promote weight loss.
- Avoiding refined oils, sugars, and flours eliminates lots of mindless calories from your diet
- Practice reconnecting your mind to your body's hunger and satiety signals. The more carefully you listen, the more natural it will become.

Dodging Disease with Diet

Health-care costs are rising in harmony with disease incidence rates. Billions of dollars are being poured into new therapies, medications, procedures, and more while the patients for whom these therapies are intended grow sicker and sicker. Evidently, a key element is missing. That element is our food.

Awareness is growing rapidly that whole food, plant-based nutrition is an inexpensive, pain-free, and effective alternative. It's been hypothesized that lifestyle change—as a form of prevention and treatment—can cut health-care costs by as much as 70 to 80 percent. Because researchers and health-care practitioners are seeing great successes, we're at the tipping point where food is making a comeback as preventative "medicine."

In This Chapter

- Overnourished and chronically ill
- Your GI tract: the gateway to good health
- Nutritional implications of common illnesses

Eradicating Chronic Disease

Chronic disease is considered an incurable illness. Medically speaking, for physicians treating chronic disease, the goal is symptom management, accomplished by balancing and modifying medications and offering procedures when appropriate.

According to the Centers for Disease Control, chronic diseases such as diabetes, cardiovascular disease, and cancer are the most common, costly, and preventable of all health problems in the United States. However, each of these conditions can be prevented—and many of them completely reversed—simply by adjusting lifestyle. Remember, genetics may load the gun, but lifestyle pulls the trigger.

Diabetes

More than 29 million Americans have diagnosed diabetes, and more than one in four people don't know they have it. Moreover, an additional 86 million have prediabetes. The two types of diabetes—type 1 and type 2—are different in terms of origin and mechanism. They may share symptoms such as high fasting blood glucose or elevated postprandial (after eating) rise in blood glucose, but the pathology is different in each: type 1 diabetes is an autoimmune disease—meaning it's caused by the body attacking itself—that typically is diagnosed during childhood and results in the pancreas being unable to produce insulin. Type 2 diabetes is a metabolic disease that occurs when the cells become resistant to insulin. In the past, type 2 diabetes was considered an adult-onset disease, but nowadays, it's being diagnosed at progressively younger ages.

Immediate health complications of diabetes include the following:

- Diabetic ketoacidosis, a life-threatening situation caused from insufficient insulin and uncontrolled ketone formation that leads to high blood-sugar levels, nausea, vomiting, abdominal pain, dehydration, ketones in the urine, acidosis, and the potential for coma and death

- Increased incidence of infections

- Insulin shock, when too much insulin is in the blood, which leads to severely low blood sugar (hypoglycemia) and possibly results in convulsions or coma

- Coma

- Death

Diabetes is the number-one cause of amputations and blindness. Additional long-term outcomes of diabetes include the following:

- Kidney disease

- Cardiovascular disease

- Retinopathy, a disease of the small blood vessels in the retina of the eyes that can eventually result in impaired vision and blindness

- Skin infections

- Neuropathy, or damage to the nerves that causes tingling, weakness, pain, and/or numbness usually in the legs, feet, toes, arms, and fingers

- Foot ulcers

Type 2 diabetes can be prevented and even reversed with diet and exercise. Obesity is the most common factor predisposing someone to type 2 diabetes, so weight management is a crucial issue. High levels of body fat, particularly *intramyocellular lipids*, lead to insulin resistance and progressively increase the need for more insulin. Eventually this need for extra insulin exhausts the pancreas, resulting in decreased secretion of insulin. Losing weight and exercising improve insulin sensitivity, thereby minimizing the amount of insulin necessary.

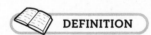 **DEFINITION**

> In contrast to adipose tissue (fat), which functions to store lipids until needed, **intramyocellular lipids** (*intra*, "within" and *myo*, "muscle") are droplets of lipids within muscle tissue cells. It is suggested that these accumulated lipids interfere with normal glucose utilization (insulin resistance) which leads to the accumulation of glucose in the bloodstream after a meal. Paradoxically, a diet low in saturated fat and high in whole-food starches can reverse this action, restoring normal insulin sensitivity.

Although type 1 diabetes is an autoimmune disease, some studies have found that insulin dosing can be decreased and long-term health outcomes can be controlled with a whole-food, plant-based diet.

Around the globe, the prevalence of diabetes increases in populations that consume more saturated fat, animal fat, and animal protein. On the contrary, prevalence decreases with greater intakes of fiber and vegetable fat. Studies show an increased risk for diabetes with meat intake and with higher blood cholesterol levels. Careful control of blood sugar levels over the long haul reduces the risk of several of the complications of diabetes.

Dietary recommendations for people with diabetes used to focus on minimizing intake of carbohydrates, causing the diet to be shifted toward more protein and fat. Currently, this advice is changing due to accumulating evidence of the harm of high intakes of saturated fat and animal protein. Nutrition plans are more individualized now, and success in using whole-food, plant-based diets to reverse diabetes has been incredibly promising.

 PLANT PITFALL

Many studies indicate an association between early exposure to dietary cow's milk proteins and an increased risk of developing type 1 diabetes. Gut influence such as inflammation and variations in gut permeability may interplay, further exacerbating these autoimmune issues. The immune system attacks these foreign proteins and fragments, eventually mistaking our own cells and proteins for invaders. Ultimately this may destroy pancreatic cells, leading to the inability to produce insulin and thereby resulting in a lifetime of type 1 diabetes.

Heart Disease

Heart disease, or coronary heart disease (CHD), is the number-one cause of death in America and around the world. It is estimated that one person dies every 40 seconds from cardiovascular disease in the United States alone. In most cases, heart attacks are due to a narrowing of the coronary arteries, the blood vessels that supply the heart with oxygen and nutrients. Atherosclerotic plaque—a buildup of cholesterol, calcium, cellular debris, and fatty materials—accumulates over many years, even starting in childhood for some people, and causes this narrowing.

Heart disease is mostly a foodborne illness, brought about by the overconsumption of saturated and trans fats, animal protein, and highly processed foods and the underconsumption of whole-plant foods. Coronary artery disease—the condition resulting from atherosclerosis in the arteries—is virtually nonexistent in cultures with a plant-based diet.

Therapy options for heart disease—drugs, stents, and bypasses—offer no more than a bandage effect. Truly treating the disease requires the cessation of consistently applying the source. If a sink is overflowing with water, mopping up the mess on the floor isn't going to stop the problem. That's precisely what current medical treatment does for heart disease—it mops up the water. Eating a whole food, plant-based diet along with exercising is the equivalent of turning off the faucet.

Cancer

Cancer is the second-leading cause of death in the United States. Almost 600,000 people die from the disease every year. As poorly understood as the development and spread of cancer is, the disease itself is rather simple on the surface. New cells routinely divide and grow as the body needs them. Old or damaged cells die as they are no longer needed. This cellular symphony of just-in-time birth and death of cells is normally well regulated, but what happens if the conductor loses the beat? New cells grow without control where they aren't needed (tumors), and old cells aren't dying when they are damaged or no longer needed. Sometimes these cells can break off, travel to new tissue, and begin growing there; this is called *malignancy*. Cancer is unlike bacterial or viral infections, as there is no foreign invader. With cancer, the problem is a genetic signaling breakdown within your own DNA that particularly impacts how cells divide and grow. These mixed signals may be inherited genetic defects or they may be associated with epigenetic modifications, as discussed in Chapter 15. Recall that this expression and silencing of genes is highly influenced by environmental conditions, especially diet.

The treatments for cancer may sometimes be worse than the cancer itself, so living to avoid cancer is a prudent choice. When treating cancer, once again, the symptoms are targeted instead of the disease mechanism. Choosing among amputating parts of your body, flooding your system with powerful toxins, and radiating your cells, or a combination of all three, is likely one of the most difficult decisions you could ever need to make. Even more tragic is the fact that these treatments don't always work. Although, they are aimed at stopping the progression of the cancer, sometimes these options simply buy you time.While cancers take on a wide range of variables outside the scope of this book, lifestyle habits that have been associated with a decreased risk for developing cancer include maintaining a healthy body weight, avoiding smoking, minimizing consumption of alcohol, reducing intake of processed and red meats, eating plenty of fruits and vegetables, and staying consistent with exercise.

It should be pointed out that the cruciferous greens such as broccoli, Chinese broccoli, broccoli rabe, cauliflower, kale, collard greens, bok choy, cabbage, kohlrabi, mustard, turnip, radish, watercress, and arugula have a potent anticancer compound called *sulforaphane*. Sulforaphane is transformed by the enzyme myrosinase when cruciferous greens are cut, chopped, or chewed, creating the active anticancer form. If you've ever eaten some fresh broccoli sprouts or mustard greens, you can taste the "spicy" flavor resulting from this chemical reaction. Note that myrosinase is deactivated by heat, so be certain to chop greens and allow them to sit for a few minutes before cooking so that the reaction can take place. Mustard powder, wasabi, and daikon radish also contain the same enzyme, myrosinase, and can be added to cooked cruciferous vegetables to jumpstart the reaction.

MIXED GREENS

Certain cancers, such as those found in the breast, are dependent on the amino acid methionine. Studies have found that cultures of normal breast tissue survive methionine restriction, but cultures of cancerous breast tissue quickly die. This relates to our discussion in Chapter 4 on amino acid restriction. A whole food, plant-based diet naturally restricts some amino acids, such as methionine, and may help prevent or slow the progression of cancerous growths even before they are large enough to be detected.

Because there are many types of cancers, multiple variables contributing to its initiation and progression, and a long lag time between the initiation of the disease and the development of symptoms, it is extraordinarily challenging to connect dietary patterns to cancer outcomes. However, you have absolutely nothing to lose by using food as part of your prevention or treatment plan. At worst, it's inexpensive, painless, and nutritious; but, at best, whole plants may help.

Hypertension

More than one third of the U.S. population has diagnosed hypertension, or high blood pressure. Defined as a blood pressure greater than 140/90 mmHg, this condition is a primary risk factor for heart disease and stroke. Hypertension is also both a cause and a result of kidney disease.

Diet and lifestyle have been consistently found to contribute significantly to elevated blood pressure. Plant-based eaters have lower blood pressure and lower incidence of hypertension than non-plant-based eaters.

Reducing sodium intake has long been promoted as a treatment for people with hypertension. However, this conventional wisdom is controversial. For salt-sensitive individuals, this dietary adjustment may certainly be beneficial. For optimal efficacy, treatment emphasis should be on weight management, exercise, and eating a whole food, plant-based diet.

High Cholesterol

Another primary risk factor for heart disease is a high cholesterol level. Over 100 million U.S. adults have total cholesterol higher than 200 mg/dL (considered the threshold for diagnosis of hyperlipidemia) and almost 31 million have a total cholesterol level above 240 mg/dL. The American Heart Association recommends maintaining a blood cholesterol level of less than 200 mg/dL, but the research shows that heart attacks very rarely occur in people with a total cholesterol level of under 150 mg/dL. Ideally, your LDL (low-density lipoprotein) should be less than 100 mg/dL, and your HDL (high-density lipoprotein) should be above 40 mg/dL.

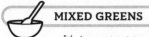 **MIXED GREENS**

It's important to note that with a lowering of total cholesterol, HDL, the "good" cholesterol, commonly decreases, too. The role of HDL is to remove cholesterol from the blood. With less cholesterol to be removed, the need for HDL is naturally lessened. Although lower HDL levels are typically seen in plant-based populations, this is accompanied by a decreased incidence of coronary heart disease.

Cholesterol-lowering medications, especially statins, are among the most widely used drugs. Although they do what they intend (lower blood cholesterol levels), they fail to address the source of the high cholesterol. Worse, they can be toxic to the liver. No medication comes without side effects. Always opt for the drug-free path, if possible.

Cholesterol levels respond rather rapidly to diet change. Within 3 weeks of following a whole food, plant-based plan, especially one with plenty of fiber, your cholesterol profile can take a dramatic turn for the better. Fiber acts like a sponge in your body. It soaks up cholesterol and accompanies it out of your body.

Osteoporosis

Bone is living, dynamic tissue made up of protein embedded with minerals. Calcium is the most abundant mineral found in bone, but phosphorus, magnesium, sodium, potassium, fluoride, and chloride are also present.

Bone strength is determined by bone mineral density (BMD), or the amount of minerals in any volume of bone. After age 25 or 30, bone minerals naturally start to break down. When this process appears to be accelerated, one of two diagnoses is made: osteopenia or osteoporosis. Osteopenia is a condition in which BMD appears to be lower than normal and is considered a precursor to osteoporosis. Osteoporosis is a crippling disease that increases your risk of bone fractures. Pain, disability, diminished quality of life, and—with hip fractures—increased risk of mortality are all potential complications of osteoporosis. The disease is most common in postmenopausal women. Clinically diagnosed osteoporosis is similar between strict plant eaters and omnivores; abstaining from animal products doesn't increase risk of osteoporosis.

Claims of osteoporosis becoming epidemic have made headline news recently. Bone-building medications are flying off the physician's prescription pads as quickly as milk off supermarket shelves. However, several caveats are evident. For the pharmaceutical, medical, supplement, and food industries, tremendous financial opportunities can be gained with medical tests, medications, supplements, and dairy products. More people with diagnosed osteoporosis equal more money to be made.

Ironically, the medications used to treat osteoporosis are not as effective as the drug manufacturers lead you to believe. Some have even been found to be dangerous. Reports have surfaced of these drugs causing esophageal cancer, heart damage, muscle pain, and other complications.

Many factors are at play when it comes to optimizing bone health, as described in Chapter 7. To reduce your risk of osteoporosis and support optimal bone mineralization, emphasize …

Daily exercise, especially resistance-based exercise.

Plenty of sunshine and possibly vitamin D supplements, if you're deficient.

Foods rich in calcium, vegetable protein, isoflavones, phytoestrogens, omega-3 fatty acids, and vitamins K, C, and B_{12}.

Gastrointestinal Illnesses

What you put into your body via your gastrointestinal (GI) tract is your inside's direct link to the outside world. Your GI tract acts as a filter, deciding what may pass into the bloodstream and what has to keep traveling back out. In fact, the GI system plays a crucial role in immune function. Hence, your immune system is greatly determined by your gut health. Ultimately, every bite determines your overall well-being. A nutrient-deficient diet plus an influx of pro-inflammatory and pro-oxidative compounds virtually destroys your body, beginning in your mouth.

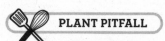

PLANT PITFALL

Carrageenan is an algae-derived ingredient used for gelling, thickening, and stabilizing food products, as well as in cosmetics, pharmaceuticals, and other applications. Some past evidence raised concerns that carrageenan may pose a risk of harmful inflammation in the intestines. More recently, authorities around the world have concluded that the use of carrageenan in food is safe. If you have intestinal issues and notice products containing this ingredient irritates you, you may consider avoiding it.

Chronic GI disorders are more prevalent than ever, and people suffer needlessly because of them. It's time to address these overly common problems by looking at the obvious—what's on your plate.

Gastroesophageal Reflux Disease

Gastroesophageal reflux disease (GERD), also known simply as reflux or heartburn, is a chronic condition caused by the regurgitation of stomach acid back up into the esophagus. Not only is GERD painful, but it can also lead to serious complications such as inflammation, ulcers, or cancer in the esophagus.

Antacids, commonly used to treat symptoms of GERD, contain high levels of aluminum, which are toxic to the brain and contribute to dementia and Alzheimer's disease. Instead of popping pills, modify your diet to avoid GERD. Behaviors that can alleviate GERD include eating a high-fiber, low-fat diet; avoiding eating past the point of comfortably full; eliminating spicy foods; sitting upright for a few hours after eating to allow the food to digest; and raising the head of your bed by 4 to 6 inches.

Inflammatory Bowel Disease

Inflammatory bowel disease (IBD) consists of two inflammatory conditions of the intestines: ulcerative colitis and Crohn's disease. Symptoms are similar between the two and include diarrhea, abdominal pain, cramping, bloody stools, and mucus. Meat, eggs, dairy, and alcohol exacerbate symptoms of these painful and debilitating diseases. Still, scientists haven't been able to establish either the cause or dietary management.

A higher prevalence of IBD is found in populations that eat meat-rich, highly processed, Westernized diets. Foods considered irritating to IBD sufferers vary, but certain ones such as alcohol, caffeine, soft drinks, wheat, sugar, high-fat foods, and yeast are common. Because of the minimized nutrient absorption found in IBD, especially during flare-ups, a nutrient-dense, plant-based diet is critical to ensure adequate intakes.

Additionally, a probiotics regimen may help support a healthy colon. Plant sources of probiotics—naturally occurring live microorganisms known to help balance the microflora in your intestinal microbiome—include miso, tempeh, sauerkraut, and plant-based yogurts. Probiotics are also available in supplement form.

Irritable Bowel Syndrome

Approximately 11 percent of adults globally suffer from irritable bowel syndrome (IBS), a chronic condition characterized by abdominal pain, cramping, bloating, and constipation and/or diarrhea. The cause of IBS perplexes health-care professionals, but it has been attributed to depression, bacterial infection, immune insufficiency, food intolerances, and stress. For some, IBS is debilitating, drastically impacting daily life.

Although medications are regularly included in treatment protocol, they're usually ineffective and, as usual, address the symptoms and not the cause. Trying to manage this disease with a high-fiber, low-fat diet along with adequate fluids may prove more beneficial. Adding foods like flaxseeds and probiotics may also improve symptoms.

Often, people suffering with IBS may have unknown food intolerances or allergies. Wheat is a common irritant, so eliminating it might help. Ask your physician to test you for possible intolerances or allergies if you've been struggling with IBS symptoms.

Diverticular Disease

Considered a fiber-deficiency disease, diverticular disease is characterized by outpouching and inflammation of the intestinal wall. Fiber increases stool bulk, thereby aiding its passage through the colon.

Higher fiber intake is one reason plant-based eaters enjoy a much lower incidence of this condition. High-fiber, low-fat diets in addition to exercise prevent diverticular disease.

Celiac Sprue

Celiac sprue, also known as *celiac disease* or *gluten-sensitive enteropathy*, is an autoimmune chronic disease of the digestive tract that interferes with the digestion and absorption of nutrients from food. Between 0.5 and 1.0 percent of the population in different parts of the world have been diagnosed with the condition. Possibly many more cases go undiagnosed because of misdiagnosis and symptoms similar to those of food intolerances and allergies. People with celiac sprue can't tolerate gluten, a protein found in wheat, barley, and rye, as well as in some oats through cross-contamination. When consumed, celiac sufferers endure damage to the *villi* that line the intestinal tract and enable nutrient absorption. Major concerns with celiac sprue include malnutrition and the onset of other diseases such as lymphoma or other cancers, type 1 diabetes, liver disease, lupus, rheumatoid arthritis, and thyroiditis.

 **DEFINITION**

Villi are tiny, fingerlike protrusions that line the small intestines and allow absorption of nutrients from the intestines into the bloodstream.

Eliminating all foods and products containing gluten is the only treatment option. With a bit of information and some practice, avoiding gluten will become second nature, and a well-balanced diet is easily attained. In recent years, a whole marketplace has opened for gluten-free living. Labeling of gluten has become mandatory, and thousands of alternatives to gluten are widely available. Entire stores dedicated to gluten-free shopping and restaurants with gluten-free menus are spreading rapidly.

Ingredients with gluten include wheat and wheat products (bran, bread, bread products, wheat germ, wheat meal, wheat pasta, wheat starch, white flour, durum, wheat berries, red wheat flakes, starch, vital wheat gluten, seitan, modified food starch, modified starch, bread flour, semolina, farina, shredded wheat, wheat protein powder, cake flour); bulgur; triticale; rye; texturized vegetable protein; texturized soy protein; hydrolyzed vegetable protein; kamut; spelt; oats; barley; couscous; graham flour and graham crackers; vegetable gum; gelatinized starch; and beers, ales, and malted drinks. Look on food labels for "contains wheat" or "gluten-free" to be certain.

Carefully watching your diet is critical with celiac sprue because of the serious health complications associated with continued villi destruction.

Other Conditions

Several other chronic medical conditions have increasingly become commonplace. As poor diets become more prevalent, resultant disease ensues. Reducing risk of and treating the following illnesses with proper nutrition have shown astonishing promise and success.

Autoimmune Disease

Your immune system is a collection of powerful tools designed to resist the constant onslaught of foreign invaders, including bacteria, viruses, and parasites. In millions of Americans (a majority of whom are women), the immune system goes awry and begins attacking itself. More than 80 diseases can be classified as autoimmune, including multiple sclerosis (MS), rheumatoid arthritis (RA), systemic lupus erythematosus (SLE), scleroderma, type 1 diabetes, and inflammatory bowel disease (IBD; discussed earlier in this chapter). Each condition bears its own set of symptoms and progression of those symptoms, some localized to one body part and others systemic.

Treatment goals are to manage symptoms, delay progression, and maintain the body's ability to fight disease. Some situations call for immunosuppressants, drugs that slow immune function and increase risk of other infections.

Certain dietary interventions have shown success in reducing inflammation and medication requirements. A strict nutrient-dense diet omitting all animal products and processed foods has been found to be effective. Hidden food intolerances or sensitivities may exist, and therefore need to be assessed so they can be eliminated. Vitamin D has been implicated in autoimmune disease, especially MS, so maintain optimal blood levels of it (see Chapter 10).

Earlier in the disease process is the time to be aggressive with your diet because once the disease progresses, whatever function has been lost cannot be reversed.

Kidney Disease

An estimated 30 million, or 15 percent of U.S. adults suffer with chronic kidney disease (CKD). More than half a million people are treated for end-stage renal disease (ESRD), an illness in which the kidneys are unable to function adequately and require dialysis and/or a transplant.

The variety of pathology—or diseases—that occurs in the kidneys is vast and can be brought about in many different ways. The two leading causes of CKD in the United States are diabetes and high blood pressure. Other common causes include various types of chronic excessive protein intake (especially animal protein), toxicity from medications (like over-the-counter pain relievers), and *metabolic syndrome.*

Plant-based diets may help prevent and manage CKD. Both the amount and type of protein consumed impact your kidneys. High protein intake (especially from animal protein) increases *glomerular filtration rate* (*GFR*). Essentially, an increased GFR means more work for your kidneys. Plant eaters also have lower blood pressure and cholesterol levels, factors known to contribute to CKD incidence and progression when high.

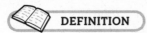 **DEFINITION**

> **Metabolic syndrome** is a cluster of conditions, including obesity, high cholesterol, hypertension, and high blood sugar, that lead to vascular and other chronic diseases. **Glomerular filtration rate (GFR),** used to measure kidney function, is the rate at which fluid filters through the kidneys.

Dementia and Alzheimer's Disease

Dementia and Alzheimer's disease are progressive diseases of the brain that are still not clearly understood. Fortunately, you have more control over the prevention and management of both diseases than you may think.

Alzheimer's disease is the most common cause of dementia and is diagnosed specifically by the presence of senile plaques, beta-amyloid tangles, and neurofibrillary tangles inside the brain.

Treat your blood vessels well to avoid dementia and Alzheimer's disease as well as heart disease, stroke, and even erectile dysfunction. Your cardiovascular system is made up of arteries, veins, and capillaries, with your heart as the pump. These blood vessels supply nutrients and oxygen throughout your entire body, from the top of your head to the tips of your toes. Atherosclerosis, the hardening of arteries, can and does occur in any of the blood vessels. Furthermore, a high cholesterol level lends itself to all the aforementioned chronic diseases.

Dementia is a chronic deterioration of cognition that usually affects the elderly. Many varied causes are attributed, including Alzheimer's disease, vascular disease (atherosclerosis, stroke), infections, structural brain disorders (like tumors or bleeding), depression, and drugs. The progression of dementia varies according to the person, and the severity lies on a continuum. Signs of dementia include short-term memory loss; impaired ability to plan, organize, or sequence abstractly; inability to articulate ideas; and inability to make purposeful movements.

High blood cholesterol levels and atherosclerosis increase your risk of developing dementia and Alzheimer's disease. Logically, these conditions are more prevalent in populations that eat a diet high in fat, dairy, and meat than in those following a plant-based diet. Consuming a diet rich in phytonutrients and antioxidants reduces your risk.

Gout

A painful inflammatory disease, gout causes painful uric acid–crystal formation in the joints, usually the toes. Uric acid is a breakdown product of purines, a class of aromatic organic compounds that are found in plant and animal tissues. Technically speaking, there are no purine-free diets, but increased risks of gout are associated with higher consumption of meat and fish, but not with high consumption of purine-rich plant foods. While there are still many guidelines that promote the restriction of purine-rich plant foods, no long-term study has ever found this to be effective. Research suggests that dietary restriction may be only applicable to purines of animal origin. In fact, purine-rich plant foods that gout sufferers are specifically told to avoid—such as beans, lentils, peas, asparagus, mushrooms, and cauliflower—have been found to be protective. This seemingly paradoxical issue may be due to the higher fiber levels that potentially bind uric acid in the gut for elimination. Furthermore, foods rich in folate and vitamin C appear to reduce the levels of uric acid accumulation. In addition to restricting animal foods high in purines, limiting alcohol is also recommended to alleviate symptoms of gout. Animal food sources high in purines include seafood, fish, red meat, and organ meats (liver, kidney, heart, and sweetbreads).

By now, you probably notice a trend. Diet plays a huge role in most illnesses common in the standard American diet and the rest of the Western world. Eating a whole food, plant-based diet prevents and reverses most of these conditions, enabling you to enjoy the freedom associated with true health.

The Least You Need to Know

- Chronic diseases like diabetes, heart disease, osteoporosis, and cancer may be prevented and even reversed by lifestyle modification.
- High blood pressure and high cholesterol are two risk factors for heart disease that are controllable with diet.
- Exercising consistently is the most important action you can take to protect your bones from osteoporosis.
- A vast majority of illnesses can be prevented and will respond favorably by eating a diet high in phytonutrients, fiber, antioxidants, vitamins, and minerals.

The Plant-Based Recipe Box

Now that you know why whole food, plant-based nutrition can rock your world in the best way possible, it's time to get cooking and eating! In Part 4, we share strategies to help you maintain an environment in which health-promoting foods are constantly available.

Being a plant eater need not turn you into a recluse. Dining out is easy if you know what to look for, as is attending social gatherings. In Chapter 17, we fill in all the odds and ends on how to master these techniques.

And for all the times you're happily at home, Chapters 18 and 19 give you a simple formula so that you're ready to cook at the first strike of hunger. You learn how to stock your kitchen and substitute ingredients so you can always have delicious plant fare at your fingertips. We also show you how to nutrify your favorite recipes, and we share some new ones—more than 45 in all!—to add to your collection. Being prepared is the key to long-term triumph.

À votre santé! To your health!

CHAPTER 17

Plant-Based in the Real World

After learning all about plant-based nutrition in the preceding chapters, your curiosity and enthusiasm must be bursting at the seams! Ready to take it on-the-go?

While the rest of the world rapidly catches up and as the buzz progressively grows louder, you'll still find a few challenges to contend with when eating away from home. Regardless, a little careful thought goes a long way and helps sustain you on your path of plant-based bliss.

In This Chapter

- An ounce of preparation is worth a pound of hunger
- Plant-based dining out and about
- Wholesome holiday eating
- Plant-based entertaining

Lessons in Preparation

In life, luck happens when opportunity meets preparation. No matter the goal, you should always be prepared to face obstacles. A little homework and planning make every situation flow smoothly.

At home, you can easily arrange to have a plethora of plants available to eat at all times by shopping regularly and preparing some basic items. A major benefit of eating at home is that you always know what's going into your meals when you're making them yourself. The stability, flexibility, and comfort of having control are key components to maintaining ease in your eating.

However, it's not always possible, or even fun, to hang out at home all the time. Being a recluse is not a prerequisite for a healthy diet! As a matter of fact, dining out and enjoying meals at the homes of your friends and family are fantastic opportunities. Not only do you get to experience dishes created by someone besides yourself, but you also have the chance to inspire and motivate others.

So let's get packing, strategizing methods to bring the plant-based world along for the ride!

Fail to Plan, Plan to Fail

Who likes being stuck in a meaty situation where you have no options? Rather than finding yourself uncomfortably starving with no whole plants to devour, plan out every adventure. Traveling? Bring enough food with you to last until you'll be near dining options. At work all day? Pack snacks and meals, or search out appropriate nearby restaurants to obtain adequate nutrition. Think like a scout, and treat every occasion as an adventure.

Planning is pleasurable because you'll derive comfort from knowing you'll have food as needed. Plus, you'll enjoy opportunities for new discoveries. Who knew a great plant-based restaurant was within walking distance from your workplace? Look at how many grab-and-eat choices are available at your local grocery store! Fine-tune your whole-plant vision, and the world will open itself to you. You need never go hungry nor feel isolated in any situation again!

Packing Meals and Snacks

When packing a to-go lunch, so many opportunities for creativity abound. You can vary your options from simple to gourmet, depending on where you're going and what you have on hand at home.

Plant foods travel exceedingly well. Some, in fact, are born ready to go straight from nature. Whole fruits are nature's portable candy—just rinse and enjoy anywhere and anytime. Visit your local farmers' market regularly to stock up on freshly picked, direct-from-the-farm produce. Raw nuts and seeds are also quick to grab and offer nutrient-dense, hunger-satiating calories.

HEALTHY HINT

In the bulk section of your supermarket, buy large bags of dried fruits, raw nuts, and raw seeds so you can whip up your own bags of trail mix. These make an easy, satisfying whole-food snack that lasts a long time, requires no refrigeration, and travels compactly.

Have you noticed the wall of nutrition bars in the market nowadays? Dozens of options line the shelves. Because of their convenience factor, nutrition bars are big sellers, and some can fit into your whole food, plant-based diet.

When selecting a bar, be sure the ingredients list contains only whole foods. Fortunately, this requirement won't limit you much because several product lines are based on whole foods. Stock up on these, and use them as an emergency snack. They'll stay fresh for months (always read expiration dates, of course, because the more whole the product, the fewer preservatives to extend freshness), and they travel extremely well.

You can even make your own bars at home, such as the Figamajigs in Chapter 23. Although they don't last as long, they're delicious, and the ingredients are 100 percent under your control.

Leftovers can make exciting and satisfying on-the-go meals. Invest in storage containers—preferably glass or stainless steel instead of plastic or aluminum—with tight-fitting lids. Last night's dinner usually tastes better the next day after the flavors have had time to meld. Casseroles, soups, stir-fries, salads, loaves, grains, legumes, and patties all travel easily with the proper storage containers.

Sandwiches offer no limit to creativity. Using tortillas, rice wrappers, or nori sheets as wraps or sprouted, whole-grain breads for classic sandwiches, you can create masterpieces. Imaginative style options include sushi, Noritos (see recipe in Chapter 20), burritos, and traditional sandwich fashion. Add spreads like hummus, guacamole, bean dip, and nut butters, and top with sliced, chopped, or whole veggies to boost phytonutrients, textures, and flavors. Banana slices with nut butter is a delicious classic. Hummus goes gorgeously with tomatoes and cucumbers. Sprouts can be added to any spread to really kick it up a nutrient notch. Of course, glorious greens should be used at any opportunity for every nutritional benefit.

If you want to forego the sandwich, turn the spreads into dips by packing them in small containers. Bring along dippers like cut carrots, bell peppers, celery, jicama, or other veggies; corn or rice thins; or homemade pita or tortilla chips.

HEALTHY HINT

Baked potatoes—any variety, but especially sweet potatoes or yams—are decadent, nutrient-filled snacks. Bake several at a time and store them in the fridge. Grab one when you're on the way out the door, and enjoy it either cold or warmed up.

Visiting the supermarket or health food store for quicker, last-minute choices is also an option. Convenience items have grown in abundance and variety. For a few extra cents (or bucks, depending on where you buy), you can have prewashed and precut veggies, salads, or fruits. These options are perfect if you have limited prep time. (To save money, prep your own in advance to grab and pack as needed.) Salad bars are more robust nowadays and brimming with healthful, whole-plant foods. If you're planning to travel by plane, train, or bus, bringing a huge salad will last you several hours and keep you happily crunching until you reach your destination. Include plenty of beans, lentils, grains, and seeds for more substantial sustainability.

Prepared foods are a little trickier to navigate because most recipes contain large amounts of oil, flour, sugar, salt, and animal products. Great take-out items at your market can include freshly made sushi vegetable rolls, plain cooked grains or legumes, steamed veggies, or baked potatoes. Sauces can be a killer, so avoid them unless you happen to know every ingredient included. Look for the cleanest, most natural choices, and don't be afraid to ask questions.

Dining Out

No restaurant is impossible to navigate, even with the strictest guidelines and highest hopes for a healthful meal. Ethnic cuisine offers tremendous variety in delicious plant-based fare. Even at a steakhouse, where the options seem narrow, you can create a meal to savor.

Check Menus Ahead of Time

Do you even remember life before the internet? Talk about the ultimate in convenience! Most restaurants now post their menus on their websites, so you have access to them at any time. Homework was never this easy! If you know ahead of time which restaurant you'll be dining at, take a look at the menu before you head out so you have time to make a careful decision.

If nothing seems to meet your criteria, you can also call ahead and ask if the chef is willing to work with you. Although the answer is almost always a resounding "Of course!", if the chef is less than accommodating, maybe choose another restaurant.

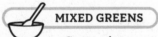 **MIXED GREENS**

Great websites are available now to help you pinpoint the type of restaurant that will cater to your needs. See Appendix D for recommendations.

Because many people have either food allergies or sensitivities, are on some sort of special diet, or have specific preferences, most food establishments are equipped to respond to such requests.

Nutrifying Any Restaurant

You're on a mission. At whichever restaurant you choose, you need to find whole-plant foods devoid of oil and other processed foods. An efficient method of selecting your perfect order should go like this: scan the menu in its entirety—from appetizers through desserts—and assess the whole-ness (or lack thereof) of the menu choices. Determine what sounds good to you by silently tuning in and asking yourself what you're hungry for. In the mood for something light? Starving and need something more substantial? If your choice is already full of colors, comes packed with fiber, and meets the criteria for the whole food, plant-based plan, you're ready to order.

Ask the waitperson if the dish can be prepared without oil and with any sauce or dressing on the side. If you plan on using sauces, be sure you know what's in them. Most sauces and dressings have oil, dairy, and a lot of salt. Ask if the restaurant has options without these ingredients. Typically safe choices include vinegars, mustard, fresh marinara sauce, fresh salsa, and fresh guacamole.

If no menu options pop off the page as plant friendly, don't worry. You can mix and match to create your own meal. Glance at all the individual items throughout the menu so you become familiar with what they have in the kitchen. Then request those items as a customized entrée.

HEALTHY HINT

Supplement whatever you order with a side salad or veggie side dishes. Ask for steamed veggies—or grilled, if the chef will prepare them without oil. Remember, the more color on your plate, the more blissful your cells.

Working with the Waitstaff and Chef

Most of the time, your waitperson and chef will be open to constructing a meal that meets your needs. Between the creativity inherent in a chef and the common endeavor for customer satisfaction, a request for something off the menu may be an inspiring challenge.

As long as you're pleasant, appreciative, and specific about what you want, a good restaurant will accommodate you as much as possible. Note that you will have a greater chance of success on a Tuesday night than on a busy Saturday. However, a good server or the manager will know what acceptable off-menu "standard" subs there are even at those busy times.

Finding Something at a Steakhouse

Surprisingly, it is sometimes easier to eat healthfully at a steakhouse than at many vegetarian or vegan restaurants, as these restaurants often give too many choices—many with excess sugar, oil, flour, and salt. Steakhouses often have amazing side dishes, and you'll be surprised how many chefs will whip up a veggie plate that will make the rest of the table drool with envy. Overall, different types of restaurants provide new prospects for whole, plant-based cuisine. Some have more options than others, but you'll almost always find enough to fill your belly. Brilliant menus at exclusively veg establishments are on the rise. Imagine what joy you'll feel when you find an entire menu that's plant friendly! All you need to be wary of is oil, agave, white breads, and other processed foods. Other than that, you can have a field day sampling inventive plant fare.

Traditional Asian cuisine is plant based. In rural Asian cultures, citizens thrive on rice, vegetables, and a bit of soy sauce for flavor. Westernized Chinese restaurants are meat-heavy but also typically offer steamed tofu, steamed vegetables, and brown rice. You can add a side salad with rice vinegar and Chinese mustard as a dressing. Beware of deep-fried dishes and rich sauces. Spring rolls with tofu and vegetables make for excellent appetizers as long as they're not fried.

Japanese food is plant friendly, with a wide variety of foods to choose from. Veggie sushi options include avocado rolls, vegetable rolls, and cucumber rolls. Other first-class choices include *sunomono* (cucumber salad); steamed, unsalted edamame (soybeans); and seaweed salad.

Many Indians traditionally maintain a vegetarian diet, so finding healthful options is easy at Indian restaurants. Additionally, Indian food is incredibly spiced, exploding with flavor, and tantalizing to the taste buds. Dishes such as *aloo gobi* (curried cauliflower and potatoes), vegetable biryani, and *chana masala* (curried, tomato-y chickpeas) are scrumptiously satisfying. Because most Indian restaurants go heavy on the oil, ask if you can have your servings oil-free or which dishes they serve already oil-free.

Nothing says "fiesta" like a Mexican meal. Screaming with the colors of the Mexican flag (red, white, and green), meals are spiced with cilantro and onion and are welcoming for plant eaters. Indulge with vegetable fajitas made oil-free and served with corn tortillas, rice and beans, and salad with salsa and guacamole—or a combination wrapped up into a burrito or taco. Be sure to ask for vegetarian beans as traditional refried beans are typically made with lard. When ordering veggie fajitas, ask if they will drop the sour cream and cheese and, perhaps, add some pineapple. You can also substitute beans in many of other Mexican dishes, for example tacos, enchiladas, or burritos. *Que rico!*

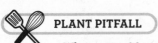 **PLANT PITFALL**

When eating Mexican, ask whether the beans are made with lard (animal fat) or pork, as this is common practice. Also be sure the rice isn't cooked in animal broth.

The biggest thing to remember is that one person's side dish is another person's entrée—you can order just sides. Explore your plant options in the side-dish category. Baked potatoes, steamed veggies, corn on the cob, brown rice, beans, salads, and asparagus are standard fare. Although this may not be your first choice, it's comforting to know you can find tasty whole foods to eat if the circumstances are out of your hands.

Holidays and Special Occasions

Holidays are cause for family and friends to unite, usually surrounding a shared meal. Once you adopt whole food, plant-based eating as a way of life, you want to tailor every aspect to optimize your well-being. Fortunately, special occasions can inspire new traditions still focused around celebration while honoring your whole-food goals.

PLANT PITFALL

Get-togethers tend to bring opportunities for others, who don't understand your journey, to question you about your choices. Respond honestly to questions, and be gentle, not preachy or judgmental. Your choices may bring to light the questioner's interest in healthful eating. Offer a copy of this book so he or she can explore the miraculous plant-based world!

Use the opportunity to explore inventive recipes and share your new world with the people closest to you. Win over your family and friends by introducing delectable foods. Woo them through their palates so they understand why you've easily revolutionized your diet. Show your loved ones how even a celebratory event presents no need for sacrifice. Whole-plant versions of almost every traditional dish you've known and loved your entire life are available—and, most importantly, are scrumptious.

How to Eat on the Holidays

Food and festivities define holiday culture. Healthful habits tend to fly out the window with the onslaught of parties, stress, and an abundance of junk foods perpetually dancing their way past your eyes and nose. So what's a whole-plant foodie to do?

To maintain consistency, focus on your goals and the pleasure of your accomplishments thus far. Eating a whole food, plant-based diet has changed your taste buds and every cell in your body. You've conquered your addictions. You may have even reversed your disease or stopped requiring medications. Using the holidays as an excuse to break your cycle of progress and achievement is counterproductive and can start a downward spiral back to your old habits. It's not worth it.

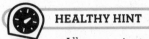 **HEALTHY HINT**

Allow exercise to be your rock throughout the holiday season (as well as the rest of the year). Rely on it, and it will consistently support your efforts to stay focused mentally, emotionally, and, of course, physically.

The allure and seduction of comfort foods originate from the situation in which you consumed them, not the foods themselves. You may crave pumpkin pie on Thanksgiving because you associate it with time spent with loved ones. The positive memories seduce your mind masked as pumpkin pie. Now is a critical time in your life to create new associations. Start an annual walk/run/hike with family and friends on Thanksgiving morning. Schedule a holiday green-smoothie competition with prizes for the yummiest concoctions. Join fellow plant eaters for potlucks and gatherings to celebrate birthdays and other special occasions. Create your new life, and make it joyful. Nothing in the world tastes better than excellent health feels.

To inspire you during the holidays, write down a specific set of goals to get you through the season. List your time-stamped, detailed, accountability-based goals on paper, and put that paper where you will see it at least once a day. Keep it in your pocket or purse, if you need to. Why do you need to maintain your new habits? What do you want to achieve in the next day, week, month, or year?

 **HEALTHY HINT**

New Year's resolutions are the perfect way for you to start your year. You can also write birthday resolutions if your birthday isn't too close to January 1. Let this be your introspective source for inspiration each year. What do you want to accomplish this year?

Logical methods can ensure plant-based holiday maintenance. You should never be in a situation where you're stuck without healthful options. Plan to succeed by thinking ahead.

When attending parties, ask the host if whole-plant options will be available, and regardless of the answer, offer to bring a dish. That way, you're guaranteed to have something you know you'll love. Most party fare includes some sort of veggies and fruit. To fill in the potential gaps, bring a hearty dish to serve as your main course. Dishes such as a lentil loaf, lasagna, or bean chili make great party favorites that will entice all the guests' curiosity. If you're extra motivated, bring a dessert as well, because whole-plant desserts are hard to come by.

At work during the holidays, the unwhole and unplant foods seem relentlessly in your face. Co-workers tend to incite sugar comas and fatty-food lethargy by inundating the office with not-so-healthy treats. No wonder people are sick so often around this time of year! The old tale of cold weather causing colds and flus is inaccurate and missing a crucial link. When your diet is inadequate, your immune system is compromised.

Fill your workspace with easy-to-grab goodies to keep temptation from taking over. Be sure you pack enough food to last you all day, and include treats you love. Remind yourself that if a piece of fresh fruit doesn't sound good, you probably aren't really hungry.

If the celebratory indulgences are becoming too much, take a walk to get some fresh air; drink hot tea; or reward yourself with a mental break by calling a friend, checking your favorite website, or listening to music with your earphones.

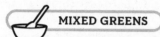

MIXED GREENS

Your support system is critical to your long-term success. Surround yourself with people who understand your intentions and who genuinely care about your outcomes.

Finally, experimenting with new recipes is always fun around the holidays, regardless of your nutrition plan. Stay tuned for tips on converting recipes to meet your needs in Chapter 19. Preparing wholesome plant cuisine stimulates all your senses and is a relaxing, educational, and pleasurable way to connect with your loved ones.

Entertaining with Veg Style

Excuses for entertaining are infinite. Whether it's for a small or large gathering, a holiday party or simple get-together, or a casual or sophisticated party, feeding gracious guests can be so satisfying. Enjoying nutritiously decadent plant fare is a superb way to bond and inspire.

If your guests aren't fellow plant eaters, don't pressure yourself into thinking this meal has to represent the be-all and end-all of whole-food cooking. Instead, choose your favorite dishes or explore new ones. You'll tantalize your visitors when you …

Use color copiously throughout the courses. Visual appeal initiates the journey of flavor.

Alter the textures and flavors among dishes. If each dish is similar in texture and/or flavor, it could get a little boring for your guests.

Choose a theme to add to the festivities. Mexican Fiesta, Poetry on a Plate, Autumnal Equinox, Beach Party, High Tea, 1980s Flashback, or Breakfast-for-Dinner are some ideas to spice up and focus your party.

Regardless of the occasion, entertain effortlessly by considering the meal a chance to share information and recipes and stimulate the senses. Open minds with a warm and welcoming home.

The Least You Need to Know

- Choose your own eating adventure by planning ahead. Be certain to bring adequate healthful choices to sustain you until you'll be somewhere plentiful in plants.

- Leftovers, sandwiches, wraps, and raw fruits and vegetables travel easily with some containers and a bit of imagination.

- Wise choices make for successful dining adventures and are possible in almost any restaurant.

- Never hesitate to ask questions when ordering at a restaurant. You need to know that what you're eating fits into your whole-food eating plan.

- Focus on your long-term goals during special occasions and holidays. Support your nutrient-dense, health-promoting diet by always having optimal food choices available, planning carefully, and surrounding yourself with support.

- Feeding friends and family wholesome plant delicacies is a decadent way to bond.

The Plant-Based Kitchen

Doesn't all this talk about wholesomely decadent plant provisions make you hungry? It's time to stock your kitchen with the staples necessary to make delicious, nutritious, plant-based meals at home.

In this chapter, we show you how to establish your new favorite foods, dishes, and tools by taking the time to try new techniques. Plus, we share tips on how you can substitute and replace some of your old ingredients—like eggs and cheese—with health-promoting versions by using a few tweaks and tricks.

In This Chapter

- Preparing your plant-friendly kitchen
- The culinary equipment you need
- Updating to wholesome alternatives

Stocking Up

Certain items should always be planted in your kitchen so you have the freedom to throw a dish together at a moment's notice. Of course, shelf- or freezer-stable ingredients can be stockpiled for longer without worrying about a rapid expiration date. Produce will naturally need to be replaced more regularly.

Stocking Your Pantry

A perfect plant-based pantry is ideally stocked with a variety of longer-lasting items, including these:

- Dried whole grains: amaranth, barley, buckwheat, bulgur, oats, millet, quinoa, rice (e.g. brown, red, purple, black, wild), teff, wheat berries

- Dried peas, lentils, and all beans (e.g. azuki, black, butter, cannellini, garbanzo, kidney, mung, navy, pinto)

- Shelf-stable almond, hemp, oat, soy, and other unsweetened, fortified plant milks

- Canned beans (ideally salt-free or low sodium and BPA-free)

- Canned or jarred corn, water chestnuts, artichoke hearts, and roasted red peppers (all packed in water)

- Canned or jarred tomato paste

- Canned tomatoes (chopped and whole)

- Fruit and vegetable purées like pumpkin, sweet potato, pear, and applesauce

- Raw nuts (e.g. almonds, Brazil nuts, cashews, walnuts) and seeds (e.g. chia, flax, hemp, pumpkin, sesame, sunflower)

- Raw nut and seed butters (e.g. almond butter, cashew butter, peanut butter, tahini)

- Olives

- Dried dates

- 100 percent pure date syrup (Find it in specialty stores.)

- 100 percent pure maple syrup

- Blackstrap molasses

- Hot sauces and salsas

- Vinegars (e.g. apple cider, balsamic, red wine, rice wine, white)

- Tamari or low-sodium soy sauce

- Whole-grain pasta (corn, brown rice, quinoa, soy, whole-wheat)

- Whole-grain crackers, corn thins, and brown-rice cakes

- Whole-grain, legume, and nut flours (almond, barley, buckwheat, chickpea, oat, and whole-wheat, for example)

- Dried fruits

- Sun-dried tomatoes

- Raw cacao nibs

- Cocoa powder

To stay well supplied, maintain ongoing shopping lists. As soon as you open the last of an item from your pantry, add it to your list for the next time you go food shopping. That way, you won't forget and will always have those ingredients ready when you need them.

What's in the Fridge?

How delightful is it to open your refrigerator and see bright, colorful options ready to be devoured whenever hunger strikes? All you need is a bit of planning and a shopping/prepping plan to keep you fully supplied. The refrigerator represents a temporary storage house where perishables move quickly and, ideally, are consumed in appropriate time.

In your fridge, store the following:

- Open plant milks, sauces, tahini, salsas, mustards, vinegars, and salad dressings

- Open packages of nuts, seeds, and nut or seed butters

- Fresh veggies

- Salads and salad mixes

- Leftovers

- Cut fruits

- Whole-fruit jams

- Fresh dill, rosemary, basil, cilantro, parsley, thyme, and other herbs

- Tofu

- Tempeh

- Jars of minced garlic and ginger

- Whole-grain corn, brown-rice, whole-wheat, or sprouted-grain tortillas and breads

To boost convenience and maintain an easy-grab situation to keep you on track, always keep cut veggies and fruits, salad, soup, and bean dip in your fridge. These foods make perfect snacks and supplements to your main dish. You can also keep batches of leftover grains or beans to toss into whatever you're preparing for dinner. Bags of prewashed leafy greens are ideal for quickly throwing together your morning green smoothie, so keep those handy, too.

Foods from the Freezer

Your freezer can be a convenience dream come true if you know how to use it the right way. Take advantage of extra time or leftovers by freezing full meals and saving them for occasions when you're too busy to cook. Make extra portions when you do have cooking opportunities or food-prep fests, and freeze the extras in freezer-friendly storage containers. Also, sustain an adequate supply in your freezer of the following:

- Frozen bananas and other fruits

- Frozen corn, peas, greens, broccoli, mushrooms, and other vegetables and mixed blends

- Precooked brown rice, oats, quinoa, and other grains

- Whole-fruit ice pops or sorbet

 **HEALTHY HINT**

Frozen bananas make green smoothies divine by hiding any bitterness from the greens and providing a creamy texture. Buy extra bananas every week, and when they reach the state of ripeness you prefer, peel them, break them into halves or thirds, and store them in freezer storage containers in the freezer.

Herbs and Spices

Plain salt and pepper are so … well, plain. Today's seasoning zing originates from creative blends, fresh herbs, and organic dried spices. Why be bland when you can explode with flavor? Bring out the essence of whole-plant foods by experimenting with seasonings.

Herbs are plants valued for their aromas, flavors, or medicinal qualities. The most commonly used fresh herbs include the following:

- Basil
- Chives
- Cilantro
- Dill
- Mint

- Oregano
- Parsley
- Rosemary
- Sage
- Thyme

These herbs can be used dried as well.

Spices are any of a variety of dried seeds, roots, bars, fruits, or leaves used to add flavors, colors, or antimicrobial properties to foods. Classic dried spices commonly used include the following:

- Allspice
- Anise
- Cardamom
- Cayenne
- Chiles
- Chipotle
- Cinnamon
- Cloves
- Coriander
- Cumin
- Curry
- Fennel
- Garlic powder
- Ginger
- Lemongrass

- Mace
- Marjoram
- Mustard
- Nutmeg
- Onion powder
- Oregano
- Paprika
- Paprika (smoked)
- Peppers (white, black, or pink)
- Red pepper flakes
- Sage
- Star anise
- Sumac
- Thyme
- Turmeric

If you're ready to have some real fun (or you need help with being daringly flavorful), spice blends are for you. Sprinkle them on any mix of legumes, grains, and veggies to create a flavor sensation. Check the ingredient list to be sure your store-bought blends are salt-free. And always remember that less is more when experimenting. You can always add more, but you can't take it out once it's in!

The following table lists the spices used to create popular spice blends. (Note that blends vary by brand.)

Popular Spice Blends

Blend Name	Ingredients
Chili powder	Garlic powder, onion powder, ground cumin, ground oregano, ground allspice
Chinese five-spice powder	Ground star anise, ground fagara, ground cassia seeds, ground cloves, ground fennel seeds
Curry powder	Ground red chiles, ground coriander seeds, ground mustard seeds, ground black peppercorns, ground fenugreek seeds, ground ginger, ground turmeric
Garam masala	Ground cumin, ground coriander seeds, ground cardamom, ground black peppercorns, ground cloves, ground cinnamon, ground mace, ground bay leaves
Herbes de Provence	Basil, fennel, marjoram, rosemary, sage, thyme
Jerk seasoning	Minced dried chiles, ground thyme, ground cinnamon, ground ginger, ground allspice, ground cloves, minced dried garlic, minced dried onions
Pickling spice	Mustard seeds, red pepper flakes, allspice berries, dill seed, cinnamon stick, mace, whole cloves, bay leaves, dried ginger
Quatre-Épices	Grated nutmeg, ground whole cloves, ground ginger, ground black peppercorns
Zahtar	Ground sumac, roasted sesame seeds, dried thyme

Dried herbs and spices are stronger in flavor than their fresh counterparts due to a concentration of phytochemicals in the dried form. Basically, you're getting more of the herb or spice because the water is taken out. Store dried varieties in a cool, dark, dry location to maintain freshness.

The general rule for measuring fresh versus dried herbs is that 1 tablespoon fresh is the equivalent of 1 teaspoon dried. Powdered versions are even more potent than crumbled because they disperse throughout the food more easily. You can alternate between the two based on the recipe requirements and what you have in your kitchen or garden. Fresh is ideal in terms of flavor but much less convenient than dried. Dried spices are shelf-stable for 2 or 3 years when kept in a cool, dry place in airtight containers. You can tell that a dried spice is no longer good when its aroma disappears.

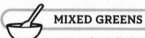 **MIXED GREENS**

User-friendly kits to grow your own herb garden abound. You can cultivate your own herbs in your kitchen, backyard, or anywhere else you like. Whether you have a green thumb or not, fresh and fragrant herbs can be yours with ease.

New to herbs and spices and not sure what to use with what? No problem! The following table outlines some commonly recognized herbs and spices used around the world in traditional cuisines.

Spices Around the World

Region	Herbs and Spices
Asian	Cinnamon, cloves, fennel, peppers, star anise
Indian	Coriander, cumin, curry, mustard, turmeric
Italian	Basil, oregano, parsley, rosemary, thyme
Mediterranean	Cumin, garlic, onion, pepper, turmeric
Mexican	Basil, chili powder, cilantro, cumin, onion
Southwestern United States	Chili powder, garlic, onion powder, paprika
Thai	Chili, cilantro, lemongrass, Thai basil

Equipped to Veg Out

Nothing special is required to be a full-fledged whole-plant foodie. Any basically equipped kitchen is adequate to get you started. Of course, gadgets and equipment are available to do all sorts of fancy tricks and to make life easier. So you can stay basic or indulge your technical or curious side, depending on your budget and preferences.

Basic Appliances

Two of the most valuable small appliances for your kitchen are a food processor and a blender. Your food processor doesn't have to be top-of-the-line to get the job done, but having something to chop, mix, slice, grate, mince, and shred saves you time and increases your productivity.

If you can invest in one item for your kitchen, it should be a high-powered blender. This appliance is so strong, it could turn a hockey puck into liquid. Making green smoothies with one of these powerhouses is simple because nothing combines and liquefies with the same gusto. There are smaller "bullet" blenders that do a fantastic job on dressings and sauces. You can even travel with them on longer trips.

An immersion blender is an inexpensive, super-handy tool that allows you to bring the blender to the food instead of the other way around. Ideal for puréeing hot soup right in the pan, it's easy to use and clean.

Rice/vegetable steamers are useful because they enable you to make whole grains as simply as possible. Just add the grain and the water in the appropriate ratio, and push the setting. Voilà! Within minutes, you have perfectly steamed grains without a mess, a burnt pot, or the need to stir every few minutes. Plus, the steamer keeps it warm until you're ready to serve your meal. You can also throw in your veggies at the end for an easy steam. Also consider the newer Asian "fuzzy logic" rice cookers. These use microcomputers to generate more complex cooking profiles and really change the texture and flavor of rice, especially brown.

Slow cookers are ideal in the plant-based kitchen. Slow cookers' set-it-and-forget-it ease of use makes cooking meals effortless. If you can open ingredients, you can have delicious dishes ready to eat whenever you are.

Other equipment, like pressure cookers, juicers, dehydrators, and coffee grinders, are some beyond-the-basic small appliances that will inspire you or save you time.

Handy Utensils

A good set of knives is crucial. Plant eaters spend much time chopping away and need to maximize efficiency as much as possible. Most important are a chef's knife, a serrated bread knife, a smaller serrated knife (for cutting tomatoes), and a paring knife. Your chef's knife will become an attachment to your hand because you need it to chop and prep veggies frequently. Invest in one you love, and to make chopping time trouble-free, keep it sharp with an effective sharpener.

Kitchen scissors are a must-have for cutting veggies and herbs and opening bags. You may consider doubling up on the scissors, reserving one for food only to prevent cross-contamination.

You'll also need a cutting board. Bamboo is a sustainable material, it's beautiful, and it doesn't contain the harmful chemicals found in plastic. Another perk of omitting animal products is that you don't need separate cutting boards for meats and produce to prevent cross-contamination.

 **PLANT PITFALL**

Plastics are ubiquitous, found in everything from wrappers, storage containers, and food products to baby bottles and toys. As convenient and accommodating as plastic is, it also comes with health implications. Chemicals found in plastics, such as dioxins, phthalates, and bisphenol A (BPA), are known to damage the immune system, alter hormones, and cause cancer.

Peelers, zesters, and graters are utensils mandatory for certain effects. You'll need one of each to help massage the phyto-fabulous complexes out of citrus, roots, potatoes, and more.

Must-Haves and Lovely Luxuries

Pots, pans, and mixing bowls are essential in any kitchen. Depending on how many people you're cooking for and what types of recipes you typically conjure up, the sizes and shapes you need may vary. The materials these items are made from matter most. Plastics, many metals (like aluminum), and nonstick coatings release toxins into your foods as they cook or as foods just come into contact with these surfaces. Choose cast iron, stainless steel, bamboo, glass, enamel, or silicone as safe and functional options.

Measuring cups and spoons are also kitchen fundamentals. Aim for glass or stainless steel with clearly defined measurements.

You'll also need a colander, a can opener, spatulas, large wooden spoons, a ladle, tongs, a whisk, baking sheets, and oven mitts.

Now for the "lovely luxuries." These items aren't critical but add opulence and flair. Included in this category are the following: wooden citrus reamer, apple corer, veggie chopper, tofu press, mandoline, spiral slicer, (plant) milk frother, garlic press, mezzaluna, melon baller, and silicone bakeware.

Plant-Based Substitutions

Afraid you'll miss your go-to favorites? Hooked on meat or cheese? Wonder how to bake without eggs? If so, check out the sparkling substitutions in the plant world. These alternatives not only taste luscious but are also healthful!

Egg Replacements

Eggs are versatile in both cooking and baking. The high protein and fat content help bind, leaven, and thicken and also increase tenderness, volume, and richness. Fortunately, you have several options when it comes to egg substitutions, depending on what type of recipe you're creating.

Commercial egg replacers (like Follow Your Heart, Ener-G, or Bob's Red Mill), commonly found in most health food stores, are typically flavorless and can, therefore, be used in a sweet or savory dish. You must add water to these powders to create an egg-like consistency. Follow the directions on the package for the accurate ratio.

Soft tofu works magnificently in quiches, scrambles, frittatas, or egg salads. Sometimes crumbled firmer tofu provides a more similar texture to cooked egg. Adding turmeric turns the tofu yellow and, in some dishes, might be unrecognizable to unsuspecting tasters. For baked good, blending silken tofu with liquid ingredients until smooth doesn't change the flavor but makes the result heavier. This technique is ideal for brownies. When making substitutions, ¼ cup blended soft tofu is the equivalent of 1 large egg.

When baking, smashed or puréed fruits work wonders. Substitute ½ banana or ¼ cup puréed fruit like applesauce per 1 egg.

Flax "eggs" are awe-inspiring. When made correctly, they look, feel, and act exactly like egg whites, but without the health burden! Blend, mix, or whisk 1 tablespoon ground flaxseed with 3 tablespoons water until the mixture turns into a thick, white milkshake consistency. Use for dressings, sauces, mayonnaise, or baked goods.

Chia seeds have an identical effect and can be used in the same way as flax, 1 teaspoon ground chia seeds to 3 tablespoons water.

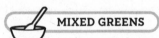 **MIXED GREENS**

Flaxseeds and chia seeds are chock-full of omega-3 fatty acids, fiber, and other phyto-nutrients. Plus, the cost of making an egg substitute with these ingredients is pennies.

Plant Milks

A plethora of plant-based milks have flooded the marketplace in response to consumer demand. Whether for lactose intolerance or other health reasons, many people are turning to these delicious and nutritious dairy substitutes.

Each type of milk provides its unique texture and flavor, and most are fortified to the extent that nothing is lacking nutritionally when compared to the dairy version. Here are some options you might want to check out:

Soy milk is velvety, smooth, and rich—perfect for adding to your morning coffee or tea. It is rich in nutrition and substitutes directly (with the same ratio) for milk in all recipes.

Rice milk is grainier and thinner and is lower in protein and other nutrients. However, rice is the least allergenic food available, so this product works well for people with allergies or who simply prefer the texture.

Oat milk is even grainier, but it's thicker than rice milk. Plus, it provides some fabulous fiber to the mix.

Hemp milk, which is easy to blend up at home (just blend hemp seeds with water), offers some of hemp's famous omega-3 fatty acids and a delicately nutty flavor.

Coconut milk is really creamy and has a distinctive flavor that's used often in Thai, Indian, and other traditional cuisines. Note it is high in saturated fats and should be used sparingly.

Cashew milk is a more recent addition to the club, serving up a neutral, light, and smooth consistency.

Milks made from different legumes, vegetables, nuts, and grains each offer distinct nutritional and culinary profiles.

New and exciting products continue to line the shelves, providing a plethora of possibilities. Regardless of your preference, select the unsweetened version to avoid added sugars. Also, confirm that the product is fortified with vitamins B_{12} and D by reading the ingredients list.

Mock Meats

Odds are, you were raised on the standard American diet based on meat and potatoes. Meat and meat products are typically the centerpiece of the dinner plate, with a potato and maybe some veggies on the side. Because of this tradition, switching to an entirely new plate display may be difficult at first. This is where mock meats or meat analogues—intended to imitate the texture, flavor, and appearance of meats but made from non-animal-based ingredients—come into play.

Every time we visit the supermarket, it appears as though new plant-based products have popped onto the shelves. The creativity and quality of these meat-imitating items are rather impressive, making perfect transition foods or special treats.

Truth be told, these meat alternatives aren't definitive of health foods. However, the fact that they replace animal products makes them, by default, *healthier* foods. Although they're processed, mock meats are devoid of animal protein, dietary cholesterol, and (most of the time) those other compounds, such as carnitine, choline, and TMAO (trimethylamine N-oxide), which we are trying to minimize exposure to. Plus, their contribution to enabling meat eaters to go meatless offers inherent benefit.

MIXED GREENS

Mock meats have expanded in an unprecedented way, with everything from plant-based versions of chicken nuggets, burgers, and seafood, to so much more. Most major retailers are not only selling these options, many even have their own lines of animal-free alternatives.

Once you're past the transition state, more whole foods will naturally take precedence in your diet as your taste buds change and your plant-based recipe box grows. Ultimately, mock meats should be thought of as an occasional indulgence.

Tofu, Tempeh, and Seitan

Nutritionally, tofu is a rich source of protein, omega-3 fatty acids, calcium (if prepared with calcium sulfate), iron, and isoflavones. Tofu comes in a range of firmness from soft to extra-firm. Generally, the softer the tofu, the lower it is in fat.

A prized attribute of tofu is its versatility. Because it imparts virtually no flavor on its own, its capacity to absorb flavors is heightened. Intermingling flavorfully into any recipe with a variety of textures, tofu is a celebrity in plant-based cooking.

Tofu lends itself to a plethora of possibilities. Silken or soft tofu blends well with other ingredients to become a custard, pudding, or dip. Firm or extra-firm tofu is excellent crumbled into chilies, stews, and scrambles, or cubed and added to stir-fries and soups. Seasoned with a marinade or herbs and spices, tofu can be baked and served on its own as an entrée.

Traditionally a staple in Indonesia, tempeh is a cultured and fermented soybean cake. Distinguishable from tofu by its nutty flavor and chewy texture, tempeh is a delicious, nutrient-dense substitute for meat that's very high in fiber and protein.

Tempeh comes in varieties made with grains, flax, and vegetables and can be used in a variety of ways to add consistency and taste. Crumble tempeh as an alternative to ground meat in a pasta sauce or chili. Slice it and broil, bake, or stir-fry it with sauce and veggies for a satisfying meal.

When you rinse away all the starch granules from the wheat grain, the protein is left over. This wheat protein, known as *gluten*, is the basis for a meat analogue called *seitan*. Prized for its meaty characteristics, seitan is used in hundreds of products that are directly intended to mimic meat.

Plain seitan can be used as a meat alternative when cooked at home with other whole foods. Braised, baked, or cooked in a pressure cooker, seitan works well in stews and sautés.

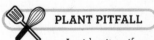 **PLANT PITFALL**

Avoid seitan if you have celiac sprue, gluten intolerance, or any wheat allergies or sensitivities.

Commercial items made from seitan include faux shrimp, chicken, shredded pork, and ground beef. Inundating the marketplace and vegan restaurants (particularly Asian), seitan exemplifies the intention of a meat analogue.

At home, you can use these seitan-based products as transition foods for the meat-missing members of your family and also as occasional treats. However, be forewarned that most of these foods are processed and contain large amounts of sodium, oil, sugars, and fillers.

Mushrooms

Mushrooms have a hearty, dense mouthfeel similar to meat. Because of their immense nutritional contributions—fiber, folate, copper, potassium, niacin, selenium, riboflavin, and hundreds of phytonutrients—mushrooms make the perfect meat alternative.

Besides their nutrient prowess, mushrooms offer a vast diversity in culinary options. Throw some portobello mushroom caps on the grill for succulent "burgers." Mince mushrooms and use them as you would ground meat in lasagna, stews, casseroles, or sauces. Slice them and add them raw to salads, as sushi, or on crudités platters. Scoop out the stems and stuff mushrooms with fillings like nut cheeses, pestos, or vegetable medleys.

 **MIXED GREENS**

Mushrooms are touted for their anticancer and immune-enhancing properties. Used in Eastern medicine in elixirs and teas, mushrooms are high on the list of must-haves in a healthy eating plan.

Un-Cheeses

Now that you know why dairy is best left off your plate and out of your body, it's time to face the repercussions. Cheese has inundated the culinary world with roots deeper than any other food. Besides its seductive properties signaling you to consume more, it's nearly impossible to avoid the presence of cheese in your daily life. Restaurants add cheese to as many dishes as possible. Pizza places work hard to find ways to increase the cheesiness of their products. In television ads, companies go out of their way to provide a tantalizing visual of cheese in their pizzas, burgers, and quesadillas. From these advertisements to the pervasive addition of cheese, the allure of cheese is inescapable. You may have grown to love the flavors and textures of cheeses, as most people do.

But after you break your seduction to cheese by abstaining for just a few short weeks, you'll hardly miss it, thanks to myriad plant-based substitutes you can quickly create in your kitchen. With certain flavorings combined with tofu, beans, and other ingredients, you'll never miss cheese again.

If you're not there yet and still need a cheese "crutch," several vegan cheese products are available. These cheese alternatives have really developed over time, and improvements have been made in their melt-ability, flavor, and texture. A couple brands have even been inducted into pizza joints offering plant-based options. In the grocery store, you can now find dairy-free block cheeses, Parmesan flakes, and cheese shreds. Frozen pizzas with vegan cheeses are infiltrating the vast frozen food world as well.

Remember, however, that these products are processed foods. They don't fit the category of whole foods. These faux cheeses still contain oil, sodium, and added flavors. Use them for transition and rare treats only.

> **HEALTHY HINT**
>
> More and more creative companies are offering decadent whole food, plant-based cheeses from nuts, seeds, and other ingredients. Keep your eyes out as these options continue to grow with consumer discovery and demand.

A popular favorite in the raw food community is a cheese made of fermented seeds and nuts. Typically, raw sunflower seeds, pumpkin seeds, cashews, pine nuts, macadamia nuts, or almonds are soaked and cultured for a period of a day or two. Preparing these recipes at home enables you to dictate your desired flavor, level of sourness, and consistency.

Blending ingredients like onion powder, garlic powder, miso, and other seasonings with cooked potatoes, chickpeas, or whole-grain flours creates cheesy textures and flavors that satisfy the palate and appease cravings. See Chapter 19 for some examples.

Nutritional Yeast

Although the name might be less than enticing, nutritional yeast is a magnificent staple that will "cheese" up your dishes while providing your daily recommended dose of B vitamins. An excellent source of vitamin B_{12} and protein, nutritional yeast is a primary cultured yeast grown on sugarcane and beet molasses. Unlike other yeasts, it doesn't have leavening power.

The versatility of nutritional yeast is boundless. On its own, it tastes nutty and cheesy and is delicious sprinkled on popcorn. When combined into recipes like hummus, un-cheese spreads, pasta sauce, casseroles, stews, and pizza, nutritional yeast lends a lovely flavor and huge nutrient boost.

You can find nutritional yeast at your local or larger-chain health food stores in tubs by supplements or in the bulk section. Start experimenting, and soon you'll love all the secret beauty in this plant-based essential.

Miso

Salty, pungent, flavor-rich miso is fermented soybean paste usually made in combination with a grain or bean. (It also comes in a soy-free variety made with chickpeas.) Originally from Japan, miso has a rather impressive nutrient report card for a flavoring agent. High in protein, vitamin K, manganese, zinc, and fiber, miso paste boasts the same grade for nutritional value as it does for flavor.

PLANT PITFALL

Miso is very high in sodium and should be minimized if you have elevated blood pressure. Or look for a low-sodium miso, which eliminates half of the original's amount.

Most famously used to make soup, miso is also delicious as a spread and in dressings, sauces, and sushi. Miso paste provides a zest similar to sharp cheeses and can be blended with other ingredients to create a dairy-free spread. Flavors of miso vary from light and delicate to dark and bold, each offering its own flair.

Look for miso in your supermarket's refrigerator section, opting for organic with the soy-based varieties. For some ideas on how to incorporate miso into your diet, try the recipes in Chapters 21 and 22.

Do you see the vastness of the plant-based world? So many delicious ingredients exist that it's impossible to miss your old standards. Maintain your kitchen with a variety of options, and decadent whole food, plant-based cuisine is always at your fingertips.

The Least You Need to Know

- A well-stocked kitchen enables you to be ready to create, prepare, and consume delicious plant-based foods whenever hunger and creativity strike.
- Essential equipment in the kitchen includes a high-powered blender, a food processor, and a fine set of knives.
- You can effortlessly replace eggs, milk, meats, and cheeses with health-promoting ingredients.
- Certain processed meat alternatives and cheese substitutes make the transition to a plant-based diet easier for some eaters as they move from a plate heavy in animal products to one full of whole-plant foods.

CHAPTER 1

How to Nutrify Any Recipe

A recipe is a formula of combined ingredients that, ideally, nourishes and satisfies the senses simultaneously. You may have some favorite recipes but need to improve or adapt them to fit your plant-based diet. No problem.

You need to know how to find beautiful, health-promoting ingredients that are also void of beastly, disease-promoting ones. And, of course, the end product has to be delicious. So you need to identify what needs to change in order to create a nutritious masterpiece. In this chapter, you learn how to inject nutrients into a dish and make healthy taste delicious.

In This Chapter

- Honing your "nutrification" skills
- Manipulating ingredients
- Spicing up your recipes with color, flavor, texture, and nutrients
- Simple substitutions and home-grown tricks

Analyze, Assess, and Amaze Your Friends

You needn't be a chef or have graduated from culinary school to do this. Nor do you have to attain a degree in nutrition to hone your nutrification skills. All you need is an investigative eye, a hungry curiosity, and a smidgen of practice to master this skill.

Instead of narrowing your focus to seek out only whole food, plant-based recipes, widen your possibilities by learning to nutrify any dish. Train your eyes to discern easily substituted ingredients, and you'll be pleasantly surprised by your options. Sharpen your skills by practicing, creating, and thinking outside your realm of comfort.

 **HEALTHY HINT**

The best ideas usually emerge by accident. Always keep a pen and paper handy while playing in the kitchen so you can take notes and expand your repertoire every time you learn a new trick.

How many times have you flipped through a cookbook or heard about a new recipe and thought, *Too bad I can't make this because I can't have [fill in the blank]?* It's time to switch to a glass-half-full mentality! A vast plant-based universe with endless choices of ingredients awaits you. With a detective's scrutiny and some creativity, you can master the art and science of plant-based cooking. After all, a great chef is defined not by what he or she can cook, but by what he or she can fix.

Beauty Boosters

What makes a recipe beautiful? A multitude of colors, aromas, flavors, and textures. Nature is bountiful with her infusion of all these characteristics in her plants. Combining them can be magical for both your tongue and your cells.

When analyzing a recipe, identify the power foods—those dense in nutrients, as described in Chapter 4. Greens, beans, other vegetables, fruits, and spices need to take center stage. If not, add them.

Leafy Greens

You can include leafy greens in virtually any dish. Think with your green goggles on whenever preparing any dish to see how you can sneak in more marvelous, leafy green veggies. Here are a few tricks:

Immediately before your whole-grain pasta is done cooking, add greens to the pot to wilt them. Then drain pasta and greens all together, and continue with your preparation.

Stir greens in the form of a vegetable or fresh herb into any type of soup. Cilantro perks up Thai- or Latin-flavored soups. Basil makes Italian and Mediterranean soups fresh.

Boost your salads by adding more than one type of green. In addition to or instead of classic romaine, introduce shredded kale, dandelion greens, and mixed lettuce varieties.

Include leafy greens in any smoothie or extracted juice you make to enhance nutrients exponentially.

Spruce up your spreads and dips by processing greens into them for color, flavor, and supernutrition.

Make ice cream by blending frozen fruit with green cabbage or iceberg lettuce in a high-powered blender.

Finely chop greens and combine with whole grains such as brown rice or quinoa, some herbs or spices, and nutritional yeast for a flavor-rich, nutrient-varied dish.

Blend greens into stews, stir-fries, casseroles, and sandwiches.

Bountiful Beans

Bring beans back to your dinner plate with gusto. They're as multitalented in the kitchen as they are in your body. With a wide variety of colors, sizes, shapes, textures, and flavors, bump them up in your selection criteria (if you haven't already). Here are a few tips:

Make fresh beans by cooking them on your stovetop or in a pressure cooker.

Try bean spreads and dips by processing them with herbs, spices, nutritional yeast, and miso paste (see hummus recipes in Chapter 22).

Combine beans with grains, or add beans to soups and salads.

Have a bean festival in a pot by making a chili (see recipe in Chapter 21).

 **HEALTHY HINT**

Because beans contain oligosaccharides—sugars that aren't digestible by the human GI tract—they may cause gas in some individuals. To reduce this effect, soak dry beans in water for several hours. Rinse them well before cooking in a fresh batch of water, and add a strip of kombu seaweed to the pot when you start cooking.

Healthful Herbs and Spices

Some herbs and spices have anticancer and antimicrobial properties. They add more than just flavor to your foods!

Used in traditional Chinese and Indian medicine for centuries, turmeric is potent as an anti-inflammatory. It has also been found to contribute anticancer effects, improve liver function, protect the heart, lower cholesterol, and perhaps work against cognitive decline (dementia and Alzheimer's disease). It's even high in iron. Sounds pretty powerful, right?

Turmeric is also easy to consume, with its mild, warm, peppery flavor and bright, staining, yellow color. Add turmeric to curry dishes, lentils, and tofu scrambles to make them yellow. Sauté cauliflower, onions, and other vegetables, and stir in turmeric. Whisk it into salad dressings and sauces, and use it to spice up tofu or tempeh salads.

Versatile and pungent, garlic has long been touted for its health advantages. Known as the "stinking rose," garlic acts as an antioxidant, anti-inflammatory, antibacterial, antiviral, anti-parasitic, antifungal, and as a blood thinner. It lowers blood pressure and cholesterol, reduces cancer risk, and improves iron metabolism. When chopped, chewed, or crushed, garlic releases its enzymes and converts the compound alliin into allicin, the active, health-promoting phytonutrient.

Use garlic in spreads, sauces, soups, dressings, sautés, stir-fries, and dips. Roast an unpeeled head at 400°F for about 30 minutes or until the cloves are soft. Peel and spread the garlic on whole-grain breads, tortillas, and crackers. Use this flavor-rich gem to enhance any savory recipe.

Warm and aromatic, zesty and spicy, ginger is a beautiful addition to your ingredient inventory. An effective gastrointestinal reliever, ginger has been used historically to reduce nausea. Ginger also acts as an anti-inflammatory, boosts immunity, and may even prevent cancer by inhibiting the growth of and/or killing cancer cells. Enjoy ginger as a pungent tea, or add it to rice dishes, sauces, dressings, soups, stir-fries, and baked goods.

Cinnamon, a bark that elicits a bite, also has healing capabilities. Cinnamon can improve insulin sensitivity, helping normalize blood sugar levels in diabetics. The oils in cinnamon are antimicrobial and can also inhibit inflammation and blood clotting. Warm up your oatmeal; baked goods; plant milks; pancakes; Indian, Middle Eastern, and African stews; and baked apples with a sprinkle or more of cinnamon.

Speaking of adding warmth, cayenne adds a fiery kick to recipes. Capsaicin is the compound responsible for the heat and health benefits found in cayenne. Another anti-inflammatory, capsaicin also offers relief to those suffering with painful chronic diseases like osteoarthritis, headaches, and diabetic neuropathy. Cayenne clears congestion, boosts immune function, helps dissolve blood clots, decreases cholesterol, and helps you lose weight. Heat up your recipes with a careful dash of cayenne.

 **HEALTHY HINT**

For a warming, spicy treat that also enhances your well-being, make a tea with sliced ginger root and a pinch of cayenne.

Basil is one of the most popular herbs worldwide. Fragrant and familiar, basil is loaded with flavonoids capable of protecting your DNA, and it acts as a potent antibacterial agent and anti-inflammatory. Basil is used to make pesto and virtually all Italian dishes. With more than 60 varieties, this versatile herb is a must-have in your kitchen.

Other phytonutrient-dense seasonings include mustard seed, oregano, sage, parsley, rosemary, and onion. Each one offers its own unique personality, lending flavorful undertones to any dish.

Texture Tricks

Besides phytonutrients and seasonings, you can also improve a recipe by influencing textures. In culinary terms, shapes are supposed to stay consistent. If you julienne one vegetable in a dish, you're advised to julienne all the vegetables. This adds to visual and textural appeal.

Create some interest in your dishes by adding textures from chewy to crunchy, soft to firm, dense to light, or thin to thick. Mouthfeel adds a significant layer to food likes and dislikes, so think about varying textures in your dishes. Take tempeh versus tofu, for example. Similar nutritionally and tastewise, their consistencies are completely different. If you prefer (or just happen to be in the mood for) a smoother, silkier texture, opt to use tofu. Tempeh is chewier and grainier, satisfying a different mouthfeel.

Experiment with textures as well as flavors, aromas, and colors to get the most out of a recipe. Beautify your plate and your palate with all of nature's gorgeous gifts to stimulate your senses and inspire your culinary competence.

Beast Busters

You should now know what the "beasts" are when it comes to healthful eating. When preparing your own plant-based dishes, find and replace or simply eliminate these ingredients. These include any animal or processed products.

Some recipes are easily nutrified. For example, if you find a chicken stir-fry you're interested in trying, you can simply switch the chicken to tofu, tempeh, or seitan cubes and follow the rest of the recipe.

Of course, not everything is that cut and dried. A steak dinner can be switched for a tempeh steak, but you're better off with a new recipe. In this case, if you can't beat 'em, substitute 'em! Here are some examples:

Dishes like casseroles and lasagnas are easy to modify. Finely chopped mushrooms, cooked lentils, or crumbled tempeh mimic the mouthfeel of ground meat.

Swap 1 tablespoon gelatin for 1 tablespoon *agar agar* flakes or ½ teaspoon agar powder (thickens 1 cup liquid).

Exchange a dairy yogurt with soy-, almond-, coconut-, or rice-based yogurt. Be wary of sugar-filled products. Instead, buy the plain flavor, and add fresh fruit and date paste for a whole-food version. Plain, plant-based yogurt works well as a moisture-adding ingredient in baking. It can also add a creamy texture when cooking sauces, curries, or soups.

Make buttermilk by adding 2 teaspoons lemon juice or vinegar (e.g. white or apple cider) to 1 cup plant milk.

Vegetable broth can easily replace chicken, meat, or fish broth. For a meatier flavor, add tamari sauce or miso paste to water or vegetable broth to taste, or use a mushroom-based broth or stock.

For frozen desserts, choose whole-fruit sorbet or ice pops, or blend frozen fruit in a high-powered blender.

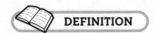 **DEFINITION**

Agar agar is a gelatinous substance derived from seaweed that works as a thickening agent and can replace gelatin, an animal-based substance, as a plant-based substitute.

Hundreds of products free of animal ingredients are currently on the market, such as sour cream, butter, mayonnaise, whipped cream, ice cream, creamer, mock meats, cheese, and cream cheese. Although these goods are a step up in terms of harmfulness, they're still processed foods. Oils, sugars, sodium, added flavors, and colors are used to mimic the original versions. Instead of allowing these items to populate your daily diet, use them sparingly.

If you have a serious medical condition like diabetes, heart disease, or cancer, stay away from the processed foods entirely to allow your body to gain maximum benefit from whole food, plant-based nutrition. Moderation is inadequate when your body needs to heal and recover. You need to keep your diet at the highest level of purity and nourish yourself properly.

You can look at vegan recipes for a ton of ideas, too. To convert a vegan recipe into a whole-food recipe, use these simple substitutions:

Replace oil in stovetop cooking with equal amounts of water, vegetable broth, vinegar, wine, beer, plant milks, pure juice, tea, or coconut water. Usually 1 tablespoon of oil can be replaced by ¼ cup of liquid. Monitor closely to avoid sticking or burning. In sauces or dressings, oil can be replaced with silken tofu, flaxseeds, hempseeds, chia seeds, plant milks, or cannellini beans for creaminess; and water, vegetable broth, vinegar, wine, beer, plant milks, pure juice, tea, or coconut water for moisture. In baking, replace 1 cup oil with 1 cup applesauce or other fruit purée (such as pumpkin, banana, squash, or prunes), mashed banana, silken tofu, or mashed avocado.

Swap salt for powdered or flaked sea vegetables (such as dulse and nori) in equal amounts. (You may need more kelp powder if you're still used to eating high amounts of salt.) You can also use any of the wide variety of salt-free seasonings found in the store or online and experiment with using other herbs and spices to expand your palate's repertoire of flavor.

For any sweetening, opt for dates, date paste (see the next section for how to make your own), date syrup, fruit purees, or fruit.

DIY Ingredients

You can easily whip up several ingredients at home, providing you with 100 percent whole-food options. These quickies are a superior investment and save you from apprehension and label-reading time—and provide better taste.

Date Paste

Date paste is the ultimate sweetener. This easy DIY whole food can replace sugars in baking and add sweetness to dressings, smoothies, and sauces.

Dates   Water or unsweetened almond milk

1. Soak dates in water or unsweetened almond milk for several hours to soften. Add only enough liquid to cover dates so your end paste isn't too thin.

2. When dates appear flaky and swollen, pour off a little liquid. In a blender or food processor, blend remaining liquid with dates for 1 or 2 minutes or until smooth, stopping to scrape down the sides as needed.

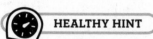 **HEALTHY HINT**

> If you're in a rush or decide to make a recipe with date paste before you've had time to soak the dates, use hot water to expedite the process.

Parmesan Shake

Who needs dairy when you can make this plant-perfect Parmesan Shake in less than a minute?

1 cup raw almonds	4 TB. raw sesame seeds
1 cup nutritional yeast flakes	2 tsp. sea vegetable (dulse or nori) flakes or powder

1. Add almonds, nutritional yeast flakes, sesame seeds, and sea vegetable flakes to a food processor, and process for 45 to 60 seconds or until mixture turns into a powder.

2. Use on everything from pasta dishes and lasagnas, to salads, soups, spreads, dips, casseroles, and anywhere else you'd use the dairy version.

 MIXED GREENS

> This shake is high in calcium, magnesium, vitamin E, all the B vitamins, protein, and healthy fats. Best of all, you avoid the saturated fat, cholesterol, sodium, and other no-no's in the original version.

Plant-Based Sour Cream

Sour cream can be nutrified and tastes even better than store-bought when you make it at home with whole-plant foods.

14 oz. silken tofu	1½ tsp. sea vegetable (dulse or nori) flakes or powder
¼ cup unsweetened soy milk	1 TB. chopped fresh parsley (or 1 tsp. dried parsley)
4 TB. freshly squeezed lemon juice	
2 TB. nutritional yeast flakes	

1. In a food processor, combine tofu, soy milk, lemon juice, nutritional yeast flakes, sea vegetable flakes, and parsley for 2 minutes or until smooth.

2. Keep tightly covered in the refrigerator for 3 or 4 days.

You can also save some bucks by making your own flours. Simply grind whole grains like oats and buckwheat in a high-powered blender until the mixture is fine and powdery.

Or you can make nut flour by processing raw nuts alone or in combination. (And if you find you've overprocessed the nuts, enjoy your homemade nut butter!) Nut flours are great for dessert bases like pie crusts, cookies, and bars. They provide dense nutrition along with rich flavor. Process them with dried fruit for a homemade nutrition bar.

A new perspective breeds creativity. Challenge and excite yourself to explore, mix, match, blend, and combine. Avoiding and substituting the beasts has never been so easy. Take some time investigating products and ingredients. Focus on Mother Nature's boundless beauties to add color, texture, and flavor in ways that may be new to you. You never know what you may discover!

The Least You Need to Know

- Be on the lookout for ways to sneak more power foods like leafy green veggies, beans, herbs, and spices into your meals.
- Many recipes can be easily converted to whole food, plant-based versions by avoiding animal and processed foods as main ingredients.
- Nutrify your favorite recipes by substituting whole-plant food ingredients for the originals. Homemade imitation products like sour cream, Parmesan cheese, and date paste taste superior to the original, processed versions.
- One of the easiest ways to create a new work of genius is to take a vegan recipe and substitute the oil or sweeteners with a whole-food version.
- Have fun playing with plant-based ingredients. You have nothing to lose and only delicious cuisine and ingenious culinary tricks to gain!

Morning, Noon, and Light Fare

The first meal of the day is by definition when we break our fast. It doesn't matter what time that occurs nor what food we choose to eat. The idea that we name meals and have standard times that they are served has more to do with the business of food service and very little to do with health. With that said, one can find a wide range of conflicting recommendations that tell us what, when, and how often to eat. Some choose to skip eating first thing in the morning, while others consider it their favorite meal. Both approaches can be very successful in health and weight management.

In this chapter, we have a collection of recipes that range from on-the-go nourishing drinks to traditional breakfast and lunch fare to energy bars for endurance athletes. We won't limit you to the time of day you can eat these delicious, plant-based meals. No matter how rushed your day is, be sure to take time to smell the spinach!

In This Chapter

- Delicious breakfast starters
- Delightful early day options
- Food to support athletes
- Bright and colorful soups and salads

It's Easy Being Green Smoothie

Fruity and sweet, frosty and creamy, this smoothie is so delectable.

Yield:	Prep time:	Serving size:	
6 cups	10 minutes	1 smoothie	
Each serving has:			
460 calories	13g total fat	0.5g saturated fat	0g trans fat
0mg cholesterol	460mg sodium	82g total carbohydrates	20g dietary fiber
46g sugars	11g protein	536mg calcium	5mg iron

4 cups packed green leafy vegetables (spinach, dandelion greens, collard greens, kale, or other favorite greens)

2 TB. hempseeds and/or flaxseeds

1 cup frozen blueberries

¼ cup frozen cherries

¼ cup frozen raspberries

¼ cup frozen pineapple pieces

¼ cup frozen mango chunks

1 medium frozen peeled banana, broken into pieces

2 cups unsweetened plant milk

1. In a high-powered blender, combine greens, hempseeds, blueberries, cherries, raspberries, pineapple, mango, banana, and plant milk.

2. Blend on high speed for 60 seconds or until smooth. Enjoy icy cold.

Variation: You can substitute 2 cups *coconut water* or cooled green tea for plant milk.

 **DEFINITION**

> **Coconut water,** the clear liquid found inside a young coconut, is extremely high in electrolytes and makes an excellent natural sports drink.

Mint Chocolate Nib Smoothie

Minty, sweet, and decadent, this breakfast smoothie will refresh and energize you.

Yield:	Prep time:	Serving size:	
5 cups	5 minutes	2½ cups	
Each serving has:			
450 calories	13g total fat	4g saturated fat	0g trans fat
0mg cholesterol	230mg sodium	80g total carbohydrates	25g dietary fiber
35g sugars	12g protein	356mg calcium	9mg iron

3 cups packed green leafy vegetables (spinach, dandelion greens, collard greens, kale, or other favorite greens)

1 cup fresh mint leaves, chopped

2 TB. hempseeds and/or flaxseeds

2 medium pitted dates or more to taste

½ cup raw cacao nibs

1 cup frozen blueberries

2 medium frozen peeled bananas, broken into pieces

1 cup ice

2 cups unsweetened chocolate plant milk

1. In a high-powered blender, combine greens, mint, hempseeds, dates, cacao nibs, blueberries, bananas, ice, and plant milk.

2. Blend on high speed for 60 seconds or until smooth. Enjoy icy cold.

Variation: If this smoothie isn't sweet enough for you, add more dates to suit your taste.

 **HEALTHY HINT**

> Challenge yourself to pack the blender with more and more greens as your taste buds evolve through the plant-based world.

Chocolate Almond Butter in a Cup

Rich and dreamy, this candy-in-a-glass green smoothie will put a smile on your face.

Yield:	Prep time:	Serving size:	
4 cups	5 minutes	2 cups	

Each serving has:			
590 calories	30g total fat	4.5g saturated fat	0g trans fat
0mg cholesterol	230mg sodium	74g total carbohydrates	23g dietary fiber
30g sugars	19g protein	374mg calcium	5mg iron

4 cups fresh spinach, tightly packed

¼ cup raw almond butter

2 TB. hempseeds and/or flaxseeds

2 medium pitted dates or more to taste

½ cup raw cacao nibs

2 medium frozen peeled bananas, broken into pieces

1 cup ice

2 cups unsweetened chocolate plant milk

1. In a high-powered blender, place spinach, almond butter, hempseeds, dates, cacao nibs, bananas, ice, and chocolate plant milk.

2. Blend on high speed for 60 seconds or until smooth. Enjoy icy cold.

Variation: Feel free to use a different raw nut butter in place of almond butter. Try ¼ cup unsweetened peanut butter or cashew butter instead.

 **HEALTHY HINT**

You can make your own nut butter by processing raw nuts and/or seeds in your food processor until pasty.

Basil-Lemon Switchel

Switchel is the original sports drink and goes back to the eighteenth century. Matt Frazier, the No Meat Athlete, created this tart, refreshing, and healthful twist on the mass-marketed sports drinks.

Yield:	Prep time:	Serving size:	
4 cups	5 minutes	4 cups	
Each serving has:			
123 calories	0g total fat	0g saturated fat	0g trans fat
0mg cholesterol	687mg sodium	26g total carbohydrates	0g dietary fiber
18g sugars	2.4g protein	450mg calcium	1.8mg iron

½ cup fresh basil leaves

4 cups water

zest of 1 small lemon

1 TB. fresh lemon juice

1 TB. apple cider vinegar or to taste

2 TB. molasses

¼ tsp. salt

1. Bring basil, 1 cup water, and lemon zest to a boil over medium-high heat. Once boiling, remove mixture from heat and allow to steep for 10 minutes.

2. Strain out basil leaves and zest. Stir in lemon juice, apple cider vinegar, molasses, salt, and remaining 3 cups water (to make up for evaporation, bring to 4 cups total). Chill before adding to water bottle or serve over ice.

Variation: Maple syrup may be substituted for molasses for a milder taste.

 MIXED GREENS

This recipe comes from Matt Frazier, the No Meat Athlete. He is a marathoner, ultra-marathoner (50 miles), and even a 100-mile runner, and he's fueled by an exclusively plant-based diet. He is the author of *No Meat Athlete: Run on Plants and Discover Your Fittest, Fastest, Happiest Self* and *The No Meat Athlete Cookbook*, which was named one of 7 best health and wellness books of 2017 by *Sports Illustrated* and *People* magazines.

Peanut Butter–Chocolate Bean Bars

This new take on energy bars by No Meat Athlete Matt Frazier will fuel athletes in the most grueling endurance competitions. Packed with calories, classic chocolate-peanut-butter flavor, and plenty of plant phytonutrients, not only is the flavor better than the packaged and highly processed store-bought variety, it can be adjusted to meet your desired level of sweetness.

Yield:	Prep time:	Cook time:	Serving size:
12 bars	10 minutes	20 minutes	1 bar

Each serving has:			
234 calories	8.5g total fat	1.5g saturated fat	0g trans fat
0mg cholesterol	190mg sodium	34g total carbohydrates	8.1g dietary fiber
9.2g sugars	9.4g protein	55mg calcium	2.6mg iron

1 (15-oz.) can black beans, drained	¼ tsp. sea salt
½ cup natural peanut butter (no sugar added)	1½ cups rolled oats
¼ cup maple syrup	½ cup unsweetened cocoa
¼ cup chopped dates	½ cup oat flour
1 tsp. vanilla extract	¼ cup hemp seed hearts
	½ cup raisins

1. Preheat the oven to 350°F.

2. In a food processor, combine black beans, peanut butter, maple syrup, dates, vanilla extract, and salt until smooth. Add rolled oats, cocoa, and oat flour to mixture and pulse until combined.

3. Stir in hemp seed hearts and raisins. Spread mixture into a 13x9-inch non-stick or silicone baking pan.

4. Bake for 15 to 18 minutes. Cool on a wire rack and cut into 12 bars.

 MIXED GREENS

Making energy bars at home is not only a cost saver, but it's a flavor savior as well. There are many combinations of these bars by varying the ingredients. In general Matt's energy bars have these basic ingredients: beans (15-oz can), binder (½ cup), sweetener (¼ cup), extract (1 tsp.), soft sweet fruit (¼ cup), dry spice (1 tsp.), oats (1 ½ cups), dry base (½ to 1 cup), salt (¼ tsp.), and stir ins (½ to 1 cup). Get creative and design your perfect on-the-go snack.

Blueberry Banana Pancakes

Hearty and syrupy, these fruity pancakes make a great weekend morning treat.

Yield:	Prep time:	Cook time:	Serving size:
4 large pancakes	10 minutes	10 minutes	2 large pancakes

Each serving has:			
190 calories	2g total fat	0g saturated fat	0g trans fat
0mg cholesterol	40mg sodium	40g total carbohydrates	6g dietary fiber
13g sugars	7g protein	611mg calcium	2mg iron

1 medium banana	2 tsp. baking powder
¼ cup plant milk	1 TB. pure maple syrup
1 cup whole-grain flour (oat, whole-wheat, etc.)	1 cup fresh or thawed frozen blueberries

1. In a large bowl, mash banana with a fork. Add plant milk and mix until lump-free.

2. Add whole-grain flour and baking powder to banana mixture, and mix with a fork just until dry ingredients are moistened. Stir in maple syrup and blueberries until incorporated.

3. Heat a medium skillet over medium-high heat until hot. Pour ½ cup batter into the skillet. Reduce heat to medium, and cover. Cook for 2 to 4 minutes or until pancake starts to brown at the edge. Using a spatula, turn pancake and cook other side for 1 or 2 minutes or until golden brown. Repeat with remaining batter.

4. Drizzle with additional maple syrup, if desired, to serve.

 MIXED GREENS

Whole-grain flour mixes are available commercially. You can probably even find gluten-free options easily. Experiment with different varieties to see which you prefer.

Veggie Tofu Scramble

This scramble offers skillet-sizzled classic tastes. Buttery and silky, the garlicky, onion bite will induce long-term cravings.

Yield:	Prep time:	Cook time:	Serving size:
4 cups	10 minutes	12 to 16 minutes	1 cup

Each serving has:			
140 calories	4.5g total fat	0g saturated fat	0g trans fat
0mg cholesterol	470mg sodium	10g total carbohydrates	3g dietary fiber
2g sugars	14g protein	174mg calcium	3mg iron

1 small yellow onion, chopped

5 medium baby bella mushrooms, sliced

¼ cup vegetable broth

1 (12-oz.) pkg. firm or extra-firm tofu, drained and crumbled

1 TB. tamari

1 TB. dried parsley flakes

1 TB. nutritional yeast flakes

½ tsp. garlic powder

½ tsp. onion powder

½ tsp. turmeric

½ tsp. freshly ground black pepper

1 cup chopped fresh spinach

½ cup salsa

1. In a medium saucepan over medium heat, sauté onions and mushrooms in vegetable broth for 5 minutes or until onions are translucent.

2. Stir in tofu, tamari, dried parsley flakes, nutritional yeast flakes, garlic powder, onion powder, turmeric, and black pepper, and simmer for 10 to 12 minutes or until moisture has evaporated. Add spinach and salsa, and scramble for 2 to 4 more minutes or until brown at the edges.

3. Serve hot with warmed corn tortillas or a side of brown rice or quinoa, if desired.

 MIXED GREENS

Dried mushrooms have an intense, rich, umami flavor that can be used in many different ways. Grind them into a powder, and sprinkle it into soups, casseroles, or stews as a seasoning. Or reconstitute them for use as you would fresh mushrooms.

Breakfast Rice Pudding

Knowing this cozy and enticing pudding is on the menu, you'll love waking up on a cold day. The cinnamon undertones are warming, while the crunch of the smooth almonds mixed with the chewiness of the raisins makes this dish hearty.

Yield:	Prep time:	Cook time:	Serving size:
6 cups	5 minutes	20 minutes	1½ cups

Each serving has:			
420 calories	11g total fat	1g saturated fat	0g trans fat
0mg cholesterol	70mg sodium	72g total carbohydrates	6g dietary fiber
36g sugars	12g protein	304mg calcium	3mg iron

2 cups cooked brown rice

1 cup raisins

½ cup slivered raw almonds

¼ cup pure maple syrup

1 TB. alcohol-free vanilla extract

1 TB. ground cinnamon

3 cups unsweetened plant milk

1. In a medium saucepan over medium heat, combine brown rice, raisins, raw almonds, maple syrup, vanilla extract, ground cinnamon, and plant milk.

2. Bring to a boil, and reduce heat to low. Simmer over low heat, stirring occasionally, for 20 minutes or until pudding thickens.

3. Serve hot, or refrigerate to serve chilled.

Variation: Dates or bananas are easily substituted for maple syrup. Puree 1 or 2 pitted dates with 1 tablespoon warm water and use in place of maple syrup. Or substitute ¼ cup puréed ripe banana thinned with a small amount of water.

 **HEALTHY HINT**

This pudding is the perfect dish to use up your leftover rice. Or in a pinch, microwave single-ingredient, ready-cooked brown rice packets to use instead.

Japanese Noritos

Crispy nori sheets make for a delightfully light wrapper, surrounding the crunchy and savory filling. Blending these textures will remind you of sushi but with a heartier feel.

Yield:	Prep time:	Serving size:	
2 noritos	10 minutes	2 noritos	
Each serving has:			
140 calories	2g total fat	0g saturated fat	0g trans fat
0mg cholesterol	460mg sodium	20g total carbohydrates	4g dietary fiber
2g sugars	6g protein	62mg calcium	1mg iron

2 sheets nori

1 tsp. low-sodium miso paste

¼ cup cooked brown rice

½ small Persian cucumber, julienned

1½ TB. shredded carrots

1 tsp. tamari

1 tsp. sesame seeds or gomashio

1. Place nori sheets on a flat surface. Gently and evenly place miso paste on ½ of each nori sheet.

2. Add brown rice, Persian cucumber, and shredded carrots on top of miso paste. Drizzle with tamari, and lightly sprinkle sesame seeds over top.

3. Tightly roll nori like a burrito from ingredient-filled side.

Variation: For Mexican Noritos, substitute filling with 3 tablespoons Sweet Pea Guacamole (recipe in Chapter 22), ¼ cup julienned jicama, ½ tablespoon chopped fresh cilantro, and 2 tablespoons salsa.

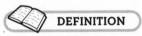 **DEFINITION**

The word **norito** is a combination of nori and burrito, because these rolls, filled with crunchy and savory filling and wrapped in crispy nori sheets, ultimately end up looking, and being eaten, like burritos. Persian cucumbers are mini seedless cucumbers that are crisp, refreshing, and available throughout the year.

Holy Kale with Herbed Tahini Dressing

You won't be able to stop eating oh-so-good-for-you kale after you try this fresh, sweet, and herbed delightful dressing. Rich and creamy, zesty and nutty, the garlic and cilantro tones will make you an instant fan.

Yield:	Prep time:	Serving size:	
12 cups	20 minutes	2 cups	
Each serving has:			
270 calories	8g total fat	<1g saturated fat	0g trans fat
0mg cholesterol	252mg sodium	43g total carbohydrates	5g dietary fiber
8g sugars	13g protein	353mg calcium	5mg iron

10 cups curly kale, rinsed, drained, and shredded

1 cup carrots, shredded

1 cup red cabbage, shredded

1 (15-oz.) can cannellini beans, rinsed and drained

1 cup water

1½ cups fresh cilantro, de-stemmed

1 cup fresh Italian parsley, de-stemmed

¼ cup freshly squeezed lime juice

1 TB. lime zest

2-4 pitted dates

3 TB. tahini

3 TB. hempseeds

2 TB. tamari

1 large clove garlic, peeled and crushed

½ tsp. cayenne

1. In a large salad bowl, combine kale, carrots, and red cabbage.

2. In a blender, combine cannellini beans, water, cilantro, Italian parsley, lime juice, lime zest, dates, tahini, hempseeds, tamari, garlic, and cayenne. Blend on high speed for 1 minute or until creamy and smooth.

3. Pour dressing over salad, toss to evenly distribute, and serve immediately.

Variation: You can substitute 1½ cups other fresh herbs like dill or basil for the cilantro. Either way, the herbed tahini dressing is also delicious on any vegetable salad or over a baked potato.

 **PLANT PITFALL**

Only zest citrus fruits that are organically grown or washed carefully with soap and water first. Citrus rind has a tendency to hold onto a lot of pesticide and other chemical residues on its surface.

Salted Peach Ceviche

Although ceviche is commonly associated with fish, this one bathes fresh peaches and smashed heart of palm in a lime and grapefruit sauce, creating a sweet and tangy summer treat with just a hint of peppery zing that's cooled by refreshing mint. It can be eaten with chips, turned into tacos, or even tossed with pasta. This recipe comes courtesy of Chef Jason Wyrick, *New York Times* bestselling author, culinary instructor, and the executive chef of The Vegan Taste.

Yield:	Prep time:	Serving size:	
1 cup	5 minutes	$\frac{1}{2}$ cup	
Each serving has:			
170 calories	4g total fat	1g saturated fat	0g trans fat
0mg cholesterol	602mg sodium	29g total carbohydrates	5g dietary fiber
16g sugars	7g protein	69mg calcium	1mg iron

4 to 5 pieces heart of palm, sliced into ¼-inch lengths

1 small dried guajillo chile, stems and seeds removed

2 fresh peaches, pitted and diced

¼ cup of fresh grapefruit juice

Juice and zest of 2 medium limes

2 TB. toasted and salted pepitas (pumpkin seeds)

1 tsp. minced fresh mint

¼ tsp. sea salt

1. Smash heart of palm pieces with the back of a knife or heavy spoon until flaked. Place in a medium, nonreactive mixing bowl.

2. Place guajillo chile in a small pan and cook over medium heat for 15 seconds per side until slightly cooked then remove from the pan and allow chile to cool.

3. Crush chile with your hands and add flakes to heart of palm.

4. Add peaches, grapefruit juice, lime juice and zest, pepitas, mint, and salt. Toss ceviche and allow to sit for at least 30 minutes before serving.

 PLANT PITFALL

When preparing highly acidic foods such as tomatoes or citruses, be sure to use nonreactive cookware made of stainless steel, ceramic, glass, and enamel-coated metal. Avoid pans, bowls, and utensils made of cast iron, aluminum, and copper. These metals react with the acids in these foods and impart an unpleasant metallic flavor to the final dish.

Sushi Salad with Creamy Miso Dressing

Free-style sushi all in a big bowl, this salad is refreshingly crisp and fulfilling, with gingery, pungent, and peppery flavors from the East.

Yield:	Prep time:	Serving size:	
8 cups	30 minutes	1⅓ cups	
Each serving has:			
180 calories	9g total fat	1g saturated fat	0g trans fat
0mg cholesterol	70mg sodium	21g total carbohydrates	6g dietary fiber
4g sugars	6g protein	43mg calcium	1mg iron

4 sheets nori	½ cup water
1 cup cooked brown rice	2 TB. raw tahini
2 cups chopped romaine lettuce	1-3 pitted dates
1 cup shredded red cabbage	1 TB. low-sodium miso paste
1 cup shredded carrots	3 TB. freshly squeezed lemon juice
1 cup julienned cucumbers	1 TB. unsweetened rice vinegar
1 cup frozen shelled edamame, thawed	1 tsp. minced fresh ginger
1 medium avocado, peeled, pitted, and sliced	1 medium clove garlic, minced
	⅓ tsp. red chili flakes
1 TB. pickled ginger (optional)	¼ tsp. Chinese five-spice powder (optional)

1. On a cutting board, use a pair of scissors to shred nori sheets into pieces. Line up nori sheets around the perimeter of a large bowl to create a border. Spoon brown rice into the center. Pile romaine lettuce, red cabbage, carrots, cucumbers, and edamame on top of rice.

2. Gently place avocado on the top, and add pickled ginger (if using) in the center.

3. In a high-powered blender or food processor, combine water, tahini, dates, miso paste, lemon juice, rice vinegar, ginger, garlic, chili flakes, and Chinese five-spice powder (if using). Blend or process for 1 minute or until dressing is smooth and creamy.

4. Toss dressing and salad, and serve.

 **DEFINITION**

> **Nori,** the Japanese name for seaweed, is dried, typically toasted, made into flat sheets, and used as a sushi wrapper.

Bulgur, Green Bean, and Carrot Tahini Salad

This grain salad has it all: protein and fiber-packed bulgur wheat, crisp and tender vegetables, sweet currants, and a cumin-scented, flavorful tahini dressing that brings it all together and adds healthy fat to the meal. This recipe is from Gena Hamshaw, author of *Choosing Raw* and *Food52 Vegan*, and creator of The Full Helping, a blog dedicated to plant-based recipes and a compassionate relationship with food.

Yield:	Prep time:	Cook time:	Serving size:
3 cups	15 minutes	15 minutes	1½ cups

Each serving has:			
359 calories	13g total fat	1.5g saturated fat	0g trans fat
0mg cholesterol	372mg sodium	56g total carbohydrates	12g dietary fiber
18g sugars	12g protein	178mg calcium	5mg iron

1 cup dry bulgur wheat	2 cups fresh green beans, chopped into 1-inch pieces
¼ cup tahini	1½ cups peeled and grated carrot
2 TB. fresh lime juice	½ cup finely chopped red onion (optional)
⅓ cup water	1 cup chopped parsley leaves, loosely packed
1 clove garlic, finely minced	½ cup currants
½ tsp. ground cumin	¼ cup sliced or slivered almonds (toasted if desired)
½ tsp. fine salt	
⅛ tsp. freshly ground black pepper	

1. Cook bulgur according to package instructions. Allow to cool for at least 15 minutes.

2. While bulgur cooks and cools, whisk together tahini, lime juice, water, garlic, cumin, salt, and pepper in a small bowl until well blended. Set dressing aside.

3. Bring a large pot of water to boil. Add green beans to water and cook for 2 minutes, until tender-crisp. Drain green beans.

4. In a large mixing bowl, combine cooked bulgur, cooked green beans, carrot, onion (if using), parsley, currants, and almonds. Add dressing to the bowl and toss salad until well mixed, and serve.

 MIXED GREENS

The bulgur can be cooked ahead of time for speedy assembly of this recipe, and the leftovers keep nicely for up to 3 days in the fridge.

Kale Salad with Lentils and Quinoa

This is a favorite salad. It's incredibly tasty, with both tangy and slightly sweet flavors, and also a powerhouse of nutrients that we like to make large bowls of and enjoy as a family. This recipe is courtesy of Marco Borges, author *of New York Times* best seller *The 22-Day Revolution.*

Yield:	**Prep time:**	**Cook time:**	**Serving size:**
4 cups	15 minutes	30 minutes	2 cups

Each serving has:			
341 calories	7g total fat	1g saturated fat	0g trans fat
0mg cholesterol	182mg sodium	54g total carbohydrates	9g dietary fiber
6g sugars	18g protein	100mg calcium	6mg iron

½ cup uncooked French lentils

2½ cups water

Salt

½ cup quinoa

2 cups chopped kale

1 TB. tahini

2 TB. lemon juice

1 TB. Vinegar

½ cup sliced grape tomatoes

1. Place lentils in a colander and rinse while discarding any stones. Set aside.

2. In a medium pot over high heat, add lentils, 1 ½ cups water, and a pinch salt, and bring to a boil. Reduce heat to medium-low, partially cover the pot, and simmer for 25 minutes or until lentils are tender. Drain lentils, and set aside to cool until ready to use.

3. In a medium saucepan over high heat, combine quinoa, remaining 1 cup water, and a pinch salt, and bring to a boil. Reduce heat to medium-low, cover, and simmer for 25 minutes or until water is absorbed.

4. Fluff quinoa with a fork, remove from heat, and cover until ready to use.

5. In a large mixing bowl, gently toss cooked lentils, cooked quinoa, and kale until combined.

6. In a small mixing bowl, blend tahini, lemon juice, and vinegar until dressing is smooth.

7. Drizzle dressing over kale salad and gently toss until fully coated. Garnish with grape tomatoes and enjoy.

 **HEALTHY HINT**

Kale is low in calories, high in fiber, antioxidant rich and loaded with vitamins A and K as well as iron. Quinoa is also loaded in fiber and is a complete source of protein (lots of it). Lentils are great for lowering cholesterol and stabilizing blood sugar. They're also rich in folate and magnesium which are big contributors to heart health.

Ginger-Carrot Soup with Crème Fraîche

The silky-sweet carrots in this soup are a perfect match for the subtle aromatic hints of curry. Top off this warm soup with the cool decadence of cashew crème fraîche for a delightfully fresh finish. This recipe is from Matthew Kenney, the world's leading plant-based chef; his integrated, plant-based, lifestyle company provides innovative products and services in 10 cities worldwide.

Yield:	Prep time:	Cook time:	Serving size:
8 cups	10 minutes	45-60 minutes	2 cups soup

Each serving has:			
235 calories	8g total fat	1g saturated fat	0g trans fat
0mg cholesterol	442mg sodium	38g total carbohydrates	10g dietary fiber
18g sugars	6g protein	139mg calcium	3mg iron

2 pounds carrots, peeled and cut into large pieces

¼ tsp. freshly ground black pepper

2 shallots, thinly sliced

2 tsp. minced ginger

¼ tsp. ground cumin

¼ tsp. ground fennel

¼ tsp. caraway seeds

1 tsp. coriander seeds

8 cups low-sodium vegetable broth

2 bay leaves

1 cup cashews, soaked in water overnight and drained

¼ cup water

Juice of 2 small lemons

1 tsp. nutritional yeast

Zest of 1 small lemon

1. Preheat oven to 375°F. Place carrots on a large parchment paper–lined baking sheet. Rub pepper onto carrots, and place pan in oven to roast for 45 minutes.

2. When 15 minutes of roasting time remains, in a large pot over medium-high heat, sauté shallots, ginger, cumin, fennel, caraway seeds, and coriander seeds in a small amount of vegetable broth. Try to neither flood the pan with liquid, nor let it dry completely.

3. Remove carrots from oven and add carrots, remaining vegetable broth, and bay leaves, to the pot. Bring to a boil and then reduce heat to low and gently simmer for 15 minutes.

4. While soup simmers, blend cashews, water, 2 tablespoons lemon juice, and nutritional yeast in a high-powered blender or food processor for 1 minute or until crème frâiche is smooth and creamy.

5. Remove bay leaves from soup, and season soup with remaining lemon juice (to taste) and lemon zest. Blend until smooth with an immersion blender. Serve immediately, garnishing each bowl with 2 tablespoons of cashew crème fraîche.

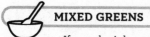 **MIXED GREENS**

If you don't have an immersion blender, carefully pour soup into a regular blender to purée. Note that this may require blending separately in more than one batch. Return soup to the pot after it's blended.

Spinach Split Pea Soup

This split pea soup can be enjoyed chunky or puréed. Its rich fragrance is bolstered by celeriac's luscious, creamy celery flavor and just a hint of sweetness from the carrots and onion. This recipe comes from Julie Morris, Los Angeles–based natural foods chef and *New York Times* best-selling cookbook author of *Superfood Kitchen*.

Yield:	Prep time:	Cook time:	Serving size:
8 cups	10 minutes	45-60 minutes	2 cups soup
Each serving has:			
251 calories	4g total fat	1g saturated fat	0g trans fat
0mg cholesterol	466mg sodium	42g total carbohydrates	16g dietary fiber
4g sugars	13g protein	61mg calcium	3mg iron

3 TB. yellow miso paste

8 cups water

1 TB. olive oil (optional)

1 yellow onion, diced

2 carrots, diced

5 cloves garlic, minced

½ pound celeriac (celery root), peeled and diced

1½ cups dried split peas

1 bay leaf

3 cups baby spinach, tightly packed

½ tsp. sea salt or to taste

½ tsp. freshly ground black pepper or to taste

1. In a small bowl, mix miso paste with 1 cup water until dissolved, and set aside.

2. In a large heavy bottomed pot over medium heat, warm olive oil (if using) or 2 tablespoons water. Add onions and carrots, and cook about 10 minutes or until soft. Add garlic and sauté for an additional minute. Mix in celeriac, split peas, bay leaf, miso mixture, and remaining 7 cups water. Stir to combine and bring soup to a boil over high heat. Cover, and reduce heat to low. Cook for 60 minutes or until peas are very soft and partially dissolved, adding additional water during cooking if needed.

3. Remove bay leaf, and add spinach, salt, and pepper. Cook for one minute or until spinach turns bright green. Remove from heat. If desired, use an immersion blender to partially or fully purée soup.

4. Serve warm. Covered and refrigerated, Spinach Split Pea Soup will last for up to 5 days.

 MIXED GREENS

Although celeriac (celery root) may not be the most alluring looking root in the vegetable aisle, it certainly compensates with its extraordinary texture and flavor. You may be pleasantly surprised at celeriac's ability to make soups, stews, and purees silky smooth. You can also enjoy them as tasty chips or "fries." Alternatively, celeriac is delicious served raw and tossed into salads.

Zel's Zesty Rainbow Salad

A lightly spiced, herb-based dressing, boosted with the nutritional benefits of nuts, tempers the distinct flavor of cilantro in this salad for the perfect balance of tang and tastiness.

Yield:	**Prep time:**	**Serving size:**	
8 cups	30 to 45 minutes	1⅓ cups	
Each serving has:			
140 calories	5g total fat	1g saturated fat	0g trans fat
0mg cholesterol	210mg sodium	19g total carbohydrates	5g dietary fiber
5g sugars	7g protein	99mg calcium	2mg iron

1 large head broccoli, cut into bite-size pieces

1 medium bunch watercress, coarsely chopped

8 medium leaves romaine lettuce, coarsely shredded

2 or 3 medium carrots, coarsely shredded

2 cups frozen peas, thawed

1½ cups shredded red cabbage

4 to 6 medium radishes, sliced

1 small whole green onion

2 cups coarsely chopped fresh cilantro, lightly packed

1 cup water

½ cup cashews or macadamia nuts

¼ cup white wine vinegar

3 TB. fresh lemon juice

2 medium cloves garlic, minced

2 tsp. red miso

¾ tsp. ground cumin

½ tsp. ground coriander

½ tsp. lemon pepper

½ tsp. guar gum or xanthan gum

Pinch cayenne

1. Fill a 3-quart saucepan ⅔ full with water, and bring to a boil over high heat. In small batches, blanch broccoli for 1 minute. Using a slotted spoon, remove broccoli to a dish or bowl to cool. Repeat with remaining broccoli pieces, and set aside.

2. In a large salad bowl, toss watercress and lettuce. Pile cooled broccoli into the center, heaping it high.

3. Surround broccoli with a circle of shredded carrots, followed by a circle of peas, filling the entire surface and covering greens.

4. Arrange red cabbage in 4 piles over peas, and place sliced radishes in spaces between cabbage. Artfully place green onion near center of salad.

5. In a blender, combine cilantro, 1 cup water, cashews, white wine vinegar, lemon juice, garlic, red miso, cumin, coriander, lemon pepper, guar gum, and cayenne. Blend on high speed for 60 seconds or until fully puréed and dressing is smooth and creamy.

6. Pour dressing into a narrow-neck bottle for easy serving. Shake well before serving with salad. (Refrigerated, dressing will keep for 1 week.)

 MIXED GREENS

Salads ought to be colorful and so visually appealing they're irresistible, luring diners to the table. The salad's health benefits are a bonus.

Daikon, Mango, and Avocado Summer Rolls with Ume-Lime Sauce

A refreshing take on traditional spring rolls with superior sweetness accompanied by a fragrant, complex sauce make a perfect appetizer that will get your guests talking. This recipe comes from Miyoko Schinner, vegan entrepreneur, cookbook author, and speaker.

Yield:	Prep time:	Serving size:	
8 rolls	30 minutes	2 rolls	
Each serving has:			
268 calories	6g total fat	1g saturated fat	0g trans fat
0mg cholesterol	429mg sodium	51g total carbohydrates	5g dietary fiber
31g sugars	4g protein	36mg calcium	1mg iron

8 rice paper rounds

Bowl of hot water (for dipping)

6 oz. daikon, peeled and julienned

1 large mango, peeled and julienned

½ English cucumber, peeled and julienned

1 large avocado, peeled and cut into thin strips

1 TB. umeboshi paste

⅓ cup date or maple syrup

⅓ cup fresh lime juice

1. Dip one rice paper round in hot water for 5 to 10 seconds to soften. Place rice paper on a clean surface.

2. Working quickly, place a small and equal amount each of daikon, mango, cucumber, and avocado on rice paper at the end closest to you.

3. Fold in sides of rice paper and then roll as tightly as possible. Cut each roll in half.

4. Dilute umeboshi paste with syrup and whisk in lime juice. Serve as a dipping sauce with rolls.

 **DEFINITION**

Daikon is a large, elongated radish used especially in Asian cuisine and enjoyed raw, pickled, or cooked. **Umeboshi paste** is a sour condiment made from pickled, pureed umeboshi plums and used in dips, dressings, sauces, sushi, and for seasoning vegetables.

Mouthwatering Mains

A proper dinner involves sitting relaxingly at the table after a long, productive day, slowly savoring a delicious, nutritious meal. Yet this isn't always the case.

Some of the recipes in this chapter are quick and simple, while others yield large batches so you can refrigerate or even freeze the leftovers for future dinners when you may be too tired or pressed for time to cook. Supplementing these meals with salads and soups—or mixing and matching for a sample-style meal—is a great way to enhance variety and satiate your hunger.

The recipes in this chapter, from all around the world, are staples in our homes. We sometimes even eat them for breakfast. (But shhh, don't tell anyone!)

In This Chapter

- International noodle dishes
- Classic legume and grain combos
- Hearty herbaceous helpings

Japanoodles

Miso adds a savory, salty component that, together with garlic and sesame, provides the perfect amount of flavor to coat the silky rice noodles.

Yield:	Prep time:	Cook time:	Serving size:
4 cups	5 minutes	5 minutes	1 cup

Each serving has:			
290 calories	1g total fat	0g saturated fat	0g trans fat
0mg cholesterol	710mg sodium	56g total carbohydrates	2g dietary fiber
0g sugars	6g protein	80mg calcium	1mg iron

4 qt. water	2 tsp. gomashio or sesame seeds
1 (8-oz.) pkg. dry rice noodles	4 cups chopped mixed leafy green vegetables (chard, dandelion greens, collard greens, spinach, and/or kale)
½ cup low-sodium miso paste	
2 or 3 medium cloves garlic, crushed	

1. In a medium saucepan over medium-high heat, bring water to a boil. Add rice noodles and boil for 4 or 5 minutes.

2. Meanwhile, in a large bowl, mix together miso paste, garlic, and gomashio.

3. About 30 seconds before noodles are done, add greens to the pan and allow to wilt. Drain noodles and greens in a colander.

4. Add noodles and greens to miso paste mixture, and stir to combine. Serve warm.

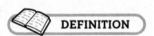 **DEFINITION**

> **Gomashio** is a Japanese condiment made of a blend of toasted sesame seeds, salt, and sometimes sea vegetables.

Herbed Balsamic Pasta

Garden-fresh herbs complemented by balsamic zest inspire the feel of a stroll through Tuscany—an altogether satisfying Italian experience.

Yield:	Prep time:	Serving size:	
6 cups	20 minutes	1½ cups	
Each serving has:			
280 calories	1.5g total fat	0g saturated fat	0g trans fat
0mg cholesterol	40mg sodium	58g total carbohydrates	5g dietary fiber
5g sugars	8g protein	57mg calcium	2mg iron

4 qt. water

1 (12-oz.) pkg. whole-grain pasta

1½ cups chopped fresh basil

1 TB. minced fresh or 1 tsp. dried oregano

1 TB. minced fresh or 1 tsp. dried rosemary

Pinch sea salt (optional)

¾ tsp. freshly ground black pepper

½ cup balsamic vinegar

2 cups chopped fresh spinach

1. In a medium pot over medium-high heat, bring water to a boil. Add pasta and cook according to the package directions.

2. Meanwhile, in a large bowl, combine basil, oregano, rosemary, sea salt (if using), black pepper, and balsamic vinegar.

3. About 1 minute before pasta is done cooking (test it to be sure it's soft), add spinach to the pot with pasta.

4. After 1 minute maximum, drain pasta and spinach in a colander. Add to balsamic vinegar mixture and toss well, coating pasta adequately. Serve warm.

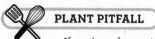 **PLANT PITFALL**

If you're salt-sensitive or have been diagnosed with high blood pressure or kidney disease, omit the salt in recipes.

Buttery Sweet Potato Pasta with Smoky Breadcrumb Topping

The use of caramelized sweet potatoes in a puréed pasta sauce gives a luscious, buttery texture. Topped off with a little smoky crunch, it's purely delicious! This recipe is courtesy of Dreena Burton, recipe developer and cookbook author; visit plantpoweredkitchen.com for more of her recipes.

Yield:	Prep time:	Cook time:	Serving size:
5 servings	30 minutes	70 minutes	1 cup

Each serving has:			
595 calories	7g total fat	0.5g saturated fat	0g trans fat
0mg cholesterol	677mg sodium	118g total carbohydrates	17g dietary fiber
11g sugars	20g protein	58mg calcium	5mg iron

2 medium or 1 very large sweet potato

2 medium to large cloves garlic, roughly chopped

1¼ tsp. sea salt or to taste

Freshly ground black pepper

2 TB. tahini

1 TB. chickpea miso (or another mellow miso like brown rice miso)

2 cups water

1 TB. fresh thyme leaves

¼ tsp. smoked paprika

Pinch freshly grated nutmeg

1½ TB. fresh lemon juice

1¼ lb. whole-grain pasta

4-5 cups baby spinach leaves (optional)

1¼ cup whole-grain breadcrumbs

¼ tsp. smoked paprika (well-rounded)

1. Preheat oven to 425°F. Rinse sweet potatoes but do not peel or pierce. Place potatoes on a parchment paper–lined baking sheet lined and bake for 40 to 60 minutes or until potatoes are fully softened and beginning to caramelize. (Baking time will depend on whether you are using smaller or larger sweet potatoes.) Remove potatoes from oven and cool slightly. Reduce oven temperature to 375°F. Remove sweet potato skins and discard. Set sweet potatoes aside.

2. Prepare pasta according to package directions, cooking it *al dente* (retaining a slight bite, not fully soft).

3. While pasta cooks, in a blender, add cooked sweet potatoes, garlic, 1 teaspoon salt (or less to taste), pepper, tahini, miso, 1 cup water, thyme, paprika, nutmeg, and lemon juice. Purée until smooth, and then add remaining 1 cup water and blend again until fully smooth. Set aside.

4. In a small mixing bowl, combine breadcrumbs with smoked paprika and remaining ¼ teaspoon sea salt. Spread breadcrumbs on a baking sheet and bake for 7 to 8 minutes or until breadcrumbs turn golden. Stir crumbs once or twice while baking so they brown evenly. Let crumbs cool fully and store in an airtight container in fridge until ready to use.

5. Once pasta is cooked, drain it in a colander but don't rinse. Return pasta to the pot, pour sweet potato sauce over pasta, and cook over medium-low heat for a few minutes, just until sauce thickens and is heated through. Add spinach (if using) to pasta and sauce and cook until slightly wilted. Remove from heat and serve, topping each portion with seasoned breadcrumbs.

 HEALTHY HINT

It's always helpful to bake extra sweet potatoes, since you can store leftovers in the fridge for up to 5 days or freeze them for a couple of months in an airtight container. The sweet potatoes and the breadcrumbs in this recipe may be prepared in advance and stored until needed. Many varieties of dry pasta are sold in 1-pound packages. This recipe yields a generous amount of sauce, so you can use more than 1 pound of pasta to stretch it out if you like. We typically use about 1¼ pounds dry pasta—if you use less pasta, your dish will just be a little saucier.

Easy Beans and Quinoa

This warm and hearty one-pot wonder has a very Southwestern flare.

Yield:	Prep time:	Cook time:	Serving size:
4 cups	10 minutes	30 minutes	1 cup

Each serving has:			
170 calories	2g total fat	0g saturated fat	0g trans fat
0mg cholesterol	180mg sodium	30g total carbohydrates	6g dietary fiber
2g sugars	8g protein	64mg calcium	3mg iron

1 small yellow onion, chopped

2 medium cloves garlic, minced or crushed

¼ cup vegetable broth

½ cup dry quinoa

1 (15-oz.) can no-salt-added pinto or black beans, rinsed and drained

1 cup water

½ tsp. ground cumin

¼ tsp. sea salt (optional)

¼ tsp. freshly ground black pepper

½ cup frozen corn kernels, thawed

¼ cup chopped fresh cilantro

1. In a medium pot over medium heat, sauté onion and garlic in vegetable broth for 5 minutes or until onions are translucent.

2. Add quinoa, pinto beans, water, cumin, sea salt (if using), and black pepper. Bring to a boil, lower heat to low, and simmer for 20 minutes, stirring frequently, or until all liquid is absorbed.

3. Stir in corn and cilantro until heated through. Remove from heat and serve.

 MIXED GREENS

Cilantro is actually the stems and leaves of the coriander plant. Popular in the Southwestern and Western regions of the United States, cilantro has a pungent odor many people don't appreciate. Italian parsley can be used instead of cilantro if you're not a fan.

Baked Lentils and Rice Casserole

Rustic and hearty, this simple baked dish will be a regular staple in your home.

Yield:	Prep time:	Cook time:	Serving size:
10 cups	5 minutes	90 minutes	1¾ cups

Each serving has:			
250 calories	1g total fat	0g saturated fat	0g trans fat
0mg cholesterol	190mg sodium	48g total carbohydrates	14g dietary fiber
3g sugars	13g protein	66mg calcium	4mg iron

1 medium yellow onion, chopped

1 cup uncooked wild and/or brown rice

1 cup dried lentils (red, green, and/or caviar)

1 (14-oz.) can crushed tomatoes, with juice

1 TB. chopped fresh or 1 tsp. dried rosemary

1 TB. chopped fresh or 1 tsp. dried basil

1 tsp. chopped fresh or 1 tsp. dried oregano

4 cups vegetable broth

1. Preheat the oven to 350°F.

2. In a large, deep baking dish, combine onion, rice, lentils, tomatoes, rosemary, basil, oregano, and vegetable broth, and stir gently.

3. Bake, covered, for 90 minutes, stirring every 30 minutes to prevent sticking, until bubbling and browned. Serve warm.

 MIXED GREENS

Lentils are one of the most nutrient-dense foods around. With loads of fiber, protein, iron, and folate, these nutritional superstars will rock your world!

Roasted Cauliflower and Sweet Potatoes with Creamy Chimichurri Sauce

The garlicky Argentinean herb sauce, chimichurri, traditionally contains a lot of olive oil. This recipe leaves out the oil and adds cooked cannellini beans for a creamy version that adds a flavor punch to roasted vegetables and other foods. (It's great over baked tofu.) This recipe is the creation of Robin Robertson, author of more than 20 cookbooks including the best-seller *Vegan Planet.*

Yield:	Prep time:	Cook time:	Serving size:
4 servings	15 minutes	25 minutes	1 cup

Each serving has:			
87 calories	0.6g total fat	0g saturated fat	0g trans fat
0mg cholesterol	94mg sodium	18g total carbohydrates	4g dietary fiber
4g sugars	4g protein	55mg calcium	2mg iron

1 small head cauliflower, cored	3 garlic cloves, crushed
1 large sweet potato, peeled and cut into ¼-inch-thick slices	⅓ cup fresh parsley leaves
Olive oil cooking spray (optional)	¼ cup fresh basil leaves
½ tsp. salt or more to taste	2 tsp. fresh thyme
½ tsp. freshly ground black pepper or more to taste	½ cup cooked or canned cannellini beans (or other white beans), drained and rinsed
2 shallots, quartered	2 TB. lemon juice

1. Preheat the oven to 425°F. Line 2 large, rimmed baking sheets with parchment paper and set aside.

2. Place cauliflower on a cutting board, cored-side down, and cut it into ½-inch-thick slices using a serrated-edge knife. Arrange cauliflower slices in a single layer on the prepared baking sheets, spray with olive oil cooking spray (if using), and season with salt and pepper. Arrange sweet potato slices on the second baking sheet. Spritz with olive oil cooking spray (if using) and season with salt and pepper.

3. Roast vegetables 20 to 25 minutes or until tender and browned, turning once with a large metal spatula about halfway through.

4. While vegetables are roasting, place shallots and garlic in a food processor and pulse until minced. Add parsley, basil, thyme, ½ teaspoon salt, and ¼ teaspoon black pepper to shallot and garlic mixture and pulse until finely minced. Add the cannellini beans and lemon juice to mixture and blend until sauce is smooth.

5. Remove vegetables from oven and serve with sauce poured over the top.

 HEALTHY HINT

Blended cannellini beans (cooked from scratch or canned) are a perfect substitute for oil in terms of adding creaminess to a dressing, dip, or sauce. Swapping them in a recipe for oil reduces the fat and calorie content and also adds in healthful fiber and phytonutrients.

Steamed Veggie Sampler

Steaming vegetables until they're just crisp-tender is one of the healthiest ways to prepare them because it preserves more of the nutrients than boiling or oven-roasting. Tossed with fresh herbs and a little vegetable broth, and given a squeeze of fresh lemon juice at the end, perks up their naturally sweet and unique flavors.

Yield:	Prep time:	Cook time:	Serving size:
6 cups	10 to 15 minutes	8 to 15 minutes	1 cup

Each serving has:			
45 calories	0g total fat	0g saturated fat	0g trans fat
0mg cholesterol	40mg sodium	9g total carbohydrates	2g dietary fiber
3g sugars	3g protein	47mg calcium	1mg iron

4 large cloves garlic, peeled

1½ cups small cauliflower florets

1½ cups small broccoli florets

1 cup (¼-in. thick) diagonally cut carrots or diagonally halved baby carrots

1 cup sugar snap peas, ends trimmed

1½ cups (2-in. long) diagonally cut asparagus, ends trimmed

¼ cup low-sodium vegetable broth

¼ cup chopped fresh parsley

1 TB. chopped fresh dill or thyme, or to taste

Sea salt

Freshly ground black pepper

1 lemon, cut into wedges

1. In a large pot with a collapsible steamer basket or a steamer rack insert, add garlic and set over medium-high heat. Add enough water so it just touches the bottom of the collapsible steamer, or add 1 or 2 inches water if using a rack insert (garlic should not come into direct contact with the water). Cover and bring to a boil.

2. Depending on the steamer setup, steam vegetables separately in batches or all together. Cauliflower and broccoli florets take 5 to 7 minutes, carrots and sugar snap peas take 3 to 5 minutes, and asparagus takes 2 or 3 minutes to steam. If steaming all together, add them in order, starting with cauliflower and broccoli florets, after 2 minutes add carrots and sugar snap peas, and when they're crisp-tender, add asparagus and steam for 2 minutes.

3. Transfer steamed vegetables to a large bowl. Remove garlic cloves from water with a slotted spoon, slice or chop, and add to steamed vegetables, if desired.

4. Add vegetable broth, parsley, dill, sea salt, and black pepper, and toss well to combine. Squeeze fresh lemon juice over individual servings, and serve hot.

Variation: Feel free to substitute other vegetables in this recipe such as potatoes, turnips, artichokes, Brussels sprouts, green beans, corn, greens, mushrooms, or zucchini that have been cut into bite-size pieces and steamed until crisp-tender. Omit fresh herbs and vegetable broth, if desired, and instead season with sea salt and black pepper to serve with your favorite vinaigrette or creamy salad dressing.

 HEALTHY HINT

When steaming, be sure to use a pot that's large enough to hold items and allows the steam to fully circulate around them. Be sure the water is boiling and producing steam before adding the vegetables, and keep the pot tightly covered to prevent the steam from escaping. When removing the lid, lean back to avoid being burned by the steam, and use pot holders to remove the steamer basket or insert. Finally, you can use the liquid that remains in the pot to flavor soups, stews, and sauces.

Salsa Falafel Burgers

These burgers are filled with zesty flavors, yet they take only 7 minutes to prep for the oven. Now that's my kind of burger! This recipe comes from Laura Theodore, a nationally recognized public television food personality, radio host, and popular vegan cookbook author; learn more at jazzyvegetarian.com.

Yield:	Prep time:	Cook time:	Serving size:
6 burgers	10 minutes	45 minutes	1 burger

Each serving has:			
161 calories	1g total fat	0g saturated fat	0g trans fat
0mg cholesterol	710mg sodium	56g total carbohydrates	2g dietary fiber
0g sugars	6g protein	80mg calcium	1mg iron

1 can chickpeas (garbanzo beans), drained and rinsed	½ tsp. turmeric
1 TB. (well-rounded) sesame tahini	¼ tsp. ground cumin
½ tsp. smoked paprika	⅓ cup plus 2 TB. prepared salsa
	⅔ cup rolled oats

1. Preheat the oven to 400°F. Line a medium-sized rimmed baking pan with parchment paper.

2. In a medium mixing bowl, mash chickpeas, tahini, paprika, turmeric, and cumin with a potato masher or large fork until crumbly. Add salsa and continue to mash until well combined. Stir in rolled oats and mix until incorporated.

3. Scoop one-sixth of chickpea mixture and place it on the prepared pan. Flatten with your hands and form mixture into a burger shape. Continue with remaining chickpea mixture until you've made 6 patties.

4. Bake patties for 25 minutes. Remove the baking pan from the oven, flip burgers, and bake for an additional 10 to 12 minutes or until patties are almost set and slightly golden. Let cool for 5 to 7 minutes before serving.

 MIXED GREENS

Simple, delicious recipes such as these burgers with only four ingredients plus spices make eating plant-based easy and accessible for everyone. Bonus: it is almost always the rule that the simpler the ingredients, the healthier the recipe.

Fiesta Fantastica

The earthy spices enrich the warm, hearty lentils and are contrasted by fresh crisp greens and all the blended flavors of the accoutrements.

Yield:	Prep time:	Cook time:	Serving size:
4 tostadas	10 minutes	55 minutes	1 tostada

Each serving has:			
340 calories	10g total fat	1.5g saturated fat	0g trans fat
0mg cholesterol	740mg sodium	52g total carbohydrates	14g dietary fiber
5g sugars	16g protein	125mg calcium	4mg iron

1 medium yellow onion, chopped

2 medium cloves garlic, crushed

3 cups vegetable broth

1 cup green lentils, dried and rinsed

1 tsp. ground cumin

1 tsp. turmeric

1 tsp. freshly ground black pepper

1 tsp. chili powder

4 large or 8 small whole-grain tortillas

4 cups chopped mixed greens

1 cup Sweet Pea Guacamole (recipe in Chapter 22)

1 cup Plant-Based Sour Cream (recipe in Chapter 19)

1 cup low-sodium salsa

1. In a medium saucepan over medium heat, sauté onions and garlic in ¼ cup vegetable broth for 5 minutes or until onions are translucent.

2. Add lentils, cumin, turmeric, black pepper, chili powder, and remaining 2¾ cups vegetable broth. Simmer for 40 to 50 minutes or until all liquid is absorbed.

3. Warm tortillas on the stovetop, in the microwave, or in a toaster oven until heated through. Spoon lentils onto tortillas, and layer mixed greens, Sweet Pea Guacamole, Plant-Based Sour Cream, and salsa on top. Serve immediately.

Variations: For more of a taco or burrito, use less stuffing and roll it up. To make a Fiesta Fantastica Salad Extraordinaire, add more raw veggie strips like cucumbers, bell peppers, tomatoes, and jicama.

 **HEALTHY HINT**

When shopping for salsa, why not try one of the delicious commercially prepared salsas available? You can find sweet, fruit-based salsas (like peach or mango), ones with added beans, and freshly made salsas stocked in the produce section of many supermarkets.

Kathy's Easy Quinoa Burrito Bowl

This spicy, earthy bowl is hearty, fresh, and full of traditional Mexican flavors and comes from Kathy Patalsky, the author of *Healthy Happy Vegan Kitchen* and *365 Vegan Smoothies*, as well as the founder of the popular food website FindingVegan.com.

Yield:	Prep time:	Cook time:	Serving size:
4 bowls	30 minutes	30 minutes	1 bowl

Each serving has:			
622 calories	22g total fat	3.2g saturated fat	0g trans fat
0mg cholesterol	857mg sodium	88g total carbohydrates	21g dietary fiber
8g sugars	24g protein	166mg calcium	8mg iron

1 cup plus 2 TB. dry quinoa

1⅔ cups water

⅓ cup medium sweet onion, diced

¼ tsp plus pinch sea salt

1½ cups canned black beans
(15oz. can), drained and rinsed

1 avocado, diced or mashed

Juice of 1 small lime or lemon

Pinch ground black pepper

1 tsp. cumin

⅛ tsp. chipotle powder

1 TB. nutritional yeast

4 cups chopped romaine lettuce

1 tomato, diced

¼ cup chopped, pitted black olives

½ cup chopped fresh cilantro

Salsa (optional)

2 to 4 corn tortillas, warmed

1. In a medium saucepan over high heat, add quinoa, water, onion and ¼ teaspoon salt. Stir, and bring to a boil. Cover with a lid, reduce heat to low, and simmer for 15 minutes or until most liquid is absorbed.

2. While quinoa is cooking, warm black beans in a small sauce pan over low heat, or in a microwave-safe dish in the microwave oven until just heated through.

3. In a small bowl, toss avocado and lime juice. Season with a pinch salt and pepper.

4. Remove quinoa from heat and allow it to rest, still covered, for 5 additional minutes. Remove lid. Add cumin, chipotle powder, and nutritional yeast to quinoa and fluff with a fork.

5. Build bowls: Divide romaine, diced tomatoes, and olives evenly among 4 bowls, followed by a few large scoops quinoa and black beans in each bowl. Top with avocado and garnish with cilantro and salsa (if using). Serve with warm corn tortillas.

Variation: Serve your Burrito Bowl with cashew sour cream. Soak ¾ cup raw cashews overnight and drain. Blend cashews with 2 tablespoons lime or lemon juice, ⅛ teaspoon sea salt (or to taste), and ½ cup water (or as needed to blend) in a food processor or blender until smooth. Chill for a minimum of 20 minutes before serving.

 MIXED GREENS

Burrito bowls are one of our favorite go-to meals. They can be whipped up swiftly on a busy weeknight, and the flavors are incredible. You can get fancy and add accents like cilantro or cashew sour cream, or keep things simple with just the basics. We like to serve burrito bowls with tortillas to create a fajita-like effect! Using quinoa in place of rice is a smart move because it is packed with protein and has a fluffy texture to love.

Wacky Wild Rice

With its Mediterranean flavors and mixture of textures, this grainy, slightly acidic rice dish hits the spot.

Yield:	Prep time:	Cook time:	Serving size:
6 cups	10 minutes plus 2 hours to soak	60 minutes	1 cup

Each serving has:			
250 calories	2g total fat	0g saturated fat	0g trans fat
0mg cholesterol	220mg sodium	50g total carbohydrates	10g dietary fiber
7g sugars	12g protein	47mg calcium	3mg iron

5 cups water or vegetable broth

1 cup sun-dried tomatoes

1¼ cups wild rice, rinsed well

1 (15-oz.) can no-salt-added chickpeas, rinsed and drained

1 (14-oz.) can artichoke hearts packed in water, rinsed and drained

1. In a small bowl, combine 2 cups water and sun-dried tomatoes, and set aside to soak for 2 hours. Drain off and discard water.

2. In a medium saucepan over high heat, bring remaining 3 cups water to a boil. Add wild rice, reduce heat to low, and simmer, partially covered, for 45 to 50 minutes or until nearly all liquid is absorbed.

3. Turn off heat and allow rice to stand for 10 minutes or until remaining liquid is absorbed.

4. Stir in sun-dried tomatoes, chickpeas, and artichoke hearts. Serve warm.

 PLANT PITFALL

Wild rice needs to be rinsed very well before cooking because it has a tendency to hold on to pebbles, hulls, and dirt. Soak in warm water for a few minutes to allow any debris to be loosened. Then skim off what you can and use a colander or a sifter to wash away the rest.

Collard Greens with Beans and Barley

The delightful blends of textures, sweet and pungent flavors, and bright colors of this staple dish will keep you thinking about seconds.

Yield:	Prep time:	Cook time:	Serving size:
6 cups	10 minutes	10 minutes	1½ cups

Each serving has:			
400 calories	2.5g total fat	0g saturated fat	0g trans fat
0mg cholesterol	570mg sodium	84g total carbohydrates	19g dietary fiber
4g sugars	15g protein	171mg calcium	4mg iron

4½ cups water	3 cups vegetable broth
1 large bunch collard greens, rinsed and chopped	1 (15-oz.) can cannellini beans, rinsed and drained
1 large yellow onion, chopped	¼ tsp. freshly ground black pepper
2 large cloves garlic, minced	4½ cups cooked barley
2 TB. whole-grain oat flour	

1. In a medium pot over medium-high heat, bring 4 cups water to a boil. Add collard greens, and blanch for 1 or 2 minutes or until cooked down and starting to darken in color. Drain.

2. In a separate large pot over medium heat, sauté onion and garlic in remaining ½ cup water for 5 minutes or until onion is translucent.

3. In a medium bowl, whisk together oat flour and vegetable broth, and add to onion mixture. Bring to a boil, and add cannellini beans and black pepper. Reduce heat to low, and simmer, stirring, for 1 minute.

4. Add blanched greens and cooked barley, and simmer, stirring frequently, until flavors are melded and nearly all liquid is absorbed. Serve warm.

 **HEALTHY HINT**

Blanching is an excellent way to preserve nutrient content and alter the texture of vegetables. When used instead of boiling, baking, or roasting, more of the vitamins, minerals, and phytonutrients remain.

Roasted Cheesy Cauliflower

This may be the simplest dish you've ever made, and yet you won't be able to stop yourself from finishing the whole thing! Think warm and toasty sprinkled with nutty cheese.

Yield:	Prep time:	Cook time:	Serving size:
2 cups	5 minutes	20 to 25 minutes	1 cup

Each serving has:			
84 calories	0.5g total fat	0g saturated fat	0g trans fat
0mg cholesterol	88mg sodium	16g total carbohydrates	8g dietary fiber
7g sugars	8g protein	63mg calcium	1mg iron

1 medium head cauliflower, cut into florets	1 TB. nutritional yeast flakes

1. Preheat the oven to 400°F. Line a baking sheet with a silicone baking mat.

2. Lay cauliflower florets on the baking sheet, and place in the oven. Bake for 20 to 25 minutes or until soft edges are golden brown.

3. Remove from the oven, and sprinkle with nutritional yeast flakes. Serve warm.

Variation: For a richer dish, substitute 2 tablespoons Parmesan Shake (recipe in Chapter 19) for the nutritional yeast flakes.

 **HEALTHY HINT**

Cauliflower provides almost a day's worth of vitamin C and is a member of the extremely health-promoting, cancer-fighting cruciferous vegetable group. Roasting it brings out the subtle sweet flavors and is a truly enjoyable treat.

Beans and Greens Chili

This warm and spicy chili is earthy and fiery and will fill you up no matter how hungry you are.

Yield:	Prep time:	Cook time:	Serving size:
8 cups	10 minutes	50 to 60 minutes	1⅓ cups

Each serving has:			
320 calories	2g total fat	0g saturated fat	0g trans fat
0mg cholesterol	180mg sodium	63g total carbohydrates	21g dietary fiber
13g sugars	18g protein	206mg calcium	5mg iron

1 medium yellow onion, chopped

2 medium carrots, chopped

3 ribs celery, chopped

2 cups vegetable broth

2 (15-oz.) cans kidney beans, drained and rinsed

1 (15-oz.) can chickpeas, drained and rinsed

1 (28-oz.) can chopped tomatoes, with juice

1 (6-oz.) can tomato paste

8 to 12 medium baby bella mushrooms, sliced

1 (15-oz.) can corn, rinsed and drained

2 or 3 TB. chili powder

1 TB. freshly ground black pepper

1 TB. curry powder

4 cups chopped leafy green vegetables

1. In a large soup pot over medium heat, sauté onions, carrots, and celery in ½ cup vegetable broth for 5 minutes or until onions are translucent.

2. Add kidney beans, chickpeas, chopped tomatoes, tomato paste, mushrooms, corn, chili powder, black pepper, curry powder, and remaining 1½ cups vegetable broth. Stir to combine. Reduce heat to medium-low, and simmer for 40 to 50 minutes, stirring occasionally.

3. When chili appears soft, mix in leafy greens and turn off heat. Serve warm.

 **HEALTHY HINT**

Feel free to experiment with different combinations of beans, veggies, and spices in this chili. Use it as a template to highlight your favorites or whatever you have in your cupboard.

CHAPTER 2

Grab-and-Go Foods

The indulgent dips and spreads in this chapter are your ticket to whole-food heaven. Turn these recipes into a meal by spreading them on whole-grain breads, topping your salads with them, or eating enough to make you feel fulfilled.

There are many times that food isn't simply for squelching hunger, but is being served for entertainment and celebration. Dips and spreads are certainly a big part of those occasions. As you omit all the old-school food rules about how many meals and snacks to eat in a day, you'll tune in to your body's actual needs. Many times, you may notice you only feel like eating something light, while other occasions will call for something more substantial. The light fare in this chapter lends itself to those lighter times.

However, if you happen to be voraciously hungry, these dishes can be enjoyed as sides, appetizers, or as an entire meal. One of our favorite midday meals is Simply Hummus with cucumbers ... but we eat half of the entire recipe, at least! Dipping and scooping is fun and satisfying, and can fill you up for hours!

In This Chapter

- Healthful hummus
- Sassy spreads
- Delicious dips

Simply Hummus

This velvety spread delights with lemon accents and garlic undertones.

Yield:	Prep time:	Serving size:	
3 cups	5 minutes	½ cup	
Each serving has:			
150 calories	1g total fat	0g saturated fat	0g trans fat
0mg cholesterol	30mg sodium	26g total carbohydrates	6g dietary fiber
less than 1g sugars	9g protein	63mg calcium	2mg iron

2 (15-oz.) cans chickpeas, rinsed and
    drained

¼ cup freshly squeezed lemon juice

2 medium cloves garlic, peeled

2 TB. nutritional yeast flakes

½ cup water

¼ tsp. freshly ground black pepper

¼ tsp. ground paprika

1. In a food processor fitted with an S blade, combine chickpeas, lemon juice, garlic, nutritional yeast flakes, water, black pepper, and paprika. Process for 2 or 3 minutes or until
   finely ground.

2. Scrape down the sides of the food processor bowl with a wooden spoon, and process for
   1 minute longer.

3. Transfer mixture to a serving bowl, and serve with whole-grain crackers or tortillas; with
   sliced Persian cucumbers, tomatoes, and carrots; or on salad as a dressing, if desired. Store
   any leftovers in the refrigerator, covered, for up to 4 days.

Variation: For added color, nutrients, and a flavor kick, top with microgreens, sprouts, or
shredded leafy greens. Before adding the garlic into the food processor, try roasting it for a
smokier flavor. To do this, slice the top off of the entire head and place it on a silicone baking
mat– or parchment paper–lined baking sheet. Roast in a 400°F oven for 20 to 25 minutes or until
cloves are soft.

 **HEALTHY HINT**

Chickpeas are filled with soluble and insoluble fibers, protein, and a ton of flavor.
Making hummus from dried beans is easy and tastes even better than the canned
version. Try rinsing and then soaking them for a few hours first. Then rinse again.
Finally, cook at a ratio of 3 cups water per 1 cup beans. They become tender after
cooking for 1 to 1½ hours.

Indian Hummus

If you like curry, you'll love the unique flavor combination of this hummus. Sweet, strong, and spicy, this hummus can complement less intense items or stand on its own.

Yield:	Prep time:	Serving size:	
2¼ cups	10 minutes	½ cup	
Each serving has:			
250 calories	4.5g total fat	1g saturated fat	0g trans fat
0mg cholesterol	10mg sodium	46g total carbohydrates	8g dietary fiber
20g sugars	9g protein	60mg calcium	3mg iron

2 (15-oz.) cans chickpeas, rinsed and drained

2 TB. freshly squeezed lemon juice

2 medium cloves garlic, minced

2 TB. cashew butter

1 tsp. curry powder

1 tsp. turmeric

¼ tsp. freshly ground black pepper

2 medium pitted dates or 4 TB. Date Paste (recipe in Chapter 19)

½ cup water

1 cup loosely packed raisins

1. In a food processor fitted with an S blade, combine chickpeas, lemon juice, garlic, cashew butter, curry powder, turmeric, black pepper, dates, and water. Process for 2 or 3 minutes or until finely ground.

2. Scrape down the sides of the food processor bowl with a wooden spoon, and process for 30 more seconds. Sprinkle in raisins, and pulse for 10 seconds or until well combined.

3. Transfer hummus to a serving bowl, and serve with whole-wheat naan bread, whole-grain crackers, or raw vegetables, if desired. Store any leftovers in the refrigerator, covered, for up to 4 days.

Variation: You can use currants instead of the raisins if you like. Natural peanut butter or raw tahini are also good in place of the cashew butter.

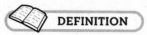 **DEFINITION**

Curry powder is a blend of spices native to India. Although you'll find many different variations, most include turmeric, ginger, paprika, coriander, cumin, pepper, cloves, fenugreek, fennel seeds, curry leaves, and garlic.

Sweet Pea Guacamole

If you love guacamole, you'll delight in this sweeter, milder version. Garlicky and zesty, the sweetness of the peas balances out the flavors.

Yield:	Prep time:	Serving size:	
4 cups	20 minutes	½ cup	
Each serving has:			
180 calories	11g total fat	1.5g saturated fat	0g trans fat
0mg cholesterol	110mg sodium	18g total carbohydrates	8g dietary fiber
1g sugars	6g protein	55mg calcium	2mg iron

3 medium ripe avocados, peeled and pitted

¼ cup freshly squeezed lemon or lime juice

1 tsp. chili powder

½ tsp. freshly ground black pepper

1 cup frozen peas, thawed

1 (15-oz.) can no-salt-added cannellini beans, rinsed and drained

1 or 2 medium cloves garlic, peeled (optional)

½ cup commercially prepared oil-free, low-sodium salsa

1. In a large bowl, mash avocados with a fork until less lumpy. Add lemon juice, chili powder, and black pepper, and smash with the fork until creamy.

2. In a food processor fitted with an S blade or a blender, combine peas, cannellini beans, and garlic (if using). Process or blend for 10 seconds or only until mixed well but still grainy.

3. Add avocado mixture and salsa, and process or blend for 5 to 10 seconds. Scrape down the sides of the food processor bowl with a wooden spoon, and process for 5 to 10 more seconds or just until evenly combined.

4. Transfer to a serving bowl, and serve with homemade chips, corn thins, or whole-grain tortillas; on a baked potato; or in a salad, if desired. Store any leftovers in the refrigerator, covered, for up to 2 days.

Variation: You can also use a commercially prepared guacamole or one from a restaurant if you can't find ripe avocados. Just replace the avocados, lemon juice, chili powder, and black pepper with 1 cup guacamole.

 **HEALTHY HINT**

To peel and pit an avocado easily, slice it open from the stem vertically around the circumference of the fruit. Pry it in half, and pluck out the pit by stabbing it with the end of a sharp knife or scooping it out with a large spoon. Slide a spoon between the flesh and the peel to remove.

Marinara Corn Cakes

This simple snack is tangy and mild. Basil overtones keep your taste buds content.

Yield:	Prep time:	Serving size:	
4 corn cakes	5 minutes	4 corn cakes	
Each serving has:			
200 calories	5g total fat	0.5g saturated fat	0g trans fat
0mg cholesterol	230mg sodium	23g total carbohydrates	5g dietary fiber
2g sugars	12g protein	84mg calcium	2mg iron

¼ cup oil-free marinara sauce, at room temperature or heated

4 corn or rice thins

2 TB. minced fresh basil

3 oz. extra-firm tofu, thinly sliced

1. Spread 1 tablespoon marinara sauce onto each corn thin.

2. Sprinkle ½ tablespoon basil onto each corn thin, and cover with sliced tofu.

Variation: Corn thins are similar to rice cakes, as they're simply puffed corn. You can substitute rice cakes instead or make these on a whole-grain cracker, tortilla, or bread.

 **HEALTHY HINT**

Opt for an oil-free marinara sauce when buying commercial brands. The label should indicate "fat-free" or "oil-free," but to be certain, read the ingredients list.

Savory Nut Spread

Cheesy and pungent, this spread brings out tastes of the Mediterranean, thanks to the sun-dried tomatoes and *tahini*.

Yield:	Prep time:	Serving size:	
1½ cups	10 minutes plus 2 hours for soaking	¼ cup	

Each serving has:			
160 calories	12g total fat	2g saturated fat	0g trans fat
0mg cholesterol	60mg sodium	10g total carbohydrates	2g dietary fiber
2g sugars	6g protein	13mg calcium	2mg iron

2⅓ cups water	1 TB. freshly squeezed lemon juice
1½ cups raw cashews	½ tsp. tamari
4 sun-dried tomatoes	½ tsp. garlic powder
2 TB. nutritional yeast flakes	½ tsp. ground paprika
1 TB. raw tahini	¼ tsp. freshly ground black pepper (optional)

1. In a small bowl, combine 2 cups water with cashews and sun-dried tomatoes. Set aside to soak for 2 hours. Drain off water and rinse well.

2. In a food processor fitted with an S blade, combine cashews, sun-dried tomatoes, nutritional yeast flakes, tahini, lemon juice, remaining ⅓ cup water, tamari, garlic powder, paprika, and black pepper (if using). Process for 2 or 3 minutes or until smooth.

3. Scrape down the sides of the food processor bowl with a wooden spoon, and process for 10 more seconds or until smooth.

4. Transfer mixture to a serving bowl. Serve on whole-grain crackers, with sliced veggies, or on whole-grain bread as a sandwich spread, if desired. Store any leftovers in the refrigerator, covered, for up to 4 days.

Variation: Try this spread using other nuts, like almonds or walnuts, or a combination of different nuts and seeds like sunflower or hempseeds to measure 1½ cups.

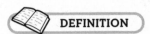 **DEFINITION**

Tahini is a thick, smooth, Middle Eastern paste made of raw, ground, hulled sesame seeds.

Hot "Cheesy" Vegetable Dip

A perfect party dish, this dip is zesty, spicy, and a rainbow of colors. You'll find excuses to make this flavor-filled bubbling delicacy on normal occasions, too.

Yield:	Prep time:	Cook time:	Serving size:
6 cups	10 minutes	50 minutes	1 cup

Each serving has:			
180 calories	3g total fat	0g saturated fat	0g trans fat
0mg cholesterol	410mg sodium	27g total carbohydrates	15g dietary fiber
3g sugars	15g protein	62mg calcium	2mg iron

1 (14-oz.) pkg. silken tofu	¼ cup freshly squeezed lemon juice
2 (14-oz.) cans artichoke hearts packed in water, rinsed and drained	2 medium cloves garlic, peeled
	6 TB. nutritional yeast flakes
2 large roasted red peppers packed in water, rinsed and drained	2 TB. tamari
	1 TB. chopped fresh or 1 tsp. dried parsley
2 cups loosely packed fresh spinach, rinsed and dried	1 tsp. freshly ground black pepper
	½ tsp. cayenne

1. Preheat the oven to 350°F.

2. Crumble tofu into a food processor. Add artichoke hearts, roasted red peppers, spinach, lemon juice, garlic, nutritional yeast flakes, tamari, parsley, black pepper, and cayenne. Process for 45 to 60 seconds or until unified and silky.

3. Pour mixture into an 11×7×2-inch baking dish. Bake, covered, for 30 minutes. Uncover and bake for 20 more minutes or until golden brown.

4. Serve hot with whole-grain crackers, pita bread, and cut vegetables, if desired.

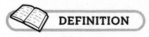 **DEFINITION**

Tamari is a wheat-free, naturally fermented soybean sauce.

Sensational Sweets

Ahh, dessert. The sweets in this chapter are even more indulgent because they're filled with health-promoting ingredients. Delight in the fact that you can satisfy your sweet tooth with these guilt-free treats.

If you love sweets, you'll be pleasantly amazed at how many decadent desserts can be made using only whole-food sweeteners, dates, fruit purées, and maple syrup. Date paste can easily be made (as seen in Chapter 19), purchased in Middle Eastern markets, or ordered online (see Appendix D). Just be sure no added ingredients are included.

From simple fresh fruit to fancy desserts, a whole food, plant-based diet will satisfy your sweet tooth more than any refined, processed item will. Reintroduce your taste buds to nature's sweetness, and enjoy the flavors and their accompanying health benefits!

In This Chapter

- Cookies to satisfy your cravings
- Sweet brownies and breads
- Fantastic fruit desserts

Sweet Cream Dip

Redefine comfort food with this velvety sweet combination.

Yield:	Prep time:	Serving size:	
3 cups	5 minutes	½ cup	
Each serving has:			
190 calories	2g total fat	0g saturated fat	0g trans fat
0mg cholesterol	30mg sodium	35g total carbohydrates	0g dietary fiber
34g sugars	5g protein	216mg calcium	1mg iron

1 (14-oz.) pkg. silken tofu

2 TB. alcohol-free vanilla extract

½ cup Date Paste (recipe in Chapter 19)

1. In a blender or food processor, combine tofu, vanilla extract, and Date Paste, and blend for 45 to 60 seconds or until creamy.

2. Use as a topping for baked goods, as a dip for fresh fruits, or as a yogurt, if desired.

Variation: You can use maple syrup instead of Date Paste in this recipe, but the consistency will be thinner. If you prefer the thickness, decrease the amount of maple syrup to ⅓ cup. Or substitute almond (or other-flavored) extract for a more distinctive flavor.

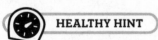 **HEALTHY HINT**

Within seconds, you can indulge your senses with this versatile dessert or snack. Treat this recipe as a topping, dip, or yogurt for an irresistible pleasure. It also works with fruits throughout the year. Dip apples and bananas in the winter and peaches and berries in the summer.

Unclassic Oatmeal Raisin Cookies

Light and fluffy, these cookies are maple-rich with raisin accents—a new unclassically classic treat.

Yield:	Prep time:	Cook time:	Serving size:
36 cookies	10 minutes	7 to 10 minutes per batch	2 cookies

Each serving has:			
130 calories	1g total fat	0g saturated fat	0g trans fat
0mg cholesterol	75mg sodium	30g total carbohydrates	1g dietary fiber
22g sugars	1g protein	126mg calcium	1mg iron

1 medium ripe banana, peeled and mashed	½ tsp. salt
1 cup Date Paste (recipe in Chapter 19)	½ tsp. aluminum-free baking powder
1 TB. alcohol-free vanilla extract	½ tsp. baking soda
¾ cup oat flour	2 cups old-fashioned rolled oats
	1 cup raisins, packed

1. Preheat the oven to 350°F. Line a baking sheet with a silicone baking mat.

2. In a large bowl, mash banana with a fork. Mix in Date Paste and vanilla extract.

3. Slowly stir oat flour, salt, aluminum-free baking powder, and baking soda into banana mixture. When mixture is smooth, add old-fashioned rolled oats and raisins, and stir until evenly distributed.

4. Scoop dough by tablespoons onto the baking sheet. Bake for 7 to 10 minutes per batch or until edges are golden brown.

5. Cool on a wire rack and serve.

Variation: You can add in 1 cup grain-sweetened chocolate chips, found in health food stores or online (see Appendix D) and/or ½ cup chopped walnuts or pecans for a richer dessert.

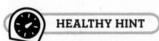 **HEALTHY HINT**

Although famous for their high soluble fiber content, oats are also rich in other nutrients, such as manganese, selenium, phosphorus, thiamin, and magnesium.

Figamajigs

This recipe takes fig bars to a whole new level! Hard to believe raw nuts and dried fruits can combine to create such sweet and chewy goodness.

Yield:	Prep time:	Serving size:	
12 bars	5 minutes	1 bar	
Each serving has:			
220 calories	13g total fat	<1g saturated fat	0g trans fat
0mg cholesterol	2mg sodium	26g total carbohydrates	6g dietary fiber
19g sugars	6g protein	34mg calcium	0.5mg iron

2 cups raw almonds

1 cup dried figs

1 cup pitted dates

1 TB. alcohol-free vanilla extract

1. In a food processor fitted with an S blade, process almonds for approximately 30 to 45 seconds or until they form a flourlike consistency.

2. Add dates and figs, and process until mixture begins to clump together.

3. Add vanilla extract, and process for 10 more seconds or until well combined.

4. Spoon mixture into an 8×8-inch silicone baking pan and press down with your hands. Cut into 12 bars, and serve.

Variation: You can also roll the mixture into balls instead of bars or shape them with cookie cutters to make them fun for kids.

 MIXED GREENS

Save beaucoup bucks by using these Figamajigs as energy bars. They cost a fraction of the price when compared to commercial bars. Plus, these have no preservatives or isolated, concentrated vitamins or minerals. Just deliciously au natural!

AJ's Peanut Bites

Peanuty and chewy, these are quick treats you'll be making for your friends. This recipe comes from Chef AJ, author of *Unprocessed*.

Yield:	Prep time:	Serving size:	
20 bites	5 minutes	1 bite	
Each serving has:			
130 calories	7g total fat	1g saturated fat	0g trans fat
0mg cholesterol	0mg sodium	14g total carbohydrates	2g dietary fiber
10g sugars	4g protein	14mg calcium	0mg iron

2 cups unsalted, roasted peanuts

2 cups pitted dates

1 TB. alcohol-free vanilla extract

1. In a food processor fitted with an S blade, process peanuts for 60 seconds or until a flourlike consistency forms. Don't overprocess, or you'll end up with peanut butter.

2. Slowly add dates, a few at a time, until mixture clumps together. Stop the food processor; if you can easily roll a ball from the mixture in your hands and it sticks, you don't need to add any more dates.

3. Add vanilla extract, and process for 10 more seconds or until well combined.

4. Using your hands, roll mixture into 20 balls, and place on a flat surface. Serve.

Variation: To make Brownie Bites, use the same technique, but use these ingredients instead: 2 cups raw walnuts, 2 cups pitted dates, ½ cup cocoa powder, and 1 tablespoon alcohol-free vanilla extract. Add cocoa powder with nuts at the beginning. To make either of these bite variations fancier, you can roll the balls in raw cocoa or carob powder, crushed nuts, or shredded coconut.

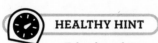 **HEALTHY HINT**

Take these bites as a fresh and homemade on-the-go snack. Treat them like you would a nutrition bar.

Fruity Nut Balls

Take these tangy, tart, sweet, and crunchy portable treats with you wherever you go.

Yield:	Prep time:	Serving size:	
14 balls	10 minutes	1 ball	
Each serving has:			
160 calories	7g total fat	1g saturated fat	0g trans fat
0mg cholesterol	1mg sodium	21g total carbohydrates	2g dietary fiber
14g sugars	4g protein	23mg calcium	1mg iron

2 cups raw cashews	1 cup pitted dates
1 cup dried unsweetened cherries	1 TB. alcohol-free vanilla extract

1. In a food processor fitted with an S blade, process cashews for approximately 30 to 45 seconds or until they form a flourlike consistency.

2. Add dates and cherries, and process for 2 to 4 minutes or until mixture begins to clump together.

3. Slowly drizzle vanilla extract into mixture, and process for 10 more seconds.

4. Using your hands, roll dough into balls, and serve. Keep covered in the refrigerator for 4 or 5 days.

Variation: Use the same amount of raw peanuts instead of cashews for Peanut Butter and Jelly Balls.

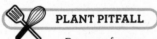 **PLANT PITFALL**

Beware of sugar and oil in dried fruits. Look for unsweetened versions, and be sure the only ingredient listed is the fruit itself.

Chef AJ's Outrageous Brownies

Indulge your sweet tooth while still eating nutrient-dense. These rich, chocolaty treats will shock your family and friends when they find out how healthful they are. Just be sure you tell them *after* they taste them!

Yield:	**Prep time:**	**Cook time:**	**Serving size:**
16 brownies	10 minutes	30 to 35 minutes	1 brownie

Each serving has:			
240 calories	5g total fat	1.5g saturated fat	0g trans fat
0mg cholesterol	40mg sodium	44g total carbohydrates	3g dietary fiber
33g sugars	3g protein	264mg calcium	2mg iron

1 (15-oz.) can no-salt-added black beans, rinsed and drained

1¼ cups Date Paste (recipe in Chapter 19)

2 TB. ground flaxseeds

1 TB. alcohol-free vanilla extract

½ tsp. caramel extract (optional)

1 tsp. aluminum-free baking powder

½ tsp. baking soda

½ cup alkali-free cocoa powder

¾ cup barley flour

1 cup nondairy, grain-sweetened chocolate chips

½ cup finely chopped raw, unsalted pecans

1. Preheat the oven to 350°F.

2. In a food processor fitted with an S blade, combine black beans and Date Paste, and process for 45 seconds or until smooth.

3. Add flaxseeds, vanilla extract, caramel extract (if using), aluminum-free baking powder, baking soda, and cocoa powder. Process for 30 more seconds. Add barley flour, and process for 5 to 10 more seconds or just until combined. Stir in chocolate chips.

4. Pour batter into an 8×8-inch silicone baking pan. Sprinkle pecans on top. Bake for 30 to 35 minutes or until middle does not jiggle and a toothpick inserted comes out clean. Cool on a wire rack for 20 minutes before serving.

Variation: You can use 1¼ cups maple syrup instead of the Date Paste and also substitute ½ cup hempseeds for the pecans. A few extra chocolate chips sprinkled on top add visual and textural appeal.

MIXED GREENS

Caramel extract is a specialty item that's not readily available on your local grocer's shelf. If you can't find it, try other extracts like mint, almond, or lemon in the same quantity to vary the flavor.

Chocolate-Chip Pumpkin Bread

This spicy, fudgy bread will tantalize your taste buds. A mix between a pudding and a cake, it's the perfect item to bring to parties … or just keep to yourself at home!

Yield:	Prep time:	Cook time:	Serving size:
1 (9×5-inch) loaf	15 minutes	1 hour	1 slice (5¼×1¾×¼-inch)

Each serving has:			
312 calories	6g total fat	2.5g saturated fat	0g trans fat
0mg cholesterol	160mg sodium	62g total carbohydrates	4g dietary fiber
45g sugars	3g protein	258mg calcium	1mg iron

1 cup Date Paste (recipe in Chapter 19)

1 (15-oz.) can pumpkin purée

3 TB. flax eggs (see instructions in Chapter 18)

½ cup pure maple syrup

1 TB. alcohol-free vanilla extract

1½ cups oat flour

½ tsp. aluminum-free baking powder

½ tsp. baking soda

½ tsp. salt

1 tsp. ground cinnamon

¼ tsp. ground cloves

¼ tsp. ground nutmeg

¼ tsp. ground ginger

1½ cups grain-sweetened chocolate chips

1. Preheat the oven to 350°F.

2. In a large bowl, combine Date Paste, pumpkin purée, flax eggs, maple syrup, and vanilla extract until smooth.

3. Gently stir in oat flour, aluminum-free baking powder, baking soda, salt, cinnamon, cloves, nutmeg, and ginger. Mix until no lumps remain. Add chocolate chips, and evenly distribute throughout.

4. Pour batter into a 9×5-inch loaf pan, and bake for 1 hour. Allow bread to cool before cutting and serving.

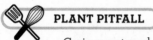 **PLANT PITFALL**

Grain-sweetened chocolate chips are not technically a whole food, and they're a specialty item. But if you can find them, feel comfortable using them in baked goods because the ingredients are completely plant-based as well as sugar- and oil-free. You can also opt for raisins or other dried fruits in place of the chocolate chips.

Dried Fruit Compote

Stewing or simmering dried fruits is a great way to rehydrate them as well as infuse them with extra flavor. This warm fruit compote makes it easy to get your servings of fruit during the cold winter months in a sweet and spicy way.

Yield:	Prep time:	Cook time:	Serving size:
5 cups	5 to 10 minutes	10 to 12 minutes	1¼ cups

Each serving has:			
441 calories	1g total fat	0g saturated fat	0g trans fat
0mg cholesterol	10mg sodium	113g total carbohydrates	13g dietary fiber
83g sugars	5g protein	104mg calcium	4mg iron

1½ cups dried peaches or other large dried fruit, cut in half

⅔ cup dried figs, cut in half

⅔ cup dried prunes, pitted and cut in half

⅔ cup dried dates, pitted and cut in half

⅓ cup raisins

⅓ cup dried cranberries or cherries

1 large orange

1½ cups water

1 (3-in.) cinnamon stick

1 (½-in.) slice fresh ginger

1. In a medium saucepan, combine peaches, figs, prunes, and dates. Add raisins and cranberries.

2. Using a vegetable peeler, remove long strips of peel from orange and then juice orange using a reamer or juicer. Add orange peel and orange juice to the saucepan, along with water, cinnamon stick, and ginger.

3. Place the saucepan over medium heat, and cook for 10 to 12 minutes or until dried fruit is plump and soft. Remove from heat. Remove cinnamon stick and ginger slice, and discard. Serve warm or cold as desired.

Variation: Individual servings can also be topped with soy yogurt and chopped nuts, if desired. You can also replace ½ cup water with apple juice, white grape juice, or white wine, and serve the compote as a dessert with slices of cake or scoops of nondairy ice cream or sorbet.

PLANT PITFALL

Choose untreated organic dried fruits over those that have been treated with sulfur dioxide, a controversial preservative often used to prevent discoloration of foods due to oxidation.

Baked Apples

An old-time fall dessert, these apples are filled with the flavor of sweetly spiced nuts and dried fruits.

Yield:	Prep time:	Cook time:	Serving size:
6 apples	10 to 12 minutes	35 to 45 minutes	1 apple

Each serving has:			
225 calories	4g total fat	0g saturated fat	0g trans fat
0mg cholesterol	6mg sodium	51g total carbohydrates	6g dietary fiber
40g sugars	2g protein	28mg calcium	1mg iron

½ cup apple juice	3 TB. dried cranberries
4 TB. maple syrup	1 TB. minced fresh ginger
¼ cup coarsely chopped raw walnuts	½ tsp. ground cinnamon
3 TB. raisins	6 large Gala or other apples, cut in half and cored

1. Preheat the oven to 375°F.

2. Pour apple juice and 2 tablespoons maple syrup into a 9×13-inch silicone baking pan, and stir well to combine. Set aside.

3. In a small bowl, combine walnuts, remaining 2 tablespoons maple syrup, raisins, dried cranberries, ginger, and cinnamon, and stir well.

4. Fill cavity of each apple with walnut mixture, and place filled apples into the baking pan.

5. Bake for 35 to 45 minutes or until apples are tender but not mushy, basting apples with pan juices every 15 minutes during baking. Remove from the oven.

6. Serve apples with pan juices spooned over the top. For an extra special treat, serve with scoops of nondairy ice cream or sorbet, if desired.

Variations: Replace walnuts with almonds or sunflower seeds and dried cranberries with chopped dates, apricots, or other dried fruits. For Baked Pears, cut pears in half lengthwise and remove their cores, fill cavities, and bake them open faced.

HEALTHY HINT

Silicone bakeware is a safe way to bake without oil. Nothing sticks to its surface and because it's an inert chemical, it's safe to use. Plus, it's made in many shapes and sizes to accommodate any recipe. Just be sure not to use it on direct heat sources to prevent melting.

Mango Banana Mousse

The concentrated flavor of dried fruits means no added sugar is needed to make a protein-packed, straight-from-the-pantry dessert. Choose sulfite-free dried fruits and non-GMO silken tofu in aseptic containers. This recipe is from Fran Costigan, author of *Vegan Chocolate* and director of vegan baking and pastry at Rouxbe Cooking School; visit her at francostigan.com.

Yield:	Prep time:	Cook time:	Serving size:
4 cups	15 minutes	45 minutes	1 cup

Each serving has:			
160 calories	2g total fat	0g saturated fat	0g trans fat
0mg cholesterol	79mg sodium	30g total carbohydrates	3g dietary fiber
19g sugars	7g protein	48mg calcium	1mg iron

8 oz. unsweetened dried mango (sulfite-free), torn or cut into pieces for faster rehydration

4 cups boiling water

1 (12.3 oz.) shelf-stable box firm or extra-firm silken tofu

1 small (ripe) banana, chunked

1 TB. lime juice or more to taste

1 fresh mango, chunked, about ¾ cup

1 tsp. pure vanilla extract

½ tsp. ancho chili powder or more to taste (optional)

1½ tsp. agar powder

2 TB. cornstarch or arrowroot

Fresh diced mango

1-2 TB. toasted coconut or chopped nuts (optional)

1. Put dried mango in medium heatproof bowl.

2. Pour boiling water over dried mango and set aside for 1 hour or until mango is very soft. You may find it more convenient to soak dried mango overnight in the refrigerator.

3. Drain rehydrated mango, reserving soaking liquid. (Do not wash the bowl mango soaked in.)

4. Purée mango in a food processor until smooth. Spoon puréed mango back into the soaking bowl.

5. Without rinsing the processor bowl, place tofu in the food processor and purée until creamy, scraping down the sides of bowl, if needed.

6. Add banana, 1 tablespoon lime juice, fresh mango, and vanilla to puréed tofu and process until all ingredients are incorporated. Add more lime juice to taste and ancho chili powder (if using). Keep purée in the processor while cooking agar-cornstarch mixture.

7. Pour ¾ cup of reserved soaking liquid into a small saucepan. Sprinkle agar powder over liquid and let it rest for 1 minute. In a small bowl, mix remaining 1/4 cup soaking liquid with cornstarch to create a slurry, and set aside.

8. Place saucepan with hydrated agar over medium heat and bring to a full boil, whisking a few times. Reduce the heat to low.

9. Stir cornstarch slurry and, whisking constantly, add it to agar mixture. If using arrowroot, cook only until it boils. If using cornstarch, cook for 30 seconds after a full boil is reached.

10. Pour hot agar/starch mixture over purée and pulse food processor to combine and then blend for 30 seconds.

11. Add more lime juice and/or ancho chili powder (if using) to taste.

12. To serve, spoon mousse into serving glasses and top with diced fresh mango. Garnish with a light sprinkle of toasted coconut or chopped nuts (if using). Or serve mousse in a parfait or wine glass, layering mousse with diced mango and Sweet Cream Dip.

Glossary

activities of daily living (ADL)   Self-care skills necessary for day-to-day function, including walking, sitting up, preparing meals, eating, lifting, and bending.

adaptation   Your body's physiologic response to exercise. It occurs with a persistent training regimen and means your body has learned to cope with the stress you've placed on it from your current program. To avoid plateaus, you have to change your workout frequently.

adequate intake (AI)   Defined by the Food and Nutrition Board of the Institute of Medicine as a recommended average nutrient intake. It is established when evidence is insufficient to develop an RDA and is set at a level assumed to ensure nutritional adequacy.

agar   A gelatinous substance derived from seaweed that works as a thickening agent and can replace gelatin as a plant-based substitute.

allspice   Named for its flavor echoes of several spices (cinnamon, cloves, nutmeg), allspice is used in many desserts and in rich marinades and stews.

almonds   Mild, sweet, and crunchy nuts that combine nicely with creamy and sweet food items.

artichoke hearts   The center part of the artichoke flower, often found canned in grocery stores.

arugula   A spicy-peppery garden plant with leaves that resemble a dandelion and have a distinctive—and very sharp—flavor.

atherosclerosis   The process of hardening and thickening of the arterial walls, associated with an increased risk for heart attacks, strokes, and other vascular diseases.

atherosclerotic plaque   A build-up of cholesterol, calcium, cellular debris, and fatty materials in the walls of the blood vessels as a consequence of atherosclerosis.

atrophic gastritis   A chronic inflammation of the stomach lining that interferes with vitamin B_{12} absorption. This condition affects up to half of adults over age 60.

autoimmune disease   An illness caused by the body attacking itself. This includes illnesses such as type 1 diabetes, multiple sclerosis, rheumatoid arthritis, and lupus.

balsamic vinegar   Vinegar produced primarily in Italy from a specific type of grape and aged in wood barrels. It's heavier, darker, and sweeter than most vinegars.

basal metabolic rate (BMR)   A measure of the rate of metabolism, it's the energy needed to sustain the metabolic activities of cells and tissues to maintain circulatory, respiratory, gastrointestinal, and renal processes.

basil   A flavorful, almost sweet, resinous herb delicious with tomatoes and used in all kinds of Italian or Mediterranean-style dishes.

beriberi   A thiamin deficiency resulting in difficulty walking; loss of sensation or function in the legs, hands, or feet; tingling; and mental confusion.

black pepper   A biting and pungent seasoning, freshly ground pepper is a must for many dishes adding an extra level of flavor and taste.

blanch   To place a food in boiling water for about 1 minute (or less) to partially cook the exterior and then submerge in or rinse with cool water to halt the cooking.

bone mineral density (BMD)   The amount of minerals in any volume of bone.

calisthenics   A form of exercise intended to develop strength and flexibility using resistance provided by your body and minimal or no equipment.

carbohydrate   A macronutrient within the general class of organic compounds that includes simple sugars, starches, and fibers. Based on specific food packaging and chemical structure, they may have a wide range of metabolic functions.

carcinogens   Agents or substances that cause or exacerbate cancer growth.

cardiac output   The total amount of blood flow from the heart during a specified period of time, or stroke volume multiplied by heart rate. Cardiac output is regulated by the amount of nutrients and oxygen required by the cells as well as the requirement to remove wastes.

cayenne   A fiery spice made from (hot) chile peppers, especially the cayenne chile, a slender, red, very hot pepper.

chickpeas (or **garbanzo beans**)   Yellow-gold, roundish beans used as the base ingredient in hummus. Chickpeas are high in fiber and low in fat.

chili powder   A seasoning blend that includes chile pepper, cumin, garlic, and oregano. Proportions vary among different versions, but they all offer a warm, rich flavor.

Chinese five-spice powder   A seasoning blend of cinnamon, anise, ginger, fennel, and pepper.

chop   To cut into pieces, usually qualified by an adverb such as "*coarsely* chopped" or by a size measurement such as "chopped into ½-inch pieces." "Finely chopped" is much closer to mince.

cilantro   A member of the parsley family used in Mexican cooking (especially salsa) and some Asian dishes. Use in moderation, as the flavor can overwhelm. The seed of the cilantro is the spice *coriander*.

cinnamon   A rich, aromatic spice commonly used in baking or desserts. Cinnamon can also be used for delicious and interesting entrées.

circulatory system   The heart, arteries, capillaries, and veins. This system is responsible for transporting blood, oxygen, and nutrients to all cells in the body.

coconut water   The clear liquid found inside a young coconut, which is extremely high in electrolytes and makes an excellent natural sports drink.

coenzymes   Small, nonprotein molecules that enhance the action of an enzyme.

core   The group of muscles located around the trunk of the body. Typically, this includes the abdominal muscles (rectus abdominis, transverse abdominis, external and internal obliques), pelvic floor muscles, and spinal stabilizer muscles.

coriander   A rich, warm, spicy seed used in all types of recipes, from African to South American, from entrées to desserts.

cumin   A fiery, smoky-tasting spice popular in Middle Eastern and Indian dishes. Cumin is a seed; ground cumin seed is the most common form used in cooking.

curry   Rich, spicy, Indian-style sauces and the dishes prepared with them. A curry uses curry powder as its base seasoning.

curry powder   A ground blend of rich and flavorful spices used as a basis for curry and many other Indian-influenced dishes. Common ingredients include hot pepper, nutmeg, cumin, cinnamon, pepper, and turmeric. Some curry can also be found in paste form.

detoxification   The process of cleansing and removing toxic compounds that may have accumulated in the organs over a period of time.

diabetic ketoacidosis   A life-threatening situation caused by insufficient insulin, leading to high blood sugar levels, nausea, vomiting, abdominal pain, dehydration, ketones in the urine, acidosis, and the potential for coma and death.

dietary cholesterol   A waxy steroid metabolite found in cell membranes and transported via the blood of all animals. An essential structural component of cell membranes, cholesterol is necessary for the manufacture of bile acids, steroid hormones, and fat-soluble vitamins, including vitamins A, D, E, and K.

diverticulosis   A condition in which the colon has small outpouchings that may lead to inflammation (diverticulitis).

DNA   An acronym for deoxyribonucleic acid, this nucleic acid (one of two, with the other being RNA) is found in the nucleus of every cell in the body and contains the genetic instructions for the development and function for all life forms.

electrolytes   Minerals found in the blood that help balance fluids and maintain normal functions, like your heart's rhythm and muscle contraction. The main electrolytes are sodium, potassium, chloride, magnesium, calcium, phosphate, and bicarbonate.

endorphins   Neurochemicals produced in the body that act as natural painkillers.

excitotoxins   Toxic molecules, like MSG or aspartame, that stimulate nerve cells so much they're damaged or killed.

flexibility   A joint's ability to move freely through a full and normal range of motion. Many factors influence joint mobility, including genetics, the joint structure itself, neuromuscular coordination, and strength of the opposing muscle group.

flexitarian   A contraction of "flexible vegetarian," or someone who eats mostly plant-based foods but occasionally eats meat, poultry, or fish.

free radicals   High-energy particles with at least one unpaired electron that go wild in the body, ricocheting around trying to match up their unpaired electrons. This causes damage and leads to heart disease, cancers, autoimmune disease, macular degeneration, impaired immunity, and accelerated aging.

garlic   A member of the onion family. A pungent and flavorful element in many savory dishes. A garlic bulb contains multiple cloves. Each clove, when chopped, provides about 1 teaspoon garlic. Most recipes call for cloves or chopped garlic by the teaspoon.

gestational diabetes (GDM)   Any degree of glucose intolerance that's first discovered during pregnancy. Although the condition usually resolves after delivery, it increases the risk by more than 7-fold of developing type 2 diabetes within 5 to 10 years after pregnancy. Children of moms with GDM are at increased risk of obesity, glucose intolerance, and diabetes in late adolescence and young adulthood. GDM complicates up to approximately 9 percent of pregnancies, according to the American Diabetes Association.

ginger   Available in fresh root or dried and ground form, ginger adds a pungent, sweet, and spicy quality to a dish.

glomerular filtration rate (GFR)   A measure of kidney function equal to the rate at which fluid filters through the kidneys.

goiter   An abnormally enlarged thyroid gland most commonly due to iodine deficiency in the diet but can also occur with other thyroid diseases.

gomashio   A Japanese condiment comprised of a blend of toasted sesame seeds, salt, and sometimes sea vegetables.

healthspan   The period of one's life during which one is generally healthy and free from serious disease. It is in contrast to life span, which is simply the number of years you live. We want to define proper diet with the goal of *living* longer, not just living *longer.*

hemorrhoids   Dilated veins in the anus or rectum typically caused by constipation or strains due to diarrhea or pregnancy.

herbes de Provence   A seasoning mix including basil, fennel, marjoram, rosemary, sage, and thyme, common in the south of France.

herbs   Plants valued for their aromas, flavors, or medicinal qualities.

homeostasis   The tendency to return to a stable or balanced point. It is maintained by various physiological processes. For example, the rise in blood alcohol, lipids, or glucose after a meal is returned to normal, premeal, levels in 4 to 6 hours after eating.

hyponatremia   Also known as "water intoxication," an abnormally low concentration of sodium in the blood (less than 135 mmol per liter) that can cause cells to malfunction and can be fatal. It can result from prolonged, heavy sweating with failure to replenish sodium or from excessive water consumption, making it common in high-endurance athletes.

indirect calorimeter   A device used by scientists to calculate metabolism and determine fat or carbohydrate fuel mixture. It uses sensors on a facemask or within a sealed room to measure and record oxygen consumed and carbon dioxide created with each breath.

insoluble fiber   Fiber that's not soluble in water and consists mainly of lignin, cellulose, and hemicelluloses. This type of fiber is primarily found in the bran layers of cereal grains.

insulin shock   A condition that occurs when too much insulin is in the blood, leading to severely low blood sugar (hypoglycemia) and possibly resulting in convulsions and coma.

intramyocellular lipids   Droplets of lipids within muscle tissue cells. It is suggested that these accumulated lipids interfere with normal glucose utilization, known more commonly as insulin resistance, which leads to the accumulation of glucose in the bloodstream after a meal. Paradoxically, a diet low in saturated fat and high in whole food starches can reverse this action, restoring normal insulin sensitivity.

iodine   A trace mineral required from the diet to help with metabolism.

julienne   French word meaning "to slice into very thin pieces."

lacto-ovo vegetarians   Vegetarians who consume dairy products and eggs.

lactose intolerance   The inability to digest lactose, the sugar component of milk, due to the body's failure to produce the enzyme lactase. Gastrointestinal symptoms vary from mild to extreme and can include gas, bloating, cramps, diarrhea, and extreme pain.

lentils   Tiny lens-shape pulses used in European, Middle Eastern, and Indian cuisines.

lymphatic system   Includes vessels and lymph nodes separate from the circulatory system that filter out microorganisms and other toxins before returning fluid and protein to the blood. It carries white blood cells throughout the body to help fight infection.

macrominerals   Also considered "bulk elements." Your body requires these minerals in amounts of 100mg per day or greater.

marjoram   A sweet herb, a cousin of and similar to oregano; popular in Greek, Spanish, and Italian dishes.

meat analogues   Products intended to imitate the texture, flavor, and appearance of meats and that are made from nonanimal-based ingredients.

metabolic syndrome   A cluster of conditions, including obesity, high cholesterol, hypertension, and high blood sugar, that lead to vascular and other chronic diseases.

metabolism   The whole range of biochemical processes that occur in the body and are necessary for the maintenance of life.

microminerals   Also known as "trace elements," these are present in minute amounts in the body's tissues and are essential in much smaller quantities (closer to 15mg per day or less) for optimal health, growth, and development.

miso   A fermented, flavorful soybean paste that is key in many Japanese dishes.

Neu5Gc   N-Glycolylneuraminic acid (Neu5Gc) is a nonhuman sialic acid sugar molecule found predominantly in red meat that promotes chronic inflammation and has been associated with increasing risk for cancer and other chronic diseases.

neuropathy   Damage to the nerves that causes tingling, weakness, pain, and/or numbness, usually in the legs, feet, toes, arms, and fingers.

nori   The Japanese name for seaweed; typically dried, toasted, made into flat sheets, and used for sushi as a wrapper.

norito   A combination of *nori* and *burrito,* these rolls, filled with crunchy and savory filling and wrapped in crispy nori sheets, ultimately end up looking, and being eaten, like burritos.

omnivore   A person or animal who eats anything.

osteopenia   A condition in which bone mineral density appears to be lower than normal. It's considered a precursor to osteoporosis.

oxidation   The chemical addition of oxygen to a molecule. Oxidation is the process that we use to extract energy from the macronutrient molecule. The browning of fruit flesh that happens over time and with exposure to air. Minimize oxidation by rubbing the cut surfaces with a lemon half. Oxidation also affects wine, which is why the taste changes over time after a bottle is opened.

passive immunity   The temporary protection against disease from the already-made antibodies of one human given to another.

pellagra   Illness caused by a deficiency in niacin resulting in scaly skin sores, delusions, diarrhea, inflamed mucous membranes, and mental confusion.

Persian cucumbers   Mini seedless cucumbers that are crisp, refreshing, and available throughout the year.

phytoestrogens   Plant compounds, similar to the hormone estrogen, that look and act like estrogen in the body.

plant-based milks   Beverages made from soy, almonds, rice, hemp, coconut, and oats fortified with calcium, vitamin B_{12}, and vitamin D that can be used in the same fashion as cow's milk but without the health risks.

prebiotics   Fermentable carbohydrates that encourage the growth of friendly bacteria in the GI tract. These friendly bacteria and their by-products inhibit the growth of harmful bacteria and yeasts, reduce cancer-promoting compounds, improve absorption of minerals, and perhaps reduce food intolerances and allergies.

protein combining   A practice taught by nutrition experts to ensure people consumed adequate amounts of all the essential amino acids. Certain foods were recommended to be eaten together at the same meal (grains and legumes, for example) to prevent protein deficiency. Because amino acids are abundant in nature and the essential amino acids all originate in plants, deficiency is unlikely when daily calorie needs are met eating a whole food, plant-based diet.

purines   A class of aromatic organic compounds that are components of nucleic acids (DNA and RNA) found in human and animal tissue.

refined foods   Foods stripped of their intact parts, as when whole grains have their bran and/or germ removed (leaving only the endosperm); examples include white flour and white rice. Refined products can also be called "polished" or "processed."

resting heart rate   The number of times the heart beats when you are completely inactive.

retinopathy   A disease of the small blood vessels in the retina of the eyes that can eventually result in impaired vision and blindness.

rice vinegar   Vinegar produced from fermented rice or rice wine, popular in Asian-style dishes. Different from rice wine vinegar.

sage   An herb with a musty yet fruity lemon-rind scent and "sunny" flavor.

salsa   A style of mixing fresh vegetables and/or fresh fruit in a coarse chop. Salsa can be spicy or not, fruit-based or not, and served as a starter on its own (with chips, for example) or as a companion to a main course.

satiety   The state of fullness and satisfaction after eating adequately.

sauté   To pan-cook over lower heat than used for frying.

scurvy   A disorder caused by vitamin C deficiency characterized by spongy gums, bleeding of the skin and gums, and loosening of the teeth.

semi-vegetarian   Someone who excludes some meat, usually red meat, from the diet while still consuming limited amounts of poultry, fish, and/or seafood.

simmer   To boil gently so the liquid barely bubbles.

soluble fiber   The water-soluble form of dietary fiber that has an affinity for water, either dissolving or swelling to form a gel. Soluble fiber is primarily found in fruits, vegetables, oats, barley, legumes, and seaweed.

spices   Any of a variety of dried seeds, roots, barks, fruits, or leaves used to add flavors, colors, or antimicrobial properties to foods.

standard American diet (SAD)   SAD is an acronym for *standard American diet*, alluding to the unhealthy dietary pattern heavy in animal products and highly processed foods, and lacking in nutritious whole foods typical in the country. Unfortunately, the United States is not the only country with these poor diet profiles anymore and is, therefore, more commonly referred to as the *standard Western diet* to include other countries in the western world with similar diets and chronic disease and obesity rates.

steam   To suspend a food over boiling water and allow the heat of the steam (water vapor) to cook the food. A quick cooking method, steaming preserves the flavor and texture of a food.

stir-fry   To cook small pieces of food in a wok or skillet over high heat, moving and turning the food quickly to cook all sides.

stress hormones   Substances such as cortisol, adrenaline, norepinephrine, and epinephrine secreted by the endocrine system when tension is induced.

stroke volume   The amount of blood pumped from the left ventricle of the heart with one contraction.

supergrains   A term used to represent grains extremely high in essential amino acids, including lysine and methionine, not common in other grains. They're also exceptionally high in fiber, vitamins, and minerals.

synergy   The effect of two or more units working together to produce a result not obtainable by each of the units independently.

tahini   A thick, smooth Middle Eastern paste made of raw, ground, hulled sesame seeds.

tamari   A wheat-free, naturally fermented soybean sauce.

tempeh   An Indonesian food made by culturing and fermenting soybeans into a cake, sometimes mixed with grains or vegetables, and high in protein and fiber.

thermic effect of food (TEF)   The increase in energy expenditure associated with the processes of digestion, absorption, and the metabolism of food.

tofu   A cheeselike substance made from soybeans and soy milk that is high in protein, omega-3 fatty acids, and calcium.

trimethylamine N-oxide (TMAO)   Produced in the body as a gut microbial-dependent metabolite of dietary choline (found concentrated in eggs, organ meat, white meat, seafood, and dairy) and L-carnitine (found in animal products, especially red meat), high levels are associated with inflammation, atherosclerosis, heart attack, stroke, and death..

turmeric   A spicy, pungent yellow root used in many dishes, especially Indian cuisine, for color and flavor. Turmeric is the source of the yellow color in many prepared mustards.

upper limit (UL)   Defined by the Food and Nutrition Board of the Institute of Medicine as the highest level of daily nutrient intake that is likely to pose no risk of adverse health effects to almost all individuals in the general population. As intake increases above the UL, the risk of adverse effects increases.

villi   Tiny, fingerlike protrusions that line the small intestines and allow absorption of nutrients from the intestines into the bloodstream.

whole food, plant-based diet   A way of eating that emphasizes whole, plant-based foods, including vegetables, fruits, whole grains, and legumes, while avoiding animal products and highly processed foods.

whole grains   Grains derived from the seeds of grasses, including rice, oats, rye, wheat, wild rice, quinoa, barley, buckwheat, bulgur, corn, millet, amaranth, and sorghum.

wild rice   Actually a grass with a rich, nutty flavor, popular as an unusual and nutritious side dish.

zest   Small slivers of peel, usually from a citrus fruit such as a lemon, a lime, or an orange.

zester   A kitchen tool used to scrape zest off a fruit. A small grater also works well.

Sample Meal Plans

Although there's no rhyme or reason to what you should eat or when, this meal plan can help you get started. Mix and match however you please, or based on what's in your kitchen at the time. Just eat whole plants and all will be well!

Day 1

Breakfast: It's Easy Being Green Smoothie (Chapter 20)

Lunch: Japanese Noritos (Chapter 20)

Snack: Simply Hummus (Chapter 22) with baby carrots and cucumbers

Dinner: Baked Lentils and Rice Casserole (Chapter 21)

Day 2

Breakfast: Blueberry Banana Pancakes (Chapter 20)

Lunch: Zel's Zesty Rainbow Salad (Chapter 20)

Snack: Sweet Pea Guacamole (Chapter 22) with whole-grain baked corn chips

Dinner: Japanoodles (Chapter 21)

Day 3

Breakfast: Chocolate Almond Butter in a Cup (Chapter 20)

Lunch: Wacky Wild Rice (Chapter 21)

Snack: Sweet Cream Dip (Chapter 23) with apple and banana slices

Dinner: Kathy's Easy Quinoa Burrito Bowl (Chapter 21)

Day 4

Breakfast: Veggie Tofu Scramble (Chapter 20)

Lunch: Sushi Salad with Creamy Miso Dressing (Chapter 20)

Snack: Savory Nut Spread (Chapter 22) on whole-grain crackers

Dinner: Fiesta Fantastica (Chapter 21)

Day 5

Breakfast: Breakfast Rice Pudding (Chapter 20)

Lunch: Spinach Split Pea Soup (Chapter 20)

Snack: Indian Hummus (Chapter 22) with whole-wheat naan

Dinner: Easy Beans and Quinoa (Chapter 21)

Day 6

Breakfast: Oatmeal with walnuts and berries

Lunch: Salted Peach Ceviche (Chapter 20)

Snack: Unclassic Oatmeal Raisin Cookies (Chapter 23)

Dinner: Herbed Balsamic Pasta (Chapter 21)

Day 7

Breakfast: Mint Chocolate Nib Smoothie (Chapter 20)

Lunch: Mexican Noritos (Chapter 20)

Snack: Hot "Cheesy" Vegetable Dip (Chapter 22)

Dinner: Beans and Greens Chili (Chapter 21)

Nutrition Charts

To help you determine how much of what nutrients you need on a daily basis, check out the following Dietary Reference Intakes, created by the Institute of Medicine's Food and Nutrition Board.

Dietary Reference Intakes (DRIs): Estimated Average Requirements
Food and Nutrition Board, Institute of Medicine, National Academies

Life Stage Group	Calcium (mg/d)	CHO (g/d)	Protein (g/kg/d)	Vit A (µg/d)a	Vit C (mg/d)	Vit D (µg/d)	Vit E (mg/d)b	Thiamin (mg/d)	Riboflavin (mg/d)	Niacin (mg/d)c	Vit B6 (mg/d)	Folate (µg/d)d	Vit B12 (µg/d)	Copper (µg/d)	Iodine (µg/d)	Iron (mg/d)	Magnesium (mg/d)	Molybdenum (µg/d)	Phosphorus (mg/d)	Selenium (µg/d)	Zinc (mg/d)
Infants																					
0 to 6 mo																					
6 to 12 mo		1.0														6.9					2.5
Children																					
1–3 y	500	100	0.87	210	13	10	5	0.4	0.4	5	0.4	120	0.7	260	65	3.0	65	13	380	17	2.5
4–8 y	800	100	0.76	275	22	10	6	0.5	0.5	6	0.5	160	1.0	340	65	4.1	110	17	405	23	4.0
Males																					
9–13 y	1,100	100	0.76	445	39	10	9	0.7	0.8	9	0.8	250	1.5	540	73	5.9	200	26	1,055	35	7.0
14–18 y	1,100	100	0.73	630	63	10	12	1.0	1.1	12	1.1	330	2.0	685	95	7.7	340	33	1,055	45	8.5
19–30 y	800	100	0.66	625	75	10	12	1.0	1.1	12	1.1	320	2.0	700	95	6	330	34	580	45	9.4
31–50 y	800	100	0.66	625	75	10	12	1.0	1.1	12	1.1	320	2.0	700	95	6	350	34	580	45	9.4
51–70 y	800	100	0.66	625	75	10	12	1.0	1.1	12	1.4	320	2.0	700	95	6	350	34	580	45	9.4
>70 y	1,000	100	0.66	625	75	10	12	1.0	1.1	12	1.4	320	2.0	700	95	6	350	34	580	45	9.4
Females																					
9–13 y	1,100	100	0.76	420	39	10	9	0.7	0.8	9	0.8	250	1.5	540	73	5.7	200	26	1,055	35	7.0
14–18 y	1,100	100	0.71	485	56	10	12	0.9	0.9	11	1.0	330	2.0	685	95	7.9	300	33	1,055	45	7.3
19–30 y	800	100	0.66	500	60	10	12	0.9	0.9	11	1.1	320	2.0	700	95	8.1	255	34	580	45	6.8
31–50 y	800	100	0.66	500	60	10	12	0.9	0.9	11	1.1	320	2.0	700	95	8.1	265	34	580	45	6.8
51–70 y	1,000	100	0.66	500	60	10	12	0.9	0.9	11	1.3	320	2.0	700	95	5	265	34	580	45	6.8
>70 y	1,000	100	0.66	500	60	10	12	0.9	0.9	11	1.3	320	2.0	700	95	5	265	34	580	45	6.8
Pregnancy																					
14–18 y	1,000	135	0.88	530	66	10	12	1.2	1.2	14	1.6	520	2.2	785	160	23	335	40	1,055	49	10.5
19–30 y	800	135	0.88	550	70	10	12	1.2	1.2	14	1.6	520	2.2	800	160	22	290	40	580	49	9.5
31–50 y	800	135	0.88	550	70	10	12	1.2	1.2	14	1.6	520	2.2	800	160	22	300	40	580	49	9.5
Lactation																					
14–18 y	1,000	160	1.05	885	96	10	16	1.2	1.3	13	1.7	450	2.4	985	209	7	300	35	1,055	59	10.9
19–30 y	800	160	1.05	900	100	10	16	1.2	1.3	13	1.7	450	2.4	1,000	209	6.5	255	36	580	59	10.4
31–50 y	800	160	1.05	900	100	10	16	1.2	1.3	13	1.7	450	2.4	1,000	209	6.5	265	36	580	59	10.4

NOTE: An Estimated Average Requirement (EAR) is the average daily nutrient intake level estimated to meet the requirements of half of the healthy individuals in a group. EARs have not been established for vitamin K, pantothenic acid, biotin, choline, chromium, fluoride, manganese, or other nutrients not yet evaluated via the DRI process.

a As retinol activity equivalents (RAEs). 1 RAE = 1 µg retinol, 12 µg β-carotene, 24 µg α-carotene, or 24 µg β-cryptoxanthin. The RAE for dietary provitamin A carotenoids is two-fold greater than retinol equivalents (RE), whereas the RAE for preformed vitamin A is the same as RE.

b As α-tocopherol. α-Tocopherol includes RRR-α-tocopherol, the only form of α-tocopherol that occurs naturally in foods, and the 2R-stereoisomeric forms of α-tocopherol (RRR-, RSR-, RRS-, and RSS-α-tocopherol) that occur in fortified foods and supplements. It does not include the 2S-stereoisomeric forms of α-tocopherol (SRR-, SSR-, SRS-, and SSS-α-tocopherol), also found in fortified foods and supplements.

c As niacin equivalents (NE). 1 mg of niacin = 60 mg of tryptophan.

d As dietary folate equivalents (DFE). 1 DFE = 1 µg food folate = 0.6 µg of folic acid from fortified food or as a supplement consumed with food = 0.5 µg of a supplement taken on an empty stomach.

SOURCES: *Dietary Reference Intakes for Calcium, Phosphorous, Magnesium, Vitamin D, and Fluoride* (1997); *Dietary Reference Intakes for Thiamin, Riboflavin, Niacin, Vitamin B6, Folate, Vitamin B12, Pantothenic Acid, Biotin, and Choline* (1998); *Dietary Reference Intakes for Vitamin C, Vitamin E, Selenium, and Carotenoids* (2000); *Dietary Reference Intakes for Vitamin A, Vitamin K, Arsenic, Boron, Chromium, Copper, Iodine, Iron, Manganese, Molybdenum, Nickel, Silicon, Vanadium, and Zinc* (2001); *Dietary Reference Intakes for Energy, Carbohydrate, Fiber, Fat, Fatty Acids, Cholesterol, Protein, and Amino Acids* (2002/2005); and *Dietary Reference Intakes for Calcium and Vitamin D* (2011). These reports may be accessed via www.nap.edu.

Dietary Reference Intakes (DRIs): Recommended Dietary Allowances and Adequate Intakes, Vitamins

Food and Nutrition Board, Institute of Medicine, National Academies

Life Stage Group	Vitamin A (μg/d)[a]	Vitamin C (mg/d)	Vitamin D (μg/d)[b,c]	Vitamin E (mg/d)[d]	Vitamin K (μg/d)	Thiamin (mg/d)	Riboflavin (mg/d)	Niacin (mg/d)[e]	Vitamin B6 (mg/d)	Folate (μg/d)[f]	Vitamin B12 (μg/d)	Pantothenic Acid (mg/d)	Biotin (μg/d)	Choline (mg/d)[g]
Infants														
0 to 6 mo	400*	40*	10	4*	2.0*	0.2*	0.3*	2*	0.1*	65*	0.4*	1.7*	5*	125*
6 to 12 mo	500*	50*	10	5*	2.5*	0.3*	0.4*	4*	0.3*	80*	0.5*	1.8*	6*	150*
Children														
1–3 y	**300**	**15**	**15**	**6**	30*	**0.5**	**0.5**	**6**	**0.5**	**150**	**0.9**	2*	8*	200*
4–8 y	**400**	**25**	**15**	**7**	55*	**0.6**	**0.6**	**8**	**0.6**	**200**	**1.2**	3*	12*	250*
Males														
9–13 y	**600**	**45**	**15**	**11**	60*	**0.9**	**0.9**	**12**	**1.0**	**300**	**1.8**	4*	20*	375*
14–18 y	**900**	**75**	**15**	**15**	75*	**1.2**	**1.3**	**16**	**1.3**	**400**	**2.4**	5*	25*	550*
19–30 y	**900**	**90**	**15**	**15**	120*	**1.2**	**1.3**	**16**	**1.3**	**400**	**2.4**	5*	30*	550*
31–50 y	**900**	**90**	**15**	**15**	120*	**1.2**	**1.3**	**16**	**1.3**	**400**	**2.4**	5*	30*	550*
51–70 y	**900**	**90**	**15**	**15**	120*	**1.2**	**1.3**	**16**	**1.7**	**400**	**2.4**[h]	5*	30*	550*
>70 y	**900**	**90**	**20**	**15**	120*	**1.2**	**1.3**	**16**	**1.7**	**400**	**2.4**[h]	5*	30*	550*
Females														
9–13 y	**600**	**45**	**15**	**11**	60*	**0.9**	**0.9**	**12**	**1.0**	**300**	**1.8**	4*	20*	375*
14–18 y	**700**	**65**	**15**	**15**	75*	**1.0**	**1.0**	**14**	**1.2**	**400**[i]	**2.4**	5*	25*	400*
19–30 y	**700**	**75**	**15**	**15**	90*	**1.1**	**1.1**	**14**	**1.3**	**400**[i]	**2.4**	5*	30*	425*
31–50 y	**700**	**75**	**15**	**15**	90*	**1.1**	**1.1**	**14**	**1.3**	**400**[i]	**2.4**	5*	30*	425*
51–70 y	**700**	**75**	**15**	**15**	90*	**1.1**	**1.1**	**14**	**1.5**	**400**	**2.4**[h]	5*	30*	425*
>70 y	**700**	**75**	**20**	**15**	90*	**1.1**	**1.1**	**14**	**1.5**	**400**	**2.4**[h]	5*	30*	425*
Pregnancy														
14–18 y	**750**	**80**	**15**	**15**	75*	**1.4**	**1.4**	**18**	**1.9**	**600**[j]	**2.6**	6*	30*	450*
19–30 y	**770**	**85**	**15**	**15**	90*	**1.4**	**1.4**	**18**	**1.9**	**600**[j]	**2.6**	6*	30*	450*
31–50 y	**770**	**85**	**15**	**15**	90*	**1.4**	**1.4**	**18**	**1.9**	**600**[j]	**2.6**	6*	30*	450*
Lactation														
14–18 y	**1,200**	**115**	**15**	**19**	75*	**1.4**	**1.6**	**17**	**2.0**	**500**	**2.8**	7*	35*	550*
19–30 y	**1,300**	**120**	**15**	**19**	90*	**1.4**	**1.6**	**17**	**2.0**	**500**	**2.8**	7*	35*	550*
31–50 y	**1,300**	**120**	**15**	**19**	90*	**1.4**	**1.6**	**17**	**2.0**	**500**	**2.8**	7*	35*	550*

NOTE: This table (taken from the DRI reports, see www.nap.edu) presents Recommended Dietary Allowances (RDAs) in **bold type** and Adequate Intakes (AIs) in ordinary type followed by an asterisk (*). An RDA is the average daily dietary intake level; sufficient to meet the nutrient requirements of nearly all (97-98 percent) healthy individuals in a group. It is calculated from an Estimated Average Requirement (EAR). If sufficient scientific evidence is not available to establish an EAR, and thus calculate an RDA, an AI is usually developed. For healthy breastfed infants, an AI is the mean intake. The AI for other life stage and gender groups is believed to cover the needs of all healthy individuals in the groups, but lack of data or uncertainty in the data prevent being able to specify with confidence the percentage of individuals covered by this intake.

[a] As retinol activity equivalents (RAEs). 1 RAE = 1 μg retinol, 12 μg β-carotene, 24 μg α-carotene, or 24 μg β-cryptoxanthin. The RAE for dietary provitamin A carotenoids is two-fold greater than retinol equivalents (RE), whereas the RAE for preformed vitamin A is the same as RE.

[b] As cholecalciferol. 1 μg cholecalciferol = 40 IU vitamin D.

[c] Under the assumption of minimal sunlight.

[d] As α-tocopherol. α-Tocopherol includes RRR-α-tocopherol, the only form of α-tocopherol that occurs naturally in foods, and the 2R-stereoisomeric forms of α-tocopherol (RRR-, RSR-, RRS-, and RSS-α-tocopherol) that occur in fortified foods and supplements. It does not include the 2S-stereoisomeric forms of α-tocopherol (SRR-, SSR-, SRS-, and SSS-α-tocopherol), also found in fortified foods and supplements.

[e] As niacin equivalents (NE). 1 mg of niacin = 60 mg of tryptophan; 0–6 months = preformed niacin (not NE).

[f] As dietary folate equivalents (DFE). 1 DFE = 1 μg food folate = 0.6 μg of folic acid from fortified food or as a supplement consumed with food = 0.5 μg of a supplement taken on an empty stomach.

[g] Although AIs have been set for choline, there are few data to assess whether a dietary supply of choline is needed at all stages of the life cycle, and it may be that the choline requirement can be met by endogenous synthesis at some of these stages.

[h] Because 10 to 30 percent of older people may malabsorb food-bound B12, it is advisable for those older than 50 years to meet their RDA mainly by consuming foods fortified with B12 or a supplement containing B12.

[i] In view of evidence linking folate intake with neural tube defects in the fetus, it is recommended that all women capable of becoming pregnant consume 400 μg from supplements or fortified foods in addition to intake of food folate from a varied diet.

[j] It is assumed that women will continue consuming 400 μg from supplements or fortified food until their pregnancy is confirmed and they enter prenatal care, which ordinarily occurs after the end of the periconceptional period—the critical time for formation of the neural tube.

SOURCES: Dietary Reference Intakes for Calcium, Phosphorous, Magnesium, Vitamin D, and Fluoride (1997); Dietary Reference Intakes for Thiamin, Riboflavin, Niacin, Vitamin B6, Folate, Vitamin B12, Pantothenic Acid, Biotin, and Choline (1998); Dietary Reference Intakes for Vitamin C, Vitamin E, Selenium, and Carotenoids (2000); Dietary Reference Intakes for Vitamin A, Vitamin K, Arsenic, Boron, Chromium, Copper, Iodine, Iron, Manganese, Molybdenum, Nickel, Silicon, Vanadium, and Zinc (2001); Dietary Reference Intakes for Water, Potassium, Sodium, Chloride, and Sulfate (2005); and Dietary Reference Intakes for Calcium and Vitamin D (2011). These reports may be accessed via www.nap.edu.

Dietary Reference Intakes (DRIs): Recommended Dietary Allowances and Adequate Intakes, Elements
Food and Nutrition Board, Institute of Medicine, National Academies

Life Stage Group	Calcium (mg/d)	Chromium (µg/d)	Copper (µg/d)	Fluoride (mg/d)	Iodine (µg/d)	Iron (mg/d)	Magnesium (mg/d)	Manganese (mg/d)	Molybdenum (µg/d)	Phosphorus (mg/d)	Selenium (µg/d)	Zinc (mg/d)	Potassium (g/d)	Sodium (g/d)	Chloride (g/d)
Infants															
0 to 6 mo	200*	0.2*	200*	0.01*	110*	0.27*	30*	0.003*	2*	100*	15*	2*	0.4*	0.12*	0.18*
6 to 12 mo	260*	5.5*	220*	0.5*	130*	11	75*	0.6*	3*	275*	20*	3	0.7*	0.37*	0.57*
Children															
1–3 y	700	11*	340	0.7*	90	7	80	1.2*	17	460	20	3	3.0*	1.0*	1.5*
4–8 y	1,000	15*	440	1*	90	10	130	1.5*	22	500	30	5	3.8*	1.2*	1.9*
Males															
9–13 y	1,300	25*	700	2*	120	8	240	1.9*	34	1,250	40	8	4.5*	1.5*	2.3*
14–18 y	1,300	35*	890	3*	150	11	410	2.2*	43	1,250	55	11	4.7*	1.5*	2.3*
19–30 y	1,000	35*	900	4*	150	8	400	2.3*	45	700	55	11	4.7*	1.5*	2.3*
31–50 y	1,000	35*	900	4*	150	8	420	2.3*	45	700	55	11	4.7*	1.5*	2.3*
51–70 y	1,000	30*	900	4*	150	8	420	2.3*	45	700	55	11	4.7*	1.3*	2.0*
>70 y	1,200	30*	900	4*	150	8	420	2.3*	45	700	55	11	4.7*	1.2*	1.8*
Females															
9–13 y	1,300	21*	700	2*	120	8	240	1.6*	34	1,250	40	8	4.5*	1.5*	2.3*
14–18 y	1,300	24*	890	3*	150	15	360	1.6*	43	1,250	55	9	4.7*	1.5*	2.3*
19–30 y	1,000	25*	900	3*	150	18	310	1.8*	45	700	55	8	4.7*	1.5*	2.3*
31–50 y	1,000	25*	900	3*	150	18	320	1.8*	45	700	55	8	4.7*	1.5*	2.3*
51–70 y	1,200	20*	900	3*	150	8	320	1.8*	45	700	55	8	4.7*	1.3*	2.0*
>70 y	1,200	20*	900	3*	150	8	320	1.8*	45	700	55	8	4.7*	1.2*	1.8*
Pregnancy															
14–18 y	1,300	29*	1,000	3*	220	27	400	2.0*	50	1,250	60	12	4.7*	1.5*	2.3*
19–30 y	1,000	30*	1,000	3*	220	27	350	2.0*	50	700	60	11	4.7*	1.5*	2.3*
31–50 y	1,000	30*	1,000	3*	220	27	360	2.0*	50	700	60	11	4.7*	1.5*	2.3*
Lactation															
14–18 y	1,300	44*	1,300	3*	290	10	360	2.6*	50	1,250	70	13	5.1*	1.5*	2.3*
19–30 y	1,000	45*	1,300	3*	290	9	310	2.6*	50	700	70	12	5.1*	1.5*	2.3*
31–50 y	1,000	45*	1,300	3*	290	9	320	2.6*	50	700	70	12	5.1*	1.5*	2.3*

NOTE: This table (taken from the DRI reports, see www.nap.edu) presents Recommended Dietary Allowances (RDAs) in **bold type** and Adequate Intakes (AIs) in ordinary type followed by an asterisk (*). An RDA is the average daily dietary intake level; sufficient to meet the nutrient requirements of nearly all (97-98 percent) healthy individuals in a group. It is calculated from an Estimated Average Requirement (EAR). If sufficient scientific evidence is not available to establish an EAR, and thus calculate an RDA, an AI is usually developed. For healthy breastfed infants, an AI is the mean intake. The AI for other life stage and gender groups is believed to cover the needs of all healthy individuals in the groups, but lack of data or uncertainty in the data prevent being able to specify with confidence the percentage of individuals covered by this intake.

SOURCES: *Dietary Reference Intakes for Calcium, Phosphorous, Magnesium, Vitamin D, and Fluoride* (1997); *Dietary Reference Intakes for Thiamin, Riboflavin, Niacin, Vitamin B₆, Folate, Vitamin B₁₂, Pantothenic Acid, Biotin, and Choline* (1998); *Dietary Reference Intakes for Vitamin C, Vitamin E, Selenium, and Carotenoids* (2000); and *Dietary Reference Intakes for Vitamin A, Vitamin K, Arsenic, Boron, Chromium, Copper, Iodine, Iron, Manganese, Molybdenum, Nickel, Silicon, Vanadium, and Zinc* (2001); *Dietary Reference Intakes for Water, Potassium, Sodium, Chloride, and Sulfate* (2005); and *Dietary Reference Intakes for Calcium and Vitamin D* (2011). These reports may be accessed via www.nap.edu.

Dietary Reference Intakes (DRIs): Recommended Dietary Allowances and Adequate Intakes, Total Water and Macronutrients

Food and Nutrition Board, Institute of Medicine, National Academies

Life Stage Group	Total Water[a] (L/d)	Carbohydrate (g/d)	Total Fiber (g/d)	Fat (g/d)	Linoleic Acid (g/d)	α-Linolenic Acid (g/d)	Protein[b] (g/d)
Infants							
0 to 6 mo	0.7*	60*	ND	31*	4.4*	0.5*	9.1*
6 to 12 mo	0.8*	95*	ND	30*	4.6*	0.5*	**11.0**
Children							
1–3 y	1.3*	**130**	19*	ND[c]	7*	0.7*	**13**
4–8 y	1.7*	**130**	25*	ND	10*	0.9*	**19**
Males							
9–13 y	2.4*	**130**	31*	ND	12*	1.2*	**34**
14–18 y	3.3*	**130**	38*	ND	16*	1.6*	**52**
19–30 y	3.7*	**130**	38*	ND	17*	1.6*	**56**
31–50 y	3.7*	**130**	38*	ND	17*	1.6*	**56**
51–70 y	3.7*	**130**	30*	ND	14*	1.6*	**56**
> 70 y	3.7*	**130**	30*	ND	14*	1.6*	**56**
Females							
9–13 y	2.1*	**130**	26*	ND	10*	1.0*	**34**
14–18 y	2.3*	**130**	26*	ND	11*	1.1*	**46**
19–30 y	2.7*	**130**	25*	ND	12*	1.1*	**46**
31–50 y	2.7*	**130**	25*	ND	12*	1.1*	**46**
51–70 y	2.7*	**130**	21*	ND	11*	1.1*	**46**
> 70 y	2.7*	**130**	21*	ND	11*	1.1*	**46**
Pregnancy							
14–18 y	3.0*	**175**	28*	ND	13*	1.4*	**71**
19–30 y	3.0*	**175**	28*	ND	13*	1.4*	**71**
31–50 y	3.0*	**175**	28*	ND	13*	1.4*	**71**
Lactation							
14–18 y	3.8*	**210**	29*	ND	13*	1.3*	**71**
19–30 y	3.8*	**210**	29*	ND	13*	1.3*	**71**
31–50 y	3.8*	**210**	29*	ND	13*	1.3*	**71**

NOTE: This table (take from the DRI reports, see www.nap.edu) presents Recommended Dietary Allowances (RDA) in **bold type** and Adequate Intakes (AI) in ordinary type followed by an asterisk (*). An RDA is the average daily dietary intake level; sufficient to meet the nutrient requirements of nearly all (97-98 percent) healthy individuals in a group. It is calculated from an Estimated Average Requirement (EAR). If sufficient scientific evidence is not available to establish an EAR, and thus calculate an RDA, an AI is usually developed. For healthy breastfed infants, an AI is the mean intake. The AI for other life stage and gender groups is believed to cover the needs of all healthy individuals in the groups, but lack of data or uncertainty in the data prevent being able to specify with confidence the percentage of individuals covered by this intake.

[a] *Total* water includes all water contained in food, beverages, and drinking water.

[b] Based on g protein per kg of body weight for the reference body weight, e.g., for adults 0.8 g/kg body weight for the reference body weight.

[c] Not determined.

SOURCE: *Dietary Reference Intakes for Energy, Carbohydrate, Fiber, Fat, Fatty Acids, Cholesterol, Protein, and Amino Acids* (2002/2005) and *Dietary Reference Intakes for Water, Potassium, Sodium, Chloride, and Sulfate* (2005). The report may be accessed via www.nap.edu.

Dietary Reference Intakes (DRIs): Acceptable Macronutrient Distribution Ranges

Food and Nutrition Board, Institute of Medicine, National Academies

Macronutrient	Range (percent of energy)		
	Children, 1–3 y	Children, 4–18 y	Adults
Fat	30–40	25–35	20–35
n-6 polyunsaturated fatty acids[a] (linoleic acid)	5–10	5–10	5–10
n-3 polyunsaturated fatty acids[a] (α-linolenic acid)	0.6–1.2	0.6–1.2	0.6–1.2
Carbohydrate	45–65	45–65	45–65
Protein	5–20	10–30	10–35

[a] Approximately 10 percent of the total can come from longer-chain n-3 or n-6 fatty acids.

SOURCE: *Dietary Reference Intakes for Energy, Carbohydrate, Fiber, Fat, Fatty Acids, Cholesterol, Protein, and Amino Acids* (2002/2005). The report may be accessed via www.nap.edu.

Dietary Reference Intakes (DRIs): Acceptable Macronutrient Distribution Ranges

Food and Nutrition Board, Institute of Medicine, National Academies

Macronutrient	Recommendation
Dietary cholesterol	As low as possible while consuming a nutritionally adequate diet
Trans fatty Acids	As low as possible while consuming a nutritionally adequate diet
Saturated fatty acids	As low as possible while consuming a nutritionally adequate diet
Added sugars[a]	Limit to no more than 25 % of total energy

[a] Not a recommended intake. A daily intake of added sugars that individuals should aim for to achieve a healthful diet was not set.

SOURCE: *Dietary Reference Intakes for Energy, Carbohydrate, Fiber, Fat, Fatty Acids, Cholesterol, Protein, and Amino Acids* (2002/2005). The report may be accessed via www.nap.edu.

Dietary Reference Intakes (DRIs): Tolerable Upper Intake Levels, Vitamins
Food and Nutrition Board, Institute of Medicine, National Academies

Life Stage Group	Vitamin A (µg/d)[a]	Vitamin C (mg/d)	Vitamin D (µg/d)	Vitamin E (mg/d)[b,c]	Vitamin K	Thia-min	Ribo-flavin	Niacin (mg/d)[c]	Vitamin B6 (mg/d)	Folate (µg/d)[c]	Vitamin B12	Panto-thenic Acid	Bio-tin	Cho-line (g/d)	Carote-noids[d]
Infants															
0 to 6 mo	600	ND[e]	25	ND	ND	ND	ND	ND	ND	ND	ND	ND	ND	ND	ND
6 to 12 mo	600	ND	38	ND	ND	ND	ND	ND	ND	ND	ND	ND	ND	ND	ND
Children															
1–3 y	600	400	63	200	ND	ND	ND	10	30	300	ND	ND	ND	1.0	ND
4–8 y	900	650	75	300	ND	ND	ND	15	40	400	ND	ND	ND	1.0	ND
Males															
9–13 y	1,700	1,200	100	600	ND	ND	ND	20	60	600	ND	ND	ND	2.0	ND
14–18 y	2,800	1,800	100	800	ND	ND	ND	30	80	800	ND	ND	ND	3.0	ND
19–30 y	3,000	2,000	100	1,000	ND	ND	ND	35	100	1,000	ND	ND	ND	3.5	ND
31–50 y	3,000	2,000	100	1,000	ND	ND	ND	35	100	1,000	ND	ND	ND	3.5	ND
51–70 y	3,000	2,000	100	1,000	ND	ND	ND	35	100	1,000	ND	ND	ND	3.5	ND
>70 y	3,000	2,000	100	1,000	ND	ND	ND	35	100	1,000	ND	ND	ND	3.5	ND
Females															
9–13 y	1,700	1,200	100	600	ND	ND	ND	20	60	600	ND	ND	ND	2.0	ND
14–18 y	2,800	1,800	100	800	ND	ND	ND	30	80	800	ND	ND	ND	3.0	ND
19–30 y	3,000	2,000	100	1,000	ND	ND	ND	35	100	1,000	ND	ND	ND	3.5	ND
31–50 y	3,000	2,000	100	1,000	ND	ND	ND	35	100	1,000	ND	ND	ND	3.5	ND
51–70 y	3,000	2,000	100	1,000	ND	ND	ND	35	100	1,000	ND	ND	ND	3.5	ND
>70 y	3,000	2,000	100	1,000	ND	ND	ND	35	100	1,000	ND	ND	ND	3.5	ND
Pregnancy															
14–18 y	2,800	1,800	100	800	ND	ND	ND	30	80	800	ND	ND	ND	3.0	ND
19–30 y	3,000	2,000	100	1,000	ND	ND	ND	35	100	1,000	ND	ND	ND	3.5	ND
31–50 y	3,000	2,000	100	1,000	ND	ND	ND	35	100	1,000	ND	ND	ND	3.5	ND
Lactation															
14–18 y	2,800	1,800	100	800	ND	ND	ND	30	80	800	ND	ND	ND	3.0	ND
19–30 y	3,000	2,000	100	1,000	ND	ND	ND	35	100	1,000	ND	ND	ND	3.5	ND
31–50 y	3,000	2,000	100	1,000	ND	ND	ND	35	100	1,000	ND	ND	ND	3.5	ND

NOTE: A Tolerable Upper Intake Level (UL) is the highest level of daily nutrient intake that is likely to pose no risk of adverse health effects to almost all individuals in the general population. Unless otherwise specified, the UL represents total intake from food, water, and supplements. Due to a lack of suitable data, ULs could not be established for vitamin K, thiamin, riboflavin, vitamin B12, pantothenic acid, biotin, and carotenoids. In the absence of a UL, extra caution may be warranted in consuming levels above recommended intakes. Members of the general population should be advised not to routinely exceed the UL. The UL is not meant to apply to individuals who are treated with the nutrient under medical supervision or to individuals with predisposing conditions that modify their sensitivity to the nutrient.

[a] As preformed vitamin A only.

[b] As α-tocopherol; applies to any form of supplemental α-tocopherol.

[c] The ULs for vitamin E, niacin, and folate apply to synthetic forms obtained from supplements, fortified foods, or a combination of the two.

[d] β-Carotene supplements are advised only to serve as a provitamin A source for individuals at risk of vitamin A deficiency.

[e] ND = Not determinable due to lack of data of adverse effects in this age group and concern with regard to lack of ability to handle excess amounts. Source of intake should be from food only to prevent high levels of intake.

SOURCES: *Dietary Reference Intakes for Calcium, Phosphorous, Magnesium, Vitamin D, and Fluoride* (1997); *Dietary Reference Intakes for Thiamin, Riboflavin, Niacin, Vitamin B6, Folate, Vitamin B12, Pantothenic Acid, Biotin, and Choline* (1998); *Dietary Reference Intakes for Vitamin C, Vitamine E, Selenium, and Carotenoids* (2000); *Dietary Reference Intakes for Vitamin A, Vitamin K, Arsenic, Boron, Chromium, Copper, Iodine, Iron, Manganese, Molybdenum, Nickel, Silicon, Vanadium, and Zinc* (2001); and *Dietary Reference Intakes for Calcium and Vitamin D* (2011). These reports may be accessed via www.nap.edu.

Dietary Reference Intakes (DRIs): Tolerable Upper Intake Levels, Elements
Food and Nutrition Board, Institute of Medicine, National Academies

Life Stage Group	Arsenic[a]	Boron (mg/d)	Calcium (mg/d)	Chromium	Copper (μg/d)	Fluoride (mg/d)	Iodine (μg/d)	Iron (mg/d)	Magnesium (mg/d)[b]	Manganese (mg/d)	Molybdenum (μg/d)	Nickel (mg/d)	Phosphorus (g/d)	Selenium (μg/d)	Silicon[c]	Vanadium (mg/d)[d]	Zinc (mg/d)	Sodium (g/d)	Chloride (g/d)
Infants																			
0 to 6 mo	ND[e]	ND	1,000	ND	ND	0.7	ND	40	ND	ND	ND	ND	ND	45	ND	ND	4	ND	ND
6 to 12 mo	ND	ND	1,500	ND	ND	0.9	ND	40	ND	ND	ND	ND	ND	60	ND	ND	5	ND	ND
Children																			
1–3 y	ND	3	2,500	ND	1,000	1.3	200	40	65	2	300	0.2	3	90	ND	ND	7	1.5	2.3
4–8 y	ND	6	2,500	ND	3,000	2.2	300	40	110	3	600	0.3	3	150	ND	ND	12	1.9	2.9
Males																			
9–13 y	ND	11	3,000	ND	5,000	10	600	40	350	6	1,100	0.6	4	280	ND	ND	23	2.2	3.4
14–18 y	ND	17	3,000	ND	8,000	10	900	45	350	9	1,700	1.0	4	400	ND	ND	34	2.3	3.6
19–30 y	ND	20	2,500	ND	10,000	10	1,100	45	350	11	2,000	1.0	4	400	ND	1.8	40	2.3	3.6
31–50 y	ND	20	2,500	ND	10,000	10	1,100	45	350	11	2,000	1.0	4	400	ND	1.8	40	2.3	3.6
51–70 y	ND	20	2,000	ND	10,000	10	1,100	45	350	11	2,000	1.0	4	400	ND	1.8	40	2.3	3.6
>70 y	ND	20	2,000	ND	10,000	10	1,100	45	350	11	2,000	1.0	3	400	ND	1.8	40	2.3	3.6
Females																			
9–13 y	ND	11	3,000	ND	5,000	10	600	40	350	6	1,100	0.6	4	280	ND	ND	23	2.2	3.4
14–18 y	ND	17	3,000	ND	8,000	10	900	45	350	9	1,700	1.0	4	400	ND	ND	34	2.3	3.6
19–30 y	ND	20	2,500	ND	10,000	10	1,100	45	350	11	2,000	1.0	4	400	ND	1.8	40	2.3	3.6
31–50 y	ND	20	2,500	ND	10,000	10	1,100	45	350	11	2,000	1.0	4	400	ND	1.8	40	2.3	3.6
51–70 y	ND	20	2,000	ND	10,000	10	1,100	45	350	11	2,000	1.0	4	400	ND	1.8	40	2.3	3.6
>70 y	ND	20	2,000	ND	10,000	10	1,100	45	350	11	2,000	1.0	3	400	ND	1.8	40	2.3	3.6
Pregnancy																			
14–18 y	ND	17	3,000	ND	8,000	10	900	45	350	9	1,700	1.0	3.5	400	ND	ND	34	2.3	3.6
19–30 y	ND	20	2,500	ND	10,000	10	1,100	45	350	11	2,000	1.0	3.5	400	ND	ND	40	2.3	3.6
31–50 y	ND	20	2,500	ND	10,000	10	1,100	45	350	11	2,000	1.0	3.5	400	ND	ND	40	2.3	3.6
Lactation																			
14–18 y	ND	17	3,000	ND	8,000	10	900	45	350	9	1,700	1.0	4	400	ND	ND	34	2.3	3.6
19–30 y	ND	20	2,500	ND	10,000	10	1,100	45	350	11	2,000	1.0	4	400	ND	ND	40	2.3	3.6
31–50 y	ND	20	2,500	ND	10,000	10	1,100	45	350	11	2,000	1.0	4	400	ND	ND	40	2.3	3.6

NOTE: A Tolerable Upper Intake Level (UL) is the highest level of daily nutrient intake that is likely to pose no risk of adverse health effects to almost all individuals in the general population. Unless otherwise specified, the UL represents total intake from food, water, and supplements. Due to a lack of suitable data, ULs could not be established for vitamin K, thiamin, riboflavin, vitamin B₁₂, pantothenic acid, biotin, and carotenoids. In the absence of a UL, extra caution may be warranted in consuming levels above recommended intakes. Members of the general population should be advised not to routinely exceed the UL. The UL is not meant to apply to individuals who are treated with the nutrient under medical supervision or to individuals with predisposing conditions that modify their sensitivity to the nutrient.

[a] Although the UL was not determined for arsenic, there is no justification for adding arsenic to food or supplements.

[b] The ULs for magnesium represent intake from a pharmacological agent only and do not include intake from food and water.

[c] Although silicon has not been shown to cause adverse effects in humans, there is no justification for adding silicon to supplements.

[d] Although vanadium in food has not been shown to cause adverse effects in humans, there is no justification for adding vanadium to food and vanadium supplements should be used with caution. The UL is based on adverse effects in laboratory animals and this data could be used to set a UL for adults but not children and adolescents.

[e] ND = Not determinable due to lack of data of adverse effects in this age group and concern with regard to lack of ability to handle excess amounts. Source of intake should be from food only to prevent high levels of intake.

SOURCES: *Dietary Reference Intakes for Calcium, Phosphorous, Magnesium, Vitamin D, and Fluoride* (1997); *Dietary Reference Intakes for Thiamin, Riboflavin, Niacin, Vitamin B₆, Folate, Vitamin B₁₂, Pantothenic Acid, Biotin, and Choline* (1998); *Dietary Reference Intakes for Vitamin C, Vitamin E, Selenium, and Carotenoids* (2000); *Dietary Reference Intakes for Vitamin A, Vitamin K, Arsenic, Boron, Chromium, Copper, Iodine, Iron, Manganese, Molybdenum, Nickel, Silicon, Vanadium, and Zinc* (2001); *Dietary Reference Intakes for Water, Potassium, Sodium, Chloride, and Sulfate* (2005); and *Dietary Reference Intakes for Calcium and Vitamin D* (2011). These reports may be accessed via www.nap.edu.

Resources

To support you on your journey further along the plant-based path, I've compiled this appendix full of many helpful resources to make it easier for you to connect with fellow plant-foodists, continue learning, and find more delicious recipes.

Nutrition Information Books

Barnard, Neal D. *21-Day Weight Loss Kickstart*. New York: Grand Central Life & Style, 2011.

———. *Breaking the Food Seduction*. New York: St. Martin's Griffin, 2003.

———. *Dr. Neal Barnard's Program for Reversing Diabetes*. New York: Rodale, 2007.

———. *The Cheese Trap*. New York: Grand Central Life & Style, 2017.

Brazier, Brendan. *Thrive: The Vegan Nutrition Guide to Optimal Performance in Sports and Life*. Philadelphia: Da Capo Press, 2007.

Buettner, Dan. *The Blue Zones*, 2nd ed. Washington, D.C.: National Geographic Society, 2012.

Campbell, T. Colin, and T. M. Campbell. *The China Study*. Dallas: BenBella Books, 2006.

Davis, Brenda, and Vesanto Melina. *Becoming Raw*. Summertown, TN: Book Publishing Company, 2010.

———. *Becoming Vegan*. Summertown, TN: Book Publishing Company, 2014.

Esselstyn, Caldwell B. *Prevent and Reverse Heart Disease*. New York: Penguin Group, 2007.

Fuhrman, Joel. *Disease-Proof Your Child*. New York: St. Martin's Griffin, 2005.

———. *Eat for Health*. Flemington, NJ: Gift of Health Press, 2008.

———. *End of Diabetes*. New York: HarperOne, 2013.

———. *End of Heart Disease*. New York: HarperOne, 2016.

———. *Eat to Live*. New York: Little, Brown and Company, 2011.

———. *Super Immunity*. New York: HarperOne, 2011.

Greger, Michael. *How Not to Die*. New York: Flatiron Books, 2015.

Karlsen, Micaela C. *A Plant-Based Life*. New York: Amacom, 2016.

Kessler, David. *The End of Overeating*. New York: Rodale, 2010.

Lisle, Doug J., and A. Goldhamer. *The Pleasure Trap*. Summertown, TN: Healthy Living, 2003.

Mackey, John. *The Whole Foods Diet*. New York: Grand Central Life & Style, 2017.

McDougall, John A. *The Starch Solution*. New York: Rodale, 2012.

Ornish, Dean. *The Spectrum*. New York: Ballantine Books, 2017.

Robbins, John. *Healthy at 100*. New York: Ballantine Books, 2007.

———. *The Food Revolution*. Boston: Conari Press, 2010.

Plant-Based Cookbooks

Barnard, Tanya, and S. Kramer. *How It All Vegan*. Vancouver, BC: Arsenal Pulp Press, 1999.

———. *The Garden of Vegan*. Vancouver, BC: Arsenal Pulp Press, 2002.

Bennett, Beverly Lynn, and Ray Sammartano. *The Complete Idiot's Guide to Vegan Cooking*. Indianapolis: Alpha Books, 2008.

Burton, Dreena. *Eat, Drink and Be Vegan*. Vancouver, BC: Arsenal Pulp Press, 2007.

———. *Let Them Eat Vegan*. Boston: Da Capo Press, 2012.

———. *Plant-Powered Families*. Dallas: BenBella, 2015.

Campbell, Leanne, *The China Study Cookbook*. Dallas: BenBella Books, 2013.

Chef AJ. *Unprocessed*. Los Angeles: Hail to the Kale Publishing, 2011.

Frazier, Matt, and Stefanie Romine. *The No Meat Athlete Cookbook*. New York: The Experiment, 2017.

Fuhrman, Joel, *Eat to Live Cookbook*. New York: HarperOne, 2013.

Hever, Julieanna, and Beverly Lynn Bennett. *The Complete Idiot's Guide to Gluten-Free Vegan Cooking*. Indianapolis: Alpha Books, 2011.

Kenney, Matthew, *PLANTLAB*. New York: Regan Arts, 2017.

Kramer, Sarah. *Vegan A Go-Go*. Vancouver, BC: Arsenal Pulp Press, 2008.

Moskowitz, Isa C., and T. H. Romero. *Veganomicon: The Ultimate Vegan Cookbook*. New York: Marlowe and Company, 2007.

Patrick-Goudreau, C. *Color Me Vegan*. Beverly, MA: Fair Winds Press, 2010.

———. *The Vegan Table*. Beverly, MA: Fair Winds Press, 2009.

Reinfeld, Mark. *Healing the Vegan Way*. Boston: Da Capo Press, 2016.

Robertson, Robin. *1,000 Vegan Recipes*. Hoboken: John Wiley and Sons, 2009.

———. *Vegan on the Cheap*. Hoboken: John Wiley and Sons, 2010.

Schinner, Miyoko. *Artisan Vegan Cheese*. Summertown, TN: Book Publishing Company, 2012.

———. *The Homemade Vegan Pantry*. Berkeley: Ten Speed Press, 2015.

Stepaniak, Jo. *The Ultimate Uncheese Cookbook, 10th Edition*. Summertown, TN: Book Publishing Company, 2003.

Theodore, Laura, Jo. *Vegan-ease*. Bloomington: Jazzy Vegetarian, 2015.

Nutrition and Health Information, Recipes, and Support

American College of Lifestyle Medicine
www.lifestylemedicine.org

Brenda Davis, R.D.
www.brendadavisrd.com

Chef Beverly Lynn Bennett
www.veganchef.com

Complete Health Improvement Program
www.chiphealth.com

Dr. Dean Ornish
www.ornish.com

Dr. Joel Fuhrman
www.drfuhrman.com

Dr. McDougall's Health and Medical Center
www.drmcdougall.com

Fatfree Vegan Recipes
www.fatfreevegan.com

Fran Costigan
www.francostigan.com

HappyCow (searchable database of plant-based restaurants and stores)
www.happycow.net

Healthy Happy Life
kblog.lunchboxbunch.com

Jazzy Vegetarian
www.jazzyvegetarian.com

Julie Morris
www.juliemorris.net

Just Sides
www.justsides.com

Marco Borges
www.marcoborges.com

Matthew Kenney Cuisine
www.matthewkenneycuisine.com

No Meat Athlete
www.nomeatathlete.com

Nutrition Facts
www.NutritionFacts.org

Physicians Committee for Responsible Medicine (PCRM)
www.pcrm.org

Plant-Based Dietitian
www.plantbaseddietitian.com

Plant-Powered Kitchen
www.plantpoweredkitchen.com

T. Colin Campbell Center for Nutrition Studies
www.nutritionstudies.org

The Full Helping
www.thefullhelping.com

TrueNorth Health Center
www.healthpromoting.com

U.S. National Library of Medicine
www.nlm.nih.gov

USDA Food Composition Databases
ndb.nal.usda.gov/ndb

Vegetarian Nutrition Dietetic Practice Group
www.vegetariannutrition.net

Vegetarian Resource Group
www.vrg.org

Vegetarians in Paradise
www.vegparadise.com

VegNews **magazine**
www.vegnews.com

Review Papers

Cronise, Raymond, et al. "Oxidative Priority, Meal Frequency, and the Energy Economy of Food and Activity: Implications for Longevity, Obesity, and Cardiometabolic Disease," *Metabolic Syndrome and Related Disorders,* Volume 15, Number 1, 2017. DOI: 10.1089/met.2016.0108. (easy access: bit.ly/oxidativepriority)

Cronise, Raymond, et al. "The 'Metabolic Winter' Hypothesis: A Cause of the Current Epidemics of Obesity and Cardiometabolic Disease," *Metabolic Syndrome and Related Disorders*, Volume 12, Number 7, 2014. DOI: 10.1089/met.2014.0027. (bit.ly/WinterNeverComes)

Hever, Julieanna. "Plant-Based Diets: A Physician's Guide," *Perm J,* 2016, Summer, 20(3): 15-082. DOI: dx.doi.org/10.7812/TPP/15-082. (easy access: bit.ly/PlantBasedNutrition)

Hever, Julieanna, and Raymond Cronise. "Plant-Based Nutrition for Healthcare Professionals," *Journal of Geriatric Cardiology*, 2017, 14:355-368. (easy access: bit.ly/GeriatricPBN-pdf)

Melina, Vesanto, et al. "Position Paper on Vegetarian Diets," *Journal of the Academy of Nutrition and Dietetics*, Volume 16, Number 12, December 2016. (easy access: bit.ly/VegANDPosition)

Index